Early Modern Genres of 1

Bringing together an international group of literary scholars, intellectual historians, and cultural historians, this book discusses history in its various forms, either as texts or images in the early modern period (1500–1800).

Early Modern Genres of History explores different genres and representational modes regarded as *history* before history became a scientific discipline during the nineteenth century. It does not seek to show how the modern discipline of history as an academic study developed, but rather to examine the ways in which historical texts and images became part of a wider field of early modern knowledge formations. This volume demonstrates how history was connected to the developments in the public sphere, how antiquarian historians used genres in their work, how history evolved and functioned in the visual field, and how historical genres travelled across different contexts. Overall, *Early Modern Genres of History* reveals how the diversity of historical representations in the early modern period has contributed to the broader foundations of history as it is understood in the twenty-first century.

This volume is of great use to upper-level undergraduates, postgraduates, and scholars interested in early modern Europe and the history of knowledge across both the history and literature disciplines.

Emil Nicklas Johnsen, PhD History of Ideas, University of Oslo (UiO), Norway. Johnsen has published extensively in Nordic intellectual history, with particular interest in historiography and the dynamics of the public sphere. In addition, he has long experience as editor in *Arr. Idéhistorisk tidsskrift* (*Journal of the History of Ideas*) and is currently writing the textbook *Vestens idéhistorie fra 1800 til i dag* (*History of Ideas in the Western World from 1800 until today*).

Ina Louise Stovner, PhD Cultural History, University of Oslo (UiO), Norway. Stovner's research interests include topics within cultural history, understanding of history, and memory studies, and she has special expertise in visual sources 1750 to 1840. She has extensive teaching experience in cultural history and museology at UiO and several years of experience as a member of the editorial team in *Tidsskrift for kulturforskning* (*Journal of Cultural Studies*).

Early Modern Themes

Books in the *Early Modern Themes* series are aimed at upper level undergraduate and postgraduate students who are looking more deeply at thematic topics in the early modern period. They combine chapters offering a synthesis of the topic as it stands, the key historiographical debates, and the cutting edge research which is driving the field forward.

Early Modern Childhood
An Introduction
Edited by Anna French

Early Modern Things
Objects and their Histories, 1500–1800, 2nd edition
Edited by Paula Findlen

Early Modern Court Culture
Edited by Erin Griffey

Early Modern Streets
A European Perspective
Edited by Danielle van den Heuvel

Early Modern Toleration
New Approaches
Edited by Benjamin J. Kaplan and Jaap Geraerts

Early Modern Jewish Civilization
Unity and Diversity in a Diasporic Society. An Introduction
Edited by David Graizbord

Early Modern Genres of History
Edited by Emil Nicklas Johnsen and Ina Louise Stovner

For more information about this series, please visit: https://www.routledge.com/Early-Modern-Themes/book-series/EMT

Early Modern Genres of History

Edited by Emil Nicklas Johnsen and
Ina Louise Stovner

Routledge
Taylor & Francis Group

LONDON AND NEW YORK

Designed cover image: Clio – Muse of History © The Picture Art
Collection / Alamy Stock Photo

First published 2024
by Routledge
4 Park Square, Milton Park, Abingdon, Oxon OX14 4RN

and by Routledge
605 Third Avenue, New York, NY 10158

Routledge is an imprint of the Taylor & Francis Group, an informa business

© 2024 selection and editorial matter, Emil Nicklas Johnsen and
Ina Louise Stovner individual chapters, the contributors

The right of Emil Nicklas Johnsen and Ina Louise Stovner to be identified
as the authors of the editorial material, and of the authors for their
individual chapters, has been asserted in accordance with sections 77 and
78 of the Copyright, Designs and Patents Act 1988.

British Library Cataloguing-in-Publication Data
A catalogue record for this book is available from the British Library

Library of Congress Cataloguing-in-Publication Data
Names: Johnsen, Emil Nicklas, editor. | Stovner, Ina Louise, editor.
Title: Early modern genres of history / edited by Emil Nicklas Johnsen
and Ina Louise Stovner.
Description: London ; New York, NY : Routledge, Taylor & Francis
Group, 2024. | Series: Early modern themes | Includes bibliographical
references. |
Identifiers: LCCN 2023058548 (print) | LCCN 2023058549 (ebook) |
ISBN 9781032364414 (hardback) | ISBN 9781003331971 (paperback) |
ISBN 9781003331971 (ebook)
Subjects: LCSH: Historiography--Europe--History--Case studies. |
Europe--History--1492---Historiography--Case studies. |
Europe--History--1492---Sources--Case studies.
Classification: LCC D13.5.E85 E27 2024 (print) | LCC D13.5.E85 (ebook)
| DDC 940.072/2--dc23/eng/20240327
LC record available at https://lccn.loc.gov/2023058548
LC ebook record available at https://lccn.loc.gov/2023058549

ISBN: 978-1-032-36441-4 (hbk)
ISBN: 978-1-032-36442-1 (pbk)
ISBN: 978-1-003-33197-1 (ebk)

DOI: 10.4324/9781003331971

Typeset in Times New Roman
by MPS Limited, Dehradun

Contents

Figures

Contributors

Anne Eriksen is a cultural historian and Professor at the University of Oslo, Norway. She has published widely on early modern historical writing, museums and museology, cultural memory, and uses of the past. Her new book on historic sites and national identity is to appear in 2024.

Håkon Evju is Associate Professor of Intellectual History at the University of Oslo, Norway. His main research interest focuses on eighteenth- and nineteenth-century Dano-Norwegian and Norwegian intellectual history set within a European context and spans the Enlightenment, history of political and economic thought, history of historiography, and the history of press freedom.

Anne Helness is Lecturer in Intellectual History at the University of Oslo, Norway. Her research mainly focuses on the history of knowledge in the early modern period, with particular emphasis on travel writing, history of anthropology and history of geography.

Emil Nicklas Johnsen PhD in Intellectual History at the University of Oslo, Norway. His main research is concerned with Nordic intellectual history, with particular focus on history writing, debates on education, and gender, as well as the evolution of the public sphere in Denmark-Norway in the eighteenth century.

Claire Boulard Jouslin is Lecturer in British civilization at the Université Sorbonne Nouvelle-Paris, France. She specializes in the history of women and the English press during the long eighteenth century (1660–1770). Her field of study includes women's journalism, socialization, and the education of women in the UK periodical, as well as cultural exchanges between England and France during the Enlightenment.

John Ødemark Professor of Cultural History, University of Oslo, Norway. His main research themes are cultural translation, early modern encounters, medical humanities, and the history of the human sciences. He is PI of the research project *Bodies in Translation: Science, Knowledge and Sustainability in Cultural Translation*, funded by the *Research Council of Norway*.

Sebastian Olden-Jørgensen is Associate Professor of Modern History at the University of Copenhagen, Denmark. He has written extensively on court history, historiography, and the history of religious and political thought in Danish and European contexts. Together with Knud Haakonssen, he has edited and contributed to *Ludvig Holberg (1684–1754): Learning and Literature in the Nordic Enlightenment* (Routledge, 2017).

Mark Salber Phillips is Professor of History Emeritus at Carleton University in Ottawa, Canada, and a fellow of the Royal Society of Canada. As a historian of ideas, his publications focus primarily on Renaissance and Enlightenment historiography. His book, *On Historical Distance* (2015), won the Canadian Historical Association's Ferguson prize.

Svein Atle Skålevåg is Professor of History of Science at the University of Bergen, Norway. His main research interest is in the history of psychiatric and medical knowledge, as well as the history of historical knowledge.

Thomas Slettebø is Associate Professor of History at Western Norway University College of Applied Sciences in Bergen, Norway. Among the main areas of focus in his research are the political culture of the Danish-Norwegian absolute monarchy, early modern memory cultures, and the intersection of religion, politics, and memory.

Ina Louise Stovner PhD Cultural History at the University of Oslo, Norway. Stovner specializes in historiography, exemplarity, and the uses of the past, focusing on visual sources including history painting and portraiture in Denmark-Norway in the eighteenth century.

Angus Vine is Associate Professor of Early Modern Literature at the University of Stirling (UK). He works on early modern cultural and intellectual history, with a focus on book history, material culture, and the history of science. He is the author of *In Defiance of Time: Antiquarian Writing in Early Modern England* (Oxford University Press, 2010), *Miscellaneous Order: Manuscript Culture and the Early Modern Organization of Knowledge* (Oxford University Press, 2019), and the forthcoming *Early Modern Merchants and Their Books* (Oxford University Press).

Daniel Woolf is Professor of History at Queen's University in Kingston, Ontario, Canada, where he served for ten years as Principal and Vice-Chancellor. He is the author or editor of several books on the history of historical writing and on early modern British cultural history, including most recently *A Concise History of History* (2019), and has published essays in such journals as *History and Theory*, *The Journal of the History of Ideas*, *Past and Present*, and *The American Historical Review*.

Acknowledgements

The authors of this book acknowledge the support and funding from the Research Council of Norway ("Forskergrupper ved Universitetet i Oslo – Det humanistiske fakultet", Project number 284393).

Introduction

Early modern genres of history

Emil Nicklas Johnsen and Ina Louise Stovner

The study of history has a history itself. Before the 19th century, when history became a professionalized academic discipline, a wide range of genres and modes of representation carried the name of history. This diversity of genres and forms was accompanied by a corresponding variety of agents. If history was not a specialised type of research, composing, writing and publishing history was not restricted to persons trained in specific academic methods. According to Jean Bodin (1530–1596) and other early modern theorists, the best historian was the experienced statesman, with close connections to the political and military events that he described. But women, clergy, merchants and, in some cases, peasants also wrote histories of their family, life, profession or village. Though marginalised by later professionalisation of history, this diversity of texts and even images from the 16th to the 18th century is a rich and fruitful source not only to early modern life, but also to early modern understandings of history, memory and the past and to its categories and genres of knowledge.

This book explores the various forms and shapes that history took during the early modern period (1500–1800), offering valuable insights not only into early modern culture but also into our understanding of history, memory, the past and categories of knowledge. The aim of this book is not to trace the development of the modern discipline of history as an academic study but rather to examine the various ways in which historical texts and images became part of a broader field of early modern knowledge formations and cultural contexts. Our contention is that the diversity of historical representations in the early modern period shaped the idea of history in significant ways and that it contributed to the foundations of history as we think about it today.

The lens of historical genres can help us understand the kinds of histories that were told in the early modern period, with what aims and to whom. Once we become aware of the diffusion of historical genres, it is hard to ignore that historical narratives vary in type and could include travelogues, biographies, letters, "relations", descriptions, memoirs, funeral orations, history paintings or portraits—in addition to essays of political or "perfect" history. This multiplicity of narratives presented the history of states and realms, but just as frequently focused on important individuals or powerful families, foreign

DOI: 10.4324/9781003331971-1

countries and towns or other remarkable particularities. Their aim could be religious, moral, political, educational or simply made to entertain and amuse. By bringing to light the histories and genre types that flourished in the period, we seek to draw attention to how these different practices shaped ideas about knowledge and science, political thought and culture. Through different case studies, the chapters in this volume explore how genres and text hierarchies were formed, maintained and changed, and how this diversity of early modern genres of history continues to impact our understanding of history today.

Existing literature on genres of history in the early modern period

There already exists a body of scholarly work on history writing in the early modern period, with a predominant emphasis on Britain. In his two books, *Society and Sentiment: Genres of Historical Writing in Britain, 1740–1820* (2000) and *On Historical Distance* (2013), Mark Salber Phillips has explored the interplay of ideas and genres in a variety of historical representations in the early modern period. These two books, however, deal exclusively with Britain and Italy and do not explore the development of historical genres in other parts of Europe or the world. Similarly, Daniel Woolf writes about changing historical culture in England in *The Social Circulation of the Past. English Historical Culture, 1500–1730* (2003), with more emphasis on the place of history writing in print culture. In the more recent publication *Miscellaneous Order: Manuscript Culture and the Early Modern Organization of Knowledge* (2019), Angus Vine sheds new light on transcriptive and archival practices, as well as on the broader intellectual context of manuscript culture and its scholarly afterlives. Like Phillips and Woolf, Vines contribution concerns early modern Britain. In contrast to these writers, Håkon Evju focuses on Denmark-Norway. In his recent book, *Ancient Constitutions and Modern Monarchy. Historical Writing and Enlightened Reform in Denmark-Norway 1730–1814* (2019), Evju addresses the issue of historical thought and historical enquiry in debates on political reforms, though he does not explore historical genres as such or discusses it in a wider European perspective.

Other significant contributions to our understanding of history in the early modern period focus on the place of history in the history of knowledge. An edited collection that discusses knowledge and history in early modern scholarly pursuits in a more international perspective is *Historia. Empiricism and Erudition in Early Modern Europe* (eds. Gianna Pomata and Nancy G. Siraisi, 2005). This study centres mostly around the connections between the study of nature and the study of culture. Its scope is not the discussion of various historical genres, but rather the links between the culture of humanism and the scientific revolution. More recently, *Empires of Knowledge* (ed. Paula Findlen, 2019) has charted the emergence of different kinds of scientific networks in the early modern world. This book puts greater emphasis on the history of science and medicine and looks at the changing relationship between knowledge and community. Another contribution to this field is Judith Pollmann's *Memory in Early Modern Europe, 1500–1800* (2017) is an introduction into the ways in which Europeans practiced memory in the three centuries between 1500 and 1800.

Another vein of the established research on historical cultures in the early modern period springs from older contributions on the history of the philosophy of history. In his seminal article, "Philosophy of history before historicism",[1] Georg Nadel points to the strong ties between rhetoric and history, a classical heritage that was present all through the early modern period. Nadel claims the existence of a theory of exemplarity. History was never written or studied for its own sake, but for the effects, moral or political, it could produce. This point was further developed by Reinhart Koselleck, who famously mapped the transformation of the concept of history in the so-called *Sattelzeit* between 1750 and 1850. According to Koselleck, the *Sattelzeit* can be defined as a transitional time when the term "Historie" (histories in the plural) was replaced by the singular form, "Geschichte" (history), and the belief in progress became dominant. This shift in understanding and usage of the term "history" also marked a temporalization, where history was seen as a coherent, unified process rather than a collection of stories.[2]

This anthology expands upon established perspectives in the aforementioned research, with a particular emphasis on exploring the meanings and functions of diverse forms of historical production. It explores different historical genres in history writing and painting, and it discusses the phenomenon of historical genres itself from a theoretical perspective as well as situates a broader array of examples of how genres operated. It presents a diverse range of international source material, including both written and visual sources, from various contexts in Europe, and employs a variety of methods and perspectives though, with a focus on Northern Europe and Denmark-Norway. The focus on Scandinavia is a result of the book's origin as a conference, "Genres of Historical Writing in Early Modern Europe", which was planned to take place in March 2020 in Oslo by the research group "History and Histories" at the University of Oslo. However, the conference was cancelled due to the outbreak of COVID-19 and the imposition of government restrictions. Despite this setback, the book project emerged from the ongoing research efforts of the University of Oslo's milieu, which has been dedicated to the study of early modern histories for several years.

Genres and history

What is a genre? The term is notoriously difficult to pin down or define. Scholars have different ideas about how to define and classify genres, and the boundaries between them can be blurry and subjective. The novel, for instance, serves as an illustrative a genre that encompasses many different sub-genres. Likewise, within the realm of historical representation, one can discover a multitude of genres at varying levels of specificity.

"Genre" comes from the Latin genus, which means "class of things" and refers to a system of categorisation. The term is also related to the Latin word gene, which means "to generate" or "to create something". This dual meaning reflects the fact that genres are both categorisations and creative acts.[3] Genres can mean styles, shapes, forms of expression in a given media (texts, pictures) and can contain many types of stylistic expressions. The classification and taxonomy of genres is a complex and often contentious process. Still, it remains a useful term in historical analysis of texts in the past. Genres are a way of categorising different types of texts, but there is no one universally accepted system for doing so. Viewed this way, genres become a useful tool to decipher both how knowledge and discourses have been organised as well as continually negotiated.

Through his research on early modern British history and Italian history writing, Mark Salber Phillips has proposed that history was not a uniform or singular form of representation, but rather a diverse and multifaceted "family of historical representation" consisting of various genres with differing forms and expectations.[4] He has compared this variety of genres to a crowded Thanksgiving dinner where multiple conversations are occurring simultaneously among a diverse group of relatives.[5] These genres serve as frameworks or structures that shape and guide both creation and interpretation, providing a set of conventions and expectations that allow audiences and authors to understand and engage in a particular way. However, genres are not static or fixed, and they can evolve and change over time as writers and audiences experiment with and challenge their conventions.[6] Viewing historical representations as genres allows for an exploration of both the structures of representation and how different actors have experimented within these structures, providing a more nuanced understanding of the relationship between form and content in historical representations.

The question of how rigid the structure of a genre is or has been a topic of ongoing scholarly debate. One potential issue in the study of genres is that, when an explicit examination of form takes place, it may threaten the perceived stability of the genre's structure. However, when genres are not actively under discussion or description, they may continue to thrive and represent a vital cultural pattern, albeit one that is based on unarticulated foundations. The problematisation or description of genre characteristics can make it difficult to chart the evolution of genres. In our view, the perception of genres in different contexts is always an empirical question. Different forms of historical representations can be understood as mediations of past events, processes and phenomena into the present, but they can also be seen as actively shaped expressions, whether literary, stylistic or narrative in nature.[7]

Philips has argued that historicising history has been a challenge for historians and that the field of historical thought and expression is one in which historians have been the least capable of historicising the genre itself.[8]

Writing about historical genres in more recent times, Jaume Aurell has also claimed historians have been reluctant in viewing the past of their own field of study as a part of historical change, as well as denying or not neglecting to focus on the ways in which the products of history—forms of writing or painting—have had changing forms. The idea of differentiating between scientific and creative writing has resulted in a perceived division between the texts created by historians and those generated in other disciplines. However, when one examines historical expression in the past, it becomes apparent that the distinction between prose and fiction is not always clear-cut. Furthermore, it raises the question of whether such a distinction will ever truly exist. This also implies that analysing historical genres can provide insights into the interconnectedness between history, historical texts and various other forms of text and knowledge production, which can be thought of as genres themselves.

Antiquarian and material negotiations

The book is organised into four sections, each of which examines different aspects of the genres of historical writing and representation during the early modern period. The discussion of historical genres is broad, but the book specifically focuses on four main areas. The first of these areas is the field of antiquarian forms of history. A rich tradition of historical writing, with a culture of studying various historical subjects such as objects of the past and historical events. Antiquarianism was widespread in early modern knowledge production, but it also produced texts of different genres.

In her article "Antiquarian Poetry and Royal Performance", cultural historian Anne Eriksen investigates a specific "genre of historical writing": a topographic descriptive poem that was written to welcome King Frederik V to the Eiker region of Norway by vicar Christian Grawe's in 1749. In the poem, Grawe provides a detailed description of the area's history and culture, using footnotes to provide additional information. The poem is an example of how historical writing in the early modern period often took the form of literature, and how this type of writing was used to discuss natural philosophy and the findings of natural history. The chapter examines the poem and its footnotes to understand Grawe's historical and antiquarian work, and how he used the poem as a tool for historical writing. It also explores the performative aspects of the poem and how it served as a negotiation of social and cultural codes within the context of the absolute monarchy of the Danish state.

Historian Thomas Ewen Slettebø addresses in his article the ambivalent status of compilers in Europe in the 18th century in his article "'Compiled from original authors': on the status of compilers and compilation as historiographical practice in the 18th century". Compilers collected and curated knowledge from older texts and reassembled them into new ones. Slettebø discusses the underlying assumptions and explicit justification of the work of compilers: why did compilers transcribe large amounts of text from others and present them as their own? To what degree was this an accepted practice, and when was it considered problematic? To answer these questions he explores the renowned Danish-Norwegian author, playwright and professor of history Ludvig Holberg's *Jewish History* (1742). The two-volume book aimed to provide a comprehensive history of the Jewish people from the beginning of the world to the present day. Holberg claimed that no such "general" Jewish history had previously been written, and he sought to fill this gap. Holberg's historical works have been shown to be based heavily on verbatim transcripts and translations of older works, with Holberg adding his own revisions, reflections and wit to the text. Despite his reliance on existing sources, Holberg's writing style and tone are distinctly his own, and his use of theatrical metaphors and ironical humour set his works apart from more traditional historical texts.

In his article "'History from Marble': Church Notes and Epigraphy in Early Modern England", early modern historian Angus Vine discusses the rise of epigraphy, or the study of inscriptions, in 17th-century England. The author examines three important landmarks in the history of marble, specifically the pioneering early 17th-century guides to Westminster Abbey and St Paul's by antiquary, herald and schoolmaster William Camden and printer and bookseller Henry Holland, John Weever's massive mid-century *Ancient Funerall Monuments* (1631), and finally antiquary, draughtsman and surveyor Thomas Dingley's late 17th-century eponymous work and its associated texts. These "histories from marble" were seen as a way to supplement and support the authority of traditional, text-based historical evidence. Vine also notes that this interest in material remains of the medieval past was in response to the Reformation and the destruction of monasteries. Furthermore, he highlights that the 17th-century interest in genealogy also drove this interest in church notes and funerary monuments as they provided documentary evidence of ancestors and names.

Visual understandings of history

Genres are by no means restricted to written texts. Part 2 of the book therefore shifts its focus to visual understandings and representations of history. Intellectual historian Mark Salber Phillips discusses the evolution of history painting as a genre of visual representation, from its position as the most prestigious of genres in the early modern period to its current status as one genre among others. In his article "History Painting and/as Genre", Phillips argues that the change in the understanding of history painting reflects broader historicist and democratising trends in the 19th century and that the collapse of history painting in the face of modernism has been exaggerated. The chapter also discusses the continued relevance of history painting in contemporary art, with artists using the genre for political purposes and to inscribe marginalised histories. It argues that the current revival of history painting is a new phase that builds on the foundations laid in the late 18th and 19th centuries.

In her article "Constructing a Moment in History: The Tableau as a Communicational Mode and Genre in the Late 18th Century", cultural historian Ina Louise Stovner examines the tableau as a mode of communication in 18th-century practices and production techniques such as theatre, literature, science and painting. Through an examination of various examples, including the concept of the tableau as an aesthetic expression developed by French art theorist Denis Diderot, two history paintings by Danish royal history painter Nicolai Abildgaard, the social function of the tableau in salon culture and its use in official commemorative ceremonies and parties, the article explores the characteristics of the tableau as a mode of communication. It also argues that the tableau's mode of communication should be understood in relation to the growing middle class as it met the needs of a wider audience. Additionally, the article suggests that genres are not inherent to texts but rather act as intermediaries between texts, their creators and those who interpret them.

Genres of history and the public sphere

Genres existed in public and was used and discussed there. History co-existed with other forms of writing and representation. During the early modern period, a public culture emerged, with growing readership of historical works, as emphasised by Daniel Woolf.[9] Historical writing was also shaped by developments in the public sphere. In her article "From amusement to study? Writing history in the 18th-century essay periodical press", Claire Boulard Jouslin examines the relationship between history and the essay periodical genre in 18th-century England, focusing on Addison and Steele's *Spectator* and its influence on two women's periodicals: Eliza Haywood's *Female Spectator* and Charlotte Lennox's *The Lady's Museum*. Jouslin argues that the *Spectator's* use of visual narrative made it a highly historical genre, but also perpetuated the belief that women's visual faculty was flawed and thus prevented them from producing valuable historical narratives. Jouslin discusses how Haywood and Lennox reconciled writing history with femininity and contributed to popularising history among female readers and defending women's rights to produce history. It contends that the persistence of fictionalised history in essay periodicals shows that the narration of history was always considered a major and serious study for women writers.

In his chapter "Court Intrigues Between Public and Secret History: Some 18th Century Danish Solutions", historian Sebastian Olden-Jørgensen examines the treatment of court history, or the history of royal, princely and ecclesiastical courts, by mainstream historians in the 19th and 20th centuries. These historians tended to disregard court history, viewing the driving forces of history as located in the "progressive" elements of society such as the state, nation and economy. In contrast, in the 18th century, court history was seen as an important topic, as demonstrated by Voltaire's inclusion of four chapters on court intrigues in his book "Le Siècle de Louis XIV". In this article, Olden-Jørgensen examines how Danish 18th-century historians approached court history and the various genres they used, including public history, memoires and secret history, to incorporate it into their narratives. Olden-Jørgensen also discusses the challenges faced by these historians, including the need to consider their patrons and the constraints of their positions and the ways in which their approaches have been misunderstood and mischaracterized by later historians.

Intellectual historian Emil Nicklas Johnsen investigates how the Danish historian Niels Ditlev Riegels' (1755–1802) journalism influenced his historical writing and how Riegels manoeuvred the public sphere with different historical genres, in his chapter, "Royal historiographer without the title". This article explores the various strategies employed by Riegels to revitalise his historical writing after failing to secure the position of royal historiographer in the 1780s. It examines his engagement with the Copenhagen press in the late 18th century and analyses the genre designations used by Riegels which shed light on what he intended to achieve with his history writing and how he understood his role as an historian in the public sphere. In the historiographical discourse of the 18th and 19th centuries, Riegels has been perceived as a paradigmatic case of an inadequate historian. Johnsen argues that, by examining more closely the case of his writings as genres in the public sphere, we get a clearer understanding of the possible roles and ways of navigating the public sphere with historical writing in the late 18th century.

Travelling historical genres

In part 4, the focus is on the genre of travel writing and its relationship to history. The chapter by Håkon Evju is an examination of Ludwig Albrecht Gebhardi (1735–1802) and his contributions to the historiography of the kingdoms of Denmark and Norway. Gebhardi's two-volume work, which was part of a larger universal history in German, published in Halle, travelled to the north through translations. Evju investigates the reception of Gebhardi's text as it was translated, marketed and printed in Denmark and its transformations. The text received considerable attention in Copenhagen and among the historians at Sorø, notably the influential historians Peter Frederik Suhm and Gerhard Schøning. Gebhardi's history gained considerable popularity in the early 1780s due to its alignment with prevailing trends, such as the efforts to cultivate a patriotic identity. Its success was also largely attributed to Gebhardi's connections with Danish and Norwegian historians and antiquarians during the composition of his history. Gebhardi's work exemplifies the transnational nature of historical writing in the 18th century, and Evju traces the transformations within the text and its publication history.

In her article "'For no other cause than the lack of writers': Travel Knowledge and the Preservation of Memory" Intellectual historian Anne Helness discusses *Navigationi et viaggi*, a collection compiled by Venetian humanist Giovanni Battista Ramusio, as an example of a genre of historical writing in the early modern period. During this time, Europeans needed new ways to conceptualise the world in light of changing paradigms of world trade and communication, leading to the emergence of new genres of writing, including the travel collection. Helness argues that the empirical material and editorial commentary in the *Navigationi et viaggi* combine to form an historical genre.

In 1791, Georg Høst, a Danish secretary in the foreign affairs department, published the first biography of Moroccan Emperor Mohammed ben Abdallah. In his essay "Histories from Barbary: Empirical and imperial aspirations in an 18th-century history", historian Svein Atle Skålevåg highlights the significance of this book, as well as another about the Danish administration of St Thomas, in the development of "area studies" and the expansion of European knowledge about modern Barbary. Høst's works, which were based on archival sources and marked the beginning of modern historiography with their emphasis on the causes of historical events and a more critical approach to sources, established his epistemic authority.

In his essay "Between Vico and the Virgin—Image and Historiography on Lorenzo Boturini's History of New Spain", cultural historian John Ødegaard focus on Lorenzo Boturini publication *Idea de una nueva historia general de América septentrional* from 1746. Boturini had based the publication on a collection of Mesoamerican manuscripts he had gathered. The collection was confiscated by the authorities in New Spain and Boturini was sent to Spain, where he presented his Idea to the Council of the Indies. According to Ødegaard Boturini played a significant role in the early reception of G. Vico's *New Science,* quoting extensively from it without acknowledging Vico as his source. In this chapter, Ødegaard examines the encounter of Vico and Boturini in early modern Spain and New Spain and its reception in modern historiography. It looks at the relationship between Vico's historical "paradigm" and Boturini's praise of Mesoamerican script and historiography and considers whether Vico's "influence" explains this praise.

*

The purpose of bringing together these scholarly contributions is to provide a new perspective on how genre functioned within the historical culture of the early modern period, specifically in regards to how form was intertwined with the production of knowledge, as well as the role historical genres played in political and cultural negotiations. We acknowledge that this anthology on the genres of history in the early modern period is not meant to be the final word on the subject. There is certainly potential for further exploration of the use of the genre lens in studying historical producers, writers and painters from other countries and time periods. We would be delighted if this anthology inspires further research, even if the establishment of a new genre of the study of past historical genres remains an aspiration.

Notes

1 George Nadel, "Philosophy of History before Historicism" in: *History and Theory*, 1964.
2 Reinhart Koselleck first introduced his idea in his 1967 article "Historia magistra vitæ. Über die Auflösung des Topos in Horizont neuzeitlich bewegter Geschichte". He subsequently expanded upon this idea in his seminal work, "Vergangene Zukunft. Zur Semantik geschichtlicher Zeiten" (1979), which was later translated into English as "Futures Past: On the Semantics of Historical Times" in 2004 [1985].
3 Bawashi & Reif 2010, *Genre: An Introduction to History, Theory, Research, and Pedagogy*, 3.
4 Mark Salber Phillips, *On historical distance*, 59.
5 Mark Salber Phillips, *On historical distance*, 60.
6 Mark Salber Phillips, *On historical distance*, 20.
7 Jaume Aurell, *Rethinking historical genres*.
8 Mark Salber Phillips, *On historical distance*, 59.
9 Daniel Woolf, *Reading History in Early Modern England*.

Bibliography

Bawashi Anis, S. and Jo Reif, eds. *Genre: An Introduction to History, Theory, Research, and Pedagogy*. Anderson: Parlor Press LLC, 2010.
Evju, Håkon. *Ancient Constitutions and Modern Monarchy: Historical Writing and Enlightened Reform in Denmark-Norway 1730–1814*. Leiden: Brill, 2019.
Findlen, Paula, ed. *Empires of Knowledge: Scientific Networks in the Early Modern World*. London: Routledge, 2019.
Koselleck, Reinhart. *Futures Past: On the Semantics of Historical Times*. New York: Columbia University Press, 2004 [1985].
Nadel, George. "Philosophy of History before Historicism." *History and Theory* 3, no. 3 (1964): 291–315.
Phillips, Mark Salber. *On Historical Distance*. New Haven & London: Yale University Press, 2013.
Phillips, Mark Salber. *Society and Sentiment: Genres of Historical Writing in Britain, 1740–1820*. Princeton: Princeton University Press, 2000.
Pomata, Gianna and Nancy G. Siraisi, eds. *Historia: Empiricism and Erudition in Early Modern Europe*. Cambridge, MA, and London: MIT Press, 2005.
Pollmann, Judith. *Memory in Early Modern Europe, 1500–1800*. Oxford: Oxford University Press, 2017.
Vine, Angus. *Miscellaneous Order: Manuscript Culture and the Early Modern Organization of Knowledge*. Oxford: Oxford University Press, 2019.
Woolf, Daniel. *Reading History in Early Modern England*. Cambridge: Cambridge University Press, 2001.
Woolf, Daniel. *The Social Circulation of the Past: English Historical Culture, 1500–1730*. Oxford: Oxford University Press, 2003.

Part 1

Antiquarian and material negotiations

1 Antiquarian poetry and royal performance

Anne Eriksen

In 1749, King Frederik V visited Norway, the northernmost part of his kingdom. It was a short journey, restricted to south-eastern Norway and accomplished in a couple of weeks. From Christiania (present-day Oslo), the King travelled to Kongsberg to inspect the silver mines. He also visited the cities of Fredrikstad and Fredrikshald with their fortresses before returning to Denmark. *En route*, he was celebrated by his loyal subjects and shown all the tributes worthy of a monarch. The King himself is nonetheless reported to have been mostly interested in gambling and in the theatrical company that he had brought with him for his entertainment.[1]

When the royal entourage stopped at Hokksund in Eiker on its way to Kongsberg, the vicar Christian Grawe welcomed the King with a poem of his own composition. It bore the title *Salve & Vale—Prisca & nova Egerana* (*Hail and Farewell—Ancient and New Eiker*). In 55 four-lined stanzas and with a large array of footnotes, Grawe delivered a description of the parish with numerous antiquarian details. When the poem appeared in print some months later, he could sign it not only as a vicar but also with his newly acquired title: *professor antiqvitatis patriae*. In the present world, poetry is not often used to communicate research results or to document scientific work. In the early modern period, on the other hand, as the present volume abundantly shows, historical writing employed a wide range of genres and forms. During the same period, literary forms were also used to discuss natural philosophy and the findings of natural history, even if such expressions long have been overlooked in the history of science.[2] The heyday for this type of literature was the seventeenth century. The genre to which Grawe's poem more particularly belongs, topographic descriptive poetry, was established during the same period, developing into romantic landscape poetry in the subsequent century.[3]

The aim of this chapter is to look into the specific "genre of historical writing" that Grawe chose for conveying his topographical and antiquarian knowledge about the parish: The poem with footnotes. The first part of this chapter will examine the poem and the knowledge it presents. What does it tell us about Grawe's historical and antiquarian work? And how did he make the rhymed stanzas and their apparatus of notes serve as tools for historical

DOI: 10.4324/9781003331971-3

writing? The point of this investigation is not to present literary criticism but rather to examine Grawe's work as an historian. For this reason, the explicitly historical and antiquarian parts of the poem will be given the most attention. The discussion will then move on to include the performance that the poem represented. This applies to its actual delivery during the royal visit, but equally much to the performative dimensions of the poem itself and to performance as related to an understanding of genre. The argument that I want to make rests on an approach to genre that includes more than the form and substance of a text. As "social action",[4] genre is also a negotiation of social and cultural codes. Paying attention to performativity, I will argue, is a way of investigating the workings of such codes. With this as the point of departure, I will explore how Grawe made use of both historical knowledge and cultural competence to produce a work that served him as legal tender within the social system of the absolute monarchy of the Danish state.

The ethnography of genres

In her influential article "Genre as social action", Carolyn Miller criticises purely formalist approaches to genre and advocates ethnomethodological perspectives, arguing that the "'de facto' genres, the types we have names for in everyday language, tell us something theoretically important about discourse".[5] This approach does not presuppose a limited and finite set of genres. Instead, the number of genres to be considered will grow to include mundane and vernacular speech forms. The aim is to "take seriously the rhetoric in which we are immersed, and the situations in which we find ourselves".[6] An implication is also that the social setting of the discourse not only is considered as context, but as an integral part of the genre itself. Consequently, Miller pays much attention to the typologization of recurrent social situations, and to how the experience of situations *as* recurrent is possible. "Exigence" is presented as a key term in this argument, standing at the core of the rhetorical situation and defining it. Miller argues that "exigence must be located in the social world, neither in a private perception, nor in material circumstance [...] Exigence is a form of social knowledge—a mutual construing of objects, events, interests, and purposes that not only links them but also makes them what they are: an objectified social need".[7] Exigence is a social motive: It motivates by connecting the private with the public and the singular with the recurrent.[8] It follows from these perspectives that genres are historically and culturally specific. They will change and develop over time as social situations and exigencies do. Moreover, they will also change due to the speakers more or less successful work to bring about change, to adapt to new situations and to make use of these situations. Seeing genre as social action consequently means seeing genres as negotiated, as sometimes contested and always as part of social networks.

Similar perspectives have been suggested by folklore scholars. Working comparatively with oral material from different cultural contexts, they point to the necessity of distinguishing analytical from ethnic genres. On the one hand, analytical genres make it possible to explore and compare oral material globally, to compose motive indexes and develop other scholarly tools for cross-cultural comparative research. Focusing on ethnic genres, on the other hand, helps to understand the cultural grammar particular to a specific cultural group. American folklorist Dan Ben-Amos has stated that [oral] "genres are modes of verbal symbolic interaction, having rules and structures which involve para-linguistic communicative components and established cultural attitudes. These are essential to the concepts of genres, as much as themes and verbal structure are to literary-linguistic analysis" (Ben-Amos 1976:xxxvi).[9] Even more than Miller, folklore scholars consequently have pointed out that genres have fundamental performative aspects. Moreover, this understanding of performance is not restricted to the delivery of the speaker but includes interaction with an audience. The character of this interaction will vary, from active participation in so-called conversational genres to the more passive listening to a formal speech, a complex story or an epic poem. William H. Jansen described this in terms of a continuum from performance to participation. He pointed out that genres with the lowest degree of performance have the highest degree of participation, while the opposite is the case with genres demanding well-developed specialised skills.[10] Roger D. Abrahams has later argued that performance is a constant factor in all genres but that the extent and type of interaction will vary. Elaborating on the genre continuum presented by Jansen, Abrahams develops an overview of oral genres in terms of performer-audience relationships. This approach has the advantage, he maintains, of focusing on "genres as sets of performance pieces that performers employ to affect, to *move* the audience". He also points out that "each item is performed in an attempt to influence future action by appealing to past usage".[11] As Miller pointed out, genres are recurrent performances.

Grawe's antiquarian poem will be explored with these perspectives in mind. The poem obviously referred to the past, considering its historical content but also considering its use of well-established rhetorical forms and conventions. Just as obvious, it had significant performative aspects in seeking to move its audience in the present by connecting the singular event—the King's visit—to the recurrent: The conventions for royal tribute. More profoundly, the performance that the poem represents connects the private aspects of Grawe's interest and knowledge with the public sphere, his role as civil servant and loyal subject of the king. The following examination will explore how Grawe made use of the poetic form to present his antiquarian knowledge, and how this knowledge was successfully shaped and fashioned into a performance that both included and moved his audience.

Christian Grawe—vicar, poet and antiquary

The main source of information about the life and work of Christian Grawe is a topographic description of the parish of Eiker, produced by Grawe's son-in-law and later successor to the incumbency, the natural historian Hans Strøm. This topography incorporates the historical information given by Grawe in his poem and also contains biographical information about the incumbents of the parish. Grawe was born in Denmark around 1700 and came to Norway as a young man. As a student, he worked as a private tutor, and then, after passing his exams at the University of Copenhagen, as a teacher in the city of Bragernes (present-day Drammen), not far from Eiker. In the mid-1720s, he was engaged by the Danish East India Company as a ship's chaplain. After surviving a shipwreck off the coast of Ireland, he managed to make his way to Oxford and spent a period of time there as a student, living in great poverty. In 1732, Grawe returned to Denmark and was assigned a parish there but succeeded in exchanging it for a position in Norway. He came to Eiker as a vicar in 1747 and remained there until his death in 1763. During this period, he was also involved in the development and improvement of glassworks in Norway and owned part of one of them himself. Combined with his interest in agriculture, his activities made him a wealthy man (Strøm 1784).[12]

Grawe is not known to have written any other historical works. He was, however, among the very first members of the *Royal Danish Society for Patriotic History*, founded in Copenhagen in 1745 by the historian and royal archivist Jacob Langebek. A main interest for this society was to collect and publish historical documents in its journal *Danske Magazin*. Images of seals and inscriptions were also printed. Commentaries and short articles presenting the published material were mostly written by the editor himself, Langebek. A list of the members of the *Society* was presented in each volume; in the early years, it was a very short list. From 1747 we find Christian Grawe among the twelve names listed. This year the magazine also published a document that had been donated by Grawe, a letter concerning a murder in Copenhagen in 1570 (cf. later). The same volume also presented a picture of a large silver cross reported to be in the collection of Bishop Peder Hersleb. The short article claims that it formerly had belonged to Grawe, who is referred to as "a very careful man, both in his search for all kinds of Norwegian antiquities and in collecting documents and texts to the illumination of Nordic history".[13] The respectful phrase indicates that Grawe's antiquarian interests, as well as his contact with other collectors, must have been of some standing. Letters from Grawe to Langebek also show continued contact after this. No more direct donations of manuscripts from Grawe to the *Society* have been traced, but he seems to have played a role in the arrival of a large collection of sixteenth-century manuscripts in Copenhagen in 1748. The so-called visitation protocols of the humanist and early Lutheran Bishop Jens Nilssøn (1538–1600) were included in Hersleb's collection, probably through Grawe's intervention or as a gift.[14] The *Society* for its part later received another gift, a tall and richly decorated goblet from the glassworks at Nøstetangen, in which Grawe had part ownership. The goblet is adorned with the *Society*'s seal as well as with its device, and the vignette from *Danske Magazin*. The gift was probably made as late as between 1751 and 1753, which was the period when Grawe himself was the director of the glassworks. It is still owned by the *Society*.[15]

As a topographic poet, Grawe may have had models to follow. In 1727, Johannes Schrøder published a descriptive poem about Frederikshald, also adding historical details to rhymed stanzas. There are no indications that Grawe knew this work, but its existence proves that a poem with notes was no idiosyncratic whim of Grawe's. A work of greater fame was Thomas Kingo's descriptive poem about the Danish island of Samsø, *Samsøs korte Beskrivelse*, from 1675. It had been composed in honour of the new owner of the island and estate of Samsø, Peder Schumacher Griffenfeld, who in his turn made Kingo his protégé. Of modest bourgeois origins, Peder Schumacher had made a brilliant career at court, was elevated into nobility with the name Griffenfeld and had been appointed chancellor of Denmark in 1673. Kingo's poem has no notes comparable to those of Grawe but builds directly on a contemporary topographic text in prose by Hans Resen.[16] Another possible model may have been *Nordlands Trompet*, a work by the Norwegian parson Peter Dass, published in print in 1739.[17] This poem also lacks notes, but its topographic contents make it comparable to Grawe's poem. The work presents an extensive description of the northern parts of Norway based on Dass' thorough knowledge of these regions. Beyond their topographic and descriptive content, there are also other similarities between the poems by Kingo, Dass and Grawe. They were all written for a patron—Frederik V, Peder Griffenfeld and, in the case of Dass, the Governor-general of Norway, Ditlev Vibe. This means that they all have elements of the panegyric, addressing the respective patrons in flattering tones. Furthermore, this also implies that the poems have worked as elements in those networks of client- and patron-relations that were important parts of the social structure during this period, and which at times could be decisive for achieving promotions, positions and privileges.

The poem which Grawe presented at the royal visit now exists in two versions, one hand-written and one printed. The manuscript version is in the Norwegian University Library. It is in folio format and probably in Grawe's own hand but is not signed. The printed version is dated the same year as the royal visit, 1749, and is a small booklet in octavo format. Both versions have a large and ornate title page, which in the printed version is folded together and glued in at the front to fit the modest format of the book. The print version has an additional front page which carries Grawe's name as well as his titles as the vicar of Eiker, member of the *Royal Danish Society for Patriotic History* and professor.

Local knowledge

The poem has four distinct sections. First comes its elaborate title page, addressing the King in Latin. Most of the rest is in Danish. The second section has fifteen stanzas expressing words of welcome and tribute. Then follows the section of antiquarian and topographic stanzas, altogether twenty. The final section is Grawe's prayer for the King and his House, ending with words of farewell. The three last stanzas of this section are announced as "monk's verse"[18] and are again in Latin. Notes are dispersed throughout the entire work, including the title page.

The antiquarian section, which will be the main focus of exploration here, begins with Grawe's presentation of himself. He explicitly "appears"[19] as the antiquarian in search of ancient things, and as the clergyman who daily asks for God to bless his King[20] and now is ready to present the results of his searches. The first of the antiquarian stanzas refers to a royal letter from 1350, in which King Magnus granted the monks in Oslo the exclusive right to the salmon fisheries in the Eiker River. The next stanza refers to a papal letter from 1311, naming a total of 14 chapels, and of them—according to Grawe—the one situated at Eiker. The phrase in the Pope's letter was "kapellam S:Laurentii ad Aikarn Sund", and it is Grawe's own conjecture that this refers to the sound in Lake Eikern. When the letter later was printed in *Danske Magazin*, it was pointed out that the name "Aikarn Sund" might just as likely refer to Egersund, an ancient settlement on the southern coast Norway, later growing into a town.[21] The notes of both stanzas are supplied with references to the letters and quote from them. The first of these two letters was the one that was published in *Danske Magazin* in 1747 (cf. earlier). Grawe mentions his gift in a note and names Terkel Klevenfeldt as the person he corresponded with on the occasion. Klevenfeldt, originally Kleve, was one of the original members of the *Society* and well known as a great collector himself.

After a brief mention of the glassworks in the region, Grawe then takes his listener—the King—to the church, pointing to its stonework and its mark of two crossed keys. It refers to a model of the church supposedly sent from Rome with the Pope's blessing and grant. The notes in this case refer to further medieval sources for this practice. Grawe also says that such a model, made from richly gilt copper, was given to him the other year by the neighbouring vicar Niels Bernhoft. This model came from the small chapel of Vatnås, which was undergoing restoration work at the time. In his capacity of member of the *Society*, Grawe had transferred this object to its collections, where it now can be seen. The object was long identified with a reliquary, now in the collections of the Danish National Museum (Grinder-Hansen 2003). These notes, then, again indicate the close connections between Grawe and the *Royal Danish Society for Patriotic History*, with documents and objects being sent from Eiker to Copenhagen and correspondence with the *Society's* leading members. The information confirms that Grawe was well situated within the small and rather exclusive antiquarian community of the twin kingdoms and communicated with people in its inner circles.

Grawe goes on to describe the most prominent old objects inside the church. The first is a remarkable cope with golden ornaments, "so grand, so rich from gold".[22] Another medieval letter is quoted in a note to document that the parish came under the wealthy Bishop of Oslo and that the local vicar and user of the cope thus was his *vicarius*. A costly altarpiece, two candelabra and some magnificent graves with silver ornaments are also mentioned. In addition to their costliness and conspicuous nature, these objects have direct connections to leading nobility and grand estates in the area. The candelabra had been donated by Dorthe Urne, married to the powerful statesman Ove Gedde, in 1618. In a note, Grawe presents its Latin inscription referring to Gedde in his position as the Governor of Trankebar in India, then a Danish colony. The graves are those of the feudal lord Peder Hanssøn Basse (Litle) and his wife Ingeborg Gyldenløve, of ancient Norwegian nobility. Their son later became the Chancellor of Norway. The embalmed body of an old woman, said to have been long kept on display in the sacristy, is also mentioned. In the poem, this appears more as a curiosity, but in the note, Grawe adds that this woman once was the mistress of one of the large estates in the area. From here, Grawe takes his reader back outside the church and starts pointing out the locations of the more significant farms and estates, again naming their noble proprietors. Supplemental information about the families, their genealogy and privileges then follows in the notes. Grawe gives little information about the sources that he bases this information on, but mentions the work *Danmarckis oc Norgis Fructbar Herlighed* by the historian Arnt Berntsen, published in 1656 and containing rich and detailed information about landed property in both parts of the twin kingdoms Denmark-Norway.

From the wealth of the landed nobility, Grawe turns to the wealth of the mountains themselves. Beyond a summer farm belonging to the Skjelbred estate, he writes, there was once a rich silver mine. Today, it is suspended and closed, due to richer findings elsewhere. Two other ancient mining locations are also mentioned, Gravdal and Bingen. Only ruins are left of the mines there now, Grawe says. In the final part of the antiquarian section, he then leaves the past and turns to the future: Once again, Grawe declares—though he does not know when—the Lord will bless the country and its King with new riches from the "night" of the mountains. The meagre soil of Norway will prove to hide more riches than anybody could believe.[23] A note explains that among the miners, "night" is a common expression for ore. The King, who had stopped at Eiker with his retinue, was on his way to inspect the silver mines at Kongsberg—where mint was struck with his portrait on each coin, as Grawe points out. Eiker sends its farewell to the passing monarch but also its "comfort": If—or even when—the mines at Kongsberg are exhausted, the Eiker region may prove to compensate for this. Numerous legends in oral tradition carried a similar message, as did the popular saying that "the calf is at Kongsberg, but the cow is at X"—naming a location where immense riches supposedly could be discovered, far exceeding those of the mines presently in use. For the King and the government, it was a constant worry that the Kongsberg mines were not yielding as much silver as could be wished for, which in its turn initiated exploration for new resources, and for legends or popular knowledge that might give pointers for the hunt.

In the final section of the poem, Grawe turns to the second of the tasks he has announced: To pray for the King and ask God's blessings for him. This also includes prayers and rich praise for the absent Queen Louise. Grawe asks God to make the House of the King as permanent and solid as "store Jonas Knude", explaining in a note that this was the name of the tallest and largest mountain outside Kongsberg. Even this section of the poem is rich in antiquarian knowledge. The notes are used to explain specific Norwegian words and units of measure, to present the traditional rights and privileges of the church and to discuss the Norwegian national character: brave and patriotic. Grawe finds the reason for these qualities in the ancient custom and law of *odel,* i.e., the peasants' heritable property rights to the farms, and the independence which followed from this. These notes are so long and elaborate that they fill the larger part of each page, leaving little room for the stanzas. With the notes in this section, Grawe leaves explicitly local history and topography behind, and turns to the country itself, with its language, customs and law, and a history of its own. Norway was part of the Danish conglomerate state during this period but also had an ancient history as an independent kingdom. With his notes, Grawe draws attention to issues and phenomena that were distinctively Norwegian, and which made this part of the realm different from the Danish.

The prayer which rounds off the poem also ends on this note, with its farewell to the travelling monarch: "So leave, in the name of God, but Oh, do not forget about Norway".[24] In both the hand-written and the printed versions this stanza is set in larger letters, making it visually notable and signalling the King's departure and the end of the poem. Nonetheless, the poem has a kind of appendix. Somebody is calling out from the convent of St. Laurent, a following stanza tells. This again refers to the building mentioned in the Papal letter of 1311, in which King Haakon was granted the privileges of fourteen churches or chapels. Despite its historical foundation, however, Grawe's poem makes a passage into the fantastical on this point. Even if the Papal letter should have referred to Eiker, no material traces of a building existed in Grawe's own time. Nonetheless, he makes use of this antiquarian conjecture to stage a fictitious event, a verse in Latin sent by an imaginary monk from the equally imaginary convent. The verse consists of yet another tribute to the King and his Queen, lamenting their departure from Norway. Grawe has added notes even here, in this case explaining biblical references and terms that refer to Catholic religious practice.

Poetry and antiquarianism

The combination of four-lined stanzas and elaborate footnotes is the major structural principle of Grawe's poem. The notes do not only occur in the antiquarian middle section, but run throughout the entire work, which consequently must be considered a real union of prose and poetry. The two strands of texts—poetry and prose—serve different tasks: The notes are not poetical interpretations but present elucidations of what has been said, or rather alluded to, in the stanzas. They explain the meaning of names, words and phrases, and present more specific and detailed information on the places, figures and events that are mentioned far more briefly in the stanzas. Moreover, they present Grawe himself in the role of the learned antiquarian and bear witness to his work. The knowledge he demonstrates and the historical material that he refers to tell a story of a great amount of diligent work. At the time of the royal visit, Grawe had been the vicar of Eiker for a mere two years, but he shows that he knows the parish and its historical sites and figures well and has obviously succeeded in tracing both documents and objects of historical value. The rhymed verses, for their part, give an aesthetically pleasing form to the presentation of the parish, its history and its most remarkable features. They also serve to approach and celebrate the monarch more effectively than dry antiquarian facts were likely to do on their own—the King was not known for his love of erudition. The poetry signals an appropriate address in the high rhetorical style, while also offering Grawe an opportunity to demonstrate his own mastery of such expression.

However, it should also be noted that the two types of text supplement each other and most effectively work together. The poetic form supplies a frame that gives coherence to the antiquarian information. It has often been pointed out that early modern antiquarians usually did not publish that much. One reason for this is that they first and foremost were collectors. Even the antiquarians who were most famous in their own time were known for their collections and erudition, and for their networks of friendship and correspondence rather than for published works.[25] An additional and important point stems from the very structure of antiquarianism as a tradition of knowledge. As described by Arnaldo Momigliano, antiquarian knowledge was systematic rather than narrative; historians writing in the rhetorical tradition and seeing history as the teacher of life told stories about people and their deeds.[26] And, as Anthony Grafton has pointed out, for a long time they did not make much use of notes or refer to their sources.[27] Antiquarians, for their part, collected what Francis Bacon had once called the "shipwrecks of time": documents, inscriptions and other material fragments from the past.[28] If they wrote anything at all, it was catalogues. Antiquarians would inventory and comment on their own collections or similar material elsewhere. They exchanged letters, notes and in some cases also objects and documents—just as Grawe sent antiquarian material to Copenhagen. Antiquarian writing practice thus was eminently fit for producing notes, but as they lacked a frame or an overarching story they would also lack coherence, even meaning that the notes would have to be notes *to* something.

Grawe does not present any grand story about Eiker and its history, but even without this, the poem constitutes a frame that connects different and disparate bits of information and turns them into parts of an overall and intelligible picture of the parish, including both historical and topographic elements. The poetic form represented a rhetorical tool to present his antiquarian knowledge in a way that was far more pleasing to his audience than any catalogue or collection of erudite comments would have been, but it also offered him a practical way of ordering his notes and perhaps somewhat piecemeal learning.

Footnotes, which today represent the very hallmark of historical scholarship, were used for other purposes during this period. In the same way that indexes developed as a "book part" in the early modern period,[29] notes served to insert a metalevel or second voice into books and texts. Exploring the history of indexes, Dennis Duncan has shown how they not only were a practical device that enabled readers to quickly grasp the main contents of a book but also served as a tool for irony and subversive comments.[30] A prerequisite for this to work, however, was the development of a corresponding reader competence: The readers must know what to look for and how to approach the index to enjoy its more or less subtle commentaries. Footnotes could be used in much the same way, supplying a potentially ironic or critical voice-over.

Some months before the royal visit at Eiker, the reading public in Denmark-Norway had been presented with a case of this kind. In December 1748, a panegyric cantata had been performed in honour of the royal couple at the theatre in Copenhagen, composed by the Frenchman Laurent Angliviel de la Beaumelle. He was also known as the ("anonymous" and "female") editor of the moral weekly *La Spectatrice Danoise*. Shortly after, this weekly published a harsh critique of the cantata, arguing that it could be understood as ironic. To this critical attack on both the cantata and its composer, *la Spectatrice* herself added a series of notes, defending both and including even more voices in the discussion. The competent reader of the resulting polyphony would know that all the texts—the cantata, the critique and the defending notes—were written by the same person. In a kingdom of absolute rule, this elegant construction supplied a way of discussing social and political issues not allowed in any open, public debate.[31]

Grawe's work does not seem to have been as subtle in his address to the King. Apart from the traditional double role of the panegyric to offer both praise and admonition, his tribute to the notoriously drinking and gambling King carries no signs of a double meaning. In this case, the second voice of the notes had other tasks to attend to. As pointed out earlier, they served to communicate historical learning, but in the poem's final section, they obviously also serve another aim. This is where Grawe leaves local topography and turns to national issues. The notes here are about Norway: Its history, its nature and natural wealth, its ancient language and laws and the correspondence between the two, and the resulting brave and independent character of its people. These notes differ from the bits of information in the antiquarian stanzas by adding up to a larger and far more comprehensive picture. In doing so, they also add a political dimension to the poem: The King is exhorted to "never forget about Norway", nor is he to be allowed to forget that Norway is different from Denmark and an ancient historical and political entity of its own.

Seen from such perspectives, Grawe's choice of genre for his historical writing was both instrumental and highly efficient. The four-lined rhymed stanzas with running notes worked well as a rhetorically elaborate tribute to the King, as a frame for the antiquarian knowledge and as a national plea. The work as a whole presented Grawe both as a competent poet and rhetorician and as an erudite antiquarian. The genre of the work, then, should not only be put down to being topographic. From a formal point of view, it can more precisely be designated as a specific subgenre: The erudite descriptive poem with (in this case antiquarian) notes.

The poem as performance

The discussion so far has emphasised that the poetic form also offered Grawe the possibility to *demonstrate* his competence, to *present* his knowledge and to *deliver* his tribute to the King. Performativity obviously also plays a part. Exigence motivates genre, Miller writes, by connecting the private with the public and the singular with the recurrent.[32] The exigence motivating Grawe's poem was the King's journey and the stop that he and his retinue made at Eiker. This event was singular and unique in the sense that Frederik V had never been to the parish before. Neither had Grawe probably met his King before. A "royal visit" is nonetheless also a recurrent event, representing a type and demanding specific kinds of action and expression. Even without any precise knowledge about the size and composition of the audience, Grawe's poetic performance and the reception of it stand out as a public event. To Grawe, the royal visit meant that he had to act as host, which did not only have a number of practical implications but also called on him to act as a representative of the loyal subjects paying their tribute to the monarch. At the same time, it was a singular event in his own life and career, and as such it offered unique opportunities. His choice of genre and the performance of his work took place exactly at this crossroads.

The poem itself has several explicitly performative references. The first fifteen stanzas, before the antiquarian information, serve as orientation. Grawe establishes his ethos and positions himself as a performer of the royal tribute. Announcing his own understanding of the appropriate way to greet a monarch, Grawe compares the King to the sun: His presence brings life and happiness to his subjects and does away with anxiety and fear. Grawe expresses his own great pleasure and calls out his words of welcome to the monarch in unison with "each peasant and each farmer".[33] Even the salmon in the river leap for joy at the royal visit.[34] From this initial positioning, Grawe then literally enters the stage in the first stanza of the antiquarian section. Leaving peasants and salmon behind, he "steps forward" and asks permission to "tell what I know".[35] From this point on, Grawe's poem holds the floor.

An important part of the performance that follows consists of showing, not merely telling. As pointed out by John W. Foster, topographic poetry is not only descriptive, but often tries to create a three-dimensional effect by making use of "stage directions". Adverbs like "here" and "there" are much used, together with other words that serve to locate specific elements and place them in relation to the standpoint of the performer and the audience (Foster 1970:396).[36] Furthermore, acts of seeing and moving about are often explicitly mentioned. Phrases and expressions of this kind are frequent in Grawe's poem. "Here" the monarch "will see", while "close by" and "to the left" other remarkable things likewise can be observed. Grawe "leads" his audience towards the church and then into the building itself. Here the cope with its golden ornament is exhibited, and "one notes" its costliness. After the visit, the poem lets us "step out" of the church. Standing outside it again, Grawe goes on to point out the farms and estates that can be "seen" from the front of the church, before addressing the King directly again with his prayer and his words of farewell.

Foster sees the verbs and the stage directions as elements of the way topographic poems work to create an experience of space. They obviously also have a role to play when the poem and the genre are considered from a performative point of view. Such directions do more than describe space, they situate the poet and his/her audience *in* it. Generally speaking, nothing much happens in descriptive poetry, but these markers turn topography into a place for movement, visual impression and the expression of feeling. The poem will describe this but also perform it and call on its audience to take part. As a formalised type of speech in the high rhetorical style, an address to the King demands specialised skills. It has a high degree of performativity and a correspondingly low degree of audience participation.[37] The way Grawe creates space and invites his audience into it nonetheless changes this and opens for a kind of intratextual participation that includes the audience in the performance. As a performer, Grawe employs the genre of his choice "to affect, to *move* the audience".[38] In this case the movement is spatial and physical rather than affective or intensely emotional, but it nonetheless means including the audience in the topography the poem describes, inviting engagement in the sites, objects and stories that it presents.

The most explicitly performative element of Grawe's poem is nonetheless the closing section, with the fictitious monk appearing from the imagined convent and presenting his Latin poem, at the same time creating an elegant end to Grawe's own work. The scene also fills other performative functions: It speaks directly to the King's strong interest in theatre and the theatrical, which was why he brought his own actors to entertain him on his Norwegian journey. Playing up to this, Grawe seeks to capture the attention and interest of the monarch. The scene also serves to merge past and present in Eiker. The monk appears as a sudden and surprising materialisation of the antiquarian information that Grawe so far has presented through his stanzas and notes. The past is performed. It steps into the present in the shape of a living being. And in doing so, it also lifts the royal visit out of the present and into a world of wonder and dreams. It transforms antiquities from being dry, dusty and worm-eaten erudition to something far more colourful, lively and catchy, and it creates a direct connection between the glorious world of kings and royalty and that of a dreamed past of romance and imagination.

The performative elements that have been discussed so far are all in the text itself. Not much is known about the actual delivery of the poem, the performance that took place as part of the King's visit to Eiker. It is difficult to imagine how the poem was recited. Were the notes read aloud together with the stanzas? The rhymed stanzas alone can be difficult to understand because they often merely allude to events, persons and customs from the past. The notes are the key to an understanding of what it all means, but how were they communicated? And did a monk-like figure really emerge on the hill outside the church, sending his Latin poem down to be read at the end of Grawe's? Had Grawe staged some kind of theatrical performance in honour of the King?

Some information about the performance can be inferred from the text itself. The front page of the print version of the poem declares the address to the King to have been delivered on the royal journey "through Eiker to Kongsberg, by the church on the hither side of Hougsund ferry landing 1749".[39] The phrasing supplies the performance with a precise location: It took place in front of the church at Hougsund, today's Hokksund. Moreover, the term "hither"[40] identifies the site of the performance with that of the interlocutor, making them one and the same place. Hither becomes here. This position also indicates that during the performance, the attention and gaze of the audience would actually have been directed as the poem indicates. The stage instructions "here", "there", "to the left" and so on in the poem appear to correspond with the movements and directions that have actually been part of the performance, involving the audience by catching their attention and gaze. Frederik V and his retinue have turned and looked, turned back and looked at something else, strained their gaze to see the mountains far away and again returned their attention to the site of the church and to Grawe himself. They may even have moved around and walked. According to the testimony of Grawe's son-in-law, Strøm, the King and his retinue were much impressed when shown the cope with its golden ornaments. It made them marvel, Strøm writes, even if much of its original splendour had been lost.[41] This information, again probably a tradition that had been passed on by Grawe himself as a memory of the visit, tells us that the King and his men actually visited the church where the cope was kept. This indicates that even the other objects from the church mentioned in the poem actually were shown, not merely described, and the recital of the poem at the "hither side of Hougsund ferry landing" included a visit to the church. Despite the high degree of formality that characterises both the royal visit as a "recurrent social situation" (cf. earlier) and the royal tribute in poetic form, it can be inferred that the performance engaged and involved those who were present, creating a real interaction between performer and audience. Grawe moved his audience, both physically and by awakening their awe and admiration.

Final remarks

The performance was a success. Not long after the royal visit, Grawe could sign the printed version of his poem with his new title *professor antiqvitatis patriae*—Professor of the Antiquities of the Fatherland. On the printed front page Grawe also expressed "a candid hope for lasting grace" and together with his "most humble and heartfelt gratitude and subservience".[42] The King's bestowal of an honorary professorship at the University of Copenhagen must have taken place during or shortly after the visit to Eiker. The honour can be seen as the result of the poetic performance but is perhaps more rightly considered as *part* of it. It represents the King's part in the performance, his response in kind. For a travelling monarch, bestowing grace and gifts—both symbolic and substantial—on the subjects who met him and paid him tribute was part of the task and what was expected of him. More generally, patronage, favours and recommendations were also all elements in the regular system of obtaining positions, advancements and privileges. As Emma C. Spary has pointed out, "eighteenth-century educated individuals needed to compete for patronage in order to gain advancement. Patronage stretched downward throughout society in a network of complex ramifications which controlled the getting of finances and posts".[43] Consequently, when working with source material that addresses persons who may have had favours to bestow, the historian must bear in mind the codes of the "honorific language" involved.[44] When addressing an absolute monarch, "honorific language" was a prerequisite, and not difficult to uncover in the material. What should be observed, however, and what this research has tried to show, is also the performative qualities of the poetic address, making it a "social action" in Miller's terminology. Grawe's presentation of his poem, and his antiquarian knowledge, was no mere recital of monological erudition. It was fundamentally dialogic and performative. The performance involved Grawe, the King, his retinue and every other person who might have been present "by the church on the hither side of Hougsund ferry landing 1749". It represented interaction, involvement and movement. To Grawe, it also represented a possibility to demonstrate his skills as an erudite antiquarian, as a rhetorician, but equally as much as a competent performer who was able to activate and involve his audience, to elicit response and interaction, to move and to influence future action.

Notes

1 Anne-Mette Nielsen, *Kongeferder i Norge gjennom 300 år* (Statens vegvesen: Norsk vegmuseum, 1999), 13.
2 Frédérique Aït-Touati, *Fictions of the Cosmos: Science and Literature in the Seventeenth Century* (Chicago: University of Chicago Press, 2011).
3 Robert Arnold Aubin, *Topographical Poetry in XVIII-Century England* (London: H. Milford, 1936).
4 Carolyn Miller, "Genre as Social Action", *Quarterly Journal of Speech*, 70:151–167.

5 Miller, "Genre," 155.
6 Miller, "Genre," 155.
7 Miller, "Genre," 157.
8 Miller, "Genre," 163.
9 Dan Ben-Amos, "Introduction", in *Folklore Genres*, ed. Dan Ben-Amos (Austin, Texas, University of Texas Press, 1976) ix–xlv.
10 William H. Jansen, "Classifying Performance in the Study of Verbal Folklore," in *Studies in Folklore. In Honor of Distinguished Service Professor Stith Thompson*, ed. W. Edson Richmond (Bloomington: University of Indiana Press 1957), 110–118.
11 Roger Abrahams, "The Complex Relation of Simple Forms", in *Folklore Genres*, ed. Dan Ben-Amos (Austin, Texas: University of Texas Press, 1976), 207, italics in original.
12 Hans Strøm, *Physisk-oeconomisk Beskrivelse over Eger-Præstegiæld i Aggershuus Stift i Norge* (København, Gyldendal, 1784).
13 … en meget omhyggelig Mand, saa vel i at opsøge alle Salgs Norske Antikviteter, som i at samle Documenter og Skrifter til den Nordiske Histories Oplysning (Danske Magazin 1747, vol. 3:3).
14 Yngvar Nielsen, *Jens Nilssøns Visitasbøger og Reiseoptegnelser 1574–1597* (Kristiania: Brøgger, 1885), cxx; Roar Tank, "Fra bisp til konge 1595–1749. Glimt av Eikers fortid", *Eikerminne*, 26.
15 Om Selskabet, https://danskeselskab.dk/en-norsk-glaspokal/, visited 25 May 2022.
16 Dag Finn Simonsen, *Diktet og makten. En analyse av et Kingo-dikt og en historisk drøfting av dansk-norsk barokkdiktning* (Oslo: Aschehoug, 1984), 9.
17 Hanne Lauvstad, *Helicons bierge og Helgelands schiær. Nordlands Trompets tekst, repertoar og retorikk* (Oslo: Universitetet i Oslo, 2007).
18 Grawe 1749, "Munke Vers".
19 Grawe 1749, "fremtriner".
20 Grawe 1749, "… Antiqvarius der gamle Ting opleder, som Præst der hver dag got fra Gud til Kongen Beder".
21 Danske Magazin 1745, 322.
22 Grawe 1749, "Saa stor, saa riig af Guld".
23 Grawe 1749, "Een stor Velsignelse af Jordens dyre Skatt; Op fra sin dybe gang den rige Bierge Natt.
     For Lyset komme skal i Danner-Kongens giemme; Naar Skoven siger nej skal Biergene istemme; Glüch aus, nu er vor Tiid, hvo tænkte vel derpaa; Saa megen Fedme i det mavre Norge laa".
24 Grawe 1749, "'Saa reis i Herrens Navn, ach! glem dog aldrig NORGE".
25 Peter N. Miller *Peiresc's Europe. Learning and Virtue in Seventeenth Century Europe* (New Haven and London: Yale University Press, 2000); Waldemar Hedelykke Grambye, *Antikvaren som samler i det tidlig moderne museumslandskab* (Odense: Syddansk universitet, 2020).
26 Arnaldo Momigliano, *The Classical Foundations of Modern Historiography* (Berkely: University of California Press, 1990).
27 Anthony Grafton, *The Footnote. A Curious History* (Cambridge, Mass.: Harvard University Press), 23.
28 Francis Bacon, *The Works of Francis Bacon*, eds. J. Spedding, R.L. Ellis and D.D. Heath (New York: Garrett Press, 1968 [1857–74]) vol IV: 303.
29 Dennis Duncan, "Indexes", *Book Parts*, eds. Dennis Duncan and Adam Smyth (Oxford: Oxford University Press, 2019).
30 Dennis Duncan, *Index, A History of the. A Bookish Adventure from Medieval Manuscripts to the Digital Age* (London: W.W. Norton & Co, 2022), 142–146.
31 Ellen Krefting, "La Spectatrice Danoise dans son contexte scandinave", in: Klaus-Diethler Ertler et al. (eds), *La Spectatrice Danoise de la Beaumelle* (Frankfurt: Peter Lang), 23–38.

32 Miller, "Genre," 163.
33 Grawe 1749, "... hver Landmand og hver Bonde."
34 Grawe 1749, "Selv Laxen springer op af Glæde udi Strand."
35 Grawe, "... sige hvad jeg veed."
36 John Wilson Foster, "A Redefinition of Topographical Poetry", *The Journal of English and Germanic Philology*, vol. 69, no. 3: 394–406.
37 Abrahams, "Complex Relations".
38 Abrahams, "Complex Relations", 207.
39 Grawe 1749, "... igiennem Eeger til Kongsberg ved Capelle-Backen denne Side Hougsunds Færgestæd 1749".
40 Grawe 1749, "denne Side."
41 Strøm, *Physisk-oeconomisk Beskrivelse*, 259.
42 'Et frimodig Haab af vedvarende Naade og allerdybeste taknemmelig Hiertens Underdanighed'
43 Emma C. Spary, *Utopia's Garden. French Natural History from Old Regime to Revolution* (Chicago: Chicago University Press, 2000), 34.
44 Spary, *Utopia's Garden*, 37.

Bibliography

Abrahams, Roger. "The Complex Relation of Simple Forms", in Dan Ben-Amos (ed.). *Folklore Genres*, 19–214. Austin: University of Texas Press, 1976.

Aït-Touati, Frédérique. *Fictions of the Cosmos: Science and Literature in the Seventeenth Century*. Chicago: University of Chicago Press, 2011.

Aubin, Robert Arnold. *Topographical Poetry in XVIII-Century England*. London: H. Milford, 1936.

Bacon, Francis. [1857–74]. *The Works of Francis Bacon*, eds. J. Spedding, R.L. Ellis and D.D. Heath, 14 vols. New York: Garrett Press, 1968

Ben-Amos, Dan. "Introduction", in Dan Ben-Amos (ed.). *Folklore Genres*, ix–xlv. Austin, Texas: University of Texas Press, 1976.

Danske Magazin 1745 and 1747 (vols. 1 and 3) (Copenhagen: C.G. Glassing).

Det Kongelige Danske Selskab for Fædrelandets Historie, https://danskeselskab.dk

Duncan, Dennis and Adam Smyth (eds). *Book Parts*. Oxford: Oxford University Press, 2019.

Duncan, Dennis. *Index, A History of the. A Bookish Adventure from Medieval Manuscripts to the Digital Age*. New York: W.W. Norton & Co, 2021.

Foster, John Wilson. "A Redefinition of Topographical Poetry." *The Journal of English and Germanic Philology*, 69, no. 3 (1970): 394–406.

Grafton, Anthony. *The Footnote. A Curious History*. Cambridge, MA: Harvard University Press, 1997.

Grambye, Valdemar Hedelykke. *Antikvaren som samler i det tidlig moderne museumslandskab*. PhD-avhandling. Odense: Syddansk universitet, 2020.

Grawe, Christian. *Salve & Vale. Nova & prisca Egerana*. Hougsund, 1749. No page numbers.

Grinder-Hansen, Poul. "Den Gyldne kirke fra Vatnås – og Oldsagssamlingen fra Det kongelige Danske Selskab for Fædrelandets Historie", in P. Grinder-Hansen (ed.). *Arvesølvet. Studier fra Nationalmuseet tilegnet Fritze Lindahl*, 159–173. København: Nationalmuseet, 2003

Jansen, William H. "Classifying Performance in the Study of Verbal Folklore", in W. Edson Richmond (ed.). *Studies in Folklore. In Honor of Distinguished Service Professor Stith Thompson*, 110–118. Bloomington: University of Indiana Press, 1957.

Krefting, Ellen. "La Spectatrice Danoise dans son contexte scandinave", in Klaus-Diethler Ertler et al. (eds.). *La Spectatrice Danoise de la Beaumelle*, 23–38. Frankfurt: Peter Lang, 2020.

Lauvstad, Hanne. *Helicons bierge og Helgelands schiær. Nordlands Trompets tekst, repertoar og retorikk*. Oslo: Universitetet i Oslo, 2007.

Momigliano, Arnaldo. *The Classical Foundations of Modern Historiography*. Berkeley: University of California Press, 1990.

Miller, Carolyn R. "Genre as Social Action." *Quarterly Journal of Speech* 70 (1984): 151–167.

Miller, Peter N. *Peiresc's Europe. Learning and Virtue in Seventeenth Century Europe*. New Haven and London: Yale University Press, 2000.

Nielsen, Anne-Mette. *Kongeferder i Norge gjennom 300 år*. Statens vegvesen: Norsk vegmuseum, 1999.

Nielsen, Yngvar. *Jens Nilssøns Visitasbøger og Reiseoptegnelser 1574–1597*. Brøgger: Kristiania, 1885.

Simonsen, Dag Finn. *Diktet og makten. En analyse av et Kingo-dikt og en historisk drøfting av dansk-norsk barokkdiktning*. Oslo: Aschehoug, 1984.

Spary, Emma C. *Utopia's Garden. French Natural history from Old Regime to Revolution*. Chicago: Chicago University Press, 2000.

Strøm, Hans. *Physisk-oeconomisk Beskrivelse over Eger-Præstegiæld i Aggershuus Stift i Norge*. København: Gyldendal, 1784.

Tank, Roar. "Fra bisp til konge (1595–1749). Glimt av Eikers fortid." *Eikerminne* (1950): 15–29.

2 "Compiled from original authors"

On the status of compilers and compilation as historiographical practice in the eighteenth century

Thomas Ewen Daltveit Slettebø

In 1742, the Danish-Norwegian author, playwright, and professor of history Ludvig Holberg (1684–1754) published his *Jewish History* ("Jødiske Historie"), a large work in two volumes that in total counted almost 1500 pages. As the full title of the work disclosed, the history also covered a vast period of time: *Jewish history from the beginning of the world, continued to the present day*. In the preface, Holberg presented his reasons for producing a work such as this. First, he wrote, the Jewish history is the most "pleasant and useful" of all histories. Second, he claimed that no "general" Jewish history had previously been written in any language. The ancient historian Josephus' works had ended with the destruction of Jerusalem, the English clergyman Humphrey Prideaux's *The Old and New Testament connected in the History of the Jews and Neighbouring Nations* (1715–1717) covered the period from the last kings to Herod, whereas Jacques Basnage's *Histoire des Juifs* (1706) picked up where Prideaux left off and ended in the present day. Holberg's Jewish history, or so he claimed, was the first work of any depth that treated the Jewish past in its entirety.[1]

An anecdote published in a Danish periodical almost a century later purported to reveal the circumstances surrounding Holberg's research process when writing his *Jewish history*. The story had been related to one Peder Wöldike, a principal at a Danish provincial school, by his father Marcus Wöldike (1699–1750), who had been a Hebraist and professor of theology at the University of Copenhagen. According to professor Wöldike, Holberg's library contained almost no theological works or ecclesiastical histories. Upon deciding to write a history of the Jewish people, he had contacted his learned colleague, asking him to loan him the books required for such an undertaking. Wöldike promised to send them and, believing Holberg wanted a "complete scholarly apparatus", he consequently spent a few weeks assembling the necessary literature. When he was finally finished, he sent some men with a big laundry basket full of books and papers to his colleague. Holberg, however, swiftly returned the basket with the following message to Wöldike: "Tell my dear colleague that this was not what I meant: I only wanted a Josephus and a Basnage. These I have already acquired elsewhere, so you can leave now and take all that learning with you!"[2]

DOI: 10.4324/9781003331971-4

Regardless of its veracity, Professor Wöldike's little anecdote does say something interesting about Holberg's method of writing histories. Holberg was explicitly hostile towards what he perceived as dry, scholarly learning, and he indeed tended to construct his own works of history by compiling text from merely a few existing histories. A number of studies have shown that most of Holberg's historical works—including the *Jewish History*—were to a substantial degree based upon portions of verbatim transcripts of older narrative histories or direct translations of foreign works.[3] Holberg copied everything from small paragraphs to several chapters from his sources, made revisions of varying degrees of magnitude to their phrases, and bound it all together with short passages, moral reflections and witty remarks of his own. Whereas the bulk of the narrative and the substance of his histories thus often came from elsewhere, however, their style and tone nonetheless come across as distinctly "Holbergian".[4] Holberg's textual loans are sometimes openly acknowledged in references or in the text itself, but more often than not they are made invisible to the unsuspecting reader and can only be discovered through careful comparison with presumed source texts.

From a modern standpoint, Holberg's manner of writing histories is obviously problematic. His unacknowledged borrowing from sources would today be understood as derivative and lazy writing, at best, or branded as plagiarism or intellectual property theft, at worst. Modern scholars have also tended to be the most interested in the more "original" of Holberg's historical works and to devote rather less attention to the more obviously compilatory texts (such as his *Jewish History*).[5] Until very recently, moreover, the few modern scholars who have discussed Holberg's compilation in light of eighteenth-century norms of historiographical practice have simply assumed that this was the normal way of doing things in his time.[6]

In this essay I intend to use the case of Holberg as a point of departure to discuss the broader question of the status of compilers and attitudes towards compilation as historiographical practice in eighteenth-century Europe: How did compilers present their own work, and what can these instances of self-fashioning reveal about the changing function and status of historical compilations? The self-presentation of eighteenth-century compilers also has a bearing on the evolution of genres of historical writing in the same period. As Mark Salber Phillips suggests, genres are historically contingent formations that mediate the communication between writers and their readers in the literary marketplace.[7] Identifying shifts in historical genres, he argues, entails studying the self-conscious "signaling" gestures of authors in their attempts to communicate with a perceived audience. This allows us to discover what he calls "the historically specific ideal reader".[8] While compilation as a mode of writing was used across many genres in this period, it is relevant to ask whether the compilers' novel strategies of self-presentation led contemporaries to perceive historical compilations as a distinct genre of historical writing during the period discussed here. In addition to the central case of Holberg, I will discuss several more or less well-known compilers and historical compilations primarily from the French and British contexts.

Compilation had been a central mode of writing among historians and chroniclers since antiquity and clearly remained a common practice well into the eighteenth century. It was essentially a versatile method of writing that can be found in many different subgenres within the broader field of historical writing in this period. Holberg, and many other contemporary historians, continued to compile their histories for most of the eighteenth century, in some cases with great commercial success and critical acclaim. Compilation was also frequently employed in other important areas of text production not exclusively focused on the topic of history, such as encyclopaedias and learned journals.[9]

Despite the ubiquity of compilation in the eighteenth-century world of print, however, there are good reasons to question whether historical compilations were in fact deemed completely unproblematic by contemporaries. As we shall see, there arose a critical discourse already in the first half of the century, according to which the compiler was associated with various negative characteristics such as plagiarism, pedantry, dullness and a lack of originality. If compilation remained a common practice, it was increasingly frowned upon. This suggests that there is a more complicated story to be told here than merely positing a clear dichotomy between a pre-modern historiographical regime—in which compilation was quite normal and accepted—to a modern regime in which it is denounced as hack work and plagiarism. Rather, I would argue that much of the eighteenth century was a long period of uneasy transition during which a traditional and time-honoured mode of writing histories—the art of compiling—remained important and widespread yet had to face an increasing amount of criticism and derision. Historical compilers were therefore, as we shall see, induced to respond to such criticism and did so by re-branding their role and refashioning their image in new ways.

Compilation as a contested practice

While compilation largely remained a common practice in the European Republic of Letters at the turn of the eighteenth century, it nonetheless appears that the status of the compiler became increasingly contested and ridiculed by noted intellectuals.[10] An early and much-read example of negative attitudes towards compilers is found in letter 64 of Montesquieu's *Lettres Persanes* from 1721, in which Rica, one of the book's two Persian protagonists, vents his contempt against the "compilateurs" he sees all around him in Paris:

> Of all authors, I despise none more than the compilers, who go off in all directions looking for bits and pieces of other writers' works, which they then stick into their own, like pieces of turf into a lawn; they're in no way superior to those printer's typesetters, who arrange letters which, combined

together, make a book, to which they contributed only the manual labour. I would like the original texts to be respected; I feel it's a kind of profanation, to extract the pieces which make them up from the sanctuary where they belong, and expose them to a contempt they do not deserve.[11]

In an article about compilation in Abbé Raynal's *Histoire des deux Indes* (1770), C.P. Courtney quotes a series of dismissive statements about "compilateurs" from well-known French intellectuals such as Voltaire and Rousseau, all of which suggest that dismissive and contemptuous attitudes towards compilers were very widespread among French philosophes around mid-century.[12] This impression is supported by Sophie Bourgault, who argues that: "The term 'compilateur' was deployed by countless literati in the mid-eighteenth century, and (almost) never as a compliment".[13] Unacknowledged textual theft, or plagiarism, had been widely criticised as a breach of norms in the Republic of Letters at least since the seventeenth century, although the boundaries of what constituted unacceptable plagiarism remained hazy and contested.[14] Although compilation was often exempted from definitions of plagiarism, copying from other writers to create a new text was sufficiently close in practice to render compilers vulnerable to accusations of plagiarism. And although the modern notion of the professional historian as someone who constructs their narrative based on critical analysis of authentic primary sources had yet to fully materialise, the early modern antiquarian tradition with its emphasis on finding, authenticating and critically analysing textual and material remnants from the past posed a potential challenge to those that would write their historical works merely on the basis of previous histories.[15] As contemporary reception of several of Holberg's historical works indeed show, not all eighteenth-century readers were willing to accept their compilatory aspects, although his elevated status as a public figure in his native Denmark-Norway possibly prevented his contemporaries from voicing their criticism too loudly in public.[16] Ten years after Holberg's death, his close friend Johann Adolph Scheibe apparently felt the need to publicly defend the *Jewish History* from critics denigrating the work, who had claimed that Holberg had read neither Josephus nor other older sources and that the work was compiled solely from "new, French and unreliable books" ("bloss aus neuen französischen und unzuverlässigen Büchern zusammengeschrieben").[17]

Nonetheless, despite such criticism, historical compilations continued to be written as never before in the eighteenth century. Some works were indeed popular and widely read best-sellers, so much so that one scholar has recently described the period as "the golden age of historical compilations".[18] One particularly notable example is the massive, multivolume compilation, eventually consisting of an "ancient part" and a "modern part", collaboratively produced by an anonymous group of Grub Street writers in London from the early 1730s to the mid-1760s known as *An Universal History*

(1736–1765). Although most of the sizable group of authors behind this work were relatively unknown figures that attempted to scrape together a living by writing works on commission for London booksellers, the work became a resounding critical and commercial success in the eighteenth century and was translated into several major European languages.[19] The full title of the history, which attempted to narrate the history of the entire world, clearly stated that this was a work "compiled from original authors". In practice, the phrase "original authors" here entailed that the work's authors compiled not from other compilations, but rather from those authors considered most authoritative for each nation or subject that the book covered.[20] It was also manifestly a largescale compilation based on the often unacknowledged collection, abridgement and systematisation of existing books. Karen O'Brien describes it as "a work of the Enlightenment in terms of its global conception of history" but otherwise just a "hack production" lacking both a "coherent historical programme" and "a consistent editorial line".[21] Jørgen Magnus Sejersted, on the other hand, suggests that the apparent lack of a distinct authorial voice might have been one of the work's major selling points, as it therefore easily lent itself to being compiled by other authors: it was "a text that depersonalizes original authors into an objective universality in order for new authors to repersonalize the facts by adding some of their own wit and style".[22] Guido Abbatista confirms that the *Universal History* did indeed perform such a function: the work was heavily used in influential and canonised texts such as Gibbon's *Decline and Fall of the Roman Empire* and Voltaire's *Essai sur le moeurs*. In addition, the compilation was indeed compiled by other noted compilers, such as several authors of articles in the *Encyclopedie* or Abbé Raynal in his *History of the East and West Indies*.[23] Although an unusual work in its conception, scale and popularity, the *Universal History* is in many ways an exemplary work that highlights the lingering importance of compilation to the writing of history in Europe the middle decades of the eighteenth century.

Another notable compiler of the period was the French Jansenist and former professor of rhetoric Charles Rollin, whose *Histoire ancienne* (1730–1738), a multivolume work of universal history detailing the histories of several ancient peoples within an overarching providentialist narrative, also became a major bestseller in Europe and in America in the eighteenth century.[24] Rollin unabashedly admitted in the preface to his work that he had pillaged everywhere, and that he was happy to renounce "the Title and Quality of an Author" if only he was considered a "good Compiler" by his readers "who will not be in much Pain what hand it comes from, provided themselves are pleas'd with it".[25] Rollin also explicitly stated that he tended not to quote from the authors from whom he transcribed, because he had "sometimes taken the Liberty of making some slight alterations". Rather than showing precisely with footnotes when and from whom he had borrowed, he merely explained briefly in the preface that he had made much use of Bossuet's Universal History and Humphrey Prideaux's history.

Holberg's *Jewish History* is a final case in point. He explicitly stated in his preface that the work was primarily based on the histories of Josephus, Prideaux and Basnage, precisely the same works that between them covered the chronological scope he claimed his own book was the first to cover as a whole. In addition, he wrote that he had used the first two volumes of *An Universal History*. In a similar manner to Rollin, Holberg pointed out that he would not cite his references, but rather that it sufficed to state that they constituted the foundation of his own work.[26]

What these examples seem to suggest is that adopting the role of the compiler was something an intellectual could still do openly and without much embarrassment. There are, however, some important nuances of self-presentation here: Whereas Rollin explicitly adopted the scholarly persona of a "compiler", and the creators of the *Universal History* advertised their compiling on the title page, Holberg seems to have preferred to refer himself as a "historian" and was much less forthright about the amount of verbatim copying in his histories. Methodically, however, there are more similarities than differences: If their histories were well-wrought, readable and somehow useful to the public, it apparently did not matter whether or not they were based on the study of archival documents or merely compiled from other works of history. Precise references were clearly not needed, apart from the historian admitting a debt of gratitude to the most central source texts in his preface. In one sense, these historians merely fulfilled the traditional role of compilers and reproduced a mode of writing that had been used by their predecessors in previous centuries. Due to the mounting criticism against compilation, however, historical compilers became more self-conscious and this led them to define the *raison d'etre* of compilation. We shall now turn to the refashioning of the compiler.

The compiler as discerning curator

In the first half of the eighteenth century, one crucial argument in defence of compilation as a method of historical writing emerged, namely the notion of the compiler as a critical curator of existing scholarly knowledge. According to this line of thought, the compiler was a figure that sifted through dusty and erudite tomes on behalf of his readers in order to extract those facts or stories he perceived as having relevance in the present, potentially even rendering those older books completely superfluous. This line of argument could in part, as we shall see later, be couched in economic terms, ostensibly offering to the consumer the opportunity to buy one historical work rather than acquiring a "whole library". It was also, however, based on the rhetorical construction of what the compilers claimed to be a new quality of knowledge dissemination.

Underlying the model of the "compiler-as-curator" seems to have been a general sense of unease, or even exasperation, among eighteenth-century readers about the growing mass of books, pamphlets and other reading materials flooding the European market, a phenomenon that has previously been described as "early modern information overload".[27] The increase in production of printed books throughout the early modern period was everywhere accompanied by scholarly critiques of the "multitude" or "abundance" of books, sometimes articulated as calls for the policing of book production or even for the culling of books.[28] It also led many scholars to experiment with various reading and note-taking strategies to find ways to more effectively process the rising amounts of available texts.[29] Somewhat paradoxically, moreover, a commonly proposed solution to the multitude of books was the production of more books. According to Ann Blair,

> [t]he perception of an overabundance of books fueled the production of many more books, often especially large ones, designed to remedy the problem—from new genres like the universal bibliography and the book review to new (or not-so-new) contributions to well-established genres, including the florilegium, the dictionary, and the encyclopedic compilation.[30]

In other words, the perceived need to manage the vast and ever-growing production of texts was met with efforts to create new texts that either contained systematised extracts of the best and most authoritative knowledge on a given subject (i.e., an encyclopaedia) or gave short presentations and verdicts of new works in manageable format (i.e., book reviews in scholarly journals). In all these pursuits, the compiler was a central figure. The art of excerpting and collecting fragments of text from existing books in order to create new books was of course not a novelty in the eighteenth century but had, as we have seen, rather been a hallmark of humanist scholarly practice throughout the early modern period, both in the form of private commonplace books or in largescale publishing projects such as florilegia or encyclopaedias. Neither was the sense of "information overload" an entirely new phenomenon in the eighteenth century, but seems rather to have been a recurring complaint directed against the book trade since the days of Gutenberg. Even the notion of the compiler-as-curator was not novel in and of itself: as historian Caspar Hirschi points out, the "widespread acceptance of the compiler as an indispensable figure" in the seventeenth century was due precisely to the compilers role as a "curator and circulator of old learning, which enjoyed greater epistemic regard than recently produced knowledge, especially when attributed to classical authors".[31] What was new was rather the compilers' confident assertion of their own critical discernment. Compilation, in this novel reiteration, implied not merely carefully organising, re-packaging and circulating existing knowledge, but rather critically examining a useless mass of unappealing materials from the past in order to extract something that a more enlightened and philosophical century could use.

The compiler was here cast no longer as an essential but humble servant of the Republic of Letters but rather as a heroic figure of good taste and philosophy that helped disseminate knowledge to a wider, non-expert readership. This re-branding of the role of compilers often entailed throwing earlier generations of compilers under the bus for allegedly lacking the necessary qualities of taste and discernment. In a 1754 essay in the Danish periodical *Mercure Danois*, an anonymous writer asserted that compilations were the best solution to the problem of the growing multitude of books. As older historical works became less interesting and relevant, the most important facts contained in them could be compiled into a "general history" ("l'histoire Générale")—the role model for this sort of operation was the French historian Rapin Thoyras, whose history of England had allegedly rendered all previous histories of England completely superfluous. Successful compilations, however, required "just and philosophical minds" ("d'esprits justes & philosophiques"), something that earlier generations of compilers had not been blessed with, but that the writer was confident that his own century of progress was now fully able to produce:

> On s'est beaucoup recrié contre les compilateurs; on les a relégue dans la classe des manoeuvres, & des portefaix de la République des Lettres, & il faut convener que la plupart de ceux qui ont paru dans les seiziéme & dixseptiéme siècles méritoient assez ce petit reproche qu'on leur a fait dans le nôtre. [...] Mais ci comme il semble, que nous sommes en droit de l'attendre des progrès que la raison a faits dans ce siècle, s'il se trouve, dis-je, un certain nombre d'esprits justes & philosophiques qui veuillent se donner la peine de rassembler en un corps ce que nou avons deja dans chaque science de connoissances réelles & solides, il est aisé de voir que le superflu de la literature n'incommodera plus que ceux qui voudront bien s'en laisser incommoder.[32]

The Irish writer Oliver Goldsmith, similarly pointed out in the preface to his *History of England* (vol. 1, 1771) that "the business of abridging the works of others has hitherto fallen to the lot of very dull men", resulting in their abridgements becoming "more tedious than the works from which they pretend to relieve us [...]".[33] Goldsmith proclaimed his superiority to these predecessors with some gusto: "As the present compiler starts with such humble competitors, it will scarcely be thought vanity in him if he boasts himself their superior". Since earlier abridgements of histories of England had been either badly written or politically partisan, "[a] very small share of taste [...] was sufficient to keep the compiler from the defects of the one, and a very small share of philosophy from the misrepresentations of the other".[34]

A similar strategy of self-promotion has previously been pointed out by Caspar Hirschi among British and French dictionary writers in the first half of the eighteenth century. Hirschi identifies what he describes as a "rapid transformation of the public image of the lexicographer" during the first half of the eighteenth century, in which "a figure long treated as a modest compiler could now be considered an original author and scholarly hero".[35] Among the reasons for this shift, according to Hirschi, was a growing "cult of originality" among intellectuals and scholars beginning in the late seventeenth century, in which the perceived usefulness of knowledge production was increasingly tied to a demand for novelty and invention. The positive valuation of original scholarship and authorship led to a concurrent devaluation of compilers as pedants, plagiarists and unoriginal thinkers.[36] Daniel Fulda has similarly identified a new emphasis on innovation arising in German academic culture around 1700, the proponents of which were markedly hostile to the hitherto quite normal and accepted practice of copying, transcribing and excerpting from existing texts.[37]

One of the preferred strategies of lexicographers anxious to counter the rising contempt against compilers, argues Hirschi, was to promote their encyclopaedias as original works of genius, while simultaneously downplaying the efforts of their predecessors. The re-branding of lexicographers, highly successful in the case of Diderot and d'Alemberts *Encyclopédie* as well as Samuel Johnson's *Dictionary*, was thus due to aggressive self-promotion rather than any significant innovations in their actual methods of compilation. Dan Edelstein has argued that the French *Encyclopédie* was a project massively indebted to the erudite culture of early modern humanism, despite explicit hostility towards humanist scholarly learning among Enlightenment philosophes. "[T]he spirit of Enlightenment", he writes, "blew off only the topsoil of erudite culture, and [...] the humanist practices of learning were often perpetuated despite the occasional anti-humanist declarations".[38] Although humanist learning could be attacked in the *Encyclopédie*, the *philosophes* nonetheless employed the very same erudite methods, such as compilation, and frequently scavenged the works of early modern humanists for relevant materials. Whereas the methods of "classification, extraction and compilation of texts and ideas" had already been developed and perfected by previous generations of scholars, they were now employed to "serve the philosophical good of disseminating 'general Enlightenment' [...]".[39]

The historical compilers of the eighteenth century faced similar challenges as dictionary writers and editors. They largely came up with the same solution, namely to re-brand the work of compilation as a more useful pursuit than it had been before, due to the capabilities of modern compilers. A more enlightened century needed a new brand of compilers able to do the tedious work of sorting through archives and libraries to discover what readers needed to know, to discard the rest, and to update the knowledge produced in earlier centuries for a modern audience. As C.P. Courtney has pointed out, in the eighteenth century "the art of compilation" was essentially the "art of choosing".[40] Underlying the self-confident assertions of eighteenth-century compilers was a strong belief in the ascendancy of an enlightened sensibility able to create shape and order out of what they saw as the disorganised texts of their predecessors. Neil Safier precisely describes this sensibility in his study of the French revision in 1744 of the Cuzco historian Garcilaso de la Vega's Incan history *Comentarios reales de los Incas* (1609). The editor saw this work not merely as an act of translation from Spanish into French but rather conceived of the team responsible for the edition as "active compilers licensed to transform the editorial configuration of previous texts, especially those that dealt with topics about which they now claimed to know far more than the original authors".[41] They thus massively abridged the text, added footnotes and additional updated information about various subjects that would not have been available to Garcilaso when he wrote the book. In the preface to the new edition, writes Safier, the editor criticised the *Comentarios* for being a disorderly, confusing and unmethodical work that "heaped up" facts rather than presenting them in a structured fashion. This approach expressed a notion of "the perfectibility of historical texts", writes Safier, "a positivistic discourse arguing that the organizational methods employed by eighteenth-century authors, even those who produced what [the editor] called 'the most mediocre works', allowed for greater utility for the public to which the text was being disseminated".[42]

Holberg's historical production is in many ways an expression of a similar notion of the "perfectibility of historical texts". According to Holberg's self-presentation, a central part of his contribution to the public was to sift through inaccessible and voluminous texts and to repackage them in a more appealing way. In the preface to his *General Church History* (1738), for instance, Holberg compared his work of perusing medieval histories to searching for nuggets of gold in a dung heap.[43] In his history of the Norwegian city of Bergen from 1737, he acknowledged having made extensive use of the seventeenth-century rector Edvard Edvardsen's (1630–1695) antiquarian manuscript about Bergen, abridging it considerably whilst removing instances of repetition as well as what he considered especially tedious elements. Holberg whittled Edvardsen's almost 1100-page manuscript down to a neat 311 pages.[44] In the preface to the work, Holberg claimed that two-thirds of Edvardsen's work was "not fit to be included in printed books", such as "records of old churches' and monasteries' lands and income, lists of all parish ministers and chaplains, mayors, councillors, town bailiffs, town scriveners and teachers etc.".[45] As cultural historian Anne Eriksen has pointed out, the lists and enumerations in Edvardsen's work that in Holberg's opinion made it unfit for print, were in fact an essential part of Edvardsen's project, which was strongly influenced by the rhetorical traditions of renaissance humanism as well as by early modern antiquarianism.[46] According to Eriksen, the central rhetorical ideal of the work was *copia*, or verbal abundance. The wealth of material presented in the book in the form of numerous lists and lengthy extracts of primary sources contributed to the honour of its subject (Bergen) and demonstrated the learning of its author.[47] The antiquarian influence in Edvardsen's work is discernible in his tendency to collect and systematically present an abundance of materials about Bergen's past, in the form of documents and physical remains, rather than to attempt to chronologically narrate its history. For Edvardsen, whose idea of "history" was based on the seventeenth-century concept of *historia* as the systematic observation and description of natural and man-made phenomena, writing a work of "history" entailed creating a "broad

and encompassing account with an emphasis on details and particularities [...]
based on experience and on active collection of information".[48]

There is thus a substantial difference in historiographical method and
outlook between the copious antiquarian Edvardsen and Holberg, who saw
himself as a historian whose main task was to produce well-crafted
chronological narratives that included sound moral judgements of historical
actors and provided causal explanations for important historical events.
Holberg's brand of pragmatic history was based on a strict sense of relevance
that was diametrically opposite to Edvardsen's intentionally copious and
inclusive method.[49] Herein lay a renewed claim to utility for eighteenth-
century compilers, if not necessarily to authorial originality. The re-branding
of compilers was not merely based on their skills as discerning curators of
information, however. A second strong argument in favour of historical
compilers was their ability to present their compilations in an appealing and
readable fashion, to a growing audience of non-specialist readers. We shall
turn to the questions of style and narration.

The compiler as accomplished stylist and narrator

At least some eighteenth-century compilers were considered accomplished
stylists, crafting highly readable histories out of less promising materials.
From this perspective, a primary function of compilers was to re-work and
abridge the writings of previous generations of scholars and intellectuals in
order to communicate with a broader audience. An engaging and succinct
style, adapted to modern tastes, was therefore more crucial than the use of
original sources and expression of novel ideas. The importance of style to the
art of compilation is reflected in the article on abbé Mallet's article
"Compilation" in the *Encyclopedie*, where a clear distinction is made between
estimable and poor compilations: belonging to the former category were
works that, although consisting of fragments of text written by authors with
different styles, appeared to flow from the same pen. The article mentioned
Rollin as an example of a good compiler who managed to do just this. Poor
compilations, on the other hand, were merely dry, undigested and shapeless
patchworks. Whereas estimable compilations required taste, the badly crafted
compilations required only time, research and "the tireless patience to copy
word for word".[50] In other words, a successful compilation was a text written
in a what appeared to be a distinct authorial voice, whose style did not draw
attention to the fact that it was a compilation.

It should be stressed that contemporaries had their own set of standards
when ascertaining the quality of style in historical compilations. The most
successful and acclaimed historical compilations of the eighteenth century, in
other words, are not necessarily texts that would be considered the most
interesting or worthwhile works today. Tobias Smollett is a case in point.
Although his historical oeuvre is seldom read today, Smollett in fact wrote
some of the best-selling and most widely read histories of England in the

eighteenth century, *A Complete History of England* (1757–58) and *Continuation of the Complete History of England* (1760–65). When advertising his *Complete History* to potential subscribers, Smollett presented his work as the hitherto cheapest, shortest and most updated history of England on the market.[51] These were all no doubt important selling points that would have contributed to its astounding commercial success, the serialised weekly instalments of the history allegedly selling 10.000 copies a week at one point.[52] As historian Richard J. Jones points out, Smollett also construed his particular method of writing histories as a boon to contemporary readers. Smollett was critical of "any interruption in the narrative", especially what he called "useless disquisitions" that broke the chain of events and drew the reader's attention away from the story. The foil to Smollett's ideal was David Hume, whose histories contained a wealth of philosophical reflection. In contrast, Smollett defined his own method of writing history as "compilation", the strength of which was to sustain the reader's attention and to provide a sense of immediacy. "Compilation", writes Jones, "is thus presented as a superior method of writing history—one that, paradoxically, maintains the 'chain of events' but does not draw attention to itself as a method of doing so".[53] Smollett employed several techniques to ensure the smooth, uninterrupted flow of his text: he moved all discussions and reflections extraneous to the narrative itself to the footnotes, he abbreviated his sources a great deal and he employed what Jones describes as "beacon words", well-chosen and well-placed words that integrated elements of reflection into the text by compressing it into one single point in a sentence or paragraph: "Reflection is thus revealed to be present in Smollett's *History*—but in a form that supports it as both a work of compilation and continuation".[54]

Smollett is merely one of many historical compilers in the eighteenth century (although a highly successful one), so his style of writing may not be generalised to an eighteenth-century "aesthetic" of compilation. However, it does appear that certain elements of Smollett's approach, especially narrative flow and brevity as stylistic hallmarks of good compilations, recur also in the works of other noted compilers of the period. Such as, for instance, Oliver Goldsmith's *History of Greece* (1774), itself based to a large extent on Rollin's popular ancient history. According to the scholar Giovanna Ceserani "[t]he book reads as a novel, with suspense holding every chapter ending, and displays an impressionistic style with not a single footnote".[55] The historical compilers of the eighteenth century can appear almost obsessed in their quest for brevity, evidenced by examples of historical compilers compiling historical compilations, distiling and abbreviating the works of their immediate predecessors. Ceserani writes that William Robertson's *History of Ancient Greece* (1768) was largely a translation of the prolific compiler Pons Augustins Alletz' *Abrégé de l'histoire grecque* (1764), itself an abridgement of Rollins *Histoire Ancienne*. For Robertson, Rollin's work was disorganised, too loaded with observations and too full of detail. Alletz' abridgement was a clear improvement, but still in need of Robertson's own "alterations", "considerable additions" and arrangements in "a form which seemed more distinct and methodical, than that of the original".[56]

Original compilers

We have previously seen that the historical compilers' ability to critically select from and abridge older works, discussed in terms of critical information management, was posited as one major argument in favour of their work. Successful abridgment and effective presentation could also, however, be cast as a mark of *authorial originality*. Again, the eighteenth-century world of encyclopaedias and dictionaries can be instructive. In his study of English scientific dictionaries, Richard Yeo discusses the complex negotiations about authorship and intellectual property that took place following the Statute of Anne in Great Britain in 1710, which for the first time introduced the notion that the author was the owner of intellectual property. The decades following the Statute saw a range of legal cases and debates about the exact bounds of the limited protection of the author's rights to his own work. Two opposing principles, both embodied in the Statute, clashed against each other in these debates: namely the author's right to the fruits of his own intellectual labour versus the notion of the free dissemination of knowledge in the public domain.[57] Compilers of dictionaries, argues Yeo, in fact needed to appeal to both of these principles at the same time: they appealed to the public's right to free knowledge in order to justify their continued compiling from other works, while simultaneously asserting that their own compilations were in fact books written by authors, thus entitled to protection under the Statute.[58] Emerging from the tension of this specific historical situation was a set of rhetorical strategies for claiming authorship of compiled works, which Yeo summarises as "learned abridgment, presentation and organization".[59] The question these strategies attempted to settle, was whether a book composed with units of texts lifted from other books—a compilation—was in fact derivative and possibly liable for legal action, or somehow constituted a novel work that was instead worthy of protection. Abridgement, a mode of intellectual labour that was not covered by the Statute of Anne, seems to have become largely accepted as a legitimate basis for assertions of authorship, at least if it was performed with sufficient skill: "Indeed", writes Yeo, "by the second half of the century a standard point in claims for abridgements was that they improved the originals by making them more succinct".[60] The compilers could also assert authorship by stressing their own work's original organisation according to a distinct plan, system or method, superior to those of their competitors.[61] Yeo warns against viewing eighteenth-century compilations through the lens of later, Romantic notions of originality and authorship, but nonetheless argues that there was something akin to originality at play here:

> There were claims to authorship above mere compilation, but these did not rest on a profession of originality, certainly not on the kind of originality associated with some special creative personality informing the work. Rather, such claims were founded on the labour and learning invested by the compiler in the dictionary.[62]

Parallel strategies of self-presentation can be found among the historical compilers of this period who, in addition to stressing their adeptness in efficiently abridging their sources, often advertise the novelty and utility of the "plan" or "system" of their historical works.[63] This was not always mere bluster: The structure of historical compilations could, in fact, introduce some genuinely original elements to the narration of history, although much or even most of the content of the works was derivative of earlier authors.

As Giovanna Ceserani points out in a discussion of eighteenth-century compilations of ancient history following Rollin (by authors such as Robertson and Temple Stanyan), the narrative structures of these works represented a novel approach that would prove to have lasting effects on the modern historiography of classical Greece. "Despite engaging solely with ancient narratives", writes Cesarani, "the molding of diverse sources and multicentered accounts of ancient Greece into a single-threaded narrative was indeed a new challenge".[64] In selecting an "Athenocentric perspective", which allowed them to tell the story from a specific vantage point among the many city-states of the Greek world, and by dividing the history of Greece into four ages, the eighteenth-century compilers developed "an influential and long-lasting mold for narrating the history of ancient Greece" that would continue to influence professional historians in the nineteenth century.[65]

Another experiment with form was attempted by Holberg, who arranged his three-volume *History of Denmark* (1732–35) according to what he saw as five distinct periods in the history of the kingdom, each introduced by notable rupture in its political or religious conditions such as the introduction of Christianity, the Reformation and the introduction of absolute monarchy. He described this structure as a completely new "invention" that had pleased his readers.[66] Although Holberg's five periods were in fact quite novel in a Danish context, where previous national histories had simply been structured according to the reign of monarchs, it built on similar attempts at secular modes of periodisation in the works of French and English historians of the previous generation such as Pere Daniel and Laurence Echard.[67] According to Inga Henriette Undheim, Holberg would thus probably not have seen the act of periodisation itself as an original invention on his part, but rather understood that he had come up with his own, nationally specific alternative to older, Christian models of periodisation such as the Four Monarchies of the Old Testament.[68] Undheim identifies an extra layer of literary experimentation in Holberg's periodisation, arguing that his selection of five periods was inspired by the classicist notion that a drama should ideally be divided into five acts and that his history of Denmark in fact followed the basic plot structure of a comedy.[69]

Underlying many of the historical compilers' drive towards developing perspicuous and effective modes of style and narration, was clearly an attentiveness to the perceived needs of readers. The arguments presented by eighteenth-century compilers in favour of their craft—discerning curation of information, an appealing and lucid style, brevity, effective narration—can arguably be understood as strategies for adapting their works to an expanding market for works of history. In a recent study of Oliver Goldsmith as historical compiler, Yuhki Takebayashi points out that the role of compilers in the eighteenth century was very much affected by important changes in public views on the authorship, purpose and usefulness of histories, as well as in the composition of their readership, at least in the British Isles. In the eighteenth century, according to Takebayashi, the traditional expectation that the historian should be someone with "an impressive political or antiquarian resume" was gradually supplanted by "a growing sense of acceptance and appreciation for works that had been compiled from readily accessible sources by those who had the gift of writerly competence [...]".[70] In other words, whereas for earlier generations the historian had ideally been a retired statesman relating the political history of the realm to an elite audience of princes and politicians, alternatively someone who relied on the patronage of politicians and other powerful figures for their livelihood, the early eighteenth century saw the emergence of a new type of historian that relied more or less completely on the public's interest in their work.[71] Noelle Gallagher similarly argues that the field of historical writing in early eighteenth-century Britain was "dominated by the growth of a competitive literary marketplace—an environment that extended the authorship of history to enterprising writers without the social status, leisure time, or experience recommended by *artes historicae*".[72] Although the intricate relationship between the expanding role of the historian and the concomitant growth of the literary marketplace in this period has been most thoroughly studied in England, where these changes were presumably espe-cially marked, similar developments were taking place elsewhere as well.[73]

The eighteenth century saw a growth in the demand for histories coming from an increasingly heterogeneous readership, including middle-class readers, women and children, reading for leisure and entertainment. Works of history were thus fast becoming a commercially viable consumer product, and publishers, booksellers and historians experimented with new genres, forms and thematic content in order to appeal to these readers.[74] If the historical compilation came to be perceived as a distinct genre during this period, and not just as a method of writing, it was the imagined requirements of this new and broadened readership that helped define its distinguishing features: The self-fashioning of compilers emphasised the eminent readability, relative brevity and singular utility of their works. In buying one single book or a series of books, they seemed to promise, one could find all one needed to know about the ancient world, the history of the Jewish people or of the kingdom of England, presented in an entertaining and easily digestible style.[75] This was of course especially true when the compilations translated and transcribed original works in Latin or ancient Greek or in other European languages—in these cases, historical compilations written in the vernacular offered a portal to hitherto unavailable texts. Charles Rollin's ancient history, for instance, was a broad historical synthesis, compiled from a variety of classical sources, aimed at interested non-specialists. Rollin himself stated that his primary audience consisted of young people and other persons "who desire no deep Insight into the History of those ancient Times".[76] Holberg, who appreciated Rollin's work and in fact compiled parts of his ancient history, described the latter as an "important work, especially for lay persons and women in all countries".[77] He described Rollin's Roman history as a "symbolical book or canonical text for all those who cannot consult the sources themselves". According to Holberg, this included those Danish women who, thanks to Rollin's Roman history, could now exactly recount the reasons for Rome's spectacular growth.[78]

Conclusion

Posterity has generally not been kind to the work of the historical compilers of the eighteenth century. Their histories have often either received scant attention in the study of eighteenth-century historiography, or they have been explicitly criticised for their derivative nature or lack of originality.[79] As I have argued, a critique of compilation as a mode of writing and constructing histories emerged already in the early part of the eighteenth century, urging a response from historical compilers to define and advertise the utility of their activity in order to place it on a more respectable footing. The self-fashioning of the historical compilers focused, as I have argued, on their roles as discerning curators of knowledge, and as accomplished stylists able to write histories that people would want to read. In addition to constituting a more or less viable defence in the face of mounting criticism, these were also major selling points in a competitive and growing literary marketplace hungry for histories.

One may be tempted to treat some of these self-professions with a dose of scepticism. When a writer such as Oliver Goldsmith described himself "front stage" as a superior and philosophically minded compiler compared to his "tedious" predecessors, the "backstage" description of his working methods suggests something rather different. According to a contemporary account, he composed one of his histories merely by perusing and taking notes from two or three relevant histories in the morning, "spent the day generally convivially" and then brought his notes and writing materials with him to bed to write the chapter before he went to sleep: "This latter exercise cost him very little trouble, he said; for having all his materials ready for him, he wrote it with as much facility as a common letter".[80] As this account suggests (as well as the introductory anecdote about Holberg's working methods), historical compilers were rarely fastidious scholars. Their labour, however, was in any case geared more towards communicating to a broad audience or, if viewed more cynically, to sell more historical works to the greatest number of readers with the least amount of work. Whether or not one accepts at face value their high-spirited rhetoric of public service, the historical compilers could indeed function as funnels of historical knowledge and antiquarian research that they had gleaned from less accessible, more specialised literature out of reach for many among their audience. Even if Holberg did only compose his *Jewish History* on the basis of a few volumes of Josephus, Basnage, Prideaux and the *Universal History*, thus inviting the criticism from a learned, elite audience that he had merely copied these texts, he nonetheless performed a service for those of his compatriots that had neither resources and leisure nor the linguistic competence to consider these works for themselves. The readability and accessibility of some eighteenth-century compilations contributed to giving them an importance among contemporaries that probably cannot be overestimated. Some of these works have a remarkable reception history that merits further attention. They were read and appreciated not only by the general public but also by intellectuals all over Europe who made extensive use of them in their own works. In this vibrant Republic of cut-and-paste, text fragments clearly travelled rapidly between books and across borders in a vast scale.

There is also a broader question of how changing attitudes towards historical compilations relate to evolving genres of historical writing in the eighteenth century. There appears to be a distinction between those authors that explicitly described their own works as compilations in their paratextual addresses to their ideal readers (such as Oliver Goldsmith), and authors that rather downplayed the compilatory aspects of their own work, such as Ludvig Holberg. In the first case, there are grounds for denoting the historical compilation—advertised as an entertaining, easily read abridgement of earlier works—as a separate genre of historical writing that appealed to a broad readership in the period. In the latter case, the designations "compiler" and "compilation" is retrospectively applied to what was originally presented as a historian's work of history, suggesting a more complex and possibly fraught relationship between the historian's historiographical method and his self-fashioning.[81] Investigating the responses of contemporary readers would help to further elucidating whether the historical compilation was perceived as a distinct genre, and what audiences saw as its main characteristics.

Notes

1 Ludvig Holberg, *Jødiske Historie Fra Verdens Begyndelse Fortsatt Til disse Tider, Deelt udi Tvende Parter* (Copenhagen, 1742), 2r.

2 Jens Møller, *Mnemosyne eller Samling af fædrenelandske Minder og Skildringer*, vol. 4 (Copenhagen, 1833), 99.

3 For examples of recent studies that discuss copying of sources, plagiarism or compilation in Holberg's historical works, see Inga Henriette Undheim, "Introduksjon til (naturrettslig) historiefortelling", in *Historikeren Ludvig Holberg*, ed. Jørgen Magnus Sejersted & Sebastian Olden-Jørgensen (Oslo: Scandinavian Academic Press, 2014), 61–87; Tim Berndtsson, "'Hvad Contra-Parten har at sige derimod'. Historiografisk dialog mellan Holberg og Pufendorf", in *Historikeren Ludvig Holberg*, ed. Jørgen Magnus Sejersted & Sebastian Olden-Jørgensen (Oslo: Scandinavian Academic Press, 2014), 147–180; Kristoffer Schmidt, "Ludvig Holbergs Heltehistorier—mellem moralfilosofi og historie" (PhD diss., University of Copenhagen, 2015); Jørgen Magnus Sejersted, "Jewish

History", *Ludvig Holberg (1684–1754). Learning and Literature in the Nordic Enlightenment*, ed. Knud Haakonsen & Sebastian Olden-Jørgensen (Abingdon: Routledge, 2017), 196–215; Thomas Daltveit Slettebø, "Kompilatoren Holberg. Om patriotisk og protestantisk kompilasjon i Ludvig Holbergs *Dannemarks Riges Historie*", *Historisk tidsskrift* 120, no. 1 (2020): 13–46; Are Bøe Pedersen, "'En Knude, som ved Menneskelige Raisons og historiske Exempler ikke kand løses'. Hebraisk mytologi og forsvar mot religionskritikk i Ludvig Holbergs *Den jødiske Historie* (1742)" (PhD diss., University of Bergen, 2022).

4 Typical of Holberg's style is his dry wit and irony and interspersions of short, essayistic reflections, all written in a plain and understandable but also elegant Danish. Another personal touch added by Holberg, who was also a noted author of popular comedies, is the frequent employment of theatrical metaphors—the historical actors tend to wear 'masks' and 'play roles' to conceal their true motives in the 'comedies' or 'tragedies' of history. See Slettebø, "Kompilatoren Holberg", 38–42: See also Inga Henriette Undheim, "Historie og komedie. Litterære strukturer og strategier i Holbergs rikshistoriografi" (PhD diss., University of Bergen, 2019), 357–365.

5 For an elaboration of this point, see Slettebø, "Kompilatoren Holberg", 19–20; For a thorough discussion of the reception history of Holberg's *Jewish History*, which also focuses on evaluations of its compilatory character, see Pedersen, "'En Knude, som ved Menneskelige Raisons og historiske Exempler ikke kand løses'", 37–73.

6 This is the approach of Holberg's most recent biographer, Lars Roar Langslet. In his discussion of the so-called 'Hojer feud', in which Holberg's rival Andreas Hojer accused his *Introduction til de fornemste Europæiske Riges Historier* (1711) of being derivative of Samuel Pufendorf's *Einleitung zu der Historie der Vornehmsten Reiche und Staaten so itziger Zeit in Europa sich befinden* (1683), Langslet here posits a marked difference between pre-modern and modern attitudes towards intellectual property: "There is [...] no doubt that most of Holberg's overview of world history was a transcription of Pufendorf, and so derivative in relation to him that critics today would judge it to be loaned goods, bordering on plagiarism. On the other hand, we should remember that the Holberg era did not have a strict view on such loans, at least not in popular [populærvitenskapelige] texts [...] (my translation)". Lars Roar Langslet, *Den store ensomme—en biografi om Ludvig Holberg* (Oslo: Forlaget Press, 2001), 111.

7 Mark Salber Phillips, *Society and Sentiment: Genres of Historical Writing in Britain, 1740–1820* (Princeton: Princeton University Press, 2000), 10.

8 Phillips, *Society and Sentiment,* 11.

9 Martin Gierl, "Compilation and the Production of Knowledge in the Early German Enlightenment", in *Wissenschaft als kulturelle Praxis 1750–1900*, eds. Hans Erich Bödeker, Peter Hanns Reill & Jürgen Schluhmbohm (Göttingen: Vandenhoeck & Ruprecht, 1999), 69–93.

10 Caspar Hirschi, "Compiler into Genius. The Transformation of Dictionary Writers in Eighteenth-Century France and England", in *Scholars in Action. The Practice of Knowledge and the Figure of the Savant in the 18th Century, Vol. 1*, eds. André Holenstein, Hubert Steinke, and Martin Stuber (Leiden & Boston: Brill, 2013), 151–154.

11 Montesquieu, *Persian Letters*, transl. Margaret Mauldon (Oxford: Oxford University Press, 2008), 87.

12 C.P. Courtney, "L'art de la compilation de l'*Histoire des deux Indes*", in *L'Histoire des deux Indes: réécritureet polygraphie*, eds. Hans-Jürgen Lüsebrink & Anthony Strugnell (Oxford: Voltaire Foundation, 1995), 307–308.

13 Sophie Bourgault, "Philhellenism among the Philosophes: Ancient Greece in French Enlightenment Historiography", in *A Companion to Enlightenment Historiography,* edited by Sophie Bourgault & Robert Sparling (Brill: Leiden, 2013), 442.

14 Daniel Fulda, "Plagiieren als wissenschaftliche Innovation? Kritik und Akseptanz eines vor drei Jahrhunderten skandalisierten Plagiats im Zeitalter der Exzerpierkunst", *Berichte zur Wissenschaftsgeschichte* 43, vol. 2 (2020): 220–221; Tomas Zahora, "Thomist Scholarship and Plagiarism in the Early Enlightenment: Jacques Echard Reads the Speculum morale, Attributed to Vincent of Beauvais", *Journal of the History of Ideas* 73, vol. 4 (2012): 517–524.

15 For a discussion of the "antiquarian" critique of compilation in eighteenth-century Denmark, see Slettebø, "Kompilatoren Holberg", 17.

16 In a private letter in 1731 to Holberg's colleague, the professor and historian Hans Gram, the customs official and jurist Christian Stub gave a scathing review of Holberg's *Dannemarks og Norges Beskrivelse* (1729). Among other things, Stub claimed that the book's twelfth chapter was merely a Danish translation of his own latin disputation on Danish legal history. In a letter to Gram from 1733, Stub claimed that the second volume of Holberg's *Dannemarks Riges Historie* (1733) was no "opus eruditum" since it was almost exclusively based on the seventeenth-century historian Arild Huitfeldt, who Holberg "rarely cites except when he wants to refute him". Chr. Bruun, "Et samtidigt Bidrag til Bedømmelsen af Holbergs Forfattervirksomhed", *Danske Samlinger for Historie, Topographi, Personal- og Literaturhistorie*, no 1 (1865–66), 399.

17 Johann Adolph Scheibe, *Ludwigs Freyherrns von Holberg Peter Paars, ein komisches Heldengedicht* (Copenhagen & Leipzig: Franz Christian Mummens Wittwe, 1764), lxxiii.

18 Yuhki Takebayashi, "The Grounded Patriot: Oliver Goldsmith as Historical Compiler" (PhD diss., Trinity College, Dublin, 2019), 24.

19 Guido Abbatista, "The Business of Paternoster Row: Towards a Publishing History of the Universal History (1736–65)", *Publishing History* 17 (1985): 8–22; Johan van der Zande, "August Ludwig Schlözer and the English *Universal History*", in *Historikerdialoge. Geschichte, Mythos und Gedächtnis im Deutsch-britischen kulturenn Austauch 1750–2000* (Göttingen: Vandenhoeck & Ruprecht, 2003), 138–139.

20 Van der Zande, "August Ludwig Schlözer", 148.

21 Karen O'Brien, "The History Market in Eighteenth-Century England", in *Books and Their Readers in Eighteenth-Century England: New Essays*, ed. Isabel Rivers (London: Continuum, 2003), 116–117.

22 As Sejersted demonstrates, this is precisely how the work was used by Holberg. Sejersted, "Jewish History", 202.

23 Although he himself is primarily interested in the *Universal History* from the perspective of its remarkable publishing history, Abbatista makes a compelling case for studying the circulation of the Universal history in its many translations, imitations and editions all over Europe, which he describes as a "huge European project, around which the attention of cultivated Europe and the booksellers was concentrated for the whole of the eighteenth century" Abbatista, "The Business of Paternoster Row", 22; See also van der Zande, "August Ludwig Schlözer", 148–149.

24 On the many translations and great success of Rollin's ancient history, see Giovanna Ceserani, "Narrative, Interpretation, and Plagiarism in Mr. Robertson's 1778 *History of Ancient Greece*", *Journal of the History of Ideas*, 66, no. 3 (2005), 419; Mark W. Graham argues that the work was "the most widely read historical work of late eighteenth-century America before it fell out of favour", and that Rollin's vision of universal history profoundly shaped American readers' ideas of antiquity, offering a storehouse of narratives and ideas about the past that could be utilised in the political struggles during and after the American Revolution. See Mark W. Graham, "Charles Rollin and Universal History in America", *Modern Intellectual History* 17, vol. 2 (2020): 326, 340–349.

25 Charles Rollin, *The Ancient History of the Egyptians, Carthaginians, Assyrians, Babylonians, Medes and Persians, Macedonians, and Grecians*, vol. 1 (London: James, John and Paul Knapton, 1734), xxvi.

26 Holberg, *Jødiske Historie*, 2r.

27 Daniel Rosenberg, "Early Modern Information Overload", *Journal of the History of Ideas* 64, no. 1 (2003): 1–9.

28 Richard Yeo, *Encyclopaedic Visions. Scientific Discoveries and Enlightenment Culture* (Cambridge: Cambridge University Press, 2001), 87–91.

29 Ann Blair, "Reading Strategies for Coping With Information Overload ca. 1550–1700", *Journal of the History of Ideas* 64, no. 1 (2003): 11–28.

30 Blair, "Reading Strategies", 12.

31 Hirschi, "Compiler into Genius", 151.

32 Mercure Danois, Juillet 1754, 115.

33 Oliver Goldsmith, *The History of England, from The Earliest Times to the Death of George II*. Vol 1, London 1771, ii.

34 Ibid.

35 Hirschi, "Compiler into Genius", 147.

36 Hirschi, "Compiler into Genius", 151–155.

37 Daniel Fulda, "Plagiieren als wissenschaftliche Innovation?", 218–219.

38 Dan Edelstein, "Humanism, l'Esprit Philosophique and the Encyclopédie", *Republics of Letters: A Journal for the Study of Knowledge, Politics and the Arts* 1, no. 1 (2009), 2.

39 Edelstein "Humanism", 16.

40 «L'art de la compilation serait donc essentiellement l'art de choisir [...]». C.P. Courtney, "L'art de la compilation", 309.

41 Neil Safier, "'To Collect and Abridge ... Without Changing Anything Essential'. Rewriting Incan History at the Parisian Jardin du Roi", *Book History* 7 (2004): 65.

42 Safier, "To Collect and Abridge", 68.

43 Ludvig Holberg, *Almindelig Kirke-Historie* (Copenhagen: Johann Georg Høpffner, 1738), b1r.

44 Bjørn-Arvid Bagge, "Ludvig Holberg og Edvard Edvardsen—en byhistorisk komparasjon", in *Historikeren Ludvig Holberg*, eds. Jørgen Magnus Sejersted & Sebastian Olden-Jørgensen (Oslo: Scandinavian Academic Press, 2014), 241–246.

45 Ludvig Holberg, *Den Berømmelige Norske Handels-Stad Bergens Beskrivelse* (Copenhagen: J.J. Høpffner, 1737), 2 v (my translation).

46 Anne Eriksen, *Livets læremester. Historiske kunnskapstradisjoner i Norge 1650–1840* (Oslo: Pax, 2020), 54–77

47 Eriksen, *Livets læremester*, 59–66.

48 Eriksen, *Livets læremester*, 76 (my translation).

49 For a discussion of Holberg as a pragmatic historian, see Sebastian Olden-Jørgensen, *Ludvig Holberg som pragmatisk historiker. En historiografisk-kritisk undersøgelse* (Copenhagen: Museum Tusculanums Forlag, 2015), 15–26. For a discussion of his "acute sense of relevance", see Sebastian Olden-Jørgensen, "History: national, universal and dynastic", in *Ludvig Holberg (1684–1754). Learning and Literature in the Nordic Enlightenment*, eds. Knud Haakonsen & Sebastian Olden-Jørgensen (Abingdon: Routledge, 2017), 169–170.

50 Edmé-François Mallet, "Compilation", *Encyclopédie, ou dictionnaire raisonné des sciences, des arts et des métiers*, etc., eds. Denis Diderot and Jean le Rond d'Alembert. University of Chicago: ARTFL Encyclopédie Project (Spring 2021 Edition), Robert Morrissey and Glenn Roe (eds), http://encyclopedie.uchicago.edu/.

51 Richard J. Jones, "Continued Continuations of Complete Histories: Tobias Smollett and the Work of History", *Journal for Eighteenth-Century Studies* 41, no. 3 (2018): 392–393.

52 Jones, "Continued Continuations", 394.

53 Jones, "Continued Continuations", 395.
54 Jones, "Continued Continuations", 396.
55 Ceserani, "Narrative, Interpretation and Plagiarism", 419.
56 All quotes from Ceserani, "Narrative, Interpretation and Plagiarism", 421.
57 Yeo, *Encyclopaedic Visions*, 195–204.
58 Yeo, *Encyclopaedic Visions,* 204.
59 Yeo, *Encyclopaedic Visions*, 204.
60 Yeo, *Encyclopaedic Visions*, 207.
61 Yeo, *Encyclopaedic Visions*, 211–213.
62 Yeo, *Encyclopaedic Visions*, 220.
63 This was, for instance, the case with Tobias Smollett, whose *Plan of a Complete History of England* stressed that his proposed history was "formed upon a plan which was the result of the most mature deliberation". As Richard J. Jones points out, Smollett's "plan" was in part meant to differentiate it from Hume's *The History of England.* Hume's first two parts covered the Stuart monarchs and the Commonwealth, the third covered the Tudor period and the final part the earliest history of England and the Middle Ages. Smollett, however, intended to write a strictly chronological account. Jones, "Continued Continuations", 393.
64 Cesarani, "Narrative, Interpretation and Plagiarism", 435.
65 Cesarani, "Narrative, Interpretation and Plagiarism", 435.
66 Ludvig Holberg, *Dannemarks Riges Historie*, vol. 3 (Copenhagen: Johan Jørgen Høpffner, 1735), c1v.
67 Undheim, "Historie og komedie", 291–297.
68 Undheim, "Historie og komedie", 296.
69 Undheim, "Historie og komedie", 302.
70 Takebayashi, "The Grounded Patriot", 21.
71 O'Brien, "The History Market", 108–109.
72 Noelle Gallagher, "The Beginnings of Enlightenment Historiography in Britain", in *A Companion to Enlightenment Historiography*, edited by Sophie Bourgault & Robert Sparling (Brill: Leiden, 2013), 347.
73 Even Ludvig Holberg, although he was employed as a professor of history at the University of Copenhagen, essentially wrote his historical works as a private person for the general public, and with a notable degree of commercial success. Historian Sebastian Olden-Jørgensen points out that Holberg never enjoyed the position of a royal historiographer for the Danish absolute monarchy but should rather be considered "a sort of 'gentleman historian' who interacted primarily with the general reading public and only occasionally with academic or literary peers". See Olden-Jørgensen, "History", 162.
74 O'Brien"The History Market".
75 Noelle Gallagher cites several examples of English historians advertising their works in economic terms, arguing that in buying their own history, the reader would be spared the cost of buying or the work of reading a whole library. See Gallagher, "The Beginnings of Enlightenment Historiography in Britain", 355–356.
76 Rollin, *The Ancient History*, xxiii.
77 Ludvig Holberg, *Epistler*, vol. 3 (Copenhagen, 1750), 66.
78 Ludvig Holberg, *Herodiani Historie* (Copenhagen, 1746), 45.
79 Abbatista, "The Business of Paternoster Row", 5; Takebayashi, "The Grounded Patriot", 30–68.
80 William Cooke, quoted in Takebayashi, "The Grounded Patriot", 22.
81 As I have shown, some contemporaries did in fact criticise Holberg's histories as mere "compilations", but the known criticisms were either levelled in private (see note 14) or posthumously (note 15). This suggests that there was an element of taboo surrounding their compilatory aspects.

Bibliography

Abbatista, Guido. "The Business of Paternoster Row: Towards a Publishing History of the Universal History (1736–65)." *Publishing History* 17 (1985): 5–50.

Bagge, Bjørn-Arvid. "Ludvig Holberg og Edvard Edvardsen – en byhistorisk komparasjon." In *Historikeren Ludvig Holberg*, edited by Jørgen Magnus Sejersted & Sebastian Olden-Jørgensen, 231–250. Oslo: Scandinavian Academic Press, 2014.

Berndtsson, Tim. "«Hvad Contra-Parten har at sige derimod». Historiografisk dialog mellan Holberg og Pufendorf." In *Historikeren Ludvig Holberg*, edited by Jørgen Magnus Sejersted & Sebastian Olden-Jørgensen, 147–180. Oslo: Scandinavian Academic Press, 2014.

Blair, Ann. "Reading Strategies for Coping With Information Overload ca. 1550–1700." *Journal of the History of Ideas* 64, no. 1 (2003): 11–28.

Bourgault, Sophie. "Philhellenism among the Philosophes: Ancient Greece in French Enlightenment Historiography." In *A Companion to Enlightenment Historiography*, edited by Sophie Bourgault & Robert Sparling, 437–468. Brill: Leiden, 2013.

Bruun, Chr. "Et samtidigt Bidrag til Bedømmelsen af Holbergs Forfattervirksomhed i Breve fra C. M. Stub til H. Gram." *Danske Samlinger for Historie, Topographi, Personal- og Literaturhistorie*, no. 1 (1865-66), 398–400.

Courtney, C.P. "L'art de la compilation de l'Histoire des deux Indes." In *L'Histoire des deux Indes: réécriture et polygraphie*, edited by Hans-Jürgen Lüsebrink & Anthony Strugnell, 307–323. Oxford: Voltaire Foundation, 1995.

Edelstein, Dan. "Humanism, l'Esprit Philosophique and the Encyclopédie." *Republics of Letters: A Journal for the Study of Knowledge, Politics and the Arts* 1, no. 1 (2009): 1–17. https://arcade.stanford.edu/sites/default/files/article_pdfs/roflv01i01_Edelstein_072009_0.pdf

Eriksen, Anne. *Livets læremester. Historiske kunnskapstradisjoner i Norge 1650–1840*. Oslo: Pax Forlag, 2020.

Fulda, Daniel. "Plagiieren als wissenschaftliche Innovation? Kritik und Akzeptanz eines vor drei Jahrhunderten skandalisierten Plagiats im Zeitalter der Exzerpierkunst." *Berichte zur Wissenschaftsgeschichte* 43, vol. 2 (2020): 218–238. 10.1002/bewi.201900028

Gallagher, Noelle. "The Beginnings of Enlightenment Historiography in Britain." In *A Companion to Enlightenment Historiography*, edited by Sophie Bourgault & Robert Sparling, 343–371. Brill: Leiden, 2013.

Gierl, Martin. "Compilation and the Production of Knowledge in the Early German Enlightenment". In *Wissenschaft als kulturelle Praxis 1750–1900*, edited by Hans Erich Bödeker, Peter Hanns Reill, & Jürgen Schlumbohm, 69–103. Vandenhoeck & Ruprecht: Göttingen, 1999.

Graham, Mark W. "Charles Rollin and Universal History in America." *Modern Intellectual History* 17, vol. 2 (2020): 325–355.

Hirschi, Caspar. "Compiler Into Genius. The Transformation of Dictionary Writers in Eighteenth-Century France and England." In *Scholars in Action. The Practice of Knowledge and the Figure of the Savant in the 18th Century, Vol. 1.*, edited by André Holenstein, Hubert Steinke, & Martin Stuber, in collaboration with Philippe Rogger, 145–172. Leiden & Boston: Brill, 2013.

Holberg, Ludvig. *Den Berømmelige Norske Handels-Stad Bergens Beskrivelse*. Copenhagen: J.J. Høpffner, 1737.

Holberg, Ludvig. *Almindelig Kirke-Historie Fra Christendommens første Begyndelse Til LUTHERI REFORMATION, Med nogle Anmærkninger Over de udi Historien omtalte CYCLIS og Aars-Beregninger*. Copenhagen: Johann Georg Høpffner, 1738.

Holberg, Ludvig. *Jødiske Historie Fra Verdens Begyndelse Fortsatt Til disse Tider, Deelt udi Tvende Parter*. Copenhagen, 1742.

Jones, Richard J. "Continued Continuations of Complete Histories: Tobias Smollett and the Work of History." *Journal for Eighteenth-Century Studies* 41, no. 3 (2018): 391–406. 10.1111/1754-0208.12525

Langslet, Lars Roar. *Den store ensomme – en biografi om Ludvig Holberg.* Oslo: Forlaget Press, 2001.

Montesquieu. *Persian Letters.* Translated by Margaret Mauldon. Oxford: Oxford University Press, 2008.

Møller, Jens. *Mnemosyne. Eller Samling af fædrenelandske Minder og Skildringer.* Copenhagen: C. A. Reitzel, 1833.

O'Brien, Karen. "The History Market in Eighteenth-Century England." In *Books and Their Readers in Eighteenth-Century England: New Essays,* edited by Isabel Rivers, 105–133. London: Continuum, 2003.

Olden-Jørgensen, Sebastian. "History: national, universal, dynastic." In *Ludvig Holberg (1684–1754). Learning and Literature in the Nordic Enlightenment,* edited by Knud Haakonsen & Sebastian Olden-Jørgensen, 159–181. Abingdon: Routledge, 2017.

Olden-Jørgensen, Sebastian. *Ludvig Holberg som pragmatisk historiker. En historiografisk-kritisk undersøgelse.* Copenhagen: Museum Tusculanums Forlag, 2019.

Pedersen, Are Bøe. "'En Knude, som ved Menneskelige Raisons og historiske Exempler ikke kand løses'. Hebraisk mytologi og forsvar mot religionskritikk i Ludvig Holbergs *Den jødiske Historie* (1742)". PhD diss., University of Bergen, 2022.

Phillips, Mark Salber. *Society and Sentiment. Genres of Historical Writing in Britain, 1740–1820.* Princeton: Princeton University Press, 2000.

Rollin, Charles. *The Ancient History of the Egyptians, Carthaginians, Assyrians, Babylonians, Medes and Persians, Macedonians, and Grecians.* London: James, John and Paul Knapton, 1734.

Rosenberg, Daniel. "Early Modern Information Overload." *Journal of the History of Ideas* 64, no. 1 (2003): 1–9.

Safier, Neil. "'To Collect and Abridge … Without Changing Anything Essential': Rewriting Incan History at the Parisian Jardin du Roi." *Book History* 7 (2004): 63–96. https://www.jstor.org/stable/30227357

Scheibe, Johann Adolph. *Ludwigs Freyherrns von Holberg Peter Paars, ein komisches Heldengedicht.* Copenhagen & Leipzig: Franz Christian Mummens Wittwe, 1764.

Schmidt, Kristoffer. "Ludvig Holbergs Heltehistorier – mellem moralfilosofi og historie." PhD diss., University of Copenhagen, 2015.

Sejersted, Jørgen Magnus. "Jewish History." In *Ludvig Holberg (1684–1754). Learning and Literature in the Nordic Enlightenment,* edited by Knud Haakonsen & Sebastian Olden-Jørgensen, 196–215. Abingdon: Routledge, 2017.

Sejersted, Jørgen Magnus. "Ludvig Holberg." *Store norske leksikon,* last modified November 1, 2019, https://snl.no/Ludvig_Holberg#-Historiske_skrifter

Slettebø, Thomas Daltveit. "Kompilatoren Holberg. Om patriotisk og protestantisk kompilasjon i Ludvig Holbergs *Dannemarks Riges Historie.*" *Historisk tidsskrift* 120, no. 1 (2020): 13–46.

Takebayashi, Yuhki. "The Grounded Patriot: Oliver Goldsmith as Historical Compiler". PhD diss., Trinity College, Dublin, 2019.

Undheim, Inga Henriette. "Introduksjon til naturrettslig historiefortelling." In *Historikeren Ludvig Holberg,* edited by Jørgen Magnus Sejersted & Sebastian Olden-Jørgensen, 61–87. Oslo: Scandinavian Academic Press, 2014.

Undheim, Inga Henriette. "Historie og komedie. Litterære strukturer og strategier i Holbergs rikshistoriografi." PhD diss., University of Bergen, 2019.

Yeo, Richard. *Encyclopaedic Visions. Scientific Dictionaries and Enlightenment Culture*. Cambridge: Cambridge University Press, 2001.
Zahora, Tomas. "Thomist Scholarship and Plagiarism in the Early Enlightenment: Jacques Echard Reads the Speculum Morale, Attributed to Vincent of Beauvais." *Journal of the History of Ideas* 73, no. 4 (October 2012): 515–536.
Zande, Johan van der. "August Ludwig Schlözer and the English *Universal History.*" In *Historikerdialoge. Geschichte, Mythos und Gedäcthnis im Deutsch-britischen kulturellen Austauch 1750–2000*, editet by Stefan Berger, Peter Lambert, & Peter Schumann, 135–156. Göttingen: Vandenhoeck & Ruprecht, 2003.

3 "History from Marble"

Church notes and the rise of epigraphy in early modern England

Angus Vine

Introduction—of church monuments and histories from marble

In early 1600 a dedicated guide to the tombs, monuments and inscriptions of Westminster Abbey was published for the first time: *Reges, reginae, nobiles, & alii in Ecclesia Collegiata B. Petri Westmonasterii sepulti, usque ad annum reparatae salutis.*[1] The author was the antiquary, herald and schoolmaster William Camden, and the book addressed a subject of newfound interest at the time. A small and easily portable quarto, the guide quickly attracted the attention of domestic and international readers alike, and it was soon popular enough to warrant further editions in 1603 and 1606.[2] Entrepreneurial church officials took to selling it in the Abbey precincts and visitors began to tour the building with copies in their hands. Other writers and travellers also started to use it in their own descriptions of the Abbey in the accounts and journals that they wrote up afterwards.

The Bohemian nobleman Baron Waldstein (Zdeněk Brtnický Valdštejna), who toured England in July and August 1600 when he was just nineteen, was one such example. In his diary, when he recorded his visit to the Abbey that summer, Waldstein picked out Camden's guidebook for special recommendation: "The Abbey, one of the finest in the whole of England, is most magnificent and also very beautiful [...] It contains a large number of chapels and some very splendid royal monuments: with reference to these, consult a special book, which is printed in London".[3] Shortly thereafter he also quoted from the book when he described the Coronation Chair as one of the Abbey's must-see attractions: "Among other things one should see the marble throne of the Kingdom of Scotland in the royal chapel. After defeating the Scots, Edward I returned triumphant in 1297 and in the Abbey of Westminster he dedicated to God the sceptre and crown of the Kings of Scotland, and also this seat upon which the Scottish Kings used to be crowned".[4] Waldstein presumably acquired a copy when he was in London, probably from one of these entrepreneurial abbey officials.

The guide was still being touted to visitors to the Abbey a decade later. We know this because the German traveller Justus Zinzerling (Jodocus Sincerus) reported it in his *Itinerarium Galliae* (1616), an account of his travels through

DOI: 10.4324/9781003331971-5

France, Belgium and England. He recorded there that copies were "sold by the verger".[5] Valentin Arithmaeus, Professor of Poetry at Frankfurt on the Oder, noted the same thing when he visited London the following year. He, however, refused to buy the book because the verger who approached him with a copy demanded such a high price for it. In the preface to his own account of the Abbey's tombs and monuments, titled *Mausolea regum, reginarum, dynastarum, nobilium, sumptuosissima, artificiosissima, magnificentissima, Londini Anglorum* (1618), Arithmaeus wrote that "[w]hen the Verger saw I was eager after these things, he offered a copy of some Inscriptions printed several years before; but after the manner of his nation, eaten up with avarice, he demanded a great price".[6]

As the first dedicated guide to Westminster Abbey and its monuments, Camden's book was original and innovative in two interrelated ways. First, it was the first dedicated guidebook to an ecclesiastical building of any sort to be published in England. As such, it originated a form of historical writing that flourished in the seventeenth century: church descriptions. These works combined antiquarian research into the foundations and origins of churches with enumerative accounts of their tombs and monuments and observations (usually rather basic) on their architecture. Mixing church notes with checklists of funerary monuments, coats-of-arms and inscriptions, these works appealed to wealthy travellers, heralds, genealogists and antiquaries alike.

Books in the same vein that followed in the wake of Camden's guide included the printer and bookseller Henry Holland's comparable guide to St Paul's Cathedral, *Monumenta sepulchralia Sancti Pauli* (1614) (reissued in a slightly extended version in 1633 as *Ecclesia Sancti Pauli illustrata*), the antiquary William Somner's more elaborate *The Antiquities of Canterbury* (1640) and the antiquary and herald William Dugdale's much more elaborate *The History of St. Pauls Cathedral in London, from its Foundation Untill These Times* (1658). Daniel King's collection of engravings of cathedrals and abbeys from across England and Wales, *The Cathedrall and Conventuall Churches of England and Wales Orthographically Delineated* (1656), was another important landmark in this tradition.[7] King's book, which was issued in at least three different states, contains multiple engravings by him and Wenceslaus Hollar, based on original drawings by a number of artists, including Richard Newcourt, Thomas Johnson, Richard Ralinson, Stephen Anderton, Randle Holme Junior and King himself.

Camden's guide was equally significant, though, for initiating another overlapping seventeenth-century interest: epigraphy. Just as subsequent years saw a series of cathedral and church descriptions modelled on Camden's book, so they also witnessed the publication of a growing number of historical works devoted to inscriptions, funerary monuments and epitaphs, which were likewise inspired by it—what a subsequent antiquary, the draughtsman and surveyor Thomas Dingley (or Dineley as his name was also sometimes spelt) called "History from Marble".[8] Crossing confessional boundaries and incorporating works in both print and manuscript, "history from marble" became an increasingly prominent aspect of seventeenth-century antiquarian activity. As the antiquarian project turned from textual to material traces of the past, the inscriptions and monuments that historians from marble collected and documented took on a new evidentiary importance. Along with other material and visual remains such as coins and medals, these epigraphic records were able to supplement and support the authority of traditional, text-based historical evidence.[9] Moreover, this "history from marble" also constituted a significant step in early modern England's discovery of its own medieval past. Whilst their methods and approaches drew on classical scholarship, the historians of marble extended antiquarian attention from Roman remains to more recent material and archaeological traces too.

This kind of history is my subject in this chapter. Why did this "history from marble" emerge in the seventeenth century? What were the major literary and intellectual influences on it? How did it affect people's understanding of history as a practice? What were its consequences for the early modern sense of the past? How did it fit into the wider European interest in classical inscriptions? What were the effects of this new form of historical writing on historical activity more generally? How did it lead, in the British context, at least, perhaps for the first time, to a distinctly visual sense of the past? These are the research questions that the rest of this chapter sets out to answer. To do this, the chapter begins by contextualising "history from marble" and placing it within the larger culture of the material turn of post-Reformation history-writing. Subsequent sections of the chapter trace the development of this form of history, beginning with Camden's and Holland's guidebooks, before turning to the most important seventeenth-century study of inscriptions, John Weever's *Ancient Funerall Monuments* (1631). The chapter then ends with Dingley's own works, which exemplify the full potential of this new approach to the past and the books for which he coined his striking term in the first place.

Church notes and the material turn of post-Reformation history

Scholars have generally explained this rise in interest in the material remains of the medieval past as a response to the Reformation. In a now classic essay, the ecclesiastical historian Margaret Aston argued that the ruins caused by the Dissolution of the Monasteries "proved to be peculiarly fertile in stimulating consciousness of the past and in promoting historical activity" and suggested that they "fostered a growing nostalgia" for the medieval world, which "had been swept off in this break".[10] Church notes were perhaps the most obvious manifestation of this, as sixteenth- and seventeenth-century antiquaries exhaustively documented the funerary monuments, inscriptions and epitaphs and occasionally, too, the architectural features, of churches up and down the country.[11] That interest, as Alexandra Walsham has shown, numbered both Catholics and Protestants; there was, in her words, a "growing impulse" amongst conservative writers across the confessional divide "to record in writing and image remnants of a religious world that they feared would soon be lost".[12] The Worcestershire antiquary Thomas Habington, for example, who compiled an extensive collection of church notes based on his tours of that county, described his purpose as to "preasarve [...] within thease paper walles what that stronge rocke cannot keepe".[13] Habington was a Catholic convert, but the sentiment was not one just restricted to his fellow believers. Somner's *Antiquities of Canterbury*, the first extended historical study of an English cathedral, for example, reflected a High-Church Anglicanism, which was shared by many seventeenth-century antiquaries, whilst Dugdale's *History of St Paul's* was animated by an acute understanding of the fragility of historical records and a profound sense of material loss. In his case, though, this was occasioned by a more recent series of depredations as well: the neglect, even vandalism, of the church during the Commonwealth period.[14]

If seventeenth-century antiquaries increasingly sought to preserve the material remains of the medieval past through their books and collections, so those remains were also increasingly conceived in textual terms—as Dingley's term attests. The histories from marble that they started to produce did not, however, necessarily signal a dedicated medievalism, at least not in the modern understanding of that word. Rather, their works freely mixed medieval and post-medieval monuments and inscriptions, and they continued to document Roman material remains where these were unearthed too. The result was that histories from marble brought together inscribed stones from both distant and much more recent times in a universalising antiquarian project. This was entirely in keeping with the Renaissance and early modern interest in, and approach to, the medieval world more generally.[15]

The major drivers here, moreover, were not a new appreciation for medieval art and architecture, although glimpses of both did start to appear in the works of certain antiquaries, especially in the later seventeenth century. Instead, they were the senses of fear and loss expressed by Dugdale and Habington. Almost as important, too, as this chapter will go on to argue, was the widespread interest in genealogy that characterised so much seventeenth-century historical and antiquarian endeavour. Church notes, as Jan Broadway writes, "could be extremely useful for the genealogist", as they included "not only coats of arms, either drawn or in blazon, but also descriptions of funeral monuments, their inscriptions and epitaphs".[16] Churches were, therefore, one of the primary sites for both heraldic research and antiquarian activity in the period: their funerary monuments provided documentary evidence of ancestors and names, which was invaluable for drawing up pedigrees and tracing family histories.

In what follows, I examine three of the most important landmarks in this history of marble, in chronological order, to document the evolution of epigraphic activity and research in the seventeenth century and to demonstrate the changing ways in which historically minded authors made use of inscribed evidence and their shifting motives for this: Camden's and

Holland's early seventeenth-century guides to Westminster Abbey and St Paul's, Weever's massive mid-century *Ancient Funerall Monuments* and finally Dingley's late seventeenth-century eponymous work and its associated texts. What emerges from these examples is the story of a distinct form of early modern historical writing: a form whose significance scholars have noted, but whose story in long duration has rarely been told before. Before turning to these examples, though, we need to pause briefly to document the emergence of epigraphy as a discipline amongst a previous generation of continental antiquaries, whose activities instigated the study of inscriptions as historical evidence important in both their textual and material dimensions.

Two pioneering church guidebooks

As William Stenhouse has shown, there emerged across Europe in the second half of the sixteenth century a group of antiquarian scholars who "opened avenues towards the systematic exploitation of inscriptions as historical evidence", who gathered "records of examples" and "developed techniques to order and index what they found", who "produced general rules for the interpretation of epigraphic material", and whose works pioneered "ideas about the scope and potential of inscribed evidence".[17] Originating in a small community based in Rome in the 1540s and 1550s, these scholars developed ideas about the interpretation of inscriptions that had a profound influence on historical writing and, by the end of the sixteenth century, had spread across Europe thanks to a series of published collections of inscriptions and epitaphs. These works gathered examples of classical inscriptions for future scholars to use and developed approaches to and methods for interpreting that material.

By 1587, the first handbook of this subject had been published in the form of the ninth and tenth dialogues of Antonio Agustín's *Dialogos de medallas inscriciones y otras antiguedades* (1587). This work, which was published posthumously a year after its author's death, set the stall for future epigraphic research, as it mapped how, and in what circumstances, inscriptions could be used as historical evidence.[18] Agustín's book was popular and quickly met with success. An Italian translation was soon published, issued in two different editions by the Roman printer Guglielmo Facciotti in 1592, and a Latin version by the classical scholar and philologist Andreas Schott then followed in 1617. As with other scholars of the period, Agustín believed that the primary value of inscriptions was philological and lay in their potential to verify the spelling of classical Latin: what he called "el prouecho de la orthographia". However, he also recognised that inscriptions could have other uses, too, for the antiquary and historian. Notably, he argued that they could supplement, and even correct, what was obscure or false in textual records, and that in this way they could provide valuable information about subjects as diverse as Roman families, tribunes, legions, magistrates, ministers, priests, soldiers and wars.[19] Agustín's focus, as with the scholars of the 1540s and 1550s, was on classical inscriptions, but he pioneered an approach to the material remains of the past that later antiquaries would take up in considerably expanded ways.

Camden undoubtedly took his cue from this previous generation of scholars. His own book begins with a brief history of Westminster Abbey from its foundation in the seventh century ("*Fundatio Ecclesiæ Beati Petri Westmonasterij*").[20] This provides a potted account of the Abbey, in just two pages, from its first building through to the recent, post-Dissolution past. Camden's principal sources here were the sixteenth-century antiquary John Leland ("Lelandus") and, for the Abbey's foundation, a history written by the eleventh-century Norman monk Sulcard ("Sulcardus"). (He would have had access to the latter thanks to the library of his friend and fellow antiquary Robert Cotton: two manuscripts of Sulcard's history survive amongst the Cottonian manuscripts today.[21]) His own epigraphic research then follows in the form of a comprehensive collection of the Abbey's funerary inscriptions. The transcriptions of these are interspersed with brief historical notes and short biographies of the persons memorialised. He also included a list of the coats-of-arms dating from the reign of Henry III and his rebuilding of the Abbey, which could be seen on either side of the nave, reminding us of the genealogical interests of this kind of church history.

Perhaps the most distinctive aspect of the book is its guidebook format. Camden's models here were the medieval and early modern encomiastic guides to cities such as Rome, which were written for secular travellers and religious pilgrims alike. Works such as the much recopied, revised and eventually printed *Mirabilia urbis Romae* offered a model for the yoking together of touristic handbook and antiquarian description.[22] Camden's book, however, also constitutes a significant departure from these models. His work is shorn of the miraculous and wondrous elements that typify the *Mirabilia* tradition. In his guide, the antiquarian spirit predominates. After the two-page introductory history, the book transports the reader progressively, and soberly, through the interior of the Abbey, identifying numerous monuments and inscriptions in Latin and English in twenty different locations. The presentational style is strikingly "matter-of-fact": the book has, as Wyman Herendeen has noted, "the 'modern' antiquarian's and herald's concern for descriptive accuracy and the preservation of facts".[23] The result is a generically mixed book: one modelled on an earlier tradition of guidebooks, but which took its intellectual inspiration from a subsequent, more scholarly antiquarian and epigraphic tradition, and adopted its enumerative approach to monuments from contemporary topographical and chorographical works, including Camden's own, much better-known *Britannia* (1586). The *Reges, reginae, nobiles, & alii in Ecclesia Collegiata B. Petri Westmonasterii sepulti*, then, was a guidebook for the historically curious rather than the historically credulous.

Holland adopted the same approach in his book about St Paul's, which appeared fourteen years later, and was the first guide to the monuments in an English cathedral to be published. (Camden's book, whilst it initiated the genre, was not strictly speaking a cathedral guide: Westminster Abbey is not a cathedral, as in a diocesan seat, but a collegiate church.) Holland's book likewise mixes the form of a travel guide with antiquarian principles of compilation to produce a comprehensive collection of funerary monuments and inscriptions. As Camden had done, he too prefaced this collection with a short essay on the church's foundation and history ("ECCLESIÆ SANCTI PAVLI *fundatio*"). An English translation of that text then follows ("THE FOVNDATION OF SAINT PAVLES *Church*"), suggesting that he may have had a more exclusively domestic audience in mind than Camden had.[24] The book then travels through the space of St Paul's, beginning at "the entrance of the North *side or Ile of the Quire or* Chancell", and then taking the reader up and down the north and south aisles, before ending back at "the little North doore" and the "iron box for the Poore" located there. Appended to the work is a table listing the sixteen archbishops and then the eighty-seven bishops of London up to Holland's own day. The final entry in this list is the incumbent John King, "now liuing in this See of London; yea long and long may hee liue, as hee is a painfull Preacher, a vigilant Pastour, and a worthy Gouernour to Gods glory, and the Church of Englands good".[25] Holland's concluding words here are a reminder that these histories from marble were more than just exercises in antiquarian nostalgia and that they were also frequently animated by strongly held confessional identities. In Holland's case, this resulted in a guidebook that was proleptic as well as explanatory, and which served as a document of St Paul's present and future as well as a record of its past.

In the reissued edition, Holland was more explicit about why he had decided to write this kind of monumental history. He prefaced the 1633 text with an epistle "To the Reader", in which he explained why nineteen years after the first edition he had decided to return to it. One reason was because funerary monuments in St Paul's continued to be erected: this kind of compilation was, therefore, never complete and had to be continuously added to and revised. He also admitted that there were omissions in the original text, which he wanted to correct: "*Beloued, My first Collection of these Monumentall Epitaphs I published Anno. 1614. full 19 yeeres sithence: And vnto this second Edition are diuers Additions of Monuments and Epitaphs erected since that time, besides, of some omitted in the former*".[26] However, like most early modern antiquaries, he was also animated by a strongly preservationist instinct, and an awareness of the fragility of historical and material remains and of the ever-present possibility of decay and decline. In his case, the immediate trigger was the project to renovate St Paul's, which Inigo Jones had begun that same year, and a fear that this repair work might lead unintentionally to the damage of some of the church's monuments: "*And now, his* Maiesties *gracious* Commission about the Decayes and for the repayring of this famous Church, *is on foot, and in agitation* (a Worke, certes, requiring Royall helpe, and beseeming the Maiestie of so mighty a Monarch:) I haue thought good to publish this as completely as I could, lest in repairing the same, some Monuments of the dead might be defaced, if not quite raced*; but *preserued hereby to Memory and Posteritie"*.[27] As with the Worcestershire antiquary Thomas Habington, it seems, then, that Holland's aim, too, was to preserve material remains in "paper walles". That kind of wall, his words imply, could endure the ravages of humans and time far more easily than any marble or monuments could.

Ancient funerary monuments—The first English gazetteer

As with Camden's *Reges, reginae, nobiles, & alii in Ecclesia Collegiata B. Petri Westmonasterii sepulti*, Holland's guidebook appears to have met with widespread approval. In the preface to the second edition, he tells his readers that the other reason why he reissued the book was because he "*was importuned to publish this my Collection the second time*".[28] Nonetheless, popular as Camden's and Holland's guides seem to have been, both books were limited in scale and scope. Whilst they would have been useful to visitors and tourists, and to historians and antiquaries interested in the two specific churches and the individuals buried in them, they lacked the comparatist approach of the more ambitious collections of monuments and inscriptions, which had begun to appear elsewhere in Europe. Books such as Jan Gruter's monumental *Inscriptiones antiquae totius orbis Romani* (1602–03) were on an altogether different scale: this compilation brought together more than 12,000 inscriptions from across the Roman world and was a genuinely trans-European project.[29] Nor did their guidebooks contain discussions of how epigraphic material might be used and interpreted, of how inscriptions should be transcribed, or even a history of inscriptions, although elsewhere Camden himself did address all these subjects in an essay published in his antiquarian miscellany *Remaines of a Greater Worke, Concerning Britaine* (1605).[30]

Shortly before Holland reissued his text, however, a much more ambitious study of British funerary monuments had been published: John Weever's mammoth *Ancient Funerall Monuments Within the United Monarchie of Great Britaine, Ireland, and the Islands Adjacent* (1631). Weever's work is at once a collection of inscriptions, a methodical treatise in how to interpret monuments and inscriptions, a history of funerary monuments from classical antiquity to the present day and a deeply personal series of observations and reflections. Amongst its antiquarian matter, it also intersperses discussions of church history, digressions on architecture, snippets of poetry and pedigrees. It was, as such, the first comprehensive gazetteer of this kind of material to appear in English.

Such was the impact of Weever's book that Holland himself felt duty-bound to admit (but also excuse) the considerable overlap with his own much more modest project: "*I am not ignorant also that M*r. *Iohn Weever his laborious collected volume of* Funerall Monuments *is lately published: wherein I see and haply you may find many and most of my collected Epitaphs, done, doubtlesse, by his owne industry*". He hoped, though, that his readers would excuse and "*vindicate* [him] *from robbing from him or ploughing with his*

Heifer, this small piece of Ground".[31] Without Weever, history from marble might never have taken off: his work is the crucial intermediary between guidebooks such as Camden's and Holland's, which were compiled primarily for curious antiquarian-minded church visitors, and the much more elaborate church and cathedral descriptions, and collections of church monuments, that began to appear from the middle of the seventeenth century.

Weever's work was nearly 900 pages long, and it was the result of more than two decades of meticulous observation and exhaustive research. Weever combined periods of bookish study with regular journeys across Britain to make his own first-hand transcriptions.[32] Two notebooks, now in the library of the Society of Antiquaries in London, document this research, and much of the material that he copied in those manuscripts ended up in the printed text.[33] The book that emerged was commemorative, resurrectionary and explicitly focused on family history and genealogy. The letterpress title describes it as "[a] worke reuiuing the dead memory of the Royall Progenie, the Nobilitie, Gentrie, and Communaltie, of these his *Maiesties Dominions*". The same title also emphasises the variety of sources on which Weever drew and the extent to which he combined literary research with fieldwork, or as he put it "Studie" with "Trauels". It promises a work "[i]ntermixed and illustrated with variety of Historicall obseruations, anno*tations, briefe notes, extracted out of approued Authors, infallible* Records, Lieger Bookes, Charters, Rolls, old Manuscripts, and the Collections of iudicious Antiquaries".[34]

The work itself begins with a lengthy preface in which Weever explains the origins of his project, sets out his research methods and expounds his style of transcription. The preface makes clear the extent to which he conceived *Ancient Funerall Monuments* as a humanist and philological project in the contemporary continental vein. At the same time, though, the preface also signals how closely he aligned his endeavour with the particularly English form of antiquarianism that emerged as a response to the Reformation. He undertook the project, he tells his readers in the opening sentences of the book, because of the scholarly neglect of Britain's tombs and inscriptions, and because of the widespread despoliation of these monuments. The preface begins by naming three prominent, contemporary epigraphic scholars in whose footsteps he follows (Nathan Chytraeus, Franciscus Swertius and Laurentius Schraderus). Weever then turns to the execrable situation in Britain, lamenting "how barbarously within these his Maiesties Dominions" monuments have been "broken downe, and vtterly almost all ruinated".[35] The consequence of this "inhumane, deformidable act", he goes on, is that "the honourable memory of many virtuous and noble persons deceased, is extinguished". Weever's rhetoric here is far from subtle, but it makes clear his outrage at the destruction of Britain's funerary monuments in the all-too-recent past. His own antiquarian and epigraphic endeavours, he explained, were a first step to rectify this neglect. "[G]rieuing at this vnsufferable iniurie offered as well to the liuing, as the dead", and "out of the respect I bore to venerable Antiquity, and the due regard to continue the remembrance of the defunct to future posteritie", he wrote, "I determined with my selfe to collect such memorials of the deceased, as were remaining as yet undefaced; as also to reuiue the memories of eminent worthy persons entombed or interred, either in Parish, or in Abby Churches".[36]

The epistle then concludes with a brief statement and explanation of Weever's method of transcription:

> I conclude the Epitaphs and Funerall inscriptions in this booke as I finde them engrauen [...] And I write the Latine in the same manner as I finde it either written or imprinted, as *capud* for *caput*, *nichil* for *nihil*, and the like; as also E vocall, for E dipthong, dipthongs being but lately come into vse.[37]

In including this passage, Weever's aim was to underscore the documentary nature of his collection and thus signal its reliability. *Ancient Funerall Monuments*, the quotation earlier emphasises, is a diplomatic transcription and an authoritative record of monumental inscriptions and medieval manuscripts. Subsequent scholars have not always been as generous in their assessments of the work, but passages such as this do foreground Weever's commitment to a recognisably scholarly, humanist, philological method.[38] This, moreover, was not just editorial puff. As E. A. J. Honigmann has shown, "[w]hen Weever copied from a good text, he seems to have done so with a high degree of accuracy".[39] Furthermore, Weever did not just limit this approach to Latin materials. He did the same thing with Anglo-Saxon documents: "I likewise write the Orthographie of the old English as it comes to my hands; and if by the copying out of the same it be any manner of ways mollified, it is much against my will, for I hold originalls the best; whereby some may obiect the simplicitie of my vnlaboured stile, and the rough hewen forme of my writing".[40]

A Diocesan history and discourse of funerary monuments

Weever's introductory materials also include a lengthy eighteen-chapter "DISCOVRSE OF Funerall Monuments, &c.", which takes up nearly a third of the book. This discourse is a comparatist and diachronic history of funerary monuments, which moves freely across pagan and biblical, and classical and post-classical, times. Much of it is taken up with a thoroughly orthodox Anglican history of the Reformation. Echoing the tone of his preface, Weever repeatedly lambasts Protestant iconoclasm and offers a series of fierce rebuttals of monumental despoliation and neglect. In this chapter, for example, he laments that "nothing will be shortly left to continue the memory of the deceased to posteritie", and blasts "the opinion some haue, that Tombes, and their Epitaphs, taste somewhat of Poperie, hauing already most sacrilegiously stolne, erased and taken away, almost all the Inscriptions and Epitaphs, cut, writ, inlaid, or engrauen vpon the Sepulchres of the deceased; and most shamefully defaced the glorious rich Tombes, and goodly monuments of our most worthy Ancestours".[41] In Chapter 10, he similarly castigates the "too forward zeale" of the Reformers, as they "rooted vp, and battered downe, Crosses in Churches, and Church-yards", "defaced and brake downe the images of Kings, Princes, and noble estates", "crackt a peeces the glasse-windowes wherein the effigies of our blessed Sauiour hanging on the Crosse, or any of his Saints was depictured", and "despoiled Churches of their copes, vestments, Amices, rich hangings, and all other ornaments whereupon the story, or the pourtraiture, of Christ himselfe, or of any Saint or Martyr, was delineated, wrought, or embroidered". "[T]hese hote-burning in zeale officers", he went on, "got cloakes to hide their knauery, and beards to visard their hypocrisie, and thereby vnder a goodly pretence of reforming Religion, they preferred their priuate respects, and their owne enriching, before the honour of the Prince and countery; yea and before the glory of God himselfe". The worst of all, though, was that these bearded hypocrites despoiled and defaced funerary monuments: "But the foulest and most inhumane action of those times, was the violation of Funerall Monuments".[42]

Weever's "Discourse", however, is more than just tub-thumping, anti-iconoclastic rhetoric. It is also a careful and comparative history of the material form of funerary monuments. In this chapter, for example, Weever develops a taxonomy for sepulchres and monuments based on their building materials, decoration, statuary and elevation above the ground. This was a hierarchical theory, where the degree of decoration corresponded with the social status and rank of the commemorated. It was also, though, a model of memorialization that Weever saw as in decline. "Sepulchres", he warned, "should bee made according to the qualitie and degree of the person deceased, that by the Tombe euery one might bee discerned of what ranke hee was liuing". This, however, was "not obserued altogether in these times: for by some of our epitaphs more honour is attributed to a rich quondam Tradesman, or griping vsurer, then is giuen to the greatest Potentate entombed in Westminster".[43]

In the same chapter, we also hear Weever making what sound like tentative aesthetic judgements on funerary monuments. These generally accord with his conservatism and with the sense of moral and historical decline that he articulated throughout the book. He bemoaned, for example, the contemporary habit of "garnish[ing]" tombs "with the pictures of naked men and women", associating this kind of carving with the worst of pagan idolatry. Tomb-makers "now adayes", he lamented, "rais[e] out of the dust, and brin[g] into the Church, the memories of the heathen gods and goddesses, with all their whirligiggs".[44] His description of Henry VII's tomb in Westminster Abbey (carved by the Florentine sculptor Pietro Torrigiani) elsewhere in this chapter exemplifies the conservative historical and social vision behind his method of reading monuments, as well as the significance of architectural and material details for it:

Noble men, Princes, and Kings had (as it befitteth them, and as some of them haue at this day) their Tombes or Sepulchres raised aloft aboue ground, to note the excellencie of their state and dignitie; and withall, their personages delineated, carued, and embost, at the full length and bignesse, truly proportioned throughout, as neare to the life, and with as much state and magnificence, as the skill of the Artificer could possibly carue and forme the same: the materials of which were alabaster, rich marble, touch, rauce, porpherey, polisht brasse or copper.[45]

Henry VII's splendid monument, he went on, citing Francis Bacon's concluding words in his *Historie of the Raigne of King Henry the Seventh* (1622), was the pre-eminent illustration of this: "like vnto that made to the memorie of King *Henry* the seuenth in Westminster, who dwelleth more richly dead (saith *Viscount* Saint *Alban* in his history of that kings raigne) in the monument of his Tombe, then hee did aliue in Richmond or any of his palaces, it being the stateliest, and most curious daintie monument of Europe, both for the Chappell, and for the Sepulchre".[46]

By far the largest part of *Ancient Funerall Monuments*, though, are the four diocesan surveys of Canterbury, Rochester, London and Norwich that take up the remainder of the book. (Despite the promise of the title and the fact that Weever travelled as far as Scotland in search of inscriptions, the published text got nowhere near the geographical coverage that he intended.[47]) *Ancient Funerall Monuments* does in macrocosm what Camden and Holland in their guidebooks did in microcosm. Weever adopted both the copious, expansive style of contemporary antiquarian books and the peregrinatory narrative strategy of chorography. Works such as Camden's *Britannia* and topographical books such as William Lambarde's *A Perambulation of Kent* (1576; revised edition 1596) and John Norden's county surveys were his likely models here.[48] His principal aim, as with many other early modern antiquaries, was historical comprehensiveness: the four sections are, at heart, a gazetteer of the churches, abbeys and monasteries, and the funerary monuments within them, in these four dioceses. His descriptions come sometimes from direct observation, sometimes from books that he read, and sometimes from other scholarly "collections". He also sometimes included transcriptions of documents and occasionally, too, architectural descriptions. His approach to tombs and monuments was primarily genealogical. His focus, in accordance with what he set out in his prefatory epistle, was on the family histories of the individuals memorialised, and on preserving their names and fame through documenting their monuments and recording the inscriptions on them. Occasionally, though, there are also glimpses of architectural and monumental connoisseurship: as, for example, in his dating of certain inscriptions in the Minster on the Isle of Sheppey in Kent on the evidence of their style or in his description of the tomb of the fifteenth-century archbishop of Canterbury, John Kemp.[49]

Moreover, unlike Camden or Holland, Weever also explicitly included visual material in his gazetteer in the form of eighteen woodcut illustrations. The first of these occurs in his description of St Nicholas' Church in the village of Pluckley in Kent: illustrations of two of the famous Dering family brasses found in the Dering family chapel there.[50] The woodcuts depict two of the family's most notable fifteenth-century ancestors, John and Richard Dering. Weever was probably supplied with the drawings on which the woodcuts were based by one of their descendants, the seventeenth-century antiquary Sir Edward Dering.[51] Other visual material in the book includes a woodcut of a notable late-medieval monument, with a magnificent inlaid brass effigy, in St Margaret's Church, Westminster and an illustration of a near contemporary funerary monument (for Gerard D'Ewes who died in 1591) from Upminster in Essex.[52] The decision to include the former, an illustration of the tomb chest of Dame Mary Billing, a prominent fifteenth-century church benefactor, was especially prescient, as her tomb was destroyed in the mid-eighteenth century.[53] As for the latter, Weever's motivation to include that was genealogical: "whose Epitaph, because it is replenished with many particulars touching the antiquity and ensignes of this familie. I haue beene more exact in the full delineation thereof in the figure following".[54] With Weever's book, then, as well as it being a ground-breaking gazetteer and a work that exemplified the relationship between genealogy and epigraphy in historical writing at the time, there are also the first stirrings of a distinctly visual sense of the past. There are signs, too, that Weever recognised that the significance of his "church notes" lay as much in the material culture that he delineated as in the texts that he transcribed.

Conclusion—Dingley's histories from marble

This visual sense of history flourished in the later seventeenth century, taking full flight in the astonishing (but now almost entirely forgotten) work that gives its name to this chapter: Thomas Dingley's *History from Marble*. Despite not being well known today, Dingley's *History* deserves our attention because it exemplifies the ways in which seventeenth-century antiquaries and historians collected, documented and made use of church monuments and their inscriptions. In terms of genre, it is a familiar work and one in a long line of seventeenth-century antiquarian-inflected chorographies. It is yet another example of a miscellaneous collection of historical and antiquarian observations, organised along broadly geographical lines. Its coverage ranges across Gloucestershire, Wiltshire, Hampshire, Oxfordshire, Berkshire, Worcestershire and Herefordshire, with long sections on the cities of Oxford and Bath. Like many travellers at the time, Dingley journeyed with a "Journall" in his hand. From the notes and observations that he made in this notebook, he later wrote up his *History*. We know this from the following remark that he made about the church of St Mary Redcliffe in Bristol: "It was founded and finisht at the sole charges of one Canninges a citizen and merchant of Bristoll, who hath two monuments therein erected to his memory the one in sacerdotall & y[e] other in Secular habitt which I have committed to my Journall as follow".[55]

The contents of the *History from Marble* include church monuments, architectural notes on country-houses, castles and cathedrals, antiquities (classical and post-classical), onomastics, etymologies and extracts of poetry. More unexpected subjects that Dingley made notes about include the geology of hot springs and the mineralogical and medicinal qualities of their waters, campanology, prompted by a visit to one of the churches in Chippenham, and literary biography.[56] His principal interests, though, were genealogy and heraldry, and these shaped the form and contents of the entire work. A supplementary alphabetical index at the beginning of the manuscript ("An Alphabett of ARMS additionall to those w[ch] I have mett with on Funerall Monuments, Tombstones, Churches Castles Publick Buildings and Seats in this Journall") illustrates this.[57] So also do the coats-of-arms, properly tricked out, that he dutifully recorded from tombstones, seals and monuments, and which fill the pages of his *History*. Like many other seventeenth-century antiquarian and chorographical surveys, its pages are also filled with inscriptions that its author collected and transcribed. In Dingley's case, these include classical, medieval and post-medieval examples.

The *History from Marble* was not, therefore, particularly innovative in terms of its organisation, genre or subject matter. What is, however, distinctive about it, and what marks it out from the myriad other similar books written in preceding years, is the way in which it combines text and image, and the extent to which Dingley sought to document the material remains of the past visually as well as textually. The *History from Marble* is a beautifully produced manuscript, with penmanship of the highest order. By far its most striking feature are its more than one hundred fine pen-and-ink drawings. These portray churches, castles, country-houses and cathedrals; they depict antiquities, monuments and tombs; and, more frequently than anything, they document coats-of-arms, heraldic devices and other blazons.

Dingley set out his stall here with the manuscript's splendid decorative frontispiece (Figure 3.1). Personified figures of Painting and Sculpture, with some of the key tools of their respective trades (palette, brushes, chisel, try-square), face one another and hold up a curtain on which the full title is written. The frontispiece in this way signals to the reader that this will be a visual history. Elsewhere, the frontispiece also foregrounds the work's more specific interest in funerary monuments and church notes. Below the figure of Sculpture, and alongside a blank cartouche, Dingley wrote the following verses adapted from an inscription that he had found on an Oxford church monument: "Aspera vox ite, Vox | est benedicta venite. | Dicetur reprobis ite, | Venite piis" ("Harsh voice go! The voice that is blessed come! It is said to the reprobate 'go', to the pious 'come'"). He had apparently discovered this sentential distich, in a slightly different form, on an epitaph in the Church of St Mary Magdalen in Oxford, as he recorded later in the manuscript.[58] At the foot of the frontispiece, he also copied another Latin maxim, which signals even more clearly his interest in funerary monuments and epigraphy. Importantly, too, this one acknowledges his debt to previous literary and historical works: "Augustinus de Civ. Dei Sepulchrorum memoria magis virorum, est Consolatio, quam defunctorum utilitas" ("The memory of the

Figure 3.1 Thomas Dingley, "History from Marble. Being Ancient & Moderne
Funerall Monuments in England & Wales by T. D. Gen.," Bodleian
Library, Oxford, MS Top. gen. d. 19, fol. 5r. Frontispiece.

graves is more a consolation to the living than a benefit to the dead"). These
words were ultimately adapted from Book 1, Chapter 12, of St Augustine's
De civitate dei, and a passage therein which Augustine reflected on

commemorative and sepulchral practices and their significance for the living rather than the dead.[59] The more immediate source, though, was the title-page of Camden's guide to Westminster Abbey, where the maxim was given in the same form.[60] By quoting it on his frontispiece, Dingley signalled that he was writing in the same tradition and that his *History* should be seen as a direct descendant of Camden's work. Moreover, if the frontispiece indicated his debt to previous epigraphic scholarship, so also did the wonderfully suggestive title itself. The phrase "history from marble" (consciously or otherwise) echoes how pioneering earlier scholars conceived inscribed stones. Agustín, for example, described monumental inscriptions as "books on marble or bronze", whilst the Italian Jesuit historian Agostino Mascardi, in an influential treatise on the writing of history *Dell'arte historica* (1636), described classical remains more generally as *libri di marmo*.[61]

The *History from Marble* was one of six antiquarian works that Dingley compiled, all of which later ended up in the library of Sir Thomas Winnington at Stanford Court in Worcestershire, where they remained until the 1930s. The Dingley manuscripts survived the devastating fire there in December 1882, which destroyed many of the family's rare books and manuscripts. What remained of the library was then dispersed following the death of the fifth baronet, Sir Francis Winnington, in 1931.[62] All of Dingley's works combined the form of an itinerary (or, in some cases, multiple itineraries) with antiquarian observation, monumental documentation and epigraphic transcription. His *Observations in a Voyage in the Kingdom of France*, for example, which records a journey that he made in 1675, is subtitled "Being a Collection of Several Monuments, Inscriptions, Draughts of Towns, Castles, &c.".[63] His *Observations in a Voyage Through the Kingdom of Ireland*, which was bound in the same manuscript, and documents a journey that he made to Ireland five years later in 1680, possibly as a surveyor, is subtitled in exactly the same way.[64] The pages of this work, moreover, are similarly filled with church notes, architectural drawings, descriptions of tombs and funerary monuments, transcribed inscriptions and heraldic observations. Notable examples can be found in the descriptions of Tullow, Kilkenny, Cashel, Owney Abbey, Emly, Quin Abbey, Limerick and, most extensively, Dublin.[65] In short, this work, too, was a history from marble, sharing the same interests in epigraphy, funerary monuments and genealogy as Dingley's eponymous work, and the same visual approach to historical and topographical writing.

The examples of Camden, Holland, Weever and Dingley show the evolution of epigraphic research in the seventeenth century. The development from Camden's slim guidebook to Dingley's richly illustrated and lengthy manuscripts was considerable. However, there was also clearly a continuity here, as Dingley's allusive frontispiece indicates. The works discussed in this chapter all shared a common method and approach, even if in form, scope and scale, Dingley's and Weever's books had more in common with Camden's *Britannia* than his brief abbey guide. They also had a common purpose: "history from marble", these examples all suggest, was a recognisable and coherent form of antiquarian activity across the seventeenth century, and a distinct form of history. Its subject matter was church monuments, epitaphs, coats-of-arms and inscriptions. Collection, compilation, documentation and transcription were its aims. The result was a genre that drew on continental classical scholarship, and which took its inspiration from pioneering sixteenth-century work on Roman inscriptions, but which turned its attention to the medieval and post-medieval worlds as well or instead, and which resulted in something more specifically English in matter and motivation.

The drivers of this kind of history, and the principal reasons behind it, were genealogical, heraldic, antiquarian and preservationist. Thomas Habington explained in the introduction to the *Survey of Worcestershire*, his own "history from marble", that the "occasyon wheareuppon [he] fyrst undertooke this woourcke was because it was obiected by one that our countie conteygned fewe gentellmen of antiquity". He, therefore, set out to counter that objection by "s[eeing] and transcryb[ing] the Armes and monuments of all the churches in thys Shyre".[66] Exactly the same could be said for Camden, Holland, Weever and Dingley. These were the motives and methods that produced their histories from marble too. Scarred by recent memories of monumental despoliation, and all too aware that the same might happen again, they sought to preserve in their books the epitaphs and other heraldic, genealogical and monumental remains found in churches and to rescue them from the ravages of humans and time. Habington told his readers in the same place that, thanks to his exhaustive epigraphic research and his relentless transcriptions, "the face of our Shyre [was] raysed out of obscurityes". Camden, Holland, Weever and Dingley could all have made similar claims.

Notes

1 William Camden, *Reges, reginæ, nobiles, & alij in Ecclesia Collegiata B. Petri Westmonasterij sepulti, vsque ad annum reparatæ salutis* (London: E[dmund] Bollifant, 1600). The book was entered in the Stationers' Register on 21 January 1600: see *A Transcript of the Registers of the Company of Stationers of London; 1554–1640 A.D.*, ed. Edward Arber, 5 vols (London: privately printed, 1875–94), 3:56.

2 Graham Parry, *The Trophies of Time: English Antiquarians of the Seventeenth Century* (Oxford: Oxford University Press, 1995), 211; Wyman H. Herendeen, *William Camden: A Life in Context* (Woodbridge: The Boydell Press, 2007), 168–70; and Ian Atherton, "Visiting England's Cathedrals from the Reformation to the Early Nineteenth Century," in *Pilgrimage and England's Cathedrals: Past, Present, and Future*, eds Dee Dyas and John Jenkins (Cham: Springer, 2020), 88.

3 *The Diary of Baron Waldstein: A Traveller in Elizabethan England*, trans. and annot. G.W. Groos (London: Thames and Hudson, 1981), 37.

4 *Diary of Baron Waldstein*, 41; cf. Camden, *Reges, reginæ, nobiles, & alij in Ecclesia Collegiata B. Petri Westmonasterij sepulti*, A4v: "Obtulit B. Edwardo in Ecclesia Westmonasteriensi regalia regni Scotiæ, videlicet Solium inaugurationis, Sceptrum aureum cum corona, Anno 1307. mortem obijt & ad caput patrus situs est in tumulo marmoreo cum hoc Epitaphio".

5 William Brenchley Rye, *England as Seen by Foreigners in the Days of Elizabeth and James the First. Comprising the Translations of the Journals of the Two Dukes of Wirtemberg in 1592 and 1610; Both Illustrative of Shakespeare. With Extracts from the Travels of Foreign Princes and Others, Copious Notes, an Introduction, and Etchings* (London: John Russell Smith, 1865), 132; *Iodoci Sinceri Itinerarium Galliæ, Ita accomodatum, vt eius dvctv mediocri tempore tota Gallia obiri, Anglia & Belgia adiri possint: nec bis terue ad eadem loca rediri oporteat: notatis cuiusque loci, quas vocant, deliciis: cum appendice, de Bvrdigala* (Lyon: Jacques du Creux, 1616), Z7v–Z8r.

6 Rye, *England as Seen by Foreigners*, 178; Valentin Arithmaeus, *Mausoléa regum, reginarum, dynastarum, nobilium, sumptuosissima, artificiosissima, magnificentis- sima, Londini Anglorum in occidentali urbis angulo structa, H. e. Eorundem inscriptîones omnes in lucem reductæ curâ Valentinis Arithmæi, Professoris Academici* (Frankfurt: Joannis Eichorn, 1618), †5 v: "Cum verò æditimus [...] me vidit cupidum istarum rerum, obtulit exemplar inscriptionum aliquot, ante multos annos excusarum: sed pactus ex more gentis, avaritiâ ferventis ingens pretium".

7 Daniel King, *The Cathedrall and Conventvall Churches of England and Wales Orthographically Delineated by D. K. Anno M DC LVI* (London: John Overton, 1656).

8 Thomas Dingley, "History from Marble. Being Ancient & Moderne Funerall Monuments in England & Wales by T. D. Gen.," Bodleian Library, Oxford, MS Top. gen. d. 19, fol. 5r.

9 Francis Haskell, *History and Its Images: Art and the Interpretation of the Past* (New Haven and London: Yale University Press, 1993), 23.

10 Margaret Aston, "English Ruins and English History: The Dissolution and the Sense of the Past," *Journal of the Warburg and Courtauld Institutes* 36 (1973): 231–2.

11 For the rise of "church notes", see also Jan Broadway, *"No historie so meete": Gentry Culture and the Development of Local History in Elizabethan and Early Stuart England* (Manchester and New York: Manchester University Press, 2006), 133–6.

12 Alexandra Walsham, "History, Memory, and the English Reformation," *Historical Journal* 55, no. 4 (2012): 918.

13 Thomas Habington, *A Survey of Worcestershire*, ed. John Amphlett, 2 vols, Worcestershire Historical Society (Oxford: James Parker and Co., 1895–99), 2:18.

14 Parry, *Trophies of Time*, 181–5; Graham Parry and Michiyo Takano, "The Illustrations to Dugdale's *History of St Paul's Cathedral*: Subscribers and Their Sentiments," *The Seventeenth Century* 35, no. 4 (2020): 473–95.

15 For Renaissance and early modern "medievalism", see Alexander Nagel and Christopher S. Wood, "What Counted as an 'Antiquity' in the Renaissance?" in *Renaissance Medievalisms*, ed. Konrad Eisenbichler (Toronto: Centre for Reformation and Renaissance Studies, 2009), 53–74; Deanne Williams, "Shakespearean Medievalism and the Limits of Periodization in *Cymbeline*," *Literature Compass* 8, no. 6 (2011): 390–403; and Mike Rodman Jones, "The Uses of Medievalism in Early Modern England: Recovery, Temporality, and the 'Passionating' of the Past," *Exemplaria* 30, no. 3 (2018): 191–206.

16 Broadway, *"No historie so meete"*, 134. For the rise in the "genealogical imagination" more generally, see Michael Maclagan, "Genealogy and Heraldry in the Sixteenth and Seventeenth Centuries," in *English Historical Scholarship in the Sixteenth and Seventeenth Centuries*, ed. Levi Fox (London: Oxford University Press for the Dugdale Society, 1956), 31–48; and D. R. Woolf, *The Social Circulation of the Past: English Historical Culture 1500–1730* (Oxford: Oxford University Press, 2003), 99–140.

17 William Stenhouse, *Reading Inscriptions and Writing Ancient History: Historical Scholarship in the Late Renaissance* (London: Institute of Classical Studies, 2005), 115, 118.
18 For Agustín's book and its reception, see further Stenhouse, *Reading Inscriptions*, 78–80, 157–8, 161–2.
19 Antonio Agustín, *Dialogos de medallas inscriciones y otras antiguedades* (Tarragona: Felipe Mey, 1587), 2a4r: "Hai sin esto otros prouechos para ente[n] der muchas cosas q[ue] en libros estan falsas y escuras como son los nombres y prenombres y familias de los Romanos, las tribus, las legiones, los magistrados, los sacerdocios y sus ministros, los officious, el gouierno de las prouinicias, el cargo de la gente de guerra, y muchas particularidades de los soldados, y otras casas infinitas".
20 Camden, *Reges, reginæ, nobiles, & alij in Ecclesia Collegiata B. Petri Westmonasterij sepulti*, A2r–v.
21 British Library, Cotton MSS Faustina A. iii, fols 11r–16 v, and Titus A. viii, fols 2r–5 v.
22 For the *Mirabilia* and other similar guides to Rome, see Anna Blenow and Stefano Fogelberg Rota (eds), *Rome and the Guidebook Tradition: From the Middle Ages to the 20th Century* (Berlin and Boston: De Gruyter, 2019).
23 Herendeen, *William Camden*, 169.
24 Henry Holland, *Monumenta sepulchraria Sancti Pauli* (London: impensis H[enry] Holland, 1614), A3r–A4r and B1r–B2v respectively.
25 Holland, *Monumenta sepulchraria Sancti Pauli*, F3v.
26 Henry Holland, *Ecclesia Sancti Pavli illvstrata* (London: John Norton, 1633), A3r.
27 Holland, *Ecclesia Sancti Pavli illvstrata*, A3r. For the renovation project of St Paul's, see Vaughan Hart, "Inigo Jones's Site Organization at St. Paul's Cathedral: 'Ponderous Masses Beheld Hanging in the Air'," *Journal of the Society of Architectural Historians* 53, no. 4 (1994): 414–27.
28 Holland, *Ecclesia Sancti Pavli illvstrata*, A3v.
29 For accounts of Gruter's work, see Stenhouse, *Reading Inscriptions*, 149–53; and Ginette Vagenheim, "L'Epigraphie: Un aspect méconnu de l'histoire de la philologie classique au XVIIe siècle," *Les Cahiers de l'humanisme* 1 (2000): 89–91.
30 William Camden, "Epitaphes," in *Remaines of a Greater Worke, Concerning Britaine, the Inhabitants Thereof, Their Languages, Names, Surnames, Empreses, Wise Speeches, Poësies, and Epitaphes* (London: G[eorge] E[ld] for Simon Waterson, 1605), d2r–h2r.
31 Holland, *Ecclesia Sancti Pavli illvstrata*, A3r–v.
32 For the making of Weever's book, see E. A. J. Honigmann, *John Weever: A Biography of a Literary Associate of Shakespeare and Jonson, Together with a Photographic Facsimile of Weever's* Epigrammes *(1599)* (Manchester: Manchester University Press, 1987), 68–79; and Parry, *Trophies of Time*, 190–216.
33 Society of Antiquaries Library, London, MSS 127 and 128.
34 John Weever, *Ancient Funerall Monuments Written Within the United Monarchie of Great Britaine, Ireland, and the Islands Adiacent, with the Dissolued Monasteries Therein Contained: Their Founders, and What Eminent Persons Haue Beene in the Same Interred* (London: Thomas Harper, 1631), π2r.
35 Weever, *Ancient Funerall Monuments*, π3r. For Chytraeus, Schraderus, and the text-based epigraphic tradition to which they belonged, see Jan L. de Jong, "Reading Instead of Travelling: Nathan Chytraeus's *Variorum in Europa itinerum deliciae*," in *Artes Apodemicae and Early Modern Travel Culture*, eds Karl A. E. Enenkel and Jan L. de Jong (Leiden and Boston: Brill, 2019): 237–61.
36 Weever, *Ancient Funerall Monuments*, π3r.
37 Weever, *Ancient Funerall Monuments*, A2r.

38 The clergyman and historian Henry Wharton, for example, was especially damning. In *Anglia sacra* (1691), his history of the medieval church, he accused Weever of confusing the numbers in funerary inscriptions and dismissed his transcriptions as a farraginous mishmash: "Quod Weaverum attinet, is mortalium omnium infœlicissimus cunctosferè numeros ex sepulchralibus titulis in farraginem suam descriptos vitiavit" (*Anglia sacra, sive collectio historiarum, partim antiquitus, partim recenter scriptarum, de archiepiscopis & episcopis Angliæ, a prima fidei Christianæ susceptione ad annum MDXL* [London: Richard Chiswel, 1691], 4Q2v).

39 Honigmann, *John Weever*, 73.

40 Weever, *Ancient Funerall Monuments*, A2v.

41 Weever, *Ancient Funerall Monuments*, C3v.

42 Weever, *Ancient Funerall Monuments*, F1v–F2r.

43 Weever, *Ancient Funerall Monuments*, B5v–B6r.

44 Weever, *Ancient Funerall Monuments*, B6r.

45 Weever, *Ancient Funerall Monuments*, B5v.

46 Weever, *Ancient Funerall Monuments*, B5v; Francis Bacon, *The Historie of the Raigne of King Henry the Seventh*, in *The Historie of the Raigne of King Henry the Seventh, and Other Works of the 1620s*, ed. Michael Kiernan, The Oxford Francis Bacon VIII (Oxford: Clarendon Press, 2012), 169.

47 For the evidence that Weever travelled to Scotland, see his remark on the lack of surviving funerary monuments there: "As also of the Funerall Monuments which are there to be found, which will be but a few, if Sir *Robert Cottons* Librarie do not helpe me, for by my owne obseruation, in the famous maiden-citie of Edenborough, and in the Parish Churches of other Townes, the Sepulchres of the dead are shamefully abused, or quite taken away, yea and the Churches themselues, with religious houses, and other holy places, violated, demolished, or defaced" (*Ancient Funerall Monuments*, K4r).

48 For these works and their narrative strategies, see Angus Vine, "Travel and Chorography," in *A Handbook of English Renaissance Literary Studies*, ed. John Lee (Chichester: Wiley-Blackwell, 2017), 411–24.

49 Weever, *Ancient Funerall Monuments*, 2B4r and V6v. He described Kemp's tomb as a "decent Monument": a description that reflected his sense of its propriety (*OED, s.v.* "decent", *adj.* 3[a]), but was also a statement of taste (*OED, s.v.* "decent", *adj.* 2).

50 For the Dering brasses, many of which were, in fact, seventeenth-century alterations or forgeries, see R. H. D'Elboux, "The Dering Brasses," *The Antiquaries Journal* 27, nos 1–2 (1947): 11–23; and Sophie Pitman, "Prodigal Years? Negotiating Luxury and Fashioning Identity in a Seventeenth-Century Account Book," *Luxury* 3, nos 1–2 (2016): 7–31.

51 Oliver Harris, "Lines of Descent: Appropriations of Ancestry in Stone and Parchment," in *The Arts of Remembrance in Early Modern England: Memorial Cultures of the Post Reformation*, eds Andrew Gordon and Thomas Rist (London and New York: Routledge, 2016; first published 2013), 99–102.

52 Weever, *Ancient Funerall Monuments*, 2V2r and 3K3r.

53 Mackenzie E. C. Walcott, *Westminster: Memorials of the City, Saint Peter's College, The Parish Churches, Palaces, Streets, and Worthies* (Westminster: Joseph Masters, 1849), 149.

54 Weever, *Ancient Funerall Monuments*, 3K2v.

55 Thomas Dingley, *History from Marble. Compiled in the Reign of Charles II*, ed. John Gough Nichols (Westminster: Camden Society, 1867), lix.

56 Dingley, *History from Marble*, xliii–xliv, lv, and cxlvii.

57 Dingley, *History from Marble*, vii–xv.

58 Dingley, *History from Marble*, cxix: "S^T MAGDALENS CHVRCH in Oxford suburbs without the north Gate [...] It hath also the distich on the side and the other Inscripc*ion*. Aspera vox (ite) Vox est benigna (venite) Dicetur reprobis (ite) venite piis".

59 St Augustine, *De civitate dei*, 1. 12: "Proinde ista omnia, curatio funeris, conditio sepulturae, pompa exequiarum, magis sunt vivorum solacia quam subsidia mortuorum".

60 Camden, *Reges, reginæ, nobiles, & alij in Ecclesia Collegiata B. Petri Westmonasterij sepulti*, A1r. Dingley, in fact, slightly misquoted Camden and ended up mangling one of the Latin words: the text on Camden's title-page reads "Sepulchrorum memoria magis viuorum, est consolatio, quàm defunctorum vtilitas", which makes better sense and is closer to the contrast between the living and the dead that Augustine drew.

61 Stenhouse, *Reading Inscriptions*, 8; Agostino Mascardi, *Dell'arte historica d'Agostino Mascardi trattati cinque* (Rome: Giacomo Facciotti, 1636), A3v–A4r.

62 For the history of the library at Stanford Court, see Edward Walford, "Antiquarian News & Notes," *The Antiquarian Magazine & Bibliographer* 3 (1883): 97–8; and Rosemarie McGerr, *A Lancastrian Mirror for Princes: The Yale Law School* New Statutes of England (Bloomington and Indianapolis: Indiana University Press, 2011), 137.

63 National Library of Ireland, Dublin, MS 392.

64 For the reasons behind Dingley's Irish journey, see Amy Louise Harris, "New Insights into Thomas Dingley's Irish Journey 1680–81," *The Other Clare* 44 (2020), 18–19, 107.

65 Evelyn Philip Shirley, *et al.*, "Extracts from the Journal of Thomas Dineley, Esquire, Giving Some Account of His Visit to Ireland in the Reign of Charles II," *The Journal of the Kilkenny and South-East Ireland Archaeological Society*, new series 2, no. 1 (1858): 47–9; new series 4, no. 1 (1862): 107–9; new series 5, no. 2 (1865): 275, 277–82, 285–7; new series 5, no. 3 (1866): 432–8; and new series 6, no. 1 (1867): 179–81; and F. Elrington Ball, "Extracts from the Journal of Thomas Dineley, Esquire, Giving Some Account of His Visit to Ireland in the Reign of Charles II," *The Journal of the Kilkenny and South-East Ireland Archaeological Society*, sixth series 3, no. 4 (1913): 275–309.

66 Habington, *Survey of Worcestershire*, 1:34.

Figure 3.1 Thomas Dingley, "History from Marble. Being Ancient & Moderne Funerall Monuments in England & Wales by T. D. Gen.," Bodleian Library, Oxford, MS Top. gen. d. 19, fol. 5r. Frontispiece.

Bibliography

Manuscripts

Bodleian Library, Oxford
MS Top. gen. d. 19
British Library, London
Cotton MS Faustina A. iii
Cotton MS Titus A. viii
National Library of Ireland, Dublin
MS 392
Society of Antiquaries Library, London
MS 127
MS 128

Primary sources

Agustín, Antonio. *Dialogos de medallas inscriciones y otras antiguedades.* Tarragona: Felipe Mey, 1587.

Arithmaeus, Valentin. *Mausoléa regum, reginarum, dynastarum, nobilium, sumptuosissima, artificiosissima, magnificentissima, Londini Anglorum in occidentali urbis angulo structa, H. e. Eorundem inscriptîones omnes in lucem reductæ curâ Valentinis Arithmæi, Professoris Academici.* Frankfurt: Joannis Eichorn, 1618.

Bacon, Francis. *The Historie of the Raigne of King Henry the Seventh, in The Historie of the Raigne of King Henry the Seventh, and Other Works of the 1620s.* Edited by Michael Kiernan. The Oxford Francis Bacon VIII. Oxford: Clarendon Press, 2012.

Camden, William. *Reges, reginæ, nobiles, & alij in Ecclesia Collegiata B. Petri Westmonasterij sepulti, vsque ad annum reparatæ salutis.* London: E[dmund] Bollifant, 1600.

Camden, William. *Remaines of a Greater Worke, Concerning Britaine, the Inhabitants Thereof, Their Languages, Names, Surnames, Empreses, Wise Speeches, Poësies, and Epitaphes.* London: G[eorge] E[ld] for Simon Waterson, 1605.

Dingley, Thomas. *History from Marble. Compiled in the Reign of Charles II.* Edited by John Gough Nichols. Westminster: Camden Society, 1867.

Habington, Thomas. *A Survey of Worcestershire.* Edited by John Amphlett. 2 vols. Worcestershire Historical Society. Oxford: James Parker and Co., 1895–99.

Holland, Henry. *Ecclesia Sancti Pavli illvstrata.* London: John Norton, 1633.

Holland, Henry. *Monumenta sepulchraria Sancti Pauli.* London: impensis H[enry] Holland, 1614.

King, Daniel. *The Cathedrall and Conventvall Churches of England and Wales Orthographically Delineated by D. K. Anno M DC LVI.* London: John Overton, 1656.

Mascardi, Agostino. *Dell'arte historica d'Agostino Mascardi trattati cinque.* Rome: Giacomo Facciotti, 1636.

Rye, William Brenchley. *England as Seen by Foreigners in the Days of Elizabeth and James the First. Comprising the Translations of the Journals of the Two Dukes of Wirtemberg in 1592 and 1610; Both Illustrative of Shakespeare. With Extracts from the Travels of Foreign Princes and Others, Copious Notes, an Introduction, and Etchings.* London: John Russell Smith, 1865.

Sincerus, Jodocus. *Iodoci Sinceri Itinerarium Galliæ, Ita accomodatum, vt eius dvctv mediocri tempore tota Gallia obiri, Anglia & Belgia adiri possint: nec bis terue ad eadem loca rediri oporteat: notatis cuiusque loci, quas vocant, deliciis: cum appendice, de Bvrdigala.* Lyon: Jacques du Creux, 1616.

A Transcript of the Registers of the Company of Stationers of London; 1554–1640 A.D. Edited by Edward Arber. 5 vols. London: privately printed, 1875–94.

The Diary of Baron Waldstein: A Traveller in Elizabethan England. Translated and annotated by G. W. Groos. London: Thames and Hudson, 1981.

Weever, John. *Ancient Funerall Monuments Written Within the United Monarchie of Great Britaine, Ireland, and the Islands Adiacent, with the Dissolued Monasteries Therein Contained: Their Founders, and What Eminent Persons Haue Beene in the Same Interred.* London: Thomas Harper, 1631.

Wharton, Henry. *Anglia sacra, sive collectio historiarum, partim antiquitus, partim recenter scriptarum, de archiepiscopis & episcopis Angliæ, a prima fidei Christianæ susceptione ad annum MDXL.* London: Richard Chiswel, 1691.

Secondary sources

Aston, Margaret. "English Ruins and English History: The Dissolution and the Sense of the Past." *Journal of the Warburg and Courtauld Institutes* 36 (1973): 231–255.

Atherton, Ian. "Visiting England's Cathedrals from the Reformation to the Early Nineteenth Century." In *Pilgrimage and England's Cathedrals: Past, Present, and Future*, edited by Dee Dyas and John Jenkins, 75–108. Cham: Springer, 2020.

Ball, F. Elrington. "Extracts from the Journal of Thomas Dineley, Esquire, Giving Some Account of His Visit to Ireland in the Reign of Charles II." *The Journal of the Kilkenny and South-East Ireland Archaeological Society*, sixth series 3, no. 4 (1913): 275–309.

Blenow, Anna, & Stefano Fogelberg Rota, eds. *Rome and the Guidebook Tradition: From the Middle Ages to the 20th Century*. Berlin and Boston: De Gruyter, 2019.

Broadway, Jan. *"No historie so meete": Gentry Culture and the Development of Local History in Elizabethan and Early Stuart England*. Manchester and New York: Manchester University Press, 2006.

de Jong, Jan L. "Reading Instead of Travelling: Nathan Chytraeus's *Variorum in Europa itinerum deliciae*." In *Artes Apodemicae and Early Modern Travel Culture*, edited by Karl A. E. Enenkel and Jan L. de Jong, 237–261. Leiden and Boston: Brill, 2019.

D'Elboux, R. H. "The Dering Brasses." *The Antiquaries Journal* 27, nos. 1–2 (1947): 11–23.

Harris, Amy Louise. "New Insights into Thomas Dingley's Irish Journey 1680–81." *The Other Clare* 44 (2020): 18–19, 107.

Harris, Oliver. "Lines of Descent: Appropriations of Ancestry in Stone and Parchment." In *The Arts of Remembrance in Early Modern England: Memorial Cultures of the Post Reformation*, edited by Andrew Gordon and Thomas Rist, 85–102. London and New York: Routledge, 2016; first published 2013.

Hart, Vaughan. "Inigo Jones's Site Organization at St. Paul's Cathedral: 'Ponderous Masses Beheld Hanging in the Air'." *Journal of the Society of Architectural Historians* 53, no. 4 (1994): 414–427.

Haskell, Francis. *History and Its Images: Art and the Interpretation of the Past*. New Haven and London: Yale University Press, 1993.

Herendeen, Wyman H. *William Camden: A Life in Context*. Woodbridge: The Boydell Press, 2007.

Honigmann, E. A. J. *John Weever: A Biography of a Literary Associate of Shakespeare and Jonson, Together with a Photographic Facsimile of Weever's Epigrammes (1599)*. Manchester: Manchester University Press, 1987.

Jones, Mike Rodman. "The Uses of Medievalism in Early Modern England: Recovery, Temporality, and the 'Passionating' of the Past." *Exemplaria* 30, no. 3 (2018): 191–206.

Maclagan, Michael. "Genealogy and Heraldry in the Sixteenth and Seventeenth Centuries." In *English Historical Scholarship in the Sixteenth and Seventeenth Centuries*, edited by Levi Fox, 31–48. London: Oxford University Press for the Dugdale Society, 1956.

McGerr, Rosemarie. *A Lancastrian Mirror for Princes: The Yale Law School New Statutes of England*. Bloomington and Indianapolis: Indiana University Press, 2011.

Nagel, Alexander, & Christopher S. Wood. "What Counted as an 'Antiquity' in the Renaissance?" In *Renaissance Medievalisms*, edited by Konrad Eisenbichler, 53–74. Toronto: Centre for Reformation and Renaissance Studies, 2009.

Parry, Graham. *The Trophies of Time: English Antiquarians of the Seventeenth Century*. Oxford: Oxford University Press, 1995.

Parry, Graham, & Michiyo Takano. "The Illustrations to Dugdale's *History of St Paul's Cathedral*: Subscribers and Their Sentiments." *The Seventeenth Century* 35, no. 4 (2020): 473–495.

Pitman, Sophie. "Prodigal Years? Negotiating Luxury and Fashioning Identity in a Seventeenth-Century Account Book." *Luxury* 3, nos. 1–2 (2016): 7–31.

Shirley, Evelyn Philip, with John Donovan. "Extracts from the Journal of Thomas Dineley, Esquire, Giving Some Account of His Visit to Ireland in the Reign of Charles II." *The Journal of the Kilkenny and South-East Ireland Archaeological Society*, new series 2, no. 1 (1858): 22–32, 55–56.

Shirley, Evelyn Philip. "Extracts from the Journal of Thomas Dineley, Esquire, Giving Some Account of His Visit to Ireland in the Reign of Charles II." *The Journal of the Kilkenny and South-East Ireland Archaeological Society*, new series 4, no. 1 (1862): 38–52, 103–9.

Shirley, Evelyn Philip, with James Graves, George Du Noyer, John Davis White, John Windele, Herbert F. Hore, & William R. Le Fanu. "Extracts from the Journal of Thomas Dineley, Esquire, Giving Some Account of His Visit to Ireland in the Reign of Charles II." *The Journal of the Kilkenny and South-East Ireland Archaeological Society*, new series 5, no. 2 (1865): 268–290.

Shirley, Evelyn Philip, with Maurice Linehan. "Extracts from the Journal of Thomas Dineley, Esquire, Giving Some Account of His Visit to Ireland in the Reign of Charles II." *The Journal of the Kilkenny and South-East Ireland Archaeological Society*, new series 5, no. 3 (1866): 425–446.

Shirley, Evelyn Philip, with Maurice Linehan. "Extracts from the Journal of Thomas Dineley, Esquire, Giving Some Account of His Visit to Ireland in the Reign of Charles II." *The Journal of the Kilkenny and South-East Ireland Archaeological Society*, new series 6, no. 1 (1867): 73–91, 176–204.

Stenhouse, William. *Reading Inscriptions and Writing Ancient History: Historical Scholarship in the Late Renaissance.* London: Institute of Classical Studies, 2005.

Vagenheim, Ginette. "L'Epigraphie: Un aspect méconnu de l'histoire de la philologie classique au XVIIe siècle." *Les Cahiers de l'humanisme* 1 (2000): 89–91.

Vine, Angus. "Travel and Chorography." In *A Handbook of English Renaissance Literary Studies*, edited by John Lee, 411–424. Chichester: Wiley-Blackwell, 2017.

Walcott, Mackenzie E. C. *Westminster: Memorials of the City, Saint Peter's College, The Parish Churches, Palaces, Streets, and Worthies.* Westminster: Joseph Masters, 1849.

Walford, Edward. "Antiquarian News & Notes." *The Antiquarian Magazine & Bibliographer* 3 (1883): 94–99.

Walsham, Alexandra. "History, Memory, and the English Reformation." *Historical Journal* 55, no. 4 (2012): 899–938.

Williams, Deanne. "Shakespearean Medievalism and the Limits of Periodization in *Cymbeline*." *Literature Compass* 8, no. 6 (2011): 390–403.

Woolf, D. R. *The Social Circulation of the Past: English Historical Culture 1500–1730.* Oxford: Oxford University Press, 2003.

Part 2

Visual understandings of history

4   History painting and/as genre

Mark Salber Phillips

Introduction

This chapter discusses a mode of historical representation that is primarily visual rather than verbal.[2] Its subject—history painting—was long regarded as the most demanding of painterly pursuits. To trace its evolution as a painterly mode since the seventeenth century is also to trace a history of genre-construction itself, for although history painting is today regarded as one among several genres of visual representation, its lofty position in the early modern period positioned it above the other named genres. It was only in the nineteenth century that history painting came to be understood as one genre among others, if still the most prestigious. This change, as I will argue, was both the product of convergence of previously recognised genres of painterly expression with historical representation and a reflection of the broader historicist and democratising currents at large during that century.

As a coda to tracing this development, I will also argue that history painting did not collapse in the face of twentieth-century modernism, a revolution in art which, it was said until recently, caused history painting to appear obsolete and to disappear in the face of cubism, abstraction and other modernist schools.[3] As recently as 2015, when I had the opportunity to organise a colloquium on the subject at a prestigious American centre for art historical research, the director marvelled that in fifteen years in her position, she had never once heard anyone mention history painting.[4] Yet as I will argue in this paper, although history painting has undergone successive reinventions, it never in fact disappeared. Surely Picasso's *Guernica* (1937), for example, although celebrated as a masterpiece of cubism, is also a great history painting.[5] During the twentieth century, other artists also deployed history painting's narrative capacities for political ends and to inscribe marginalised histories in resistance to colonial, racialized and gendered regimes. These energies have caused history painting to gain notable momentum during the first decades of the twenty-first century, as contemporary artists again use history painting as a site of historical representation and memory.[6] We need to understand the current revival of history painting, I urge here, as a new phase that rests on a foundation laid during the late-eighteenth and nineteenth centuries when

DOI: 10.4324/9781003331971-7

history painting itself developed as a genre that responded to new currents of democratisation, secularisation and historicization.

History painting and narrativity: Text and image

Standard discussions of history painting focus on the visual aesthetics of its finest examples. After the initial identification of source texts, classical art historical analyses often turned their attention away from narrative as historical representation in order to focus on the formal aspects of the painter's work. This tendency was particularly acute through much of the twentieth century, when the modernist quest for formal purity in painterly expression was at its height. It is only recently that theorists like W.J.T. Mitchell have urged a more hybrid approach to the study of images.[7] I take up Mitchell's interest in the relationship between texts and images, but, as a cultural historian and historiographer, I am also interested in the ways these relationships have changed over time. Attention to narrative engagement—missing or muted in still life, portrait or landscape—stands out as the very foundation of history painting's majestic ambitions, whether or not they are successfully realised in any given work. Put simply, history painting as a mode of historical representation is doubly rich—a school not only of light, shape and colour but also of words and ideas, each in dialogue with the other, a movement in time as well as of thought. In opposition to the orthodoxies of artistic modernism, textual referentiality—achieved through the tight linkage of visual imagery to a known narrative evoked either through figurative compositions, titles or both—is inherent in the nature of history painting and has endured through the twentieth century to the present.

There is no simple definition of history painting, good for all times and locations. As a starter, however, we can invoke a compact definition given by a seventeenth-century English commentator, drawing upon French sources of the time. "History painting", wrote William Aglionby in 1685, "is an Assembly of many Figures in one Piece, to Represent any Action of Life, whether True or Fabulous, accompanied with all its Ornaments of Land-skip and Perspective".[8] The genre's essential quality was its dignity or elevation—a key feature of an art form that grew out of the deeply hierarchical assumptions of early modern society. As the most dignified of all the visual arts, "histories", as they were called, held a position of unique privilege. Other genres were known by the objects and materials that governed their labour. In the language of the day, their skills were considered "mechanical". By contrast, "history" called on powers of human intelligence, thus earning its place among the "liberal" arts. What gave history painting its elevation could be compared to the dignity of the court or the church—a quality of innate pre-eminence that was as natural to history painting as nobility was to the crown.

In this discussion, I build on earlier work which has focused on Renaissance and eighteenth-century historiography and, more recently, on a re-theorisation of historical distance.[9] I will draw largely on examples that emerge from my past work on British historiography in the eighteenth and nineteenth centuries. As a historian of ideas, my emphasis will be on how continuities and re-workings of this tradition have served to mediate historical representation, how a politics of democratisation has informed the evolution of genres, and how the variability of historical distance manifests itself visually. In this context, we can enlarge the art historian's question, "Is this a *good* history painting?" by asking one which may be more useful to the historian, "What *kind* of history painting is this?"

History painting and the question of genre

To begin, it will be helpful to clarify how the concept of genre has developed in the visual arts. What do we mean by genre in this context? And how does it help to give order to visual representation? There was a time when the concept seemed relatively easy to codify. In the latter half of the seventeenth century when these terms solidified in France (later in England and elsewhere), Europeans saw genre as a straightforward issue. Visual art could be divided neatly into two distinct "kinds". At the pinnacle, there was history painting in all its elevation and glory, while all the rest—portrait, still life, landscape, vignettes of popular and family life—was relegated to a lower form to which the French gave the term "genre". High art was public, genre domestic. High art was both expensive and expansive, genre limited and small scale, the domain of more ordinary folk, though often enlivened with satire and pointed social commentary. And all of this far removed from the Biblical and mythological figures who appeared on the more sober stage called history painting.

Not surprisingly, we tend to think of the genres as fixed points. Once discovered they come to seem natural categories, imbued with a kind of inevitability—something like the laws of nature. In short, they offer us the welcome sensation of a settled truth. Whether we think of still life, portrait or landscape—or, in literature, epic, novel or memoir—which of us can avoid thinking of art forms outside of these seemingly natural categories? It is hardly surprising that the genres should be understood in this way. It was all too easy, for example, to conflate the genre of landscape with the land as such—to experience the land itself as an unfinished step towards landscape in the making. In the context of deep beliefs in nature and established social hierarchies as evidencing divine providence such conflations appeared unquestionable. Even during the height of history painting's exceptional status, however, there are examples of the conflation of genres themselves that made these beliefs explicit. Poussin's famous last work *The Four Seasons* (1660–1664) appears at first to be landscapes until the viewer identifies the small figural assemblies as referencing Biblical and ancient classical narratives.[10] And a century later, as John Berger pointed out, Thomas Gainsborough juxtaposed Mr and Mrs Andrews with their acres to compose a portrait that is as much an image of the tenure of the landed gentry as of its owners' likenesses.[11]

Today this presumption of purity seems simplistic. We are now increasingly aware of the ways in which our paintings are shaped by the politics of specific times and places and our "natural" environment by countless centuries of human intervention. So much of our nutrition, for example, vegetable or animal, has been shaped and reshaped almost beyond recognition by human activity. Although only a plant biologist would be likely to think of it, the ear of corn I eat for dinner tonight has been bred to its present size and taste by humans over seven thousand years of cultivation, transforming a wild plant only a couple of inches long to its present size. Similarly, the little puppy who sits at my feet is the result of deliberate engineering. Here, however, the question becomes more complicated in ways that have a closer parallel to the genres as we conceive them. It is easy to see how much human action has shaped our dogs, but scientists tell us that the dogs themselves also played a considerable part in domesticating their "masters". Like dog breeds, the progress of the genres has been marked by proliferation leading to new identities. As each genre grew increasingly refined, the contours of the others sharpened in response. Just as cross-breeding has altered the communicative capacities of dogs and new breeds have been developed to serve new purposes—hunting, herding, therapy—so, too, have modern genres grown in variety and range to address changing social conditions. But although the graphic novel and environmental art may have emerged as new genres it does not follow that earlier forms have disappeared. We might say that a new genre is like a determined outsider looking for a way to make itself indispensable.

In short, during the eighteenth and nineteenth centuries, history painting's grandeur continued to place it well above the genres, not amongst them, and for almost four centuries the highest form of painting—the most long lasting and in many respects the most capacious—was not seen as a genre at all. As noted, however, the concept of genre elaborated itself, its "kinds" growing both in number and prestige. Although the term "history painting" never fully disappeared an ambiguity regarding its status developed with which we continue to contend. The rise of landscape painting in the eighteenth century, with its sublime and picturesque modes, provided the first real challenge, with the result that in nineteenth-century history, painting came often to be called "historical painting". While it continued to stand above any connection with the genres and to be distinguished from them by its genesis within a great tradition that was older and more distinguished than any other, it came increasingly to serve the representational needs of nations and communities, rather than to convey the eternal stories. At the same time, as we will see, minor "kinds" such as landscape and "genre" painting—scenes of ordinary folk in their homes and villages—began to be recruited to the service of historical representation, marking key events and movements in the history of the nation, and giving this august tradition a new demotic colouration.

From the modern perspective, these developments have blurred the status of history painting in two different ways. The term "historical painting"—initially intended to continue the old idea of history painting in the service of the historicism of the period—would eventually diminish the grand genre's pretentions to superiority. This shift occurred under pressure from the other genres and was never fully articulated. Thus, the historicist culture of the nineteenth century maintained history painting's height but could also appear to produce a kind of loss through the narrowing of its scope, diminishing its once uncontested power. The great mural paintings commissioned of prominent Victorian painters like William Dyce and Daniel Maclise for the redecoration of the Palace of Westminster in the 1840s, for example, continued the great tradition but now had to compete with the more lively and popular works of historical subjects by the Pre-Raphaelites and their circle.[12] As we will see, this new hybridisation of the great tradition would inject the painting of historical subjects with a new relevance and power.

The second cause of history painting's ambiguous status remains more contentious. The orthodox account of modernism, with its secular ideology and non-representational credo, could blind us to the survival of history painting and lead to a general acceptance of the idea that it had lost all relevance by the latter part of the twentieth century. While it is clear that representations of Biblical scenes and saints' lives, once at the core of the history painting tradition, have become separate genres of their own, history painting continues in new forms and retains its claim to comprehensive narrative. It is a paradox, perhaps, that in this process history painting has lost the unique prestige it once held. On the other hand, it has not abandoned its essential function as the genre most fundamentally concerned with the production of historical consciousness for a vital public domain.

Distance and re-distancing in history painting

To examine the history of history painting more closely, I want to turn to another dimension of representation that is closely linked to the evolution of the genres—the construction of distance. My purpose is to show not only that the management of distance was key to the pretensions of classic history painting but also that the need for *re*-distancing became essential to further changes in the development of this genre in subsequent periods. In common usage, *distance* refers to things that are remote or removed, but this only gives us one dimension of this important concept. As I have argued elsewhere, distance is far from the linear measure to which it is commonly reduced, nor is it confined to space and time.[13] On the contrary, it suggests a much wider range of directions. In short, whatever our point of reference, distance, like genre, is a *relational* term, open to a broad variety of affects and experiences.

With respect to history painting in particular, I offer three closely connected observations.[14] First, it is important to recognise that history painting in its classical form was an expression of an early modern society, with all the investment in hierarchical order that this implies. Whether we think of royal splendour or ecclesiastical pomp, of courts of law or the dictates of the academy, every element was tuned to an exquisite understanding of the principle of rank. Second, as the most dignified of all the visual arts, history painting held a position of unique privilege. Its elevation could be compared to the dignity of the court or the church—a quality of innate pre-eminence that was as natural to history painting as nobility was to the crown. Third, though history painting continued to claim this position well into the nineteenth century, the system of the arts was by no means static in a world governed by massive changes in economy and social class. In the nineteenth century, as already noted, the genres continued to multiply, absorbing "history" into their number. Nonetheless, the notion of distance does not lose its usefulness in the face of these changes. On the contrary, it becomes all the more necessary as an instrument for examining new complexities in the evolution of the arts. Hence the need to understand *re-distancing* as a way to track changing patterns of representation.

We need a way to parse acts of distancing in order to achieve this understanding. Every representation of history, I argue, whether textual or visual, incorporates elements of *making, feeling, acting* and *understanding*. *Making* relates to questions of formal structure and vocabulary, *feeling*, to affective impact, *acting*, to moral or political interpellation and *understanding*, to broad intelligibility. To put this in other terms, a more ramified analysis of historical representation needs to consider problems of historical mediation as they relate to these four fundamental components. First, we must examine the forms, media and conventions that give histories their structures of representation, including their aesthetic design and rhetorical address. Second, we should give attention to the work's affective character, whether (for instance) historical conditions are made accessible to us through cool appraisal or lively emotions. Third, we need to scrutinise the history's implications for action, whether the summons it issues is primarily political, religious or ethical in nature. Fourth comes the work's fundamental assumptions regarding understanding or intelligibility. These ideas guide historical practice and provide the conceptual grounds on which it depends. Combining in various ways to shape our experience of history and the social, these four overlapping but distinguishable distances—form, affect, summoning and intelligibility—provide an orientation to some of the central problems of historical representation.

History painting in Britain: A case study

The particular features of Britain's history also shaped its art. In a number of other fields—especially law, philosophy and theatre—seventeenth-century Britain had already established its own distinctive traditions. In the visual arts, however, as also in music, Britain drew heavily on the talents of foreigners. Thus it was not until the eighteenth century that Britain began to develop an ambitious visual tradition—one deeply dependent on influences from Italy, France and the Netherlands, but increasingly able to make a mark of its own. Questions of religion were especially critical. In Catholic Europe works of art were considered a natural ornament to the Church. Not so in Protestant England, where mixing art and worship in churches raised fears of Catholic practice and more sombre forms of worship were required.

Famously, in the early eighteenth century, when a group of artists offered their services gratis to the Bishop of London, the gift was refused. As the critic Francis Palgrave wrote in the mid-nineteenth century,

> In one notable way English art differs from that of all other European schools. They have their root more or less in medieval times; ours in modern. They are influenced in style or subject by native earlier masters; we, by foreigners only. Our eighteenth-century painters had to create the belief that England was able to produce Art: Italy, France, Germany, and the Netherlands could point to former triumphs with pride, or study them with emulation. The key to the first period of the British school is given by this peculiar position of circumstances.[15]

While history painting's prestige remained high through the Victorian era, it began to lose its currency in the latter part of the nineteenth century. In light of modernism's privileging of formal explorations and abstraction, artists who persisted in deploying figuration and narrative reference have tended to be disregarded or seen as localised and provincial. Another consequence has been a tendency to subsume the participation in the history painting tradition of major eighteenth- and nineteenth-century artists—Hogarth, Reynolds, West, Wilkie, Turner and others—within this formalist narrative rather than identifying their distinctive contributions to the great genre.[16] Space does not permit a full account of this long development. Instead, I will focus on several key moments in the evolution of British history painting, showing how artists negotiated genre and distance to reshape longstanding traditions.

William Hogarth is considered Britain's first great painter. His reputation rests on his conversation pieces which he used as sites for social commentary and satire. His best-known series, *A Rakes Progress* (1732–1734), represented contemporary people and drew on a popular theatrical production of his day. Yet he was anxious to establish himself as a painter capable of the highest forms and looked for opportunities to paint histories on the grand scale appropriate to the genre. Most notably, he donated works to major charitable projects underway in London during the first half of the eighteenth century. But the two biblical subjects he painted for St. Bartholomew's hospital, *Christ at the Pool of Bethesda* (1735–6) and *The Good Samaritan* (1737), failed to achieve the classical harmony and decorum expected of the genre. When, toward the end of his life, Hogarth painted his *Sigismunda Mourning Over the Heart of Guiscardo* (1759), based on a tragic heroine from Boccaccio's *Decameron,* we find a painting that answered to his highest aspirations as an artist. Yet he was bitterly disappointed when it failed to find a buyer who would pay the price given to foreign history painters. It is only recently that this and other paintings have attracted the attention of scholars long focused on his prints and satirical works.[17]

However, I would argue that we can see how Hogarth's genre paintings begin to converge with history painting in another work he presented to the Foundling Hospital. *The March of the Guards to Finchley* (1750) (Figure 4.1) is

Figure 4.1 William Hogarth, *The March of the Guards to Finchley*, 1750, oil on canvas, The Foundling Museum, London.

a lively scene that resembles his popular and successful satirical prints and paintings. Women, children and bystanders crowd around the soldiers marching toward the Scottish armies of Bonnie Prince Charlie in 1745. As a rendering of an important historical event glimpsed through its impact on ordinary people it might well be considered a history painting today, although its mid-eighteenth-century audiences would not have seen it as such. As we will see, this work seems to foretell important convergences of painting genres that would respond to a democratisation of historical narratives themselves but that were still more than half a century in the future.

The attempts of Hogarth and successive generations of British artists from the mid-eighteenth through the mid-nineteenth century to rise to the heights history painting demanded are thus revealing of critically important shifts in historical representation that were gaining momentum. Examining their works, we are able to observe their mediations of the temporal and social distances traditionally required by the genre in order to represent the changes in sentiment and historical consciousness—re-distancings—characteristic of a nation that was emerging as the most advanced democratised and industrialised society in Europe. The particular interest of history painting in Britain is that it reflects the complexities of its European counterparts and adds some distinctive features of its own.

If Hogarth's response to the rigours of history painting was occasional, though deeply felt, Joshua Reynolds' approach was neatly bifurcated. As a practitioner, he was a highly successful artist who preferred to give his talents to portraiture rather than the high road of history painting. At the same time, Reynold's importance lies in his influential *Discourses on Art*, a work written as a handbook for young students that became widely accepted as the defining text of the genre.[18] He built his idea of history painting on the strict Aristotelian distinction between the particular truths of (ordinary) history and the general truths of high art. For this reason, he preferred to speak about the "Great Style", while freely acknowledging the painter's liberty to "deviate from vulgar and strict historical truth, in pursuing the grandeur of his design". Fact and events, he insisted, "however they may bind the Historian, have no dominion over the Poet or the Painter".[19] In other words, the artist is not restricted by a merely imitative idea of truth; instead, he bent history "to his great idea of Art". And yet even Reynolds had to cede to common usage. "In conformity to custom", he wrote, "I call this part of the art History Painting; it ought to be called Poetical, as indeed it really is".[20]

As the second president of the Royal Academy, Benjamin West followed in Reynolds's footsteps, but his idea of history painting in his ground-breaking *The Death of General Wolfe* (1770) incorporated a tie to history that was alien to Reynolds's outlook[21] (Figure 4.2). As the familiar story is told in Galt's

Figure 4.2 Benjamin West, *The Death of General Wolfe*, 1776, oil on canvas, 188.5 × 268.5, Royal Ontario Museum. Photo: Courtesy Royal Ontario Museum.

biography of West, the artist responded to a visit from a sceptical Joshua Reynolds with a ringing defence of the historical grounds for his artistic choice:

> General Wolfe's victory in Quebec took place on the 13th of September, 1758, in a region of the world unknown to the Greeks and Romans, and at a period of time when no such nations, nor heroes in their costume, any longer existed. The subject I have to represent is the conquest of a great province of America by the British troops. It is a topic that history will proudly record, and the same truth that guides the pen of the historian should govern the pencil of the artist.[22]

Accordingly, West represented Wolfe and his comrades in contemporary clothing along with an Indigenous scout who observes the scene. He, too, is dressed in garments and accessories accurate to the place and period, examples of which West had in his studio to use as models.[23] West's invention would open up possibilities for history painters of the next century to represent with a new verisimilitude and immediacy the impacts of actual historical events on ordinary lives (Figure 4.3).

Figure 4.3 Benjamin Robert Haydon, *Napoleon Musing after Sunset*, before 1846, based on a work of 1830, oil on canvas 76.2 × 63.1, National Portrait Gallery, London. Photo: Wikipedia Commons.

Three very different styles of history painting emerged in the second quarter of the nineteenth century: the neoclassicism of Benjamin Haydon, the historical sublime of J.M.W. Turner and the populist historicism of David Wilkie. We can see in their work a convergence of genres that had been kept distinct and separate up until these years. Haydon combines fidelity to Reynolds formulation of the grand genre with the romanticism of his period and the psychological impulse of portraiture. In his 1820 *Napoleon Musing After Sunset*, for example, we witness the solitary brooding figure of the defeated Napoleon looking out at the last rays of the setting sun—a far cry from the many figures proposed by Aglionby or the battle scene of West. A decade later, in 1840, Turner famously developed much further the almost impressionistic approach to light and colour seen in Haydon's sky in a painting which could easily, without its title, fall into the generic category of the paintings of seascapes and ships known as "marines". In *Slavers throwing overboard the Dead and Dying—Typhoon coming on* (1840, later known as *The Slave Ship*), Turner represents the notorious incident involving the slave ship Zong, almost without any figures at all. We understand the horror of the scene primarily through its atmospheric effects. As in other works, such as *Regulus*, his 1828 painting of the torture and death of the Roman hero Regulus at Carthage (reworked 1837), it is the intense white light of the skies at the centre of Turner's composition that gives the scene the power and drama of a history painting, rather than the actions performed by the miniaturised figures in the lower righthand corner (Figure 4.4).

Figure 4.4 Joseph Malord William Turner, *Regulus*, 1828, reworked 1837, oil on canvas, 89.5 × 123.8, Tate Britain. Photo: courtesy Tate Images.

In contrast, in *The Chelsea Pensioners Receiving the London Gazette Extraordinary on Thursday, June 22, 1815, Announcing the Battle of Waterloo* (1822, retitled *The Chelsea Pensioners reading the Waterloo Dispatch*), David Wilkie celebrated Britain's conquest of Napoleon in a spirit more often attached to genre painting than to history, fully realising the convergence of genres Hogarth had explored seventy-five years earlier. In this demotic image, the artist represents a group of old soldiers joyfully receiving the report of the Waterloo Dispatch, placing the celebration of victory among figures and setting that are far from heroic. It is, however, no less a "history" for its reduction to the level of ordinary people. Commissioned by the Duke of Wellington and displayed in the Royal Academy it drew huge crowds and has been described as "the first blockbuster picture of the [Royal Academy] summer exhibitions".[24] Nor indeed was the picture any less imposing than the ruined masterpiece *The Preaching of John Knox before the Lords of the Congregation 10th June 1559* (1832) that came after, although in this case the subject was more obviously a history painting (Figure 4.5).

Despite their differences, all three artists manipulate and merge received conventions of genre and distance in order to create new kinds of historical understanding. The brooding Napoleon of Haydon, the atmospheric intensity of Turner and the reflection of a great victory in the faces of Wilkie's ordinary soldiers hybridise history painting with the portrait, the marine and the genre painting. Similarly, this democratised mode of

Figure 4.5 David Wilkie, *The Chelsea Pensioners Reading the Waterloo Dispatch*, 1818–1822, oil on canvas, 97 × 158, Apsley House, London. Photo: Wikipedia Commons.

representing history was emerging on the Continent during the first half of the nineteenth century, as seen in the success of Delacroix's *Liberty Leading the People* (1830) with its array of ordinary folk and its buxom and plainly dressed central allegorical figure. Like Hogarth and Wilkie, Delacroix brings the viewer closer to past events by constructing new modes of affect and interpellation.

The Last of England: Ford Maddox Brown and John Everett Millais

A generation later and in the wake of the realism of the Pre-Raphaelites, Ford Maddox Brown and John Everett Millais took the staging of historical subjects in a popular milieu still further. Millais's *Christ in the House of his Parents* offers up a simple domestic setting in which the young carpenter's son looks to his mother to comfort a small wound. Unusually tender though the scene may be, we have no difficulty in recognising the meaning of this child's distress and its foreshadowing of his crucifixion. Nonetheless, much of the appeal of the work resides in its deft combination of timeless symbolism and the simple innocence of the mother and child. Maddox Brown's well-known image *The Last of England* (1855) makes intimate the woes of a young family forced by poverty to seek a new life in Australia. The unpleasantness of the boat, the dejection of the father, the anxious concerns of the mother tell their story, but so does the presence of the child, barely visible under the mother's protective cloak. The tondo form of the picture gives the image of their difficult journey the aura of a Renaissance Madonna and child. No wonder

Figure 4.6 John Everett Millais, *Christ in the House of his Parents*, 1849–50, oil on canvas, 86.4 × 139.7, Tate Britain. Photo: Courtesy Tate Images.

that Brown was prepared to say of this work that it was "a history painting in the truest sense of the word". Brown's somewhat truculent statement seems to make a division between history painting that is undeniably *true* and history painting that merely follows conventional forms. If this is indeed what he had in mind, we can take it as a rebuke to those artists who did not see the need to adapt the genre to new social and political realities. The history he narrates in *The Last of England* does not focus on heroes or specific religious, political or military events but, rather, on an epochal demographic and social movement forced by poverty and deprivation. At the same time, the underlying spiritual and allegorical meanings remain central (Figure 4.7).

In his later work, Millais moved away from the complex symbolic layering of his earlier compositions. His famous painting *The Boyhood of Raleigh* (1870), for example, is anecdotal and direct in its depiction of two young boys' different reactions to the tale of an old sailor. In contrast, in Maddox Brown's *Cromwell on his Farm* (1873–4), the artist maintains the iconographic complexity and religious intensity of his earlier work. In democratising traditional history painting, all four paintings re-distance their subjects through intimate acts of individualisation. They bring the lens in close to

Figure 4.7 Ford Madox Brown, *The Last of England*, 1855, oil on canvas, 82.5 × 75, Birmingham Museum and Art Gallery. Photo: Wikipedia Commons.

alter the aspects of affect and summoning so that average viewers can relate to them in terms of interiority, psyche and experience.

History painting in modernism

With the advent of modernism, it became accepted that even such iterations of history painting no longer had a role to play—an understandable response to the dominance of avant-gardist culture. Nonetheless, we cannot ignore a nagging sense that something important has been lost from painting's scope. The notable resurgence of history painting in the contemporary art of the late twentieth and early twenty-first centuries makes us aware of a diverse but compelling body of works made alongside those of modernist and avant garde artists that have not been recognised as continuations of the history painting tradition and/or excluded from the main narratives of art and history—official war arts, feminist interventions, histories of anti-colonial resistance and survival. For this reason, I conclude by responding to one of the questions posed to contributors to this book, which I take the liberty of paraphrasing in light of my focus on history painting. "In what ways do these art works affect our idea of history today?" Many of the examples I will discuss do not, at first, appear to belong either to the classic genre of history painting or to the Romantic and realist nineteenth-century examples that, as I argue, constitute a democratised continuation of this tradition. I will argue, however, that all are lineal descendants of the great tradition because they insist on the role of the visual arts in confronting—figuratively and narratively—the essential questions raised by historical experience, now as in previous eras.

The paintings of Stanley Spencer are a good place to observe both continuity and invention. Spencer had encountered cubism as an art student before World War I, but in the paintings he made after his war service, he drew as much on Victorian realism and the deeper history painting tradition as on modernism. His paintings for the Sandham Memorial Chapel reflect the horrors of war through the mundane activities of the field hospitals in which he served—bed making, tea service, scrubbing the floor.[25] The influence of Ruben's great history painting of the *Descent from the Cross* (1612–14) informs and ennobles the compositional structure and dynamic downward movement in Spencer's far more mundane scene of *Filling Water Bottles* that Spencer painted under one of the arches. In contrast, in *We are Making a New World* (1918) Paul Nash, an official war artist, empties his canvas of figures to show us the blasted terrain of trench warfare. Here, a landscape is transformed into a history through the corrosive irony of its title, just as a title had turned Turner's marine image into a horrific revelation of the evils of the slave trade. A century later, in *The Trial of Milosevic* (2005), Dexter Dalwood would adopt a parallel strategy by representing the genocide of the Bosnian War as a stony field with an open pit in the foreground (Figure 4.8).

In the same register, during World War II, Henry Moore recorded the impact of the Blitz on ordinary civilians taking refuge in the London tube.[26] Despite the

Figure 4.8 Stanley Spencer, *Filling Water Bottles*, 1927–32, oil on canvas, 213.4 × 185.4, Sandham Memorial Chapel, England. Photo, Bridgeman Images.

modest format of the drawing, the figures have a monumentality that contemporary critics recognised as attaining the height of history painting—and even the poetic level Reynolds had defined more than a century earlier, although with very different central figures in mind. When exhibited soon after it was made, Moore's drawing, *Tube Shelter Perspective 1941*, was described as "a terrifying vista of recumbent shapes, pale as all underground life tends to be pale; regimented, as only fear can regiment; helpless yet tense, safe yet listening, uncouth, uprooted, waiting in the tunnel for the dawn to release them. This is not the descriptive journalism of art. It is imaginative poetry of a high order".[27]

Thus far I have remained within the sphere of British art, but, just as the twentieth century was one of global war and transformation, so was the artworld increasingly transnational. In this context, German artists, too, used painting to work through the terrible weight of history. In the 1930s, as he and other modernist artists experienced the rise of Nazism, Max Beckmann used the religious format of the triptych, the vocabulary of classical allusion and the representation of human violence traditional to history painting to create *Departure* (1932).[28] In the side panels we see a surreal array of contemporary figures, tortured, bound and—bizarrely—playing a drum. They convey terror, threat and unease while the mythic personages and Madonna-like woman and child in the central panel seem to hold out a glimmer of hope.

In the aftermath of the war and in the knowledge of genocide and total destruction, Anselm Kiefer adopted a strategy for representing the Holocaust as a scarred landscape in his monumental painting *Iron Path* (1986).[29] Where Beckmann presents us with powerful but enigmatic figures, the burden of Kiefer's history is carried only by the image of train tracks whose meaning is all too clear. Like Nash in his image of the devastated battlefields of World War I, Kiefer empties the land of human presence and transforms a landscape into a history painting only through a resonant title—an act of interpellation that summons the viewer to remember difficult knowledge. Equally, Gerhard Richter's painting of *Onkel Rudi* (1965) posing in his Nazi uniform could at first be understood as a photographic portrait, but the painter's blurring of the human form conveys the ambivalence of an ordinary man's roles as both oppressor and victim. In *September* (2010), Richter used a similar technique to convey the fall of the twin towers. It is a history painting that purposely adopts the small scale of the television screens on which people around the world saw this scene endlessly replayed to suggest the impossibility of representing the full magnitude of such an event. As one critic commented, because the image is "blurred and almost unseeable, you get a sense of its enormity".[30] Hybridising the genre scene, the portrait and the landscape with the history painting's thematic seriousness and duty of collective memorialization, all three German artists continue the work of their nineteenth-century predecessors. Each, however, adopts his own strategy to refuse the trope of the heroic human figure—for Beckmann an expressionist anti-aesthetic, for Keifer, the emptying of land and for Richter the blurring of the image (Figure 4.9).

Twentieth-century artists have also taken up history painting as a vehicle for representing the historical experiences of women and of colonised and disempowered subjects previously excluded from and silenced by official histories. The migration of a million African-Americans from rural poverty and racial violence in the southern United States to seek better lives in the industrialised cities of the north during the decades after World War I is one such history. In 1940, the young Jacob Lawrence set out to record this momentous movement in sixty small painted panels, each numbered and accompanied by a narrative statement. The tight relationship of text and image in *Migration Series* (1940–41) accords on the one hand with history painting's central mission and, on the other, with Lawrence's invocation of African-American story-telling traditions.[31] The need to tell stories unknown to the dominant society would lead other artists from colonised societies to use similar strategies in later years. The combination of written narrative and pictorial expression in Anishinaabe artist Bonnie Devine's *Book of Radiance* (1999) recalls Lawrence's work but also introduces the intertwined themes of Indigenous dislocation and confinement and environmental degradation that have become central to global contemporary art. As Mark Cheetham writes, "Disarmingly simple and direct, her drawings and running text relate the

Figure 4.9 Gerhard Richter, *Onkel Rudi*, 1965, oil on canvas, 87 cm × 50 cm. Lidice
Collection, Lidice, Czech Republic. Photo: Atelier Gerhard Richter.

story of her uncle's youthful discovery of the river environment on a vision
quest in 1946, its transformation into a site for uranium mining ... and the
impact of splitting the uranium atom, which unremittingly contaminates the
land, river, all inhabitants".[32]

For a long time, such works were not integrated into the history of
American and Canadian art, and it is only recently that they have been widely
accepted as historical representation on an epic scale. Thus in 2019, when
New York's Museum of Modern Art opened a major expansion and
reinstallation of its galleries of twentieth-century art, visitors found Faith
Ringgold's *American People Series #20: Die* (1967) juxtaposed with Picasso's
1907 *Demoiselles d'Avignon*, arguably the museum's most famous painting
and the point of origin of European modernism.[33] Ringgold's painting plays
with time and history in its evocation of the race riots that occurred across the
United States during the 1960s. The artist has said that "I was ... terrified
because I saw *Die* as a prophecy of our times",[34] and it stands today as a
fearful augury of continuing conflict. The juxtaposition of the canonical work
of modernist primitivism with a scene representing ongoing racial violence
endows the history painting genre with contemporary relevance (Figure 4.10).

Figure 4.10 Faith Ringgold, *Coming to Jones Road #4, Under a Blood Red Sky*, 2000, Colby College Museum of Art, acrylic on canvas with pieced fabric border, 199 × 133 cm. ©Faith Ringgold, Photo: Visual Arts-CARCC, 2023.

To me, however, a smaller work, *Coming to Jones Road #4: Under a Blood Red Sky* (2000), incorporating the homely medium of quilting, is more subtle and in some ways more compelling. Ringgold made the work after moving out of New York City to a town in New Jersey where she found herself shunned by her white neighbours. Looking out of her studio window at the woods bordering her property, she became aware that she was seeing the path trodden a hundred years earlier by slaves escaping the South via the Underground Railroad. Here again, a landscape emerges as a history, a ground that links the past to the present and can still be made to yield up its ghosts.

When commissioned to create a work for the circular top floor of the Smithsonian's Hirshhorn Museum in Washington, D.C., contemporary African-American artist Mark Bradford created another work that brings together past and present. *Pickett's Charge* (2017) is a series of eight large curving canvasses that mirror the circular panorama, or cyclorama, created in 1884 by French artist Paul Phillippoteaux to represent the Battle of Gettysburg, the turning point of the American Civil War.[35] Bradford layers a digital reproduction of the cyclorama over rows of rough cordage and covers both with layers of coloured paper; he rips and tears through the layers to disrupt the heroic imagery of the nineteenth-century representation and to suggest our fragmentary and situated vision and the unknowableness of the past.

Where Bradford defaces the history paintings of the past and points to the need for multiple perspectives, Cree artist Kent Monkman embraces and appropriates Joshua Reynolds's "Great Style" and hands it over to a new cast of characters. At the same time that he voices his admiration for the history painting tradition, he challenges it to elevate the experiences of his Canadian Indigenous community. In December 2019 New York's Metropolitan Museum of Art unveiled two mural-sized paintings it commissioned Monkman to create for its great entry hall. *Mistikosiwak—Wooden Boat People* responds both to the Met's holdings of canonical history paintings and to the nineteenth-century representations it exhibits of Native Americans as a dying race. One of the two, *Resurgence of the People*, is a repainting of Emanuel Leutze's iconic *Washington Crossing the Delaware* (1851). In Monkman's version, his gender fluid alter ego, Miss Chief Eagle Testikle, stands in the place of George Washington, leading a crowded boat of contemporary Indigenous people bearing the ancient wisdom they have to offer a world at risk.[36] The College Art Association pointed to the decolonial work Monkman accomplishes through his corpus of repaintings in the citation that accompanied its 2022 Artist Award for a Distinguished Body of Work: "Although appropriating the form of Western history painting, Monkman's artwork breaks from tradition by subverting and de-centering the Western gaze and re-presenting a perspective of history from the vantage point of Indigenous peoples … . Through his use of history painting, Monkman's project is one that reminds us of the potency of images, and the potential of the artist to provoke and challenge history and its representations"[37] (Figure 4.11).

Figure 4.11 Kent Monkman, *Mistikôsiwak Wooden Boat People: Resurgence of the People*, acrylic on canvas, 335.3 × 670.6 cm, Metropolitan Museum of Art 2020.216a, Donald R. Sobey Foundation CAF Canada Project Gift, 2020 © Kent Monkman.

Judy Chicago's *The Dinner Party*, created between 1974 and 1979, is both a pioneering and a summary work of second-wave feminism.[38] Chicago's creation is not a painting per se but rather a monumental installation that takes the form of a large triangular table with seating for thirty-nine female luminaries, ranging in time from ancient goddesses to Georgia O'Keeffe. Nonetheless, the likeness to history painting is unmistakable. It realises William Aglionby's definition of history painting in its grandeur and marshalling of many figures. Witness, too, how strongly *The Dinner Party* deploys the four dimensions of distance I identified earlier in this discussion: the formal through its imposing arrangement; affect, in the elevated feelings it evokes; interpellation, in its urgent summoning to a cause; and cognition, in its evident didactic mission. Chicago's mixture of the mythic with the modern and the fabulous with the fabled is of course deliberate. Not only does she unite the entire gender in one undivided moment, she also stamps an elevation appropriate to heroes upon all her exemplars (Figure 4.12).

I want to end with another monumental and complex work that is also realised in non-traditional media. William Kentridge's *Triumphs and Laments* (2016) contemplated history on the grandest and most comprehensive of scales and yet was designed to fade into obscurity in a matter of years. The South African artist created his frieze, fifty-five metres long and ten metres high, by overlaying stencils on the grimy patina that has built up on the high travertine stone walls that line the high banks of the Tiber River in Rome. Using high-pressure water hoses to remove the negative spaces

Figure 4.12 William Kentridge, *Triumphs and Laments* (detail), 2016, Lungotevere, Rome Courtesy of Kentridge Studio, Photo: Sebastiano Luciano.

between the figures, he composed a procession of eighty images drawn from ancient and modern Roman history, folklore and recent cinema, the sacred and the profane—Romulus and Remus, Cicero and Saint Teresa, the equestrian statue of Marcus Aurelius and the finding of Aldo Moro's body, Marcello Mastroianni and Anita Ekberg and an animated Moka espresso pot.[39] It was done, Kentridge has written, "in the knowledge that over a few years the images would fade away. The wall would darken again, through natural ageing, pollutants, graffiti; leaving a ghost of an image and a fading memory".[40]

Throughout his career, Kentridge has regularly returned to the idea of the procession to represent humanity's movements through time and space. In his 2015 video and musical work, *More Sweetly Play the Dance* (2015), for example, he drew on the medieval Dance of Death and the performances of urban African church groups to point to the violent disruptions of Apartheid, the South African mining economy and ebola. His Roman procession not only encompassed the classical, the popular and the political but also echoed and recalled the procession celebrating the Roman conquest of Jerusalem depicted on the triumphal Arch of Titus (c. 81 A.D.), one of the city's most famous monuments and an icon of the inevitable demise of all empires. As a site-specific work, adjacent to the old Jewish ghetto and on a line that also links it to St. Peter's cathedral (created, as Kentridge notes, in the same years as the ghetto), *Triumphs and Laments* invokes the Lungotevere as a lieu de memoire in which a history painting offers a path through both time and space.

I end with this recent work of historical representation because it combines so many of the innovations of other modern and contemporary artists we have looked at. As in Jacob Lawrence's *Migration Series*, Kentridge's figures move through time and space in a momentous procession. Like Judy Chicago, he used unexpected media to assemble personages from both myth and history, and like Mark Bradford, his narrative is disrupted, fragmentary and incomplete. Kentridge, like Monkman, appropriates the formal distance of canonical history painting, honouring the academic tradition through the refinement and power of his drawing while undercutting it with references to imperialism's destructive legacies. Finally, designed to fade and disappear, *Triumphs and Laments* brings to mind Richter's blurred images, Bradford's ripped, torn and partially obscured panorama of the Battle of Gettysburg, the inevitable fall of empires and the fugitive nature of historical memory.

In re-distancing the viewer, these contemporary artists dismantle and reconstruct Reynold's Great Style in different ways. They invent strategies that obscure and rupture the continuity of historical narrative—inverting early modern history painting's underlying Eurocentric premises and affirming the multiperspectival sensibility of contemporary historical writing. At the same time, twenty-first-century iterations of history painting evidence the resilience of—and continuing need for—a genre of representation that confronts us with historical narrative and memory through the distinctive union of textual and visual imagery. In this way, and in the spirit of their nineteenth-century predecessors, contemporary artists demonstrate the malleability of a genre firmly rooted in the early modern period, linking our pasts with our futures.

Notes

1 I am grateful to the Social Sciences and Humanities Research Council of Canada for its research support, to the Clark Art Institute for a fellowship and sponsorship of a colloquium on history painting and to Ruth B. Phillips for her help in preparing this chapter.
2 I am grateful to the Social Sciences and Humanities Research Council of Canada for its research support, to the Clark Art Institute for a fellowship and sponsorship of a colloquium on history painting and to Ruth B. Phillips for her help in preparing this chapter.
3 Roland Mortier, a distinguished Belgian art historian, made a point of saying that there had not been a book on this important subject since before the First World War. *Diderot et le grand gout: the presige of history painting in the 18th century* (Oxford: Oxford University Press, 1982).
4 The remark was made by Michael Ann Holly at the colloquium on history painting, Clark Art Institute, October 2015.
5 Guernica has recently been re-examined in *Pity and Terror: Picasso's Path to Guernica*. An exhibition organised by the Museo Nacional Centro de Arte Reina Sofía in Madrid.
6 See for example, Elizabeth Harney, "Reimagining Global Modernity in the Age of Neo-Liberal Patronage: The History Paintings of Julie Mehretu" and Dexter Dalwood, "What Is the History in Contemporary History Painting?" in Mark Salber Phillips and Jordan Bear eds, *What Was History Painting and What Is It Now?* (Montreal: McGill Queen's University Press, 2019).
7 W.J.T. Mitchell, *Iconology: Image, Text Ideology* (Chicago: University of Chicago Press, 1987).
8 William Aglionby, *Painting Illustrated in Three Dialogues* (London: John Gain, 1685), unpaginated.
9 Mark Phillips, *Francesco Guicciardini: The Historian's Craft* (Toronto: University of Toronto Press, 1977); Mark Salber Phillips, *Society and Sentiment: Genres of Historical Writing in Britain, 1740–1820* (Princeton: Princeton University Press, 2000); Mark Salber Phillips, *On Historical Distance* (New Haven: Yale University Press, 2015).
10 See, for example, Anthony Blunt, *Nicholas Poussin* (London: Phaidon, 1967).
11 BBC broadcast January 1972), Episode 5 "They are not a couple in Nature as Rousseau imagined nature. They are landowners and their proprietary attitude towards what surrounds them is visible in their stance and their expressions". https://www.ways-of-seeing.com/ch5 Accessed 3 January 2021. See also John Berger, *Ways of Seeing* (London: Penguin, 1972).
12 See Emma L. Winter, "German Fresco Painting and the New Houses of Parliament at Westminster, 1834–1851", *The Historical Journal* 47 (2), June 2004: 291–329; and Mitchell Frank and Mark Salber Phillips, "Historical Distance and the Nineteenth-Century Revival of Fresco", in Nicholas Chare and Mitchell B. Frank, *History and Art History: Looking Past Disciplines* (New York: Routledge, 2020).
13 Phillips, *On Historical Distance*.
14 The following paragraphs are extracted from my introductory essay in Mark Salber Phillips and Jordan Bear eds., *What Was History Painting and What Is It Now?* (Montreal: McGill Queen's University Press, 2019).

15 Francis Turner Palgrave, "The British School of Oil Painting", in *International Exhibition, 1'862, Official Catalogue of the Fine Arts Department* (London: Truscott, Son and Simons, 1862), 3.
16 A recent exception to this neglect was Tate Britain's 2015 exhibition *Fighting History* and its small publication, M.G. Sullivan ed., *Fighting History* (London: Tate Britain, 2015).
17 See Mark Salber Phillips, "Hogarth and History Painting", in Cynthia E. Roman, *Hogarth's Legacy* (New Haven: Yale University Press, 2016).
18 Reynolds Discourses on Art were delivered to the Royal Academy of Art between 1769 and 1790 and first published collectively in 1797.
19 R. Wark ed., *Discourses on Art* (New Haven, CT.: Yale University Press, 1997), 59–60.
20 Ibid.
21 The primary copy of the painting is in the National Gallery of Canada, and other copies painted by West are in the Royal Ontario Museum, the William L. Clements Library at the University of Michigan, Ickworth House, Suffolk and the British Royal Collection.
22 *The Life, Studies, and Works of Benjamin West Subsequent to His Arrival in This Country* (London, 1816; reprint 1820), 47–48. For Galt's relation to West, see Jules David Prown, *Art as Evidence: Writings on Art and Material Culture* (New Haven, Ct.: Yale University Press, 2001), 274 n.4; and Susan Rather, "Benjamin West, John Galt, and the Biography of 1816", *Art Bulletin* 86, no. 2 (June 2004): 342–45.
23 J.C.H. King, "Woodlands artifacts from the studio of Benjamin West, 1738–1820", American Indian Art Magazine 17, no. 1 (1991): 37–47.
24 Mark Hallett, co-curator of The Great Spectacle: 250 Years of Royal Academy Summer Exhibitions, 2018 https://www.royalacademy.org.uk/article/inside-the-show-the-great-spectacle accessed 9 January 2022.
25 The chapel, in Burghclere, Hampshire, was designed as a memorial by Mary and Louis Behrend (1881–1972) as a memorial, Lieutenant Henry Willoughby Sandham, Mrs. Behrend's brother, who died of disease contracted during his World War I service in Macedonia.
26 See for example, *Grey Tube Shelter* (1940) https://www.tate.org.uk/art/artworks/moore-grey-tube-shelter-n05706 and *Tube Shelter Perspective* (1941) https://www.tate.org.uk/art/artworks/moore-tube-shelter-perspective-n05709 accessed 30 April 2023.
27 Although Moore refused an invitation to be a full-time official war artist he accepted contracts to produce work for the War Artists Advisory Committee, headed by Kenneth Clark. Tate Britain website, https://www.tate.org.uk/art/artworks/moore-tube-shelter-perspective-n05709 accessed 11 January 2022.
28 See https://www.moma.org/collection/works/78367 accessed 30 April 2023.
29 See https://www.bridgemanimages.com/en/kiefer/iron-path-1986-oil-acrylic-olive-branches-lead-iron-gold-leaf-emulsion-on-canvas/nomedium/asset/1771686 accessed 30 April 2023.
30 Blake Gopnik, "Gerhard Richter's September Painting Evokes 9/11 Memories", *Newsweek*, September 5, 2011, https://www.newsweek.com/gerhard-richters-september-painting-evokes-911-memories-67367 accessed 11 January 2022. See also Robert Storr, *September: A History Painting by Gerhard Richter* (London: Tate Publishing, 2011).
31 For images see https://lawrencemigration.phillipscollection.org/ (accessed 30 April 2023) and see also Leah Dickerman ed., *Jacob Lawrence: The Migration Series* (New York: Museum of Modern Art, 2015).
32 Mark Cheetham, *Ecologies of Landscape* (Toronto: Barbara Edwards Contemporary, 2019), 10. (for pdf see https://www.academia.edu/37771109/Ecologies_of_Landscape_exhibition_ accessed 30 April 2023).

33 See Michelle Wallace, *American People, Black Light: Faith Ringgold's Paintings of the 1960s*. (New York: Neuberger Museum of Art, 2010); and Peter Schjeldahl, "The Exhuberance of MoMA's Expansion", *The New Yorker*, October 21, 2019 https://www.newyorker.com/magazine/2019/10/21/the-exuberance-of-momas-expansion Accessed 1 May 2022, and for image see https://www.moma.org/collection/works/199915 (accessed 30 April 2023)
34 https://www.moma.org/collection/works/199915, accessed 3 November 2021.
35 See Stéphane Aquin and Evelyn C. Hankins, *Mark Bradford: Pickett's Charge* (New Haven CN: Yale University Press, 2018); and for images https://hirshhorn.si.edu/exhibitions/mark-bradford-picketts-charge/, accessed 30 April 2023.
36 Ruth B. Phillips and I have discussed this work further in "Welcoming the Newcomers: Decolonizing History Painting, Revisioning History", in Kent Monkman ed., *Revision and Resistance: Mistikosiwak at the Metropolitan Museum of Art* (Toronto: Art Canada Institute, 2020), 68–77.
37 https://www.collegeart.org/news/2022/01/24/caa-2022-awards-for-distinction/ Accessed 1 May 2022.
38 See Chicago, Judy. *The Dinner Party: From Creation to Preservation*. London: Merrell (2007).
39 Kentridge designed the work to be animated by performances that have combined cinema, theatre, dance and music drawn from many traditions. At its inauguration, two processions marched toward each other, As Beatrice Zamponi observed: "In the procession a Mandinka song of African slaves, an age-old popular song from Southern Italy, and a Zulu warrior battle cry blended together to become one with the words of the poet Rilke: *That is the longing: to dwell amidst the waves / and have no homeland in time*". "William Kentridge: Triumphs and Laments", *Domus* 10 June, 2016 https://www.domusweb.it/en/art/2016/06/10/william_kentridge_triumphs_and_laments.html accessed 11 January 2022.
40 https://www.kentridge.studio/projects/triumphs-and-laments/ Accessed 1 May 2022.

Bibliography

Aglionby, William. *Painting Illustrated in Three Dialogues*. London: John Gain, 1685.
Aquin, Stéphane & Evelyn C. Hankins. *Mark Bradford: Pickett's Charge*. New Haven: Yale University Press, 2018.
Berger, John. *Ways of Seeing*. London: Penguin, 1972.
Blunt, Anthony. *Nicholas Poussin*. London: Phaidon, 1967.
Cheetham, Mark. *Ecologies of Landscape*. Toronto: Barbara Edwards Contemporary, 2019.
Chicago, Judy. *The Dinner Party: From Creation to Preservation*. London: Merrell, 2007.
Clark, Timothy J. & Anne M. Wagner. *Pity and Terror: Picasso's Path to Guernica*. Madrid: Museo Nacional Centro de Arte Reina Sofía, 2017.
Dalwood, Dexter. 'What Is the History in Contemporary History Painting?', in Mark Salber Phillips and Jordan Bear (eds.), *What Was History Painting and What Is It Now?* Montreal: McGill Queen's University Press, 2019.
Dickerman, Leah ed. *Jacob Lawrence: The Migration Series*. New York: Museum of Modern Art, 2015.
Frank, Mitchell & Mark Salber Phillips. "Historical Distance and the Nineteenth-Century Revival of Fresco," in Nicholas Chare and Mitchell B. Frank (eds.), *History and Art History: Looking Past Disciplines*. New York: Routledge, 2020.
Galt, John. *The Life, Studies, and Works of Benjamin West Subsequent to His Arrival in This Country*. London, 1816.

Gopnick, Blake. 'Gerhard Richter's September Painting Evokes 9/11 Memories.' *Newsweek*, September 5, 2011.

Harney, Elizabeth. 'Reimagining Global Modernity in the Age of Neo-Liberal Patronage: The History Paintings of Julie Mehret', in Mark Salber Phillips and Jordan Bear (eds.), *What Was History Painting and What Is It Now?* Montreal: McGill Queen's University Press, 2019.

King, J.C.H. 'Woodlands Artifacts from the Studio of Benjamin West, 1738–1820', *American Indian Art Magazine* 17 (1), (1991): 37–47.

Mitchell, W.J.T. *Iconology: Image, Text Ideology.* Chicago: University of Chicago Press, 1987

Mortier, Roland. *Diderot et le grand gout: The Prestige of History Painting in the 18th Century.* Oxford: Oxford University Press, 1982.

Palgrave, Francis Turner. 'The British School of Oil Painting', in *International Exhibition, 1862 Official Catalogue of the Fine Arts Department.* London: Truscott, Son and Simons, 1862.

Phillips, Mark Salber. *On Historical Distance.* New Haven: Yale University Press, 2013.

Phillips, Mark Salber. 'Hogarth and History Painting', in Cynthia E. Roman (ed.), *Hogarth's Legacy.* New Haven: Yale University Press, 2016.

Phillips, Mark Salber. 'Introduction: What Was History Painting and What Is It Now?', in Mark Salber Phillips and Jordan Bear (eds.), *What Was History Painting and What Is It Now?* Montreal: McGill Queen's University Press, 2019.

Phillips, Ruth B. & Phillips Mark Salber. 'Welcoming the Newcomers: Decolonizing History Painting, Revisioning History', in Kent Monkman (ed.), *Revision and Resistance: Mistikosiwak at the Metropolitan Museum of Art*, 68–77. Toronto: Art Canada Institute, 2020.

Prown, Julius David. *Art as Evidence: Writings on Art and Material Culture.* New Haven.: Yale University Press, 2001.

Rather, Susan. "Benjamin West, John Galt, and the Biography of 1816." *Art Bulletin* 86 (2), (June 2004): 324–345.

Reynolds, Joshua. *Discourses on Art*, Robert R. Wark (ed.). New Haven: Yale University Press, 1997.

Schjeldahl, Peter. *The Exuberance of MoMA's Expansion.* The New Yorker, October 21, 2019.

Storr, Robert. *September: A History Painting by Gerhard Richter.* London: Tate Publishing, 2011.

Sullivan, M.G. ed. *Fighting History.* London: Tate Britain, 2015.

Wallace, Michelle. *American People, Black Light: Faith Ringgold's Paintings of the 1960s.* New York: Neuberger Museum of Art, 2010.

Winter, Emma L. "German Fresco Painting and the New Houses of Parliament at Westminster, 1834–1851." *The Historical Journal* 47 (2), (June 2004): 291–329.

Zamponi, Beatrice. "William Kentridge: Triumphs and Laments." *Domus* 10 June, 2016.

5 Constructing a moment in history

The tableau as a communicational mode and genre in the late 18th century

Ina Louise Stovner

In the latter half of the 18th century, history painting was a significant medium for conveying history, representing a part of the era's rich diversity of historical depictions across various media. In the king's residence at Christiansborg Palace in Copenhagen, the royal power planned the adornment of the palace largest official room, the Great Hall. The Great Hall was intended to depict significant moments in the history of the dynasty and the realm. At the heart of the decorative program were ten large history paintings, narrating the virtues and good deeds of the Oldenburg dynasty from 1448 to the 1780s. Through the construction of historical examples, the political foundation of the absolute monarchy was to be reinforced. The prestigious task of creating these paintings was assigned to the young artist Nicolai Abraham Abildgaard (1743–1809), who was appointed as the royal history painter. He completed the paintings over a period of 13 years, from 1778 to 1791.

To convey these moral messages Abildgaard used a communicational strategy, widely known in the latter part of the 18th century, called the tableau. The tableau brought the didactic message to life through idealized moments that the spectator should grasp instantly. This chapter aims to delve into the communicative strategy of the tableau exploring the concept of the tableau as a genre and its influence across various media and practices. Historically, genre has been understood as a category or type of artistic or literary work that is defined by certain shared characteristics or conventions. However, recent research on genre has led to significant revisions and new ways of thinking about it. Rather than simply being a way to categorize artistic or literary works, genre is now seen as a framework for creating and interpreting meaning in various forms of communication. I will explore the idea that genres are not just inherent qualities of texts but instead act as intermediaries between texts, their creators and those who interpret them. As oral historian John Miles Foley (2012) has emphasized, comparing the types of expression found in different media and examining how they operate and vary in their interpersonal relations can provide insights into the different traditions being compared.[1]

I will start by examining the concept of the tableau as an esthetic expression, as formulated by French art theorist Denis Diderot, and its influence during the period. I will then analyze two history paintings of the Great Hall where

DOI: 10.4324/9781003331971-8

Abildgaard used the tableau in two different ways: *Christian III Succouring Denmark* (1780) and *Christian V's Danish Law of 1683* (1784). These paintings have not been fully understood by posterity, but by considering them through the lens of the tableau, I will show how the mode could compress a larger, comprehensive history into a single image in different ways. Additionally, I will examine the important social function of the tableau in salon culture and its political use in official commemorative ceremonies and parties. Ultimately, I will consider what defines the tableau's mode of communication across these various media and practices, and I will argue that the communicative device of the tableau should be seen in connection with the growing middle class, as it meets the needs of a wider audience.

The intrinsic paradox of the tableau

The word "tableau" means painting in French, but in the second half of the 18th century, the term also had another meaning. The tableau, as a form of representation, had a significant impact on various types of expression. It affected different practices and media, from artistic and literary expressions to more diagrammatic and scientific representations. Previous research on the tableau can therefore be found in different fields of study, which in different ways shed light on various aspects of tableaux and their use during the period. There is no large interdisciplinary and comprehensive presentation that discusses this representational mode. Intellectual historian Ellen Krefting has pointed out that the term tableau, semantically, has close connections to the word "table". Both the word "table" and "tableau" have a common etymological root in Latin "tabula" (tablet or plate), and they both refer to visually synthesizing representational media, where the goal is to see everything at a glance. Both are based on the didactic and epistemological role of visual expression.[2] The table presented the world as an analyzable size. Information was arranged in tables within several subject areas, it was considered a pedagogical and didactic way of providing an overview of a topic. The tableau as a form of communication attempts to achieve a specific "cognitive" effect by drawing together the particular with a larger overall and general whole. Seen in this way, the tableau embodies a kind of intrinsic paradox: it unites the specific and the unspecific, the particular and the general. This paradox is resolved in different ways in the different practices and media.

It is in his two treatises on the art of theater, *Entretiens sur le Fils naturel* (1757) and *Discours de la póesie* (1758), that Diderot defines his dramatic concept of tableau. He writes that a tableau is: "when the people on stage stand as natural and true and as pleasantly impactful as if they were portrayed by a painter on a canvas".[3] With his plays such as *Le père de familie*, Diderot wanted to adapt the drama of the theater to the expanding middle class. The tableaux were supposed to portray ordinary and everyday scenes as natural as possible, but at the same time they should be charged with intensity. In this way, a new kind of connection would emerge between stage and audience. Ideally, the actors should behave as if the audience were not present. It is as if Diderot wanted to transform the theater scene into a series of paintings, as magical as a painting by Poussin or Raphael. A famous anecdote tells how Diderot went to the theater and covered his ears to shut out the dialog, only then could he truly evaluate the scenes based on their visual expressiveness as tableaux. According to theater scholar Elin Andersen Diderot's "dramatic tableau" is centered around an idea of how the bodily subject could appear with the greatest emotional affect in an esthetic expression. The moment presented encapsulates the decisive, sublime or "pregnant moment" of the human body *in action*. Since this moment is condensed, the tableau changes and manipulates the spectator's experience of time. Time is experienced as stopped, and through this frozen moment the tableau creates a sense of presence in the viewer.[4] This vivid and visual way of representing something was meant to give the viewer a sense of presence and create a deeper emotional engagement with the subject.

Diderot's dramatic concept of the tableau had great influence, he was the most influential art critic in France in the 1750s. His ideas circulated all over Europe.[5] In his book *Absorption and Theatricality*, art historian Michael Fried describes a new notion of the relationship between painter and the beholder in French art in this period, a new kind of "radical intelligibility". According to the anti-Rococo criticism and theory, a painting ought to contain a great maxim, a lesson to the beholder. This moral message should be instantaneously apprehensible to the audience. Portraying the crucial high point of an action had traditionally been an important goal for the history painter. According to Fried, Diderot strengthens and renews this goal. He calls the tableau's ability to persuade its spectators as "absorptive". The figures are presented as completely immersed in the action of the image in such a way that the image closes in on itself so that the spectators are "drawn" into another reality. The painting should be meaningful and at the same time immediately understandable, Fried points out.[6]

In order for this communication to work, and the message to be understandable to the recipients, they had to have a certain competence: They had to be able to decode the message. This includes understanding the conventions and codes of the genre in which the message is presented. Literary critic Alastair Fowler suggests that effective communication often relies on the presence of shared conventions and genre-specific codes, emphasizing the nuanced interplay between them.[7] As a genre, the tableau is associated with moral and didactic content that is easily accessible and understood and is intended to persuade the viewer. This form was widely known in the bourgeoisie in the 1700s, which meant that the skills required to "read" a tableau—whether it was a theatrical production, a painting or a presentation in a book—were also widespread. Today, however, the tableau form is little used, and this genre expertise is far from obvious.

Ideas on immediacy and naturalness

Diderot's drama theory is grounded in his ideas and search for a more "natural language" as theater scholar Elin Andersen points out. Along with the philosophers Rousseau and Condillac, Diderot had also promoted theories about gestures as a more natural form of speech, immediately revealing the soul with the help of the body. These theories influenced practices both in theater, dance and the visual arts and they were intended to make a rigid code of conduct more natural. In parallel with this movement, the empirical investigation of mimicry and gestures was advancing with Johann Caspar Lavater's theories on physiognomy. These ideas were also popularized in the drawings of Daniel Chodowiecki. Diderot viewed gestures and mimicry as a form of "immediate" language, a more natural and genuine expression as opposed to the more artificial and mannered verbal language.[8] Diderot was particularly interested in the metonymic nature of gestures, which can express grand emotions without naming them. He believed that gestures can be complex signs that cannot be easily translated into words.[9] In this way, Diderot's concept of the tableau represents a departure from older dogmas. As Andersen has noted, it not only introduced new ideals of naturalness in theater and the visual arts, but it also broke with the doctrine of *ut pictura poesis*, which dates back to antiquity and suggests that the visual arts should be considered a form of "silent poetry". It enclosed the visual artist in a narrow circle of motifs through its iconographic codes. With Diderot's concept of the tableau,[10] the esthetic expression breaks free from these iconographic codes and becomes more rooted in sensory impressions and physicality.

The painter Jean-Baptiste Greuze was in Diderot's opinion one of the most esteemed artists in his first period as an art critic. His genre images from the 1750s illustrated the universe of Diderot's family dramas. He debuted at the Salon in 1755 with *Un Père de Familie qui lit la bible à ses enfants,* and it launched his career as a specialist in moralizing pieces regarding everyday life. The painting shows a father sitting at a table with his family, reading aloud from the Bible. It shows a moment in which he has paused in his reading since he has been moved to tears by the impact of the text. Young and old that are gathered at the table around him are gripped by the story. The painting conveys a sacred and elevated space, with a static atmosphere as if time has stopped. It is a moment that exists "outside of time".

Art historian Norman Bryson has noted that looking closer at Greuze's paintings with a modern eye, we notice several "flaws" or contradictions, as is the case in *L'Accordée de village*. For example, the father in the painting appears too old to be the father of the youngest children, the mother's body is disproportionate to her head, and her hands appear coarse and more suited to a farmer's wife. Meanwhile, the young couple that is newly engaged is dressed as fine townspeople. These contradictions can be found in all of Greuze's family genre paintings, but, as Bryson explains, they were not considered "mistakes" by contemporary viewers.[11] In the early 1760s, Greuze was considered one of the greatest painters in France. He created his figures from an existing iconography. The overly-aged father in the painting, for instance, is depicted as the typical *pater familias*. When considering the context of Diderot's drama theory, each figure in the painting represents the *essence* or a "condensed" image of what it means to be a child, sister, mother or father that the viewer could grasp instantly.[12] The painting's contemporary success and popularity indicate that the audience possessed the genre expertise necessary to comprehend it.

Evocative allegories

The esthetics of the tableau should be seen in the context of changes in the allegorical imagery of the art of the period. The function of allegory is to condense the content and create an exalted mood by connecting the theme to something universal. Artists used established imagery to express these abstract ideas figuratively. In the early modern period, members of the upper classes were educated in the interpretation of allegorical figures in art and literature. At the same time, there was a growing criticism that allegories represented an empty form of ornamentation. Allegories in art and literature were changing and becoming more didactic. Literary historian Gordon Teskey has noted that 18th-century allegories were more worldly and referred to a meaning connected to the real world, in contrast to the allegories of the Renaissance, which were often veiled in symbolism and referred to something divine.[13]

Art historian Karin Kryger advocates that in the second half of the 1700s in Denmark, the visual language in art was simplifying, becoming more immediate intelligible. The allegories of the baroque and rococo period were criticized for being enigmatic and incomprehensible, and new allegorical encyclopedias encouraged artists to study ancient coins and works of art to create a simpler visual language, closer to that of antiquity.[14] As highlighted by art historian Charlotte Christensen, the Danish artist Johannes Wiedewelt created a new emotional expression in his allegorical figures for the memorial of king Frederik V in Roskilde Cathedral in 1766. Next to the sarcophagus he portrayed the personifications of Denmark and Norway as two mourning female figures invoking a new form of "universal human affect".[15] The two crowned female figures are portrayed being in deep sorrow.

This vivid and emotional use of allegories is also apparent in the history painting *Christian III Succouring Denmark*, which Abildgaard painted for the Great Hall in Christiansborg Castle in Copenhagen in 1780 (Figure 5.1). In the painting, Abildgaard staged the dramatic moment when Christian III ended the civil war in 1536, known as the "Count's Feud". The king is reaching out his left hand to the personification of Denmark, who is kneeling in front of him. She is portrayed in a vivid and emotional way, participating in the dramatic moment depicted. With his right hand, the king is pointing toward a group of allegorical figures further back in the composition, belonging to a higher realm.

Figure 5.1 Nicolai Abildgaard, *Christian III Succouring Denmark*, 1780–81, oil on canvas, 317 × 200 cm, SMK – National Gallery of Denmark.

Together, however, all of the figures create a kind of pantomime, through their body language, gestures and mimicry they are communicating quite specific and mundane historical events. They are visualizing the exemplary effects of the king's actions. Since Christian III created peace in the kingdom, he is pointing directly to the allegorical figure *Peace*. She has her eyes fixed on the figures *Religion* and *Justice*. *Religion* is reminding us that the king created peace by introducing the Reformation in Denmark-Norway in 1536 and the figure *Justice* is telling us that this created a more just society. The allegorical figure in the very back of the composition and placed above them all is the goddess of wisdom, *Minerva*. She tells us that, as a result of these events, science and enlightenment have conquered. The allegorical figures compress these historical details that would otherwise be difficult to fit into one image. Together, all of the figures in the painting constitute a tableau, through clear gestures and mimicry, they are telling the viewers about quite specific and significant historical events. Since the king is interacting directly with the allegorical figure *Denmark* it creates an exalted and sacred atmosphere.

The painting conveys this complex history with more figures than just the king. Behind him, there are two men who are also participating in the moment through gestures and mimicry. They are also part of the overall message, and the artist has placed them there so that they could be remembered and honored. According to classicist Patrick Kragelund, the man in armor can be identified as the army general Johan Rantzau, while the man next to him is the king's chancellor Johan Friis.[16] Both Rantzau and Friis played a crucial role in the events that led to Christian III's rise to the throne and the introduction of the Reformation. They are symbolically positioned behind the king to express their significant role in the events depicted and their support to the king. Friis is pointing demonstratively toward the king while looking at Rantzau. Rantzau on the other hand has his eyes fixed on the king. He is dressed in armor and is about to grab his sword with his left hand, ready for battle.

Abildgaard's tableau catches the dramatic moment when the king saves the nation and this message is reinforced by the fact that the personification of Denmark is presented so vividly. She is desperately looking at the king for help, strongly affected by the war: her hair is disheveled, her cloak is ragged, and she is surrounded by ruins. In this way the tableau changes and alters allegorical imagery, imbuing it with more concrete, sensual and mundane qualities. One could say that through the "tableau-ian" lens, the allegorical figures become more naturalized, humanized and sensuous living beings. Similar to an allegory, the tableau operates in two layers. It refers to another speech behind the first speech, but at the same time the tableau form suppresses traditional allegorical imagery since the allegorical figure is presented with such vivid sensitivity and pathos. The portrayal of Denmark as a helpless woman in need was meant to evoke strong emotions and reactions in the viewer of the early modern period, and the king was depicted as a father protecting the kingdom. This emotional way of presenting the nation was meant to reinforce the message and the viewers emotional engagement. It was no longer sufficient to simply decode allegories analytically, through reason and thought. It was also through the viewers feelings, understanding and imagination that the allegories in the tableau moved and enlightened the beholder.

This communicative strategy and demand for instantaneousness and intelligibility should be seen in connection with the intended audience. As a representational tool, the tableau must be seen in the context of the emergence of a number of genres with a new focus on everyday life and actuality of events. Within the classical magistra vitae tradition, historical examples were intended to inspire young men of the elite to meet the tasks of public life. According to literary historian Mark Salber Phillips, this tradition in the late 18th century was replaced by a more emotional and inner version of the idea of history as "the teacher of life". Phillips points out how the growing middle class constituted a large new group within the reading public in this period. This new reading audience had a greater interest in social and inner aspects of life, and this influenced the use of examples and the didactic role of history in many different genres. The new commercial society created new boundaries between the public and private spheres and identification and empathy became an important part of storytelling.[17] The communicational device of the tableau should be seen in connection with these changes in exemplarity, as pointed out by Phillips—it met the needs of a wider audience.

Deliberate anachronisms

In his portrayal of Christian III, Abildgaard attempted to make the king easily recognizable by drawing upon famous previous depictions. However, his clothing includes a combination of historical details and anachronisms. For example, the royal cape is not from the depicted period and his shoes with red heels are not characteristic of the Renaissance.[18] These details demonstrate Abildgaard's intention to align the depiction with contemporary ideals of royalty and credibility. These anachronisms serve to establish a connection between the past and the present, making the painting more understandable to the viewer. The combination of historical details with contemporary ideals of royalty and credibility creates a sense of immediacy and reality, which helps to bring the king and the era to life, creating a more convincing tableau. Abildgaard's detailed rendering of historical details reflects the latest trends in European history painting. Prior to beginning his commission in the Great Hall, Abildgaard traveled through France and was exposed to the new style of French history painting, which emphasized the accurate reproduction of historical details in clothing and surroundings. Artists like Nicolas-Guy Brenet and Louis-Jacques Durameau were known for their attention to these details. This emphasis on historical accuracy was part of a wider movement in French art, which sought to promote patriotism and moral uplifting through art. The head of the French Academy, Antoine Joseph Dezalier d'Argenville, believed that art should be as true to historical reality as possible. He and other scholars at the Academy of Paris emphasized the importance of accurate reproduction of details, such as dress, customs and props, in creating credible and morally uplifting images. As noted by art historian Charlotte Christensen the portrayal of both Christian I and Christian III in the Great Hall shows that Abildgaard was clearly inspired by these new tendencies in French art.[19] The influential French antiquarian Anne Claude de Caylus has recently gained attention for his great influence on the art of the period. Literary historian Julie Boch describes him as one of the driving forces for a new search for "truth" and precise knowledge in art. He lectured to artists on the history of costumes at the Academy of Fine Arts in Paris. For Caylus, the historical details were an important part of the image's expressive expression, which should not be omitted, Boch points out.[20] Abildgaard valued Caylus' view of art and considered him an authority.[21] His encounter with these ideas in France likely influenced him into presenting the king as a "real historical person" and accurately rendering the historical details of their appearance and surroundings, to create a sense of credibility and closeness to the viewer. This approach reflected the contemporary view that history painting should be defined as a historical art and that the inclusion of historical details could enhance the moral effect of the image on the viewer.

Despite the fact that artists and writers in France called for historical accuracy in history paintings of the period, they also warned against exaggeration. Both Caylus and Diderot warned artists of the danger of the overly strict accuracy of reproduction when it deviated greatly from contemporary taste. "Can you recognize a prince in such a representation?" asked Caylus. "It would be misleading for an artist to portray a dress that just seems ridiculous", Diderot wrote.[22] The various adaptations should therefore be regarded as "deliberate anachronisms" to enhance the effect and under-standing of the image's content. Historian Judith Pollmann has pointed out that anachronisms can enable the communication and traffic of information between the past and the present.[23] Anachronisms in art have a long history. Art historians Alexander Nagel and Christopher Wood argue in their book *Anachronic Renaissance* that the use of anachronisms enabled artists in the Renaissance to create associations and create connections between the past and the present.[24] Peter Burke has also written about how humanists and artists in the Renaissance developed a notion of anachronisms that enabled them to bring the past closer to their own time.[25] Dress was a very important identity marker in the 1700s society. It was therefore important that the representation of the king and prince signaled their high status and dignity. The antiquarian and historical details are therefore subject to the didactic message of the image. By creating an interaction between the past and the present, the constructed moment in the tableau should be more convincing and gripping as a real historical event. According to cultural historian Anne Eriksen, the concept of truth has always been central to the study of history, but the understanding of what this truth entails has changed over time.

In traditional magistra vitae-thinking, historical truth was seen as something that is absolutely and superhistorically true, manifesting itself in concrete events or individuals who serve as exemplars. In this view, truth is situated on the moral plane. However, changes that occurred at the end of the 18th century brought historical truth closer to antiquarian accuracy, as it began to refer to specific events from the past, Eriksen notes.[26] As a genre the tableau is connected to the magistra vitae topos through its embodiment of the ideological concerns of its time and its ability to shape and reinforce moral and social values. Abildgaard's depiction of Denmark in such a ruined state was based on historical accounts of the country's condition during the civil war. The representation of the king as a paternal figure was intended to strengthen the moral message of the image and the importance of the king's actions. The tableau constructs a dramatic moment that was meant to evoke feelings of pity and sympathy in the audience, encouraging them to emotionally identify with the fatherland. The depiction of the king as a real historical person was meant to increase the sense of reality of this dramatic moment. As Phillips notes, narratives about events that occurred in the distant past can have a distancing effect on the reader.[27] To counter this, Abildgaard used deliberate anachronisms that aimed to create strong sensations in the viewer, increasing the sense of kinship and fostering sympathy.

History at a glance

Abildgaard used the tableau in a different way in other history paintings in the Great Hall. *Christian V's Danish Law of 1683* (1784) had a very central position in this grand historical program (Figure 5.2). It was placed in the very center of the room, next to a painting of his father, Frederik III, the first king receiving the right to rule as a sovereign monarch in Denmark-Norway. While the painting was lost in a devastating fire in 1794, the preserved oil sketch, along with contemporary accounts of the artwork, provides sufficient information for interpretation. The composition depicts a gathering of individuals seated around a table, including the identifiable figure of the king, and represents the assembly of the King's Privy Council in 1683. The painting does not present a dramatic moment. Instead, it aims to create a vivid and convincing illusion of the present moment in order to have an immediate and strong effect on the viewer. Unfortunately, the painting was lost in a fire when the castle burned in 1794, and it is only preserved as a sketch. The painting places the Danish Law as an important fundament for the absolute state and it honors the King for creating a fair and just kingdom based on these laws.

At first glance, the image appears as a concrete representation of a historical moment, which with a modern eye can look realistic. It presents the king and his Privy council when the Danish Law was signed in the green chamber at Copenhagen Castle in 1683. It is as if the spectator is looking into a window or is present in the room. What is striking with this

Figure 5.2 Nicolai Abildgaard, *Christian V Presents Danish Law of 1683*, 1784, oil on canvas, 61 × 37 cm, SMK – National Gallery of Denmark.

painting, is the mundane and down-to-earth atmosphere, which enhances the king's role as a political leader, not his divine power. He is presented more in a "businessman"-like manner, where he is seated around a table collaborating with his men. The painting's style is reminiscent of the genre painting popular among the bourgeoisie at the time, which often depicted scenes from everyday life. Earlier research has highlighted this painting as "a lost masterpiece in 18th-century historicism before historicism".[28] However, it can be more accurately understood within the context of the contemporary genre of the tableau, in which the emphasis is not on photographic realism, but on a more complex representation of history, in which the dimension of time is seen as secondary. As visual theorist Norman Bryson has noted, the traditional division of art into "styles" that follow each other in time can be misleading when understanding the art of the 18th century. The new tendencies in history painting have traditionally been interpreted as a precursor to later art styles. Bryson suggests that the focus on historical reconstruction gave artists a wider range of styles and expressions to work with.[29]

Through the lens of the tableau, the man in the background stands out as a key figure. The tableau communicates through clear gestures and expressions, and he clearly has an underlying message to the viewer; he is placed behind the others and is the only one looking straight at us, drawing us into the scene. The German art expert Friedrich Ramdohr described the painting when he visited the castle in 1792 and identified the man in the background as Peder Griffenfeld. Griffenfeld was Christian 5's close advisor and the *de facto* ruler of the kingdom for several years. Previous research has dismissed Ramdohr's description since Griffenfeld was in prison in 1683 and couldn't possibly have been present when the law was completed.[30] The Danish Law was not just written in 1683; however, it actually took 22 years to complete it. If we do not interpret the painting as an early form of realism, i.e., that it shows a specific moment in history but rather interpret it in the light of the contemporary tableau concept, it makes more sense.

Griffenfeld fell into disgrace seven years before the completion of the law when he was accused of treason and spent the rest of his life in prison. But looking more closely at the context and the period when this painting was made, a lot had changed. A massive effort was now being made by historians and artists to restore his reputation and clear his name.

Since he is such an essential part of the densified moment in this painting we will look a bit closer at his background. Griffenfeld was born Peder Schumacher. He was the son of a wine merchant and he had worked his way up to his high office. Following the introduction of absolutism in 1660, Griffenfeld wrote the Danish Royal Law, the *Lex Regia* in 1665. This law formed the basis for the constitution of the absolute monarchy. Apart from the king, Griffenfeld stands out as the most important man in the painting. It not only restores his reputation it also honors him by presenting him as an exemplary citizen. The artist thus seeks to instill a thought in the bourgeoisie viewer: To see themselves as an integral part of the absolutist state. This was an important political strategy of the monarchy in a time of instability and a strategy for revitalizing the absolutist regime.

As a tableau the painting communicates this moral message through many small important details: Griffenfeld is standing symbolically behind the king and the others.

He is holding a book or manuscript in his hand that represents the *Lex Regia*. He is also placed next to a cabinet with various books that refer to the initiatory work and the previous laws on which the Danish law was based. This action and his position are included in the tableau as speaking movements. Not much else happens in the painting other than the king sitting with a pen in hand, ready to sign the law. This is the pregnant moment that should enable contemporary viewers to grasp history at a glance. His background as a member of the bourgeoisie is communicated clearly since he is not dressed in the manner of a nobleman but is wearing a simple gray jacket. He also carries the white ribbon showing us the Order of the Dannebrog. In 1671, Griffenfeld initiated a new rank regulation that allowed normal citizens to be ennobled and created this new Chivalry Order. The Order of the Dannebrog was given as a reward for faithful service to the king. Griffenfeld was himself the first citizen to be ennobled and the first to receive the order.

The tableau thus shows a decisive moment that contains both past and future. In the image, the central action is illuminated from above without any visible light source, the rest of the room falls into darkness. Diderot was an advocate of the use of chiaroscuro in art. It enhances the experience of the charged moment, he wrote, the contrast between light and shadow prevented the eye from wandering, by fixing it on certain objects. The light falls most strongly on the king and Griffenfeld, who must be considered the center of the painting, both compositionally and thematically. The scene is like an allegory "loaded" with meaning, it requires a certain interpretation or decoding. The story of Griffenfeld was well-known to contemporary viewers however. Griffenfeld fell out of favor seven years before the law's completion and was accused of treason and sentenced to life imprisonment. In the period when the picture was painted, his reputation was restored. As historian Sebastian Olden Jørgensen has pointed out, a regular "Griffenfeld cult" took place in the 18th century. He was very famous during this period. As the son of a wine merchant, Griffenfeld was a good example and a role model for the kingdom's inhabitants that demonstrated what a citizen could achieve, through loyalty to the king and hard work. In order for the audience to be able to grasp this message at a glance, the references and symbols were meant to be easy to understand.

The tableau constructs the moment in two ways. First, the tableau can compress a long period of time into a single moment. In a painting, this means that people who have not been present at the same time or in the same place can appear in one and the same picture because they were important for the same event. Secondly, the tableau enables the viewer to gain information about complex events and conditions at a glance. Griffenfeld's presence tells both about the creation of the law and about his own history. The spectators should get a broader picture of the circumstances surrounding the creation of Christian V's law. Their awareness and knowledge of Griffenfeld and his efforts, which were much talked about in his day, enabled them to understand the message of the picture. In this way, the tableau's function involves both representation and perception. As a representational mode, the tableau processed and reified specific and concrete details into a more general and moral message. In this painting, it was used to strengthen and revitalize the political foundations of the monarchy.

Griffenfeld, a former member of the bourgeoisie is a crucial part of the condensed moment in this central tableau in the Great Hall. He is presented as an example of the new possibilities the bourgeoisie had gained in the absolute state—through hard work and loyalty to the king. To increase the impact of the example, Abildgaard has constructed an idea of a moment in history in order to create a feeling of immediacy and presence in the viewer. He uses the contrast of light and darkness to create a chiaroscuro effect—a way to intensify the message and create pictorial unity. The painting should be seen as an expression of what Fried calls "radical intelligibility" within the visual,[31] and what Phillips calls a new strategy[32] on the part of writers in the same period. This communicative strategy and demand for instantaneousness and intelligibility should be seen in connection with the intended audience. As a representational tool, the tableau must be seen in the context of the emergence of a number of genres with a new focus on everyday life and actuality of events. Within the classical magistra vitae tradition, historical examples were intended to inspire young men of the elite to meet the tasks of public life. According to Phillips, this tradition in the late 18th century was replaced by a more emotional and inner version of the idea of history as "the teacher of life". Phillips points out how the growing middle class constituted a large new group within the reading public in this period. This new reading audience had a greater interest in social and inner aspects of life, and this influenced the use of examples and the didactic role of history in many different genres. The new commercial society created new boundaries between the public and private spheres and identification and empathy became an important part of storytelling. The communicational device of the tableau should be seen in connection with these changes in exemplarity—it met the needs of a wider audience.

In this painting, however, it is done in a slightly different way than in the painting of Christian III. Both paintings compress time, but the connotative or symbolic level is more hidden in this painting, since the symbols are more closely connected to the action of the constructed moment, in a seemingly believable and mundane scene. The tableau created a new form of meaning since it does something with the ideal and the example that is presented. One is not only presented with a good example or a moral, the tableau was meant to evoke a moral feeling in the spectator. To interpret a tableau, both emotions, reason and imagination had to be set in motion. Through more «naturalistic» and sentimental communication the tableau met the needs of a wider audience and enabled an immediate moral identification with the beholders. This vivid and visual representational mode was meant to intensify the viewers sense of presence and create a deeper emotional engagement with the example.

The Great Hall—a magnificent tableau

The history paintings of the Great Hall convey a comprehensive message through their visual and thematic unity. Art historian Erik Fischer has noted the use of mirror symmetry in the arrangement of the paintings, with the first mirroring the last, the second mirroring the penultimate and so on. The Duchy of Holstein, depicted as the empire's southern outpost, plays a central role in this message.[33] The paintings in the Great Hall depict the kings of the Oldenburg dynasty and their great feats, with a thematic and visual combination that crosses chronological boundaries and allows the spectator to grasp the wholeness of the message at a glance. The series, as a whole, emphasizes the importance of unity and love of the fatherland in all parts of the kingdom governed by the Oldenburg dynasty, leading to peace, justice and favorable conditions for science and art. The history paintings of the Great Hall present exemplary stories chronologically, but in their entirety, time is depicted as standing still, with the images conveying timeless ideals and encapsulating time through their cyclical structure. The series also includes images that depict the center of power and the king's patriarchal role and static power, as well as representations of the nobility, clergy, citizens and even workers surrounding the king.

In 1788 a masquerade ball was held in the Great Hall, and it is reported that over 2,000 participants were in attendance. The dance floor was full of people, and the gallery was so crowded with "people of the bourgeoisie" that there was no room to spare[34] (Figure 5.3). In 1783, *Adressecomptoirs Efterretninger* announced that the ball in the Great Hall was open to all nine ranks of society, including civil officials and military leaders. The general public was also able to purchase tickets to watch the ball from the gallery, indicating that events like this were not exclusively for the highest ranks of society and that the upper middle class had access to the Great Hall, albeit as spectators. The paintings were therefore meant to reach a wide audience. The historical events and examples shown in the paintings correspond with the stories in the history books written by the historians Peter Frederik Suhm and Ove Malling written in the same period.[35] These history books were widely read by the public and were written as history school books for the Latin school. The moral histories in the paintings were therefore comprehensible and meant to reach out to a wide audience in the period.[36] The series present a "condensed" moment or example in the reign of each king. The Oldenburg dynasty is celebrated for its effort to protect the Kingdom, create peace and

INTERIEUR DE LA GRANDE SALE DU CHATEAU ROYAL DE CHRISTIANSBOURG
A COPENHAGUE ORDONNÉE PAR LE ROY FREDERIC V POUR LE MARIAGE DE CHRISTIAN VII ROY DE
DANNEMARC ET DE NORVEGE AUJOURDHUY REGNANT AVEC CAROLINE MATILDE PRINCESSE DE LA GRANDE
BRETAGNE ET TERMINÉE LORS DU MARIAGE DE LEUR MAIESTES LE VIII NOVEMBRE MDCCLXVI

Figure 5.3 Johannes Gottfred Bradt after Nicolas Henri Jardin, Court ball in
Christiansborg's Great Hall at Christian VII's wedding to Caroline Mathilde,
1768, etching, 410 mm x 435, SMK – National Gallery of Denmark.

welfare and the rise of science and culture. They are presented as the ultimate citizens, their good actions are motivated by their bravery, public spirit and their faith in God.

The kings are surrounded by famous men from their regime who are also honored for their high moral and good actions. Each painting presents moral examples of social conduct through moral lessons in patriotism, public spirit and faithfulness to the king. The two last paintings are presented as a culmination of all the good actions of the previous kings. During the reign of Frederik Vth and his son Christian 7th, peace and prosperity are presented as reaching its peak. Abildgaard used the tableau in two different ways: in some paintings, he created an exalted atmosphere with compositions where the king and his men interact with allegorical figures and personifications. Other paintings can be characterized as more mundane or down to earth, where he created a more realistic illusion of a historical moment. As moral tableaux however all of the paintings present the viewer with constructed moments that are densified, containing both the past and the future. These condensed moments, where the spectator could capture everything at a glance, were meant to increase and focus the effect of the example. The didactic message of the paintings, conveyed through the tableau form, was meant to be widely understood by the educated circles of the time. The paintings were also intended to teach future kings how to fulfill their role in the social covenant through the virtues and actions of their ancestors. Toward the end of the century, the tableau form was also expressed in a more ritualistic manner to celebrate history, patriotism, the homeland and the community.

"A grammar of emotions"

The living picture or the "tableau vivant" was considered an important part of civic ceremonies and congregations toward the end of the century in Denmark. It was used to stage abstract values such as community and patriotism in emotionally charged official celebrations and rituals and was meant to have a politically unifying effect. Ethnologist Tine Damsholt and historian Thomas Lyngby have written about this phenomenon in Denmark. These sentimental and neoclassical theatrical forms of expression were inspired by public ceremonies in the aftermath of the French Revolution. A distinctive feature of these public ceremonies was that the patriotic feelings were staged ritually.[37]

The Liberty Memorial *(Frihedsstøtten)* in Copenhagen was designed by Abildgaard and erected in memory of the abolition of the serfdom-like institution *(Stavnsbånd)* starting with agricultural reforms in 1788. The memorial symbolizes the freedom of the peasantry. According to Damsholt, the memorial can be described as a "frozen version" of a tableau vivant and the patriotic ideals. The 20-meter-high obelisk is a symbol of royal power and around the pillar there are placed four allegorical figures who, like in an exemplary patriotic tableau, represent the virtues of allegiance, bravery, civic virtue and the virtue of agricultural diligence *(agerdyrkningsflid)*.[38] The monument was completed in 1797, although the setting stone was laid by crown prince Frederik already in 1792 together with a solemn inaugural ceremony that celebrated freedom and the fatherland. During the ceremony, all the senses of the audience were set in motion, a way to "intensify the ritual space", as Damsholt points out.[39] Speeches were given praising the king's beneficial role and celebrating civic freedom followed by a musical performance. "Noble citizens" tossed flowers on the crown prince from balconies to the accompaniment of music. In this way, the ritual spoke simultaneously to different senses (the sight, ears and nose). It can be seen as a "political" enabling of sensory impressions and of the body.[40] The festivities continued on the birthday of the king and crown prince, celebrating royal power with a tableau vivant, much in the same manner as the historical paintings of the Great Hall.

Tableaux vivants were also a common part of patriotic memorial ceremonies. After the Battle of Copenhagen in 1801, Danish actor Hans Christian Knudsen traveled around the kingdom organizing commemorative ceremonies and patriotic tableaux in churches and town halls to inspire patriotism and support for the fatherland. These ceremonies were intended to create emotions in the audience and were considered more effective at expressing patriotic feelings than verbal language.[41] Lyngby describes the variant of bourgeois patriotism that characterizes the latter half of the 1700s as a "sentimental" form of patriotism—in which emotions and affect played a particularly important role.[42] During the ceremonies, Knudsen sang and proclaimed poems about the fatherland in front of a "fatherland altar". The climax of the ceremony was the "Højtids-Scene" tableau, where young girls dressed in white placed a garland of flowers with symbolic meaning on the urn that represented the heroic patriots who had died in defense of the fatherland.[43] The garland was arranged with different kinds of flowers that had different symbolic meanings.[44] It was seen as an expression of the patriotic community between the living and the dead, between death and immortality and between the sexes, Lyngby explains.[45]

Damsholt refers to the body language used in tableaux vivants as a "grammar of emotions", meaning that for an action to be recognized as an expression of feeling, it had to conform to certain rules of iconography, gestures and movement patterns. Although the rhetoric of these ceremonies emphasized unity among people of all classes, they were primarily targeted at the bourgeoisie who already understood the genre of patriotic messages and codes.[46] During patriotic ceremonies, women were often given an important role as representations of abstract ideas such as freedom and patriotism. In contrast to the men, who were typically dressed in uniform, women were often dressed in white, symbolizing the nation and its virtues. These ceremonies were part of the construction of the ideal citizen, and the contrast between the genders in these tableaux highlighted the different roles assigned to men and women as "good citizens". This "language of feeling" was meant to connect the individual with the community and the royal power.[47]

In the late 18th century, the tableau became popular in a different social context as a form of private entertainment. The "tableaux vivants", or "living pictures", were an esthetic expression that lay between painting and drama. This refined form of pantomime became a popular genre in the late 1700s and early 1800s. The idea behind these moving images was to reproduce historical scenes or famous motifs from classical art through living figures dressed in appropriate attire who mimicked the poses of famous historical or mytholog-ical figures as they appear in paintings. In his novel, *Die Wahlverwandtschaften*, from 1809, Goethe describes a social gathering amusing themselves with the entertainment of "tableaux vivants". Three famous paintings were portrayed as living pictures in a dramatic performance in three sequences with musical interludes. The motifs were widely known, and they showed magnificent scenes that had such a strong effect on the spectators in the story that they experienced it as being so deeply moving that they felt like they were brought into another world. According to literary historian Knut Ove Eliassen, this scene described in Goethe's novel offers an insight into how the tableau was used as a form of social practice and how it was considered an extremely effective medium.[48] The reason why such living images became so popular was due to the fact that works of art known only as copperplates in black and white were brought to life in a completely different way. It created a sense of presence in the viewer.

In the second half of the 1700s, tableaux vivants and attitudes were commonly used in theatrical performances such as prologues and epilogues, as well as in private social gatherings. Attitudes became especially popular within the salon culture of the period. Media researcher Karen Klitgaard Polvsen defines an "attitude" as a tableau for one person in which a dancing body pauses and stiffens in a gesture reminiscent of a statue or figure in a painting, and then moves again. The moving images could contain attitudes, which could be described as a kind of subgenre of the tableau.[49] The attitudes can be compared to the emotional allegorical figures in the visual arts. They express something more than what appears in the exterior but differ from traditional and rigid allegories with their sensitivity and pathos. Like allegories, the attitude was to be interpreted not only with reason but also with feeling and imagination.

The popularity of the genre of attitude art was not only due to its function as a form of entertainment for social gatherings but also because it served several other important social functions. For example, it provided an arena for people to showcase their skills and impress others in social settings. Additionally, the art form, which combined elements of dance, music and pantomime, was seen as an important tool for the esthetic education of girls in salon circles. By teaching them body control, musical movements and emotional expressions without the use of words, attitude art was believed to improve their social graces. The first renowned attitude artist was Emma Heart, who later became known as Lady Hamilton. Goethe, the famous German writer, saw her perform in Naples in 1787 and was reportedly impressed by her skills. Her attitudes became well-known throughout Europe and were widely distributed as printed etchings. The attitudes of Ida Brun also attracted a lot of attention. Lady Hamilton became an inspiration and role model in her upbringing. Among other things, she performed in her mother's, Friederike Bruns, salon in Copenhagen and around Europe. It was especially her naturalness[50] and grace in the presentation of the attitudes that were admired and experienced as a mixture of dance, sculpture and painting.[51] Brun described how her daughter was taught to express herself in dance, singing, attitudes and living tableaux in *Ida's ästhetische Entwickelung* (1824).[52] Throughout the 1800s, this form of entertainment was criticized for being artificial and sentimental and gradually lost its artistic reputation. However, it was still practiced as private entertainment in the lower echelons of the bourgeoisie.

Vivid historical examples

The tableau, characterized by its unique communication methods, holds several distinct traits that set it apart as a genre-spanning various practices. As indicated by media scholar John Fiske, the generic conventions of any form of expression often encapsulate the critical ideological concerns of the period in which they gain popularity.[53] In the case of the tableau, it assumes a didactic and epistemological role in visual expression, firmly grounded in the idea that history should serve as a vehicle for promoting moral uplift and civic duty.

Philosopher Stephen Neale argues that genres may also help to shape values,[54] in the case of the tableau, its focus on presenting moral examples and promoting civic duty allows it to influence and reinforce these values in society. Furthermore, Thwaites, Lloyd and Mules view the relationship between genres and social conditions as reciprocal.[55] The tableau, tied closely to the bourgeois culture of its times embodies certain ideological concerns of its time, emphasizing didacticism and the promotion of moral values. The tableau as a genre is closely tied to the bourgeoisie of its time and represents a spectator culture that may seem unfamiliar to present-day audiences. For the tableau to be effective and persuasive, the viewers were required to have a specific competence in order to decode the "charged" and expressive body language.

As I have demonstrated in this chapter, the tableau functions in two ways with regard to the moment: it shows a charged and compressed moment that must be grasped instantly, at a glance. In the visual arts, this meaningful moment can be formed by bringing allegorical figures to life, as in the image of Christian III, or by creating a more vivid and convincing illusion of a "here and now", as in the image of Christian V. These condensed moments, where the spectator could capture everything at a glance, was meant to increase and focus the effect of the historical example. Overall, the tableau can be characterized as a synthesizing and didactic form of communication. Both the narratives and the communicational devices were reshaped by new audiences and new social needs. In different practices, the tableau reconciles the particular with the universal in slightly different ways. In the visual arts, the various elements of an image are united to constitute a larger moral message. In tableaux vivants and patriotic celebrations, this occurs through charged moments conveyed using the body in frozen moments through rituals. The tableau also has a unifying effect on spectators, uniting the individual with the community—in Greuze's poignant scenes from the family and in Abildgaard's history paintings in the Great Hall where citizens are united with the king and autocracy. In the salons, the sociability celebrated their own community, and in stately patriotic ceremonies, the tableau is politically unifying, as the symbolic acts of the rituals unite the individual with the community and the community to its king. In this way, the tableau can be seen as a focal point with a unifying function in the family, social environments and more formally and politically in the state.

The tableau was intended to intensify the viewer's sense of presence and create emotional engagement, representing a break with existing dogmas and rule-based rhetoric. However, this search for a more "natural" form of expression should not be seen only as a precursor to a new form of realistic history. The concept of the tableau is firmly rooted in the idea that art and history should be morally uplifting and socially compelling. It creates a new kind of historical example by eliciting a moral response in the viewer. The viewer is not just presented to an ideal, the tableau was meant to awaken a moral feeling in the spectator, requiring the use of emotions, reason and imagination.

Notes

1 Foley, *Oral Tradtion and the Internet. Pathways of the Mind,* University of Illinois Press.
2 Krefting, "Alt i ett øyekast?", 105–106.
3 «Un incident imprévu qui se passe en action, et qui change subitement par un peintre, elle me plairait sur la toile, est un tableau» (Diderot, Entretiens sur le Fils naturel, Oevres IV, 1136) Diderot, *Œuvres Complètes,* 92.
4 Andersen *Kroppens sublime tale,* 107.
5 Abildgaard owned Diderot's *Collection complète des oeuvres philosophiques, littéraires et dramatiques, in five volumes,* from 1773. Thygesen, Kragelund, Johansen. "A History Painter's Library", Ab 517–21, 66.
6 Fried, *Absorption and Theatricality,* 89.
7 Fowler, «Genre», 216.
8 Andersen *Kroppens sublime tale,* 59–60.
9 He illustrated authors who described the new sensitivity within the bourgeoisie, among others J.W. von Goethe. Povlsen, «Standsningens attitude i krop og tekst» 96–97.
10 Andersen, *Kroppens sublime tale,* 18.
11 Bryson *Word and Image,* 138.
12 Andersen *Kroppens sublime tale,* 115–117.
13 Teskey, *Allegory and Violence,* 86.
14 In new encyclopedias such as Jean Baptiste Boudards *Iconologie tirée de divers auteurs* and Honoré Lacombe de Prezels *Dictionnaire iconologique.* Kryger, *Allegory and civic virtue,* 82–83.
15 Christensen, *Maleren Nicolai Abildgaard,* 132.
16 Kragelund, *Abildgaard,* 161.
17 Phillips, *Society and Sentiment,* 18–19.
18 Stovner, *Historiske tablåer,* 90.
19 Christensen, *Maleren Nicolai Abildgaard,* 99–102.
20 Boche, «L'esthétique du comte de Caylus: un nouveau classicisme expressif», 64.
21 Abildgaard, «Forsøg til en nye Forklaring over den Marmortavle med Solens Billede, som findes i det Matthæiske Landhuus i Rom, 279–82.
22 Loquin, *Peinture D'histoire en France de 1747 à 1787,* 169–70.
23 Pollman, *Memory in Early Modern Europe, 1500–1800,* 61.
24 Nagel & Wood, *Anachronic Renaissance,* 18, 35.
25 Burke, «The Sense of Anachronism from Petrarch to Poussin»,162.
26 Eriksen, *Topografenes verden,* 185–186.
27 Phillips, *On Historical Distance,* 86.
28 Kragelund, *Abildgaard,* 133.
29 Bryson, *Word and Image,* 240.
30 Kragelund, *Abildgaard,* 166.
31 Fried, *Absorption and Theatricality,* 89.
32 Phillips, *On Historical Distance,* 95.
33 Fischer, «Abildgaards kongebilleder i Christiansborg Riddersal», 31, 39.
34 Miranda, *Miranda i Danmark,* 119–122.

35 Suhm, *Historien af Danmark, Norge og Holsten*, Malling, *Store og Gode Handlinger af Danske, Norske og Holstenere.*
36 Stovner, *Historiske tablåer,* 38.
37 Damsholt, «Staging Emotions», 100.
38 Damsholt, «Emotions and subjectivization», 11–12.
39 Damsholt, «Staging Emotions», 110.
40 Damsholt, *Fædrelandskærlighed og borgerdyd,* 147.
41 Damsholt, *Fædrelandskærlighed og borgerdyd,* 154.
42 Lyngby, *The sentimental patriotism* 10.
43 Lyngby, *The sentimental patriotism,* 63.
44 Lyngby, *The sentimental patriotism,* 88–89.
45 Lyngby, "Fædrelandskærligheden's sensitive form of expression", 104–105.
46 Damsholt, *Fædrelandskærlighed og borgerdyd,* 153.
47 Damsholt, *Fædrelandskærlighed og borgerdyd,* 158.
48 Eliassen, «Tableau», 108, 117.
49 Povlsen, «Attitude of standsningen in body and text», 93.
50 Povlsen, «Attitude of standsningen in body and text», 105.
51 Povlsen, «Attitude of standsningen in body and text», 107–108.
52 Brown «Ideas ästhetische Entwickelung», 193–271.
53 Fiske, *Television Culture*, 110.
54 Neale, *Genre,* 16.
55 Thwaites, Lloyd & Mules, *Tools for Cultural Studies*, 100.

Bibliography

Abildgaard, Nicolai. "Forsøg til en nye Forklaring over den Marmortavle med Solens Billede, som findes i det Matthæiske Landhuus i Rom, og som Jeron, Aleander, Montfaucon og fleere have beskrevet og forklaret, Af Nicolai Abildgaard." *Minerva*, mai 1793, 277–283.

Andersen, Elin, & Karen Klitgaard Povlsen. *"Det sublime øjeblik".* In *Tableau. The sublime øjeblik*, edited by Elin Andersen and Karen Klitgaard Povlsen. Aarhus: Klim, 2001.

Andersen, Elin. *The Sublime Speech of the Body. About Tableau and Living Image at Diderot, Lessing and Lenz.* Aarhus: Aarhus University Publishing House, 2004.

Boche, Julie. "L'esthetique du comte de Caylus: un nouveau classicisme expressif." *Littératures* 36, printemps (1997): 49–69.

Brown, Friederike. "Idas ästhetische Entwickelung," in: Friederike Brun (ed.), *Wahrheit aus Morgenträumen und Idas ästetische Entwickelund.* Aarau: Sauerländer, 1824.

Bryson, Norman. *Word and Image French Painting of the Ancien Régime.* Cambridge: Cambridge Paperback Library, 1983.

Burke, Peter. "The Sense of Anachronism from Petrarch to Poussin," in: Alexandra Lianeri (ed.), *Time in the Medieval World.* Cambridge: Cambridge University Press, 2011.

Christensen, Charlotte. *The Painter Nicolai Abildgaard.* Copenhagen: Gyldendal, 1999.

Damsholt, Tine. "Staging Emotions – on Configurations of Emotional Selfhood, Gendered Bodies, and Politics in Late Eighteenth Century," *I Structures of Feeling: Affectivity and the Study of Culture*, edited by F. Tygstrup and D. Sharma, 98–115. Berlin: De Gruyters, 2015.

Damsholt, Tine. *Fædrelandskærliged og borgerdyd.* Copenhagen: Museum Tusculanums Publishing House, 2000.

Damsholt, Tine. "Fit to Stir and Lift Up the Heart. Patriotic Tableauer in 1790'rnes Copenhagen," *Tableau. Det sublime øjeblik*, edited by Elin Andersen and Karen Klitgaard Povlsen. Aarhus: Klim, 2001.

Diderot, Denis. "Pensées détachées. Sur la Peinture, la Sculpture, l'Architecture et la Poésie; Pour servir de suite aux Salons," *Œuvres Complètes de Denis Diderot. Tome quatrième*. Paris: Chez A. Belin. 1818

Diderot, Denis. *Œuvres Complètes, Tome IV, X, XIV*. Paris: Hermann [1757] 1980.

Eliassen, Knut Ove. "1809. Tableau," in: Knut Ove Eliassen and Knut Stene-Johansen (eds.), *Ledeord*. Oslo: Cappelen Akademisk Forlag, 2007.

Eriksen, Anne. *Topografenes verden. Fornminner og fortidsforståelse*. Oslo: Pax Forlag, 2007.

Fischer, Erik. "Abildgaard's royal car leader in Christiansborg Riddersal," *Kunstmuseet's Annual journal MCMXCII*. Copenhagen: Statens Museum for Kunst, 1992.

Fiske, John. *Television Culture*. London: Routledge, 1987.

Foley, John Miles. *Oral Tradition and the Internet: Pathways of the Mind*. Champaign: University of Illinois Press, 2012.

Fowler, Alastair. "Genre," in: Erik Branouw (ed.), *International Encyclopedia of Communications*, 215–217, Vol. 2. New York: Oxford University Press, 1989.

Fried, Michael. *Absorption and Theatricality*. Chicago: University of Chicago Press, 1980.

Kragelund, Patrick. *Abildgaard. The Artist between the Rebels*. Volumes 1–2. Copenhagen: Museum Tusculanums Publishing House, 1999.

Krefting, Ellen. "All at a Glance? The Tableau as a Form of Knowledge and Representation at Quesnay, Mercier and Condorcet" *I: Information. Festschrift to Knut Ove Eliassen on his 60th birthday 26 October 2019*, edited by Anne Fastrup, Gunnar Foss and Rolv Nøtvik Jacobsen, 105–118. Oslo: Novus Publishing, 2019.

Kryger, Karin. *Allegory and Civic Virtue. Studies in the Neoclassical Shrine in Denmark 1760–1820*. Copenhagen: Christian Eljers Forlag, 1985.

Leader Balle, Thomas. "Main lines. Nicolai Abildgaard. Krop and Tradition," *Nicolai Abildgaard. The Body in Rebellion*, edited by Thomas Lederballe, Morten Myrone Charlotte Christensen et al., 14–163. Copenhagen: Statens Museum for Kunst, 2009.

Locquin, Jean. *Peinture D'histoire en France de 1747 à 1787*. Paris: Henri Laurens, 1912.

Lyngby, Thomas. *The Sentimental Patriotims. Battle of Reden and H.C. Knudsens Patriotic Acts*. Copenhagen: Museums Tusculanums Forlag, 2001.

Lyngby, Thomas. "Fædrelandskjærligheden's Sensitive Form of Expression. H.C. Knudsens Patriotic Tableauer 1801–14," *Tableau. Det sublime øjeblik*, edited by Elin Andersen and Karen Klitgaard Povlsen. Aarhus: Klim, 2001.

Malling, Ove. *Store og Gode Handlinger af Danske, Norske og Holstenere*. København: Gyldendals Forlag, 1777.

Miranda, Fransisco de. *Miranda i Danmark. Francisco de Miranda's danske rejsedagbog 1787–1788*, oversatt av Kirsten Schottländer og Haavard Rostrup. København: Forlaget Rhodos, 1985.

Nagel, Alexander, & Cristopher S. Wood. *Anachronistic Renaissance*. New York: Zone Books, 2010.

Neale, Stephen. *Genre*. London: British Film Institute, 1980.

Olden-Jorgensen, Sebastian. *Griffenfeld. Prodigy, Statesman, Life Prisoner*. Copenhagen: Gads Publishing, 2006.

Phillips, Mark Salber. *On Historical Distance*. New Haven and London: Yale University Press, 2013.

Phillips, Mark Salber. *Society and Sentiment: Genres of Historical Writing in Britain, 1740–1820*. New Jersey: Princeton University Press, 2000.

Povlsen, Karen Klitgaard. "Standsningens attitude i krop og tekst," *Tableau. The sublime øjeblik*, edited by Elin Andersen and Karen Klitgaard Povlsen. Aarhus: Klim, 2001.

Pollmann, Judith. *Memory in Early Modern Europe, 1500–1800*. Oxford: Oxford University Press, 2017.

Ramdohr, F.W.B. von. *Studien zur Kenntniss der schönen Natur, der schönen Künste, der Sitten und der Statsverfassung aug einer Reise nach Dännemark*. Hanover, 1792.

Stovner, Ina Louise. *Historiske tablåer. En fortellende billedserie i Riddersalen på Christiansborg slott 1778–91*, University of Oslo, PhD thesis, 2021.

Suhm, Peter Frederik. *Historien af Danmark, Norge og Holsten udi tvende Udtog til den studerende Ungdoms Bedste*. København: Lauritz Simmelkjær, 1776.

Teskey, Gordon. *Allegory and Violence*. Itacha and New York: Cornell University Press, 1996.

Thwaites, Tony, Lloyd Davis, & Warwick Mules. *Tools for Cultural Studies: An Introduction*. South Melbourne: Macmillan, 1994.

Part 3

Genres of history and the public sphere

6 Royal historiographer without the title

Niels Ditlev Riegels (1755–1802) and the role of historical genres in the late 18th-century public sphere

Emil Nicklas Johnsen

It has been argued that history writing occupied a central place in the public sphere of late 18th-century Europe.[1] This is also the case in Denmark-Norway. That a flowering in the historical literature took place in the 1770s and onwards was noted already by prominent 19th-century scholars of the growing 18th-century public sphere[2], and it has been further observed by more recent research, that more writers and participants in the public sphere moved toward history writing in the later decades of the century.[3] But what did this history writing look like? It has also been argued that history writing took on a more political tone in the later decades of the century, and that history writing allowed different writers' opinions of the present to be cloaked as discussions of past events in an effective way.[4] What was often referred to as *pragmatic history* was a form of history writing that combined an examination of the deep causes of present or past events, which could be derived from studying the events or characters that took part in them, and a philosophical attitude that one could learn valuable moral, political lessons in the present by studying these causes.[5] Even at the end of the century, pragmatic history shaped the expectations of what history should be. An example of this in Denmark-Norway is a statement by professor of history at the university of Copenhagen, Jørgen Kierulf, who in 1799 wrote that the object of history writing was the study of "occurrences" ("Tildragelser") and that its aim was "to explain the current state of human affairs".[6] In this sense, history writing was concerned with the present as much as with the past, which partly can explain why some influential journals such as *Minerva* in Copenhagen chose to coin its' news section "History"—that is, the history of the last month.[7] This was history writing concerned with how the present came to be what it was, whatever the timeframe. And as such, in the discussions of the current state of human affairs, history writing can arguably be said to have occupied a central place for the participants in the growing public sphere of the late 18th-century Denmark-Norway.

On the other hand, history writing was—and is not—only one thing, that exists in a vacuum. One could rather claim that history writing exists in a textual ecosystem. While it can make sense to view pragmatic history as a genre, history

DOI: 10.4324/9781003331971-10

writing also existed in an evolving print culture together with other literary genres and ways of expression, which means history writing was related to a whole world of other types and forms of texts in the printed public sphere. What different genres are and how they should be understood is notoriously hard to pin down once and for all, not only because they are open to idiosyncrasies, as are all cultural expressions, but because the features of different genres are not always or even seldom explicitly agreed upon.[8] Some conventions of different types of texts or media are stable over time, while others change and are openly negotiated. Genres plays on the expectations of audiences, while merging different genres makes room for the unexpected or for new combinations, a process refered to by Mark Salber Phillips as "reframing" of genres, which underpins the instability and negotiability of literary and artistic genres and gives them a "combinatory dynamic" which can be studied in their historicity.[9] These expectations can take the form of norms or what is to be expected of the author of the text in a specific genre. Thus, I would argue that the expectations of the author and of the texts are interconnected and can be studied through the analytical lens of historical genres. Given what intellectual historian Håkon Evju has coined the eminently political mode of history writing in Denmark-Norway during the late decades of the 18th century, it is timely to investigate how textual strategies worked together with the content of historical depiction and historico-political arguments and rhetoric in the public sphere.[10]

Another important aspect connected to the role of history in the public sphere of late 18th-century Denmark-Norway is the central concern that was put on the moral demands on authors and historians. In Denmark-Norway a growing public sphere came about through political wishes. In 1770, the personal physician of King Christian VII, Johan Friedrich Struensee, sent out a Cabinet Order that explicitly ordered censorship to cease, an order which encouraged public opinion to be formed. No citizen should be hindered in "attacking abuse and exposing prejudice" and seeking the "impartial examination of the truth", it was claimed.[11] A full freedom of the press was thus introduced—the first of its kind in the world.[12] Though the period of full press freedom was short-lived and ended already in 1773, the notion that authors should be given the freedom to pursue a path of patriotic enlightened discourse, was put in motion as a real political possibility.[13] In 1784, the crown prince Frederik (later Frederik VI) came to power together with former foreign minister Andreas P. Bernstorff (1735–1797) in a bloodless coup d'état, and they made it known that they wished press freedom to flourish once more. Though they did not formalize freedom of the press, a 15-year period ensued where negotiations of the limits and conditions of the freedom of the press as well as the desired content of publications took place, which ended in a thorough statement by the government in 1799, which explicitly made it illegal to criticize the government.[14]

Though in some ways less spectacular than the Struensee period, this later 15-year period is as interesting to study to understand the development of the public sphere. Even as limits and conditions were discussed and negotiated by writers and politicians, another aspect was just as important: How should an author—or a historian—address the public sphere? Norms about how to write, how to present oneself and one's mission to public sphere, was of central concern. It is all too often assumed that people know what to do once freedom from restrictions are lifted. On the contrary, few if any forms of cultural expression, political communication, entertainment, in short, any forms of public life, develops overnight. And neither did the public sphere once press freedom was announced.[15]

In this chapter, I will explore the concept of impartiality as an ideal for authors in public sphere and how it was connected to ideals regarding the writing style of historians. Specifically, I will discuss how historical genres could be shaped by author ideals in the public sphere. In order to do this I will examine Danish historian Niels Ditlev Riegels (1755–1802), who was a controversial figure who published extensively in Copenhagen in the 1780s and 1790s, most prominently historical works but also diverse other works of natural history, journalistic pamphlets and self-edited journals. By examining Riegels' writings I aim to contribute to the exploration of the notions of what an historian could be in the public sphere in the late 18th century. By following one particular historian, it becomes possible to study and make clearer how one actor was navigating different genres. As a historian, Riegels tried to live up to ideals as well as challenges norms. It is safe to say he has been regarded as the black sheep in the family of danish historians. In the history of Danish historiography, he has been nicknamed "the most unpleasant of all our historical writers", and he has been placed firmly on the sideline of mainstream historiography when historians have tried to trace the lineage of its own discipline.[16] His attempt to become royal historiographer in Denmark-Norway also failed. But by placing his history writing in the context of the public sphere of his own time, it will be possible to shed light on what part history writing had in the general development of the public sphere in late 18th-century Copenhagen, and how the specific history writing navigated the available genres and expectations in this context.

Royal historiographer without a title

To understand this particular case, some more background on Riegels' peculiar career is necessary. He studied theology in Copenhagen and Kiel in the 1770s and developed during the span of two decades a body of work on church history, royal history, as well as writings on education and natural history. He started his career as a church historian, writing about the development of early Christianity. He was however called to court and employed as a butler for the Pages of Queen widower Juliane Marie in 1781. At court, he became involved in the beforementioned palace coup in 1784, against his employer, the queen widower, who supported the former man in power—Ove Guldberg (1731–1808). During the coup, Riegels was acting as a spy for the coup leaders Bernstorff and the crown prince. Once power had shifted hands, Riegels was awarded a yearly pension of 1200 rigsdaler for the rest of his life, as a token for his services.[17] However, as it turned out, the cost was that he had to depart from the court and seek alternative employment. (Figure 6.1)

Figure 6.1 Copper engraving by Andreas Flint (1767–1824) of historian Niels Ditlev
Riegels (1755–1802), from original painting by famous Danish portraitist
and painter Jens Juel (1745–1802). This engraving was printed in *Læsendes
Aarbog* ('Yearbook for Readers') 1800, depicting the historian as one of
the most high profile writers in Denmark-Norway.

By the time of the coup, he had already published several works of church history. Riegels' ambition was however to be appointed royal historiographer.[18] He started writing two different manuscripts on contemporary matters, meant as an application for the position. One was "A draft to the history of the education of the crown prince Frederik", and the other, "An attempt at an impartial tale of the preparation, origin, means and execution of the change of ministry the 14th of April 1784"—that is, a history of the education and upbringing of his regent and would be employer, as well as an attempt at an impartial history of a recent event in which he had played a significant role himself.[19] Histories written as eye witness accounts by statesmen or politicians was nothing new, and did not stand in the way of it being perceived as impartial. However, Riegels' attempt was seen as too controversial and was never published during his lifetime.[20]

With his ambition, he hoped to wield a substantial influence on politics as royal historiographer. This was not necessarily a given. The office of royal historiographer existed in several monarchies in Europe, from the 16th to 19th centuries.[21] One could ask what it meant to be a royal historiographer at the end of the 18th century, and what the expectations was of such an honorable title. Internationally it varied a great deal. Voltaire was appointed *historiographe de France* in 1745 and put great prestige into this position. However, it has also been claimed that the title bore no significant value other than symbolically, as an honorable post, but with no real task or importance in shaping how the crown or the government was viewed abroad.[22] In the case of Riegels, we have an interesting account by professor of History at the university of Copenhagen, Abraham Kall, who in 1786 was asked to give his opinion on Riegels as a candidate for the title. His opinions sheds light on the expectations associated with the position. Kall wrote:

> By the predicate Royal Danish historiographer, one imagines a man, to which the most important documents of the realm is trusted, from which he will use to promote true patriotic virtue, promote the esteem of the state and respect by strangers. In addition, it is required, that the person, who will carry this name with honor and public usefulness, must have a more than usual righteousness and impartiality, be known for insights into the history of the fatherland and the law of the state, as well as talents for a worthy historical lecture.[23]

The royal historiographers' role was, according to Kall, to promote "true patriotic virtue". The task of the office was to both represent the state and its history abroad, as well as to inspire the public. Kall did not find Riegels a worthy candidate, and instead recommended Peter Frederik Suhm (1728–1798), an older and more established and esteemed historian. It is interesting that Kall described the role of the historiographer in a double manner, encompassing both a representative public role while also engaging with a broader audience. The royal historiographer had both the task of representing the state power in a worthy manner to foreigners, which probably meant writing in Latin or French, as well as a task to address the domestic public and promoting patriotic virtue, more along the lines of Struensee's cabinet order mentioned earlier. Another possible understanding of Kalls statement is that it conveys a sort of double logic, integrating elements of both a sort of representative and a bourgeois public sphere—along the lines of Jürgen Habermas' ideal types.[24] And in Kalls' view, the royal historiographer was supposed to both master the dissemination of the useful and the display of the honorable.

Disappointed by not being given a chance as royal historiographer, Riegels wrote in a letter, that he could nonetheless act as a historiographer "without the title".[25] With the generous pension he was given, he could finance printing and spend his time writing histories for a broader audience. Riegels had arguably hoped to influence the center of power more directly through the office of royal historiographer. His aim was to act as a counselor, utilizing his historical scrutiny and historical narrative to shape politics by direct contact with the rulers.[26] When this did not work out through the position as royal historiographer, he turned to the public sphere and concentrated on what he could achieve there. Though, it is clear, that he continued to try to influence the crown prince through his history writing, even though he published for a larger audience. This kind of political influence wielded by the royal historiographer on the monarch, was not shared by Professor Kall. By writing a history of the education of the crown prince, and *de facto* ruler, Riegels wanted to showcase the mistakes made in the education of the prince (his employer) in a way that made it easier to correct them later. A historical examination could explain the current situation but also secure knowledge to amend them.

Textual history paintings: A journalistic historical genre?

In Riegels' extensive *oeuvre*, his royal histories were the most well known and most complete in his own lifetime. Other notable works are a three-volume church history, published between 1781 and 1786. Another is a history of surgery, that was published in both Latin and Danish in 1786 and 1788.[27] He also notably published in journals and was the editor of *Kiøbenhavns skilderie* ("The Tableau of Copenhagen"), where he wrote most of the contributions himself and where he was engaged in debates on health institutions, agriculture and education.

After being denied a direct canal to the crown as royal historiographer, Riegels instead tried his hand as an author in the public sphere—where he experimented with different roles and genres of historical writing and other writings. As a self-proclaimed royal historiographer without the title, Riegels turned to writing about the reigns of the Danish kings for the broader public. Here he used different strategies. He wrote and published more extensive works on the Danish kings Christian V (1646–1699) and Frederik 4 (1671–1730), where he sought to evaluate the reigns of these monarchs in detail.[28] On the other hand, he wrote works of shorter length, which was more focused on the kings' personal life and upbringing. Among these more biographical works, we find texts about the Danish monarchs Christian II (1481–1559) and Christian IV (1577–1648), which were published in the journal *Borger-Vennen* (*Citizen friend*), one of the journals with the highest print runs in the late 1780s and early 1790s Copenhagen.[29] In this shorter format, he also wrote about queens and other prominent female historical figures. It is not clear if he in the end of the 1780s wrote these historical texts for clearly different audiences compared to the larger volumes on Christian V and Frederik IV. Though he later showed signs that he understood these more biographically oriented historical writings, which he later coined "small historical writings", to be more suited for a larger readership—readers from all classes ("stender").[30] In the preface to *Small historical writings,* he proposed to write history for "wise mothers" and the "unlearned but well-thinking citizens" in contrast to the learned audiences, though as I have argued elsewhere, he mentions the learned audiences and fellow writers in Copenhagen circles too many times to be said to not be addressing them at all.[31] On the other hand, he later expressed hope that he could reach a similar audience with the larger more extensive works as well.[32]

What kinds of textual strategies and practices can be found in Riegels' writings for a broad audience? Here the lens of genres can be of help. Many of the texts Riegels published in his collection "Small historical writings" he called "Skilderier", which can be translated into "Paintings" or "Tableaus". This was the same designation he had used in his pioneering journal *Kiøbenhavns skilderie*, which was clearly inspired by French author Louis-Sebastian Mercier's *Tableau de Paris.* Mercier had wanted to paint a "physionomie morale" of Paris, and so Riegels wanted to do something similar in Copenhagen. The moral state of the people in the city, not the monuments was, according to Mercier, supposed to be in focus in his tableaus, and thus give a portrait of the city from different angles.[33] Riegels started to do something similar, with spectatoresque observations of the street life in market halls, shops, restaurants, etc. Though his journal is much more varied in form than the more stylistically sophisticated Mercier, and the texts in Riegels' journal consists of allegorical tales, treatises on education, journalistic reports from asylums, orphanages—basically, it may seem, whatever suited the author. Mercier sticked to his plan and form. Riegels varied his output in the journal—before he stopped publishing in 1789, after three years. However, something about the journal in its experimentation was carried on in his historical texts. Or else, it would be hard to explain why he decided to designate so many of his historical texts in the same manner as his journal. The journal turned out to be a model for the communicated genre of his historical writings.

Riegels was not the first historian in Denmark to call historical texts "skilderie", Peter Frederik Suhm had called one of his didactical texts a "Skilderie af verden"—"A tableau/painting of the world". Another text published in Danish was a eulogy of the duke Ferdinand Albrecht of Brunsvig-Wolfenbüttel and his deeds during the seven years' war. Several connotations are possible, one possibility is that this word made its way into Danish from the German "Schilderei", which means painting an escutcheon or a plaque. The historian and comedian Ludvig Holberg had also called his comedies a "skilderie" of virtues and vices. That said, there are no other historian or writer using the term as extensively as Riegels does.

The connection to Mercier suggests that "skilderie" (painting) originates from a translation of the French "tableau", but the name can simply mean painting with words. The visual side of the "skilderie" enhanced the importance of the texts capacity for impacting audiences by creating pictures in their minds and thus create an emotional effect.[34] What I would argue is that this genre designation showed that he wanted to utilize what he had developed as a journalist and publisher of the journal further in his historical works. The genre designation "skilderie" was not only a type of text, but was, I would argue, a role, with a built-in project to address audiences in certain ways. The genre was a way of communicating with the audiences, coupled with a self-understanding as author and historian.

Impartiality as an ideal

The development of the public sphere as a text culture in the period where censorship had changed or ceased, and the freedom of speech was negotiated, should also be seen as a frame which meant many authors were developing their writing style. They engaged in discussions not only about how to present their arguments but also about how to address their audiences and even how to portray themselves. Many authors, journalists as well as historians underlined their mission to the public.[35] Paratextual elements such as prefaces often underlined the projects of the authors, their motivation, etc. Even if censorship was repressive, it is not the case that once censorship was lifted, a full-grown public sphere leaped forth immediately. It took time to develop a culture of publicity.[36] So we should not be surprised to find authors experimenting with their texts, self-fashioning their roles and self-presentations as producers of published texts.

An important term for both the author in general as well as for the historian, was "impartiality". The ideal of the impartial author, which was invoked already by Struensee in 1770, was commonplace for historians, stemming from classical ideals championed by the historians of antiquity, by Polybius and Lucian, and again in the 18th century by influential figures such as Hugh Blair and Adam Ferguson.[37] It was frequently utilized to describe the unique qualifications of the historian—most famously by David Hume, who coined "impartial" the most important quality in a historian.[38] The notion of impartiality was also used to justify judgments on matters close to one's own time, but had more to do with a notion of passing a fair judgment than to be objective. It is hard to say whether the ideal of the historian's impartiality influenced the broader ideal. Nonetheless, to be considered as "impartial", the writer who published texts, often insisted that he or she worked for the common good, not his or her own private gains. Rhetorically, this meant that he or she had to make the audience sure that their intentions as authors was not to enhance their private agenda, but only that of the good of society as a whole. In this sense, the ideal of impartiality is far removed from later 19th-century liberal ideal of the public sphere as a sphere where a plurality of different voices seek the truth through rational debate. A critical assessment of this ideal along the lines of what Harold Mah has pointed out about the public sphere in the 18th century in general, is that this rhetoric of the good of society as a whole, was staging particular opinions as universal.[39] This may be the case, still it would be hard to grasp what the norms during the early stages of development of the public sphere in Copenhagen was all about, if these ideals are not taken into consideration. The ideal of impartiality placed the historian and history writing in the center of what the public sphere was all about.

Sympathy and impartiality

The journal *Kiøbenhavns skilderie—The Tableau of Copenhagen*—was on its publication in the late 1780s seen as something entirely new in the public sphere, as a sign that times had changed for the freedom of the press. A contemporary commentary called it a token that "the treasure of the freedom of press" really existed.[40] The texts were directed toward a general readership as well as toward the government—which fit with his ambition as a historiographer without the title, as described earlier. This double direction of addressing a broad audience, as well as the government, was provoking the government as well as challenging the understanding of how the freedom of the press should be used by authors. This makes it even more interesting that Riegels used the designation "skilderie" as a name for his historical works. Did the same assumptions and problems carry from his journal to his historical works?

Riegels' historical works often paint or describes characters, most often royal characters, their upbringing, reigns, deeds, virtues and vices in a way that aims to be memorable and emotionally effective, demonstrating moral or political lessons in each case. This will be more apparent if we look closer at an example.

In the 18th century, Christian II (1481–1559) was a highly controversial king, and not the most acceptable king of the Oldenburg line. Responsible for the Stockholm Bloodbath, where 60Swedish noblemen were executed, Christian II was deposed in 1523 and replaced by Frederik I. In all possible ways, Christian II was an unlikely hero for audiences familiar with the story, as he was often called "Christian the tyrant". Still, Riegels went on to portray him in a sympathetic light, in his first historical "skilderi", published in the patriotic magazine *Borger-Vennen* in 1788, and later in 1796, in the collection "Small historical writings".[41] For Riegels, Christian II brought forth "the rays of enlightenment". In Riegels' hands, Christian II became a progressive hero of the enlightenment, not the least because of what Riegels argues was his dismissive attitude toward noblemen and privileges. The story of

Christians' reign gives Riegels ample opportunity to dwell on the opposition between citizens and nobles—a theme that was well established in critiques of noblemen in the Copenhagen press.[42] This also made sense as a contribution to the journal with the name of "Citizen friend", published by one of the many active patriotic societies of the day.

To strengthen the moral lessons of the story, Riegels published source material as part of the texts. This was not restricted to learned audiences or indeed published for antiquarian reasons, but instead, he stated that he published them for the common reader to take lessons from its reading. In the middle of the biographical account of Christian II, he therefore published the kings trade laws in its entirety. This breaks the narrative in an extraordinary way and put high demands on readers. It also fits badly with the periodicity of the journal, still he insisted on the instructive and moral lessons to be gained from reading them. The trade laws of Christian II showed that a Danish king not necessarily favored the privileges of the nobility, and thus was a monument for state jurisdiction making trade available for a larger part of the population. In his own journal, Riegels did something similar, where he also published in full, the financial instructions of Frederik IV, which he asked the reader to read carefully.[43] Riegels can therefore be seen as an historian publishing source material meant for a broader audience more than an expert elite. And his project was to make the common reader learn moral and political lessons, not only from a historical narrative but also from the sources themselves, thus inviting the reader to become a co-investigator in the sources. The appendices of his larger historical works, where some source material also was published, served a similar purpose, though he is explicitly claiming the publication of several hundreds of pages in the appendix, serves the purpose of making "the Historian" more trustworthy.[44] This shows a strategy where history as *magistra vitae* is not only literary or narrative in form but also makes use of a sort of call to the common reader to go *ad fontes* together with the historian, for moral and political purposes.

After he was deposed in 1523, Christian went abroad and sought support in order to regain his throne. In 1530, he and a small army entered Norway, where he did not succeed particularly well. He was asked to go to Copenhagen to negotiate peace, but there he was arrested and made prisoner for life. The reader of Riegels' text is asked to shed a tear for the fallen king, who sails away as a prisoner from Copenhagen. He is made a hero for the common citizen and farmers—almost a revolutionary king, in the optics of Riegels. Of course, this can be discussed. The absolute monarchy in Denmark-Norway of his day was not necessarily friendly toward the privileges of nobles, and the absolute monarch could legitimize his position by claiming he secured a more just society with equal rights granted to all classes. In the later edition of 1796, Riegels claims, in reference to the events in France, that this is precisely the time to "paint the kings, as they really were, in order to stop the rage against them."[45] The historical portrayal of kings of the past could be used to stop the rage by making them heroes for the ordinary citizen, or virtuous models. But this was not without danger. As historian Marisa Linton has described in the

French context, the ideal of the virtuous citizen king which began to flourish in the latter half of the 18th century, forced kings to live up to an ideal, and thus eulogies put contrasts between ideal and reality in to play, thus contributing as much to hail as to undermine monarchs.[46]

As we have seen so far, Riegels' history writing was addressing, or at least trying to address, both a broader audience, as well as the government and the monarch. However, ideals are not the whole story. In the preface to his *Small historical writings*, Riegels writes that he has received feedback from "wise mothers" that some historical characters in his writings should be viewed as a warning. These are Cleopatra and the queen Sophia Amalia (1628–1685), who reigned together with Frederik III (1609–1670). Among the portraits in *Small historical writings*, the text about Sophia Amalia stands out as more critical to its main character. Riegels took a risk writing about Sophia Amalia and the events of 1660, the year when absolute monarchy was introduced in Denmark-Norway. The queen is here portrayed as the architect of the seizing of more power to the throne and sheds a negative light on her character, her upbringing and role in politics. She is portrayed as the corrupting force at the heart of the state. This text consisted of more critique of absolute monarchy than the heroic portrayal of Christian II.

How can this tendentious creation of heroes and villains be impartial? As I have said earlier, Riegels was rhetorically speaking not in his own name, but in the name of the journal where the text was written—the "Citizen friend". His downright attack on nobles, and blaming them for deposing a legitimate king, was also a strong one-sidedness, that did not escape readers.[47] Still the impartiality did not exclude normative judgments and political verdicts—or even personal attacks. Though Riegels seems to have gone further in testing how far one could go in critiquing the government and specific individuals, than was usual among his contemporaries.

Judging mad houses and royal courts

Many authors in 1780s and 90s Copenhagen claimed that the freedom of the press was a gift from above from the government and that gratitude should be shown. Riegels was one of the authors who challenged this view. Some worried, after reading Riegels journal *Kiøbenhavns skilderie*, that the newly won freedom of the press would lead to satire and the freedom to write pasquils.[48] Is it really necessary, wrote a young Norwegian poet Jens Zetlitz in response to the journal, "to dress truth up like a bogeyman and arm it with the scourge of satire?"[49] For Riegels, the ideal of the writer was to be a force of moral correction in society. This is where he parts more explicitly from his role model Mercier, who made it explicit that he wrote about the moral physiognomy of Paris not to pass judgments, but to study moral phenomenon like a spectator. Riegels' writings are full of concrete judgments and concrete proposals for improvements. To present abuse and disorder to a larger audience, was a central task for the writer in the public sphere he claimed.[50] (Figure 6.2)

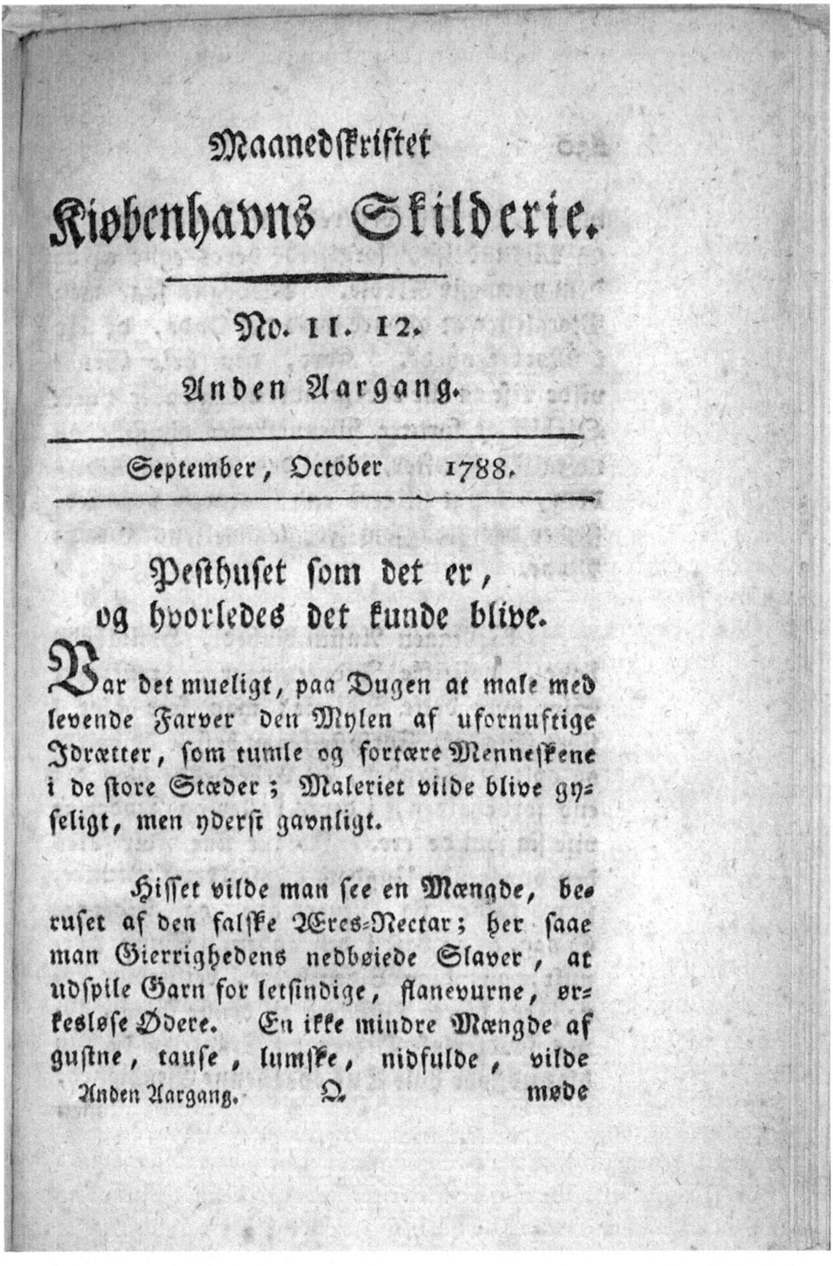

Maanedſkriftet

Kiøbenhavns Skilderie.

No. 11. 12.

Anden Aargang.

September, October   1788.

Peſthuſet ſom det er,
og hvorledes det kunde blive.

Var det mueligt, paa Dugen at male med levende Farver den Mylen af ufornuftige Idrætter, ſom tumle og fortære Menneſkene i de ſtore Stæder ; Maleriet vilde blive gyſeligt, men yderſt gavnligt.

Hiſſet vilde man ſee en Mængde, beruſet af den falſke Æres-Nectar; her ſaae man Gierrighedens nedbøiede Slaver, at udſpile Garn for letſindige, flanevurne, ørkesløſe Ødere. En ikke mindre Mængde af guſtne, tauſe, lumſke, nidfulde, vilde

Anden Aargang.   O.   møde

Figure 6.2 Titlepage for Niels Ditlev Riegels' journal *Kiøbenhavns Skilderie* (*The Tableau of Copenhagen*) number. 11 & 12 1788, where he writes about the unbearable conditions in "Pesthuset", a hospital for the mentally ill. This has been called the first journalistic reportage in Denmark.

This can be exemplified by taking a closer look at one of his most well-known text as a journalist, called "The mental hospital as it is, and as it should be", a text that has been called the first journalistic reportage in Danish.[51] The mental hospital, "St.Hans hospital" was dilapidated, and the residents there were characterized by hunger, worn-out clothes and were according to Riegels living in cramped spaces. Contrary to the intentions of both the government and the foundation that bore the name "Claudi Rosset's foundation", there was an obvious distress and misery at the hospital, and the sight of it was simply bound to move those who saw it, according to Riegels. Here you could see "humanity" being mistreated. So he wrote about the institution in a way that could make the reader witness and see the abuses that was taking place, with his or her own eyes. In the text he walks from room to room, presenting the inhabitants as figures. The hospital housed the deranged ("Gale" and "Vanvittige"), as well as patients with venereal diseases and alcoholics ("Drukkenbolter", that is "Drunkards"). A man, who is constantly banging his head against the wall, should make the reader ask himself why this innocent man who has lost his "reason", should suffer from a poor institution.

This way of showing visually to the audience and readers, what was wrong or at stake, or painting figures as moral warnings or heroes in the journalistic "tableau" ("Skilderie") is also evident in the historical "tableaus" of Riegels. Under the genre designation, Riegels writes a type of history where he uses examples. But there is more than exemplarity at stake. He is critically involved and explicit about the way warnings could be useful to society and the governing of it. This is true of the journal as well as the historical writings.

In the history writings, he is writing like a judge on behalf of posterity. "Posterity calls as a clear-sighted and impartial Judge, Denmark and Norways' King the fifth Christian, before his court of justice."[52] In Riegels view, history keeps the account of the reign of old kings and especially the absolute monarchy. The events of 1660 in Denmark, and the introduction of absolute monarchy not only made the king more powerful but also increased his responsibility for later generations—especially later historians.[53] The Kings' Law of 1665 stated that the king was only to be judged by God. Their actions and reigns were supposed to be judged on judgment day. But some historians and philosophers wanted to anticipate this day through their writings. In classical historians like Tacitus, one could find the ideal of history writing verifying the honor and virtue of persons on behalf of posterity.[54] The historian administers the judgment of posterity, because he or she is bound by the ideal of impartiality but also by the ideal of another credo found in Tacitus *sine ira et studio*—without anger or interest. Already in his first volume of Church history in 1781, Riegels had made it clear that:

Honesty instructs any history writer the same duties as a judge: first impartiality, then respect for the truth, so that he will not easily assume all witnesses accounts, neither drive his doubts too far. The witnesses are in a trial, are the sources or history writers. It is their duty to know, whether my source has the qualities, that it can pass the test, and be seen as trustworthy, to be as dependable as my daily experience to the historical certainty.[55]

The historian is impartial, and can therefore judge, both epistemologically as well as morally and politically. The impartial historian will be able to recognize and call out good and bad government, virtues and vices, in all ages. It is not unlikely this also meant the institutions and phenomenon in his own time, thus making the connection between the journalistic and historical genres of Riegels even more apparent.

Conclusion

In the late 18th century, different genres were a way of communicating with audiences as well as ways of participating in an emerging new public sphere. A soft definition of genre, as a designation of a text, shows that Riegels utilized the same designation on historical as well as other texts. His historical tableaus portrayed characters in sympathetic or critical light. Still, I have tried to show that this was a way of writing history that was shaped by his engagement as a journalist and publisher of journals—though I would also argue that the influence went both ways, that is, that his journalism also was influenced by his historical writing, and that historical writing thus was an important form of writing in the fauna of genres in the evolving public sphere of the 18th century Denmark, and that the "reframing" of different genre designations, as Riegels did, was a way of finding new ways of engaging with audiences.[56]

One could also argue that genres shaped political communication in the late 18th century. The form of the text was made to fit the purpose. Impartiality was an ideal for a writer searching for truth and moral justness. Riegels is an example of a historian who first went for a more official position as historiographer, and when that failed, found the public sphere the next best thing, a substitute for the office of royal historiographer. But as a historian in the public sphere, he discovered new ways of being a historian and found new genres such as the tableau ("skilderie") through his journalistic works. It is therefore safe to say, that his history writing would not have been the same had he not taken part in the developing public sphere of the later years of the 18th-century Denmark-Norway.

As I mentioned in the introduction, earlier research has claimed that history writing was used to conceal political discussions. In the case of Riegels, history writing did not hide political opinions, but was the preferred way to express views on the government and society. In this chapter, I have tried to highlight how the interaction of different types of genres happened in the context of the writings of this active historian in late 18th-century Copenhagen. This is of course significant for the understanding of Riegels' historical writings. But as the writer whose publications across different genres was already in his own time acknowledged as a watershed in the changes that had occurred in the press and public sphere of late 18th-century Copenhagen, it has even more implications, as it shows an important example of how different genres—historical and non-historical (then being employed as historical)—were used to navigate a developing and expanding public sphere.

Notes

1 Sophie Bourgault og Robert Sparling, *A companion to Enlightenment Historiography*, 1–22. Peter Hallberg, *Ages of liberty. Social upheaval, history writing and the new public sphere in Sweden, 1740–1792*, 95–132. Gina Dahl, *Libraries and Enlightenment*, 39–41.
2 Edvard Holm, *Nogle hovedtræk*, 134.
3 Henrik Horstbøll, "Enevælde, opinion, og opposition", 46. Horstbøll, "Civilisation og Nation", 106.
4 Jens Arup Seip. "Teorien om det opinionsstyrte enevælde", 7.
5 Sebastian Olden-Jørgensen, *Ludvig Holberg som pragmatisk historiker*, 22.
6 Jørgen Kierulf, "Professor Kierulfs Program ved Sørgehøitiden over Suhm, oversat af K.R" *Minerva*, 2 (1799): 36–43.
7 Emil Nicklas Johnsen, "I Klios forgård", 57. The instructions of king Frederik IV of 1701 regarding cencorship, stressed that opinions and news should not be mixed. This was still relevant jurisdiction in late 1780s, and may have led this news report to be described as history. Importantly, editor of the journal, Christen Pram, called his writing of the history column an impartial contribution to the public sphere. Pram, "Historien", Minerva, 3 (1787): 399–416, 400. Mona Ringvej, "Trykkefrihetens grenser—På Sporet av en flerstemmig offentlighet i Danmark-Norge før 1814", *Arr. Idéhistorisk tidsskrift* 4 (2008): 103–114, 110.
8 Carolyn Miller, "Genre as Social Action", *Quarterly Journal of Speech* 70 (1984): 151–167, 163. Mark S. Phillips, *On Historical Distance*, 155, emphasizes the "continuous self-renewal" of literary and artistic genres.
9 Mark S. Phillips, *Society and Sentiment. Genres of Historical Writing in Britain,* 20–21.
10 Håkon Evju, *Ancient constitutions and modern monarchy. Historical writing and enlightened reform in Denmark-Norway 1730–1814* (Leiden: Brill, 2019), 280.
11 Quoted in Holm, *Nogle hovedtræk*, 4–6.
12 Ulrik Langen and Frederik Stjernfelt, *The World's First Full Press Freedom. The Radical Experiment of Denmark-Norway 1770–1773*.
13 Krefting et al., *En pokkers skrivesyge*, 175–178.
14 Munck, "Absolute Monarchy in Later Eighteenth-Century Denmark. Centralized Reform, Public Expectations, and the Copenhagen Press", *The Historical Journal* 41, 1 (1998): 201–224. Munck, "Public debate, politics and print. The late enlightenment in copenhagen during the years of the French revolution 1786–1800". *Historisk tidsskrift*. 19, 5 (2014): 323–351.
15 Berge, Kjell Lars. "Developing a new political text culture in Denmark-Norway, 1770–1799", in *Eighteenth Century Periodicals as Agents of Change*, edited by Ellen Krefting, Aina Nøding, and Mona Ringvej, 175–176. (Leiden: Brill, 2015).
16 Caspar Paludan-Müller, "Dansk Historiografi i det 18de Aarhundrede", *Historisk tidsskrift*, 5, 4 (1883–84): 1–188, 148–149.
17 Johnsen, "I Klios Forgård", 141.
18 Morten Petersen, *Oplysningens gale hund,* 81–82.

19 "Udkast til Historien over Dannemarks Skiebne i de sidste 56 Aar". Manuscript in Johan von Bülows private archive, Rigsarkivet Copenhagen. The latter manuscript has only survived in fragments, and these does not concern the events of 1784 at all, but treats the reign of Frederik V only.

20 The manuscript for the education of the crown prince was not published until 2021, in Sebastian Olden-Jørgensen, "Niels Ditlev Riegels: Udkast til Kronprints Frederichs Opdragelses Historie (1786)", *Danske Magazin*, (2021): 9–44. For an in depth discussion of the first of these texts in the history of court history, see Olden-Jørgensens chapter in this volume. "An attempt at a impartial tale of the preparation, origin, means and execution of the change of ministry the 14th of April 1784" was published in 1867 in "Forsøg til en upartisk Fortælling om Forberedelserne, Oprindelsen, Midlerne og Udførelsen af Forandringen i Ministerium d 14. april 1784", trykket i J. Bang, Indbydelsesskrift til den offentlige Examen i Sorø Akademis Skole, 14– 55 (Sorø: Røhrs Bogtrykkeri, 1867). Only the beginning of the text is preserved and published here, which treats its subject up until the time of Frederik V and his government.

21 Chantal Grell, "Les historiographes en France XVe – XVIII^{e}Siècles", in *Les historiographes en Europe. De la fin du Moyen Âge à la Révolution*, edited by Chantal Grell, 127–156 (Paris: Presses de l'université Paris-Sorbonne, 2006), 146.

22 François Fossier, "La charge d'historiographe du seizième au dix-neuvième siècle", *Revue historique*, 258, 1 (1977): 73–92, 80. Chantal Grell, "Introduction", i *Les historiographes en Europe. De la fin du Moyen Âge à la Révolution*, redigert av Chantal Grell, 9–17 (Paris: Presses de l'université Paris-Sorbonne, 2006), 12–13.

23 Quoted in Christian Molbech, "Danske, hidtil utrykte Breve, af og til historisk bekiendte Personer", *Historisk Tidsskrift* 1, 4 (1843): 273–368, 350.

24 Jürgen Habermas, *The Structural Transformation of the Public Sphere*, 5–8.

25 Riegels letter to Johan von Bülow, 16 april 1786. See Johnsen, "I Klios forgård", 31.

26 For the backround for the idea of the historian as political councellor, see Daniel Woolf, *The Idea of history*, 141–145.

27 Niels Ditlev Riegels, *Fuldstændig Kirkehistorie fra Pompeji til Hadriani Tider med Trende Afhandlinger om Jøderne, Hedningene og Gnostikerne, og oplysende Anmærkninger af Riegelsen. Første Deel* (København: Nicolaus Møller, 1781). Niels Ditlev Riegels, *Fuldstændig Kirkehistorie fra Hadrian til Constantin den Stores Død, med en Afhandling om de Christnes Forfølgelser, Martyrer, deres Nytte og deraf opkomne Misbrug, og oplysende Anmerkninger af Riegelsen. Anden Deel* (København: Gyldendals forlag, 1784). Niels Ditlev Riegels, *Fuldstændig Kirkehistorie, indebefattende Arianernes Oprindelse, Skiebne, Lærdom, samt Udtog af deres Skrivter; Iligemaade om Apollinaristerne, Marcellianerne og Photinianerne med en Afhandling om Sønnens evige Fødsel af Faderen; denne Lærdoms Skiebne, især iblant de christne Philosopher; og en Indledning, visende Oplysningens Skiebne til vore Tider, efterat den med Arianerne blev i Kirken ligesom foragtet. Af Riegels. Tredie Deel. Første Bind.* (København: Christian Frederik Holm, 1786). Niels Ditlev Riegels, *Forsøg til Chirurgiens Historie, i Henseende til dens uadskillelige Foreening med Medicinen, og begges borgerlige Anseelse, fra dens Oprindelse af hos Grækerne, Romerne, Araberne, Occidentalerne, indtil 1215, da Hierarchiet foragtede og forjog den. Dernæst om sammes forskieelige Skiebne i Frankrig, indtil dens Ære der stadfæstes ved et Kongl. Academies Oprettelse. Og endelig Chirurgiens lignende Skiebne i Dannemark. Med oplysende Anmærkninger og nogle Bilag, hvoriblandt trende utrykte Breve, og en Tale af Benignus Winslöw. Af Riegels.* (Kiøbenhavn: Christian Friderik Holm, 1786). [Niels Ditlev Riegels], *De fatis faustis et infaustis Chirurgiæ. nec non ipsius interdum indissolubili amicitia cum medicina coeterisque studiis liberalioribus ab ipsius origine ad nostra usque tempora commentatio historica* (Hafniæ: P.M. Höpffneri, 1788).

28 Johnsen, "I Kios forgård", 137–167. Niels Ditlev Riegels, *Forsøg til Femte Christians Historie som en Indledning til Fierde Friderichs ved Etatsraad Høyer af N.D.Riegels* (København: P.M. Høpffner, 1792). Niels Ditlev Riegels, *Udkast til Fierde Friderichs Historie efter Høier af N.D. Riegels. Første Deel* (København: Christian Frederik Holm, 1795). Niels Ditlev Riegels, *Udkast til Fierde Friderichs Historie efter Høier af N.D. Riegels. Anden Deel* (København: C.F. Holms Enke, 1799).
29 Johnsen, "I Kios forgård", 100.
30 Niels Ditlev Riegels, *Smaa historiske Skrifter af N.D. Riegels. Første Deel.* (København: A. Soldins forlag, 1796).
31 Johnsen, "I Kios forgård", 108.
32 Riegels, *Udkast til Fierde Friderichs Historie. Første Deel*, xi.
33 Louis-Sébastien Mercier, *Tableau de Paris*. Nouvelle édition. Corrigée & augmentée. Tome I (Amsterdam, 1782), iii–iv.
34 Ina Louise Stovner, "Tablåets retorikk og estetikk. En didaktisk representasjonsform i andre halvdel av 1700tallet", *Arr. Idéhistorisk tidsskrift* 1 (2021): 79–92.
35 Johnsen, "I Kios forgård", 54 ff.
36 Kjell Lars Berge, "Developing a new political text culture in Denmark-Norway, 1770–1799", i *Eighteenth Century Periodicals as Agents of Change*, edited by Ellen Krefting, Aina Nøding, and Mona Ringvej, 172–184 (Leiden: Brill, 2015), 175–176.
37 Jeffrey Smitten, "Impartiality in Robertson's History of America", *Eighteenth-Century Studies* Vol. 19, 1 (1985): 56–77, 66.
38 Philip Hicks, *Neoclassical History and English Culture*, 9–10.
39 Harold Mah, "Phantasies of the public sphere", 168.
40 "Rigsdalers-Sedlens Hændelser". *Nyeste Kjøbenhavnske Efterretninger om lærde Sager*, 49 (1790): 778–789.
41 [Riegels, Niels Ditlev]. "Skilderie af Christian den Anden", *Borger-Vennen, 36* (1789): 279–283.[Riegels, Niels Ditlev]. "Malerie af Christian den 4de, Konge i Dannemark og Norge", in *Borger-Vennen*, 17–18 (1788):129–141.
42 Håkon Evju, "Et spørsmål om ære. Adelskritikk i dansk-norske tidsskrifter på 1790-tallet". In *Kritikk før 1814*, edited by Eivind Tjønneland, 317–328. Oslo: Dreyer, 2014.
43 [Riegels], "1700 den 9de Januarii. Instruction", Kiøbenhavns skilderie, 10–12 (1789): 232–247. [Riegels], "Hvorfore er dette sidste Nummer af Kiøbenhavns Skilderie", 215.
44 Riegels, *Fierde Friderichs Historie*, vii.
45 Riegels, *Smaa historiske Skrifter. Første Deel*, 158. Though I am not analyzing them here, Riegels published a smaller two volume work called "Historical paintings" in 1799, with an explicit moral goal of painting histories in order for the text to be "a guide to virtue on the path of life". Riegels, *Historiske Malerier, som Veiviser til Dyd paa Livets Bane, fremsatte I Fortællinger af N.D.Riegels. Første Hefte.* (København: J.H. Schubothes Forlag, 1799). Riegels, *Historiske Malerier, som Veiviser til Dyd paa Livets Bane, fremsatte i Fortællinger af N.D.Riegels. Andet Hefte* (København: J.H. Schubothes Forlag, 1799).
46 Marisa Linton, The politics of virtue (Houndmills, Basingstoke: Palgrave, 2001), 168–69. Marisa Linton, "The unvirtuous King? Clerical Rhetoric on the French Monarchy, 1760–1774", *History of European Ideas*, 1–2 (1999): 55–74, 56: "Changes in the strategic use of the concept of kingly virtue may have done as much or more to undermine the idea of a sanctified monarchy and to destabilize monarchical authority as did the scurrilous accounts of kingly vice that emanated from 'Grub street'." See this in contrast to Robert Darnton, *The Forbidden Best-Sellers of pre-revolutionary France* (Glascow: Harper Collins, 1996), 216: "(…) like the drip of water on a stone, the denunciations of dissolute kings and wicked

ministers wore away the layer of sacredness that made the monarchy legitimate in the eyes of its subjects."

47 This was the verdict of Christian Molbech (1783–1857), the Danish nestor historian of the first part of the 19th century. Johnsen, "I Klios forgård", 15.

48 Johnsen, "I Klios forgård", 95.

49 Jens Zetlitz, "Til Forfatteren af Kiøbenhavns skilderie", *Samleren,* 2, 51 (1788): 409–414. Other more senior readers reacted similarly, like the politician August Hennings.

50 [Riegels], "Om Opdragelsen, helst den huuslige", 227. Riegels, *Smaa historiske Skrifter. Tredie Deel,* 569. Riegels, Smaa historiske Skrifter. Tredie Deel, 553.

51 Petersen, *Oplysningens gale hund,* 157. [Niels Ditlev Riegels], "Pesthuset som det er, og hvorledes det kunde blive", Kiøbenhavns Skilderie 11,12 (1788): 229–286.

52 Riegels, *Forsøg til Femte Christians Historie,* 1. Carl Becker, in his *The heavenly city of the eighteenth century philosophers,* claimed the idea of "posterity" for the enlightenment replaced God and the Christian doctrine of salvation, and was an integral part of a secularized religiosity. Sven Delblanc has traced the idea of posterity as a court of appeal, as connected to a notion of the only place honor and dignity could be procured. Delblanc, "Ära och minne", 70.

53 Riegels, *Forsøg til Femte Christians Historie,* 4: "at spille en Rulle, hvorved han mægtigen forøgede sit og Efterkommernes Ansvar, som Regentere; thi han giorde ved den arvelige Enevælde næsten paa en uafbetalelig Maade dem og sig evig gieldbundne til Efterverdenen."

54 *Suum cuique decus posteritas rependit (An.,* 4.35.3). See Harold Parker, *The Cult of Antiquity and the French Revolutionaries,* for how much inspiration radical thinkers in France took from Tacitus. About Tacitus as a role model, see Bo Lindberg, "Tacitism in theory and practice", in *Acta Conventus Neo-Latini Upsaliensis,* (Leiden: Brill, 2012).

55 Riegels, *Fuldstændig Kirkehistorie,* 32–33: "Redelighed paalægger enhver Historieskriver samme Pligter, som en Dommer: først Upartiskhed, dernest Ærbødighed for Sandheden, at han ei let overtar alle Vidners Udsigende, ei heller driver sin Tvivlelyst for vidt. De Vidner ere i Rettergang, ere Kilderne eller Historieffrivere. Det paaligger da at vide, om min Kilde har de Egenskaber, at den kan udstaae Prøve og ansees for troværdig efter den bliver Historiens Vished lige saa uryggelig, som min daglige Erfaring."

56 Phillips, *Society and sentiment,* 13–14, 21.

Bibliography

Berge, Kjell Lars. "Developing a New Political Text Culture in Denmark-Norway, 1770 1799." In *Eighteenth Century Periodicals as Agents of Change,* edited by Ellen Krefting, Aina Nøding, and Mona Ringvej, 175–176. Leiden: Brill, 2015.

Becker, Carl. *The Heavenly City of the Eighteenth Century Philosophers.* Yale: Yale University Press, 2003.

Bourgault, Sophie og Robert Sparling (red.). *A Companion to Enlightenment Historiography.* Brill: Leiden, 2013.

Bülows collection of manuscripts at Sorø Akademis Bibliotek.

Dahl, Gina. *Libraries and Enlightenment. Eighteenth-Century Norway and the Outer World.* Aarhus: Aarhus University Press, 2014.

Darnton, Robert. *The Forbidden Best-Sellers of Pre-revolutionary France.* Glasgow: Harper Collins, 1996.

Delblanc, Sven. "Ära och minne." *Studier kring ett motivkomplex i 1700-talets litteratur.* Uppsala/Stockholm. 1965.

Evju, Håkon. *Ancient Constitutions and Modern Monarchy. Historical Writing and Enlightened Reform in Denmark-Norway 1730–1814*. Leiden: Brill, 2019.

Evju, Håkon. "Et spørsmål om ære. Adelskritikk i dansk-norske tidsskrifter på 1790-tallet." *I Kritikk før 1814*, edited by Eivind Tjønneland, 317–328. Oslo: Dreyer, 2014.

Fossier, François. "La charge d'historiographe du seizième au dix-neuvième siècle." *Revue historique*, 258, 1 (1977): 73–92.

Grell, Chantall (red.). *Les historiographes en Europe de la fin du moyen Âge à la Révolution*. Paris: Presses de l'université Paris-Sorbonne, 2006.

Habermas, Jürgen. *The Structural Transformation of the Public Sphere. An Inquiry into a Category of Bourgeois Society*. Cambridge: Polity, 1989.

Hallberg, Peter. *Ages of Liberty. Social Upheaval, History Writing and the New Public Sphere in Sweden, 1740–1792*. Stockholm: Stockholm Studies in Politics 92, 2003.

Hicks, Philip. *Neoclassical History and English Culture*, 9–10.

Holm, Edvard. *Nogle hovedtræk af trykkefrihedens historie. 1770–1773*. Reprografisk gjenutgitt og forlagt af Selskabet for udgivelse af kilder til dansk historie 1975. København, 1885.

Horstbøl, Henrik. "Civilisation og Nation." In *Danmarks historie. Bind 10. Historiens historie*, edited by Søren Mørch, 102–180. København: Gyldendal, 1992.

Horstbøl, Henrik. "Enevælde, opinion og opposition." *Historie/Jyske samlinger* 17, (1987): 35–53.

Johnsen, Emil Nicklas. "I Klios forgård. Forfatterroller, offentlighet og politisk evaluering i Niels Ditlev Riegels' (1755–1802) historieskriving." PhD, University of Oslo, Det humanistiske fakultet, Institutt for filosofi, idé- og kunsthistorie og klassiske språk, 2019.

Kierulf, Jørgen. "Professor Kierulfs Program ved Sørgehøitiden over Suhm, oversat af K.R." *translated from Latin by Knud Lyhne Rahbek*. *Minerva* 4 (1799): 36–43.

Krefting, Ellen, & Aina Nøding og Mona Ringvej (eds.). *En pokkers skrivesyge. 1700-tallets dansk norske tidsskrifter mellom sensur og ytringsfrihet*. Oslo: Scandinavian Academic Press, 2014.

Krefting, Ellen, & Aina Nøding og Mona Ringvej (eds.). *Eighteenth Century Periodicals as Agents of Change. Perspectives on Northern Enlightenment*. Leiden: Brill, 2015.

La Vopa, Anthony J. "Conceiving a Public: Ideas and Society in Eighteenth-Century Europe." *Journal of Modern History* 64 (1992): 79–116.

Langen, Ulrik & Frederik Stjernfelt. *The World's First Full Press Freedom. The Radical Experiment of Denmark-Norway 1770–1773*. Berlin/Boston: De Gruyter, 2022.

Lindberg, Bo. "Tacitism in Theory and Practice." In *Acta Conventus Neo-Latini Upsaliensis*. Leiden, The Netherlands: Brill, 2012.

Linton, Marisa. *The Politics of Virtue*. Houndmills, Basingstoke: Palgrave, 2001.

Linton, Marisa. "The Unvirtuous King? Clerical Rhetoric on the French Monarchy, 1760–1774." *History of European Ideas*, 1–2 (1999): 55–74.

Mercier, Louis-Sébastien. *Tableau de Paris*. Nouvelle édition. Corrigée & augmentée. Tome I. Amsterdam, 1782.

Molbech, Christian. "Danske, hidtil utrykte Breve, af og til historisk bekiendte Personer." *Historisk Tidsskrift* 1, 4 (1843): 273–368, 350.

Miller, Carolyn. "Genre as Social Action." *Quarterly Journal of Speech* 70 (1984): 151–167.

Munck, Thomas. "Absolute Monarchy in Later Eighteenth-Century Denmark: Centralized Reform, Public Expectations, and the Copenhagen Press." *The Historical Journal* 41, 1 (1998): 201–224.

Munck, Thomas. "Public Debate, Politics and Print. The Late Enlightenment in Copenhagen During the Years of the French Revolution 1786–1800." *Historisk tidsskrift*. 19, 5 (2014): 323 351.

Olden-Jørgensen, Sebastian. *Ludvig Holberg som pragmatisk historiker. En historiografisk kritisk undersøgelse.* København: Museum Tusculanums forlag, 2015.

Olden-Jørgensen, Sebastian. "Niels Ditlev Riegels: Udkast til Kronprints Frederichs Opdragelses Historie (1786)." *Danske Magazin*, (2021): 9–44.

Parker, Harold. *The Cult of Antiquity and the French Revolutionaries.* New York: Octagon Books, 1965.

Paludan-Müller, Caspar. "Dansk Historiografi i det 18de Aarhundrede." *Historisk tidsskrift* 5, 4 (1883–84): 1–188.

Petersen, Morten. *Oplysningens gale Hund. Niels Ditlev Riegels. Oprører, kirkehader og kongeskænder. 1755–1802. En biografi.* København: Aschehoug, 2003.

Phillips, Mark Salber. *On Historical Distance.* New Haven & London: Yale University Press, 2013.

Phillips, Mark Salber. *Society and Sentiment. Genres of Historical Writing in Britain, 1740–1820.* Princeton, N.J.: Princeton University Press, 2000.

Pram. "Historien." *Minerva* 3 (1787): 399–416.

Rahbek, Knud Lyhne. "Literatur." *Minerva* 1 (1785): 86.

Riegels, Niels Ditlev. "1700 den 9de Januarii. Instruction." *Kiøbenhavns skilderie* 10–12 (1789): 232–247.

Riegels, Niels Ditlev, & Niels Ditlev Riegels. *Bager Madses Brev-Taske.* København: Christian Frederik Holm, 1789.

Riegels, Niels Ditlev. Brev til Johan von Bülow, 16. April 1786. Bülows Manuskriptsamling i Sorø Akademis Bibliotek, 37d/1–6.

Riegels, Niels Ditlev, & Niels Ditlev Riegels. *De fatis faustis et infaustis Chirurgiæ. nec non ipsius interdum indissolubili amicitia cum medicina coeterisque studiis liberalioribus ab ipsius origine ad nostra usque tempora commentatio historica.* Hafniæ: P.M. Höpffneri, 1788.

Riegels, Niels Ditlev. "Forsøg til en upartisk Fortælling om Forberedelserne, Oprindelsen, Midlerne og Udførelsen af Forandringen i Ministerium d 14. april 1784.", trykket i J. Bang, *Indbydelsesskrift til den offentlige Examen i Sorø Akademis Skole*, 14–55. Sorø: Røhrs Bogtrykkeri, 1867.

Riegels, Niels Ditlev. *Forsøg til Chirurgiens Historie, i Henseende til dens uadskillelige Foreening med Medicinen, og begges borgerlige Anseelse, fra dens Oprindelse af hos Grækerne, Romerne, Araberne, Occidentalerne, indtil 1215, da Hierarchiet foragtede og forjog den. Dernæst om sammes forskieelige Skiebne i Frankrig, indtil dens Ære der stadføstes ved et Kongl. Academies Oprettelse. Og endelig Chirurgiens lignende Skiebne i Dannemark. Med oplysende Anmærkninger og nogle Bilag, hvoriblandt trende utrykte Breve, og en Tale af Benignus Winslöw. Af Riegels.* Kiøbenhavn: Christian Friderik Holm, 1786.

Riegels, Niels Ditlev. *Forsøg til Femte Christians Historie som en Indledning til Fierde Friderichs ved Etatsraad Høyer af N.D.Riegels.* København: P.M. Høpffner, 1792.

Riegels, Niels Ditlev. *Fuldstændig Kirkehistorie fra Pompeji til Hadriani Tider med Trende Afhandlinger om Jøderne, Hedningene og Gnostikerne, og oplysende Anmærkninger af Riegelsen. Første Deel.* København: Nicolaus Møller, 1781.

Riegels, Niels Ditlev. *Fuldstændig Kirkehistorie fra Hadrian til Constantin den Stores Død, med en Afhandling om de Christnes Forfølgelser, Martyrer, deres Nytte og deraf opkomne Misbrug, og oplysende Anmerkninger af Riegelsen. Anden Deel.* København: Gyldendals forlag, 1784.

Riegels, Niels Ditlev. *Fuldstændig Kirkehistorie, indebefattende Arianernes Oprindelse, Skiebne, Lærdom, samt Udtog af deres Skrivter; Iligemaade om Apollinaristerne, Marcellianerne og Photinianerne med en Afhandling om Sønnens evige Fødsel af Faderen; denne Lærdoms Skiebne, især iblant de christne Philosopher; og en Indledning, visende Oplysningens Skiebne til vore Tider, efterat den med Arianerne blev i Kirken ligesom foragtet. Af Riegels. Tredie Deel. Første Bind.* København: Christian Frederik Holm, 1786.

Riegels, Niels Ditlev. *Historiske Malerier, som Veiviser til Dyd paa Livets Bane, fremsatte i Fortællinger af N.D. Riegels. Første Hefte.* København: J.H. Schubothes Forlag, 1799.

Riegels, Niels Ditlev. *Historiske Malerier, som Veiviser til Dyd paa Livets Bane, fremsatte i Fortællinger af N.D. Riegels. Andet Hefte.* København: J.H. Schubothes Forlag, 1799.

Riegels, Niels Ditlev, & Niels Ditlev Riegels. "Hvorfore er dette sidste Nummer af Kiøbenhavns Skilderie." *Maanedsskriftet Kiøbenhavns Skilderie.* København: Christian Friderich Holm, 1787–1790.

Riegels, Niels Ditlev, & Niels Ditlev Riegels. "Malerie af Christian den 4de, Konge i Dannemark og Norge." *Borger-Vennen* 17–18 (1788): 129–141.

Riegels, Niels Ditlev, & Niels Ditlev Riegels. *Maanedsskriftet Kiøbenhavns Skilderie.* København: Christian Friderich Holm, 1787–1790.

Riegels, Niels Ditlev, & Niels Ditlev Riegels. "Om Opdragelsen, helst den huuslige." *Kiøbenhavns Skilderie* 7–10 (1788): 85–227.

Riegels, Niels Ditlev, & Niels Ditlev Riegels. "Pesthuset som det er, og hvorledes det kunde blive." *Kiøbenhavns Skilderie* 11, 12 (1788): 229–286.

Riegels, Niels Ditlev, & Niels Ditlev Riegels. "Skilderie af Christian den Anden." *Borger Vennen* 1–2, 36–10 (1789): 279–284.

Riegels, Niels Ditlev. *Smaa historiske Skrifter af N.D. Riegels. Første Deel.* København: A. Soldins forlag, 1796.

Riegels, Niels Ditlev. *Smaa historiske Skrifter af N.D. Riegels. Tredie Deel.* København: A. Soldins forlag, 1798.

Riegels, Niels Ditlev. *Udkast til Fierde Friderichs Historie efter Høier af N.D. Riegels. Første Deel.* København: Christian Frederik Holm, 1795.

Riegels, Niels Ditlev. *Udkast til Fierde Friderichs Historie efter Høier af N.D. Riegels. Anden Deel.* København: C.F. Holms Enke, 1799.

Riegels, Niels Ditlev. "Udkast til Historien over Dannemarks Skiebne i de sidste 56 Aar." Håndskrift. Johan von Bülows privatarkiv, Rigsarkivet.

Riegels, Niels Ditlev, Niels Ditlev Riegels & Aben Esra. "Udtog af en reisende Rabiners Brev, i Anledning af Medaillerne den 24 April 1798, sendte til Religionens Venner Bisp Balle og Bispinden og til Statens Ven Magister Boye i Naschau." *Politisk og physisk Magazin* 11 (1798): 744–752.

"Rigsdalers-Sedlens Hændelser". *Nyeste Kjøbenhavnske Efterretninger om lærde Sager* 49 (1790): 778–789.

Ringvej, Mona. "Trykkefrihetens grenser – På Sporet av en flerstemmig offentlighet i Danmark-Norge før 1814." *Arr. Idéhistorisk tidsskrift* 4, (2008): 103–114.

Seip, Jens Arup. *Teorien om det opinionsstyrte enevelde.* Oslo: Universitetsforlaget, 1958.

Sennett, Richard. *The Fall of Public Man.* London: Penguin, 2002.

Smitten, Jeffrey. "Impartiality in Robertson's History of America." *Eighteenth-Century Studies* 19, 1 (1985): 56–77, 66.

Stovner, Ina Louise. "Tablåets retorikk og estetikk. En didaktisk representasjonsform i andre halvdel av 1700-tallet." *Arr. Idéhistorisk tidsskrift* 1 (2021): 79–92.

Tacitus, Cornelius. *The Annals. The Loeb Classical Library.* Cambridge, Mass: Harvard University Press, 1937.

Tode, Johan Clemens. "Et Par Ord om Skriftet: Afhandling om Veisenhusets Gienoprettelse, først indrykket i Iris for Dec. 1795." *Iris og Hebe* 1 (1796): 117–119.

Woolf, Daniel. *The Idea of History in Early Stuart England.* Toronto, 1990.

Zetlitz, Jens. "Til Forfatteren af Kiøbenhavns skilderie." *Samleren* 2, 51 (1788): 409–414.

7 From amusement to study?

Historical genres in the 18th-century essay periodical press

Claire Boulard Jouslin

It seems that in 18th-century England the modern conception of history defined as distinct from fiction and as some neutral account of facts had long coexisted with more fictional historical genres such as poetry, drama, martyrologies and secret histories.[1] Recent scholarship has discussed many of these historical genres.[2] Yet, one genre, namely the genre of the essay periodical which emerged in the early 18th century, seems not to have commanded much attention in its relation to history.

This article purports to examine the interplay between history and the essay periodical in the 18th century starting with the most famous and most influential of them all, Joseph Addison's and Richard Steele's *Spectator* (1711–1712; 1714). Its aim is to trace the influence the *Spectator*'s conception of historical representation exercised on later periodicals, and particularly on two women's monthly journals: Eliza Haywood's *Female Spectator* (1744–45), and Charlotte Lennox's *The Lady's Museum* (1760–61).

To do this, this study will follow a double line of argument. First, the *Spectator*'s general use of visual narrative turned the journal into a highly historical genre which offered a national narrative in its own semi-fictional way. Second, the *Spectator* argued that women's visual faculty was flawed. The *Spectator* implicitly inferred that women's sight prevented them from producing valuable historical narratives and led them to produce immoral and deficient narratives. As a result, it seems that this discourse was currently held to denounce the scandalous subhistorical genre of secret memoirs female writers were accused of writing.

This essay therefore offers to examine the way Haywood and Lennox, who published history in their periodicals, reconciled writing history with femininity and contributed both to popularising history among female readers as well as to defending women's rights to produce and make history in the way they thought fit.

This will eventually lead to the contention that beyond the commercial imperative of entertaining readers, the persistence of various genres of fictionalised history in essay periodicals reveals that the narration of history was always considered a major and serious study for women writers. D. R. Woolf's argument

DOI: 10.4324/9781003331971-11

in his otherwise seminal article "From Hystories to the historical," that women's conception of polite history passed from an amusement to a serious object of study,[3] which was reflected by the emergence of professional female historians after 1770, needs therefore to be qualified.

The essay periodical as a historical genre

It may seem a bit farfetched to argue that the Spectatorial essay could constitute a historical genre since past historical events, and in particular, English political events are hardly mentioned in the *Spectator*. However, browsing through the 635 issues of this daily periodical one finds the following illuminating statement:

> It is the most agreeable Talent of an Historian, to be able to draw up his Armies and fight his Battels in proper expressions, *to set before our Eyes* (my emphasis) Divisions, Cabals, and Jealousies of Great Men, and to lead us Step by Step into the several Actions and Events of his History. *We love to see* the Subject unfolding it self by just Degrees, [...] I confess this shews more the Art than the Veracity of the Historian, but I am only to speak of him as he is qualified to please the Imagination. And in this respect, Livy, has, perhaps excelled all who ever went before him, or have written since his Time. He describes every thing in so lively a manner, that his whole History is an admirable Picture, and touches on such proper Circumstances in every Story, that his reader becomes a kind of Spectator, and feels in himself all the variety of Passions, which are correspondent to the several Parts of the Relation.[4]

There are three points in this quote which are striking. Firstly, it is significant the *Spectator* argues that a historical narrative is more pleasant and instructive as it is visual because it then turns historical texts into pictures and readers into spectators and eye-witnesses. As the title *The Spectator* announced, vision and sight were core values in the periodical: Mr Spectator, the editor, defines himself as "a spectator of mankind" (S.1) and transfers his observation into essays he called "speculations" (*S.* 3). The *Oxford English Dictionary* defines speculation as vision. As a consequence, it seems that essays, being a visual form of writing, are most adapted to history writing.

At the same time, Addison associates historical matter with the imagination. This quote is indeed extracted from the famous series of essays devoted to the pleasures of the imagination in which Addison explained, following John Locke, that all forms of artistic pleasures are derived from the sight [5]. A good historical narrative is therefore able to conjure up scenes in the imagination of the reader, and has the same imaginative function as fiction or art. Mr. Spectator, the eidolon, makes it clear that the dividing line between history and story, or facts and fiction may be blurred: "I confess this shews more the Art than the Veracity of the Historian" (S. 420). But he dismissed such blurring as unimportant, considering rhetoric and therefore the narrative to be more valuable than factual veracity. This interplay of fiction, history, the genre of the essay and vision is a founding element of the periodical as it is embodied by Mr. Spectator himself who "open(s) the Work with my own History," his fictitious autobiography.[6]

Lastly, it seems also quite significant that Addison should recommend to imitate the style of an ancient historian, Livy.[7] This means that whatever the subject matter of modern history, the latter is not radically different from ancient history as the aim of history is to display facts and make the reader "feel in himself all the variety of passions" to become polite.

Such definition of historical writing sheds light on the very specific way history is narrated in the *Spectator*. History features as allegories. The latter rewrite ancient historical texts which provide readers with a more general,—nearly universal—history of mankind in essays that particularly rely on visual device.

Spectator essays 433 and 434 are a case in point. They explain how the republic of the Amazonian tribe eventually incorporated with the republic of the Scythians and "became the most flourishing and Polite Government in the part of the World which they Inhabited."[8] Indeed, these two essays, which include an introductory paragraph about the complementary nature of men and women, constitute a fictional visual rewriting of Herodotus's *History*.[9] Like Livy, Mr. Spectator retells history by using two visual literary genres: allegory and character.[10] Each republic stands for the virtues and defects of each sex which are conjured up through character-like descriptions of the protagonists. Thus the Amazons are depicted as an unnatural commonwealth of viragos which trains its daughters in brutal and manly arts and which is progressively taught by men to redirect their energy to more suitably feminine activities; while the republic of men is a society of rough warriors who are encouraged to be as unrefined as possible:

> I find the Name of a Minister of State in one part of their history, who was fined for appearing too frequently in clean Linnen; and of a certain great General who was turned out of his post for Effeminacy, it having been proved upon him by several credible Witnesses that he washed his Face every Morning.[11]

The overall effect of this narrative is one that a good historical narrative is expected to produce: it entertains the more learned reader with a parody of an ancient text and the common reader with a satire of romp girls and rustic men while it gives food for thought to all readers about politeness, a subject that was both highly topical and political. Indeed, the Whig faction contended that only cultivation of manner and politeness could deflate party divisions and shelter the kingdom from potentially harmful behaviours.[12]

In that context, readers could plainly see that beneath the pleasant moral and allegorical surface, there were coded allusions targeting specific contemporary policies. The general turned out of his post was an allusion to the Whig

Duke of Marlborough, commander general of the British army who had been dismissed from the government by Queen Anne after the Tory landslide in the 1709 general election.[13] In the same way, at a time when many Tory ladies vindicated their political support to the Tory and Church faction, ridiculing the Amazonian tribe and its senate may well have been an indirect attack on Tory female political activism and a warning that it was highly unnatural and potentially dangerous.[14] To promote feminine moderation and domesticity and masculine refinement as complementary was therefore an allegorical way of recalling the necessity for both sexes but also for both political parties to reconcile and live together in harmony. It was also a way to promote commerce (understood in all its meanings—economic as well as social and moral) as the solution to guarantee the nation's harmony and prosperity, an argument that was largely held by the Whigs. Thus, these historical essays show that politeness —the most refined form of commerce—had been acknowledged since antiquity as a political and social necessity. And they reminded readers of the usefulness of history and of its capacity of giving lessons well beyond its own epoch.

Furthermore, Mr. Spectator also hinted that the spectatorial essay genre was quintessentially historical because Mr. Spectator had the qualities of a good historian: impartial, writing speculative thoughts, he, like historians, who "are obliged to follow Nature more closely, and to take entire Scenes out of her [...] ha(s)ve the high satisfaction of beholding all Nature with an unprejudic'd eye; and having nothing to do with Mens Passions or Interests, I can with the greater Sagacity consider their Talents, Manners, Failings, and Merits."[15] As *The Spectator* reports and comments upon stories relating to the everyday life of all ranks of society, each essay may be considered a part of a serialised social micro-history of early 18th-century England.

Essay 101 confirms this hypothesis. Lamenting the party spirit of contemporary historians, Mr. Spectator falls into daydreaming about what a future unbiased historian would write about the late Stuart society using the *Spectator* as a primary source of information. It is noteworthy that this essay does not provide a narrative of the main political events: instead, it brushes in various strokes the picture of the everyday life of his contemporaries. The essay thus constitutes a synecdoche of the journal and one may consider that each new essay achieves the completion of the general picture and thus transforms *The Spectator* into a history book. Mr Spectator imagines the future historian's comments on the *Spectator* essays: "as for his Speculations, notwithstanding the several obsolete Words and obscure Phrases of the Age in which he lived, we still understand enough of them to see the Diversions and Characters of the English Nation in his time."

One could object that this essay was a mere joke and that defining the *Spectator* as a social history book is stretching the analysis a little too far. Yet Addison's insistence on distancing through obsolete words along with the stress on emotional familiarity with readers created through the sense of sight suggests that he did separate past from present, which is now commonly believed to be the mark of modern history as an independent field.[16]

This essay equally shows that Addison had the intuition that the everyday and private life and mores of his contemporaries—as much as the spectacular pageantry of politics—could make the subject matter of a historical narrative that constructed a national identity too. In this, he was ahead of his time since it is one of the characteristics of social history to acknowledge that present microcosms also make a historical matter that can be analysed with historical tools. Moreover, recording this history in a two-pence periodical sheet meant that the journal popularised a type of easy-to-read (visual?) history which on the one hand, widely differed from the one recorded by historians—who transcribed "the spectacular politics" of pageantry in heavy and costly volumes. On the other hand, the periodical's spectacular and moral history also offered readers an alternative to the genre of the secret history, another type of visual and intimate history of the people that was both highly political and risqué and that described reality in fictional terms.

Now, like many of his contemporaries, the *Spectator* associated the latter type of history—considered as scandalous and fictional gossip—to women writers, an opinion that partly originated in the fact that the author of one of the best sellers of the period, the *Secret Memoirs of the New Atalantis* was a woman, Mary Manley de la Rivière. The *Spectator* also attributed the intimate connexion between the genre of the secret history and femininity to another cause. It suggested that such fraught history could only be produced by women because they had a deficient eye sight. In essay 252, Mr. Spectator published a letter from a female correspondant, Mary Heartfree, a self-proclaimed specialist of the language of women's eyes. She reported the devious ways with which her acquaintances used their sight: "The eye of Leonora is slyly watchful while it looks negligent; she looks round her [...] and yet seems to be employed on Objects directly before her [...] There is a brave soldier's Daughter in Town, that by her Eye has been the Death of more than ever her Father made fly before him."

So, it is clear that beyond denouncing the corruption of these young women's gaze, Mary Heartfree's aim is to slander her neighbours through her written observations of their private life. She too has faulty eyesight. Significantly, she concludes her letter promising: "if you do me the Honour to print this among your Speculations, I shall in my next, make you a present of secret History, by translating all the Looks of the next Assembly of Ladies and Gentlemen into Words, to adorn some future Paper." The conclusion that readers were encouraged to draw then was that, unlike Mr. Spectator who observed his contemporaries write a day-to-day history that aimed at reforming and instructing readers at once, women who attempted to dabble with micro-history were inappropriate historians.

This opinion was to prevail, for years later in his *Moral and political Essays*, the historian David Hume denounced women's improper curiosity and love for secret histories and denied that the genre was a historical genre.[17] He thus reasserted this implicit assertion that women could not write proper serious history. However, Hume also encouraged women to change their reading habits and to read standard history because, he claimed, being amusing and instructive, history is perfectly adapted to the light intellect of female readers.[18]

With this context in mind, it is, therefore, all the more remarkable that two mid-18th-century periodicals written by two women—Eliza Haywood and Charlotte Lennox—and primarily targeting a female audience, should take up the *Spectator*'s formula on the one hand, and should also deal with both social and traditional history on the other. This raises the following questions: How did they reconcile writing history with the *Spectator*'s prejudice about women's visual inability to write history? What sort of history did they write? And what was their purpose in writing history in their magazines?

Reconciling visual history and secret memoirs in the *Female Spectator* (1744–1746)

Eliza Haywood firmly grounded her twenty-four monthly issues of the *Female Spectator* within the spectatorial and spectacular moral tradition of the essay periodical. Like Mr. Spectator, the anonymous editor, the Female Spectator, opens her journal with her short autobiography; and she explains that her essays will provide readers with a visual description of the English society in order to reform the moors of her contemporaries. The magazine may therefore be described as constituting, like the *Spectator*, another social history book based on semi-fictional essays.

Yet, the eidolon states that the feminine quality of her sight prompts her to observe society in a different way from the *Spectator*: she claims to be a reformed coquet, that is a person who used to mingle in society to be seen and admired. She further explains that this position—which most people reproved—enables her to be an acute social observer and a witness to the social scene: "I shall also acknowledge, that I have run through as many Scenes of Vanity and Folly as the greatest Coquet of them all [...] The Company I kept [...] furnished me not only with the Knowledge of many Occurrences, which otherwise I had been ignorant of, but also enabled me, when the too great Vivacity of my Nature became temper'd with Reflection, to see into the secret Springs which gave rise to the Actions I had either heard or, been witness of [...]."[19]

Returning the *Spectator*'s argument that feminine eyesight is fraught, she argues that it is *because* as a woman, she had so-called deficient sight, that she has become a fine observer of the world and that she is most suited to describing the social scene and thus to becoming a social historian.

In this introductory justification of her venture, she also warns that the journal will flirt with the genre of the secret histories, by disclosing behind-the-door scenes:

It is also highly proper I should acquaint the Town, that to secure an eternal Fund of Intelligence, Spies are placed not only in all the Places of Resort in and about this great metropolis, but at Bath, Tunbridge, and the

Spaw, and means found out to extend my Speculations even as far as France, Rome, Germany, and other foreign Parts, so that nothing curious as worthy of Remark can escape me; and this I look upon to be a more effectual Way of penetrating into the Mysteries of the Alcove, the Cabinet, or Field, than if I had the power of Invisibility [...][20]

Yet she dispels any moral doubt about her writing by adding: "I would, by no means, however, have what I say be construed into a Design of gratifying a vicious Propensity of propagating Scandal: [...] for tho' I shall bring real Facts on the Stage, I shall conceal the Actors Names under such as will be conformable to their Characters; my intention being only to expose the Vice, not the Person—nor shall I confine myself to modern Transactions—Whenever I find any Example among the Ancients which may serve to illustrate the Topick I shall happen to be upon, I shall make no scruple to insert it. [...]"[21]

How then does she translate such principles in the *Female Spectator* without injuring the reputation of the journal? Haywood stresses the importance for women to read history and particularly the history of past events, even though, she conceded, women could not use their knowledge for professional purposes. History, she explains, brings moral instruction as well as entertainment.

"Affording the strongest Precept by Example:—the Rise and Fall of Monarchies;—The Fate of Princes, the Sources from which their good or ill fortune may be deduc'd;—the various Events which the Struggles for Liberty against arbitrary Power have produc'd, and the wonderful Effects which the Heroism of particular Persons has obtained, both to curb Oppression in the Tyrant, and Sedition in the Subject, afford an ample Field for Contemplation, and at the same time too much Pleasure to leave room for any Amusements of a low and trifling Nature."[22]

But most of all, reading history will enable readers to develop their critical faculty and to enable them to exercise it upon their own environment. Thus, Haywood encourages her readers to study, for three hours a day, a list of ancient authors, including Herodotus, Velleius Paterculus, Suetonius, Thucydides, Josephus and Tacitus, whose general histories and ancient biographies will help them make comparisons and assess the value of present political events. Thus equipped, "When she (the female reader) hears of any notable transaction in the Field or Cabinet, she will be impatient to look over the Annals of past Times, to find if the present really excel all that have gone before, or whether it be [...] that [...] There is nothing new under the sun."[23]

Haywood therefore clearly conceives history as a tool that could lead women to intellectual and political emancipation. At the same time, she highlights that the genres of history do not really matter, for the emancipating force of history relies not so much on the narrative form as on the strength of facts:

"I am very sensible, that the Ignorance, which the greatest Part of our Sex are in of the dead Languages, is looked upon as an Impediment to our being well read in History; because, though most of the Greek and Latin

Authors are translated either into English or French, which is, now pretty equal with People of any tolerable Education, yet we cannot expect them in the same Purity as if we understood the Originals; but this Objection is of no Force, because, even in those that are the worst done, we still find Facts such as they were, and it is the Knowledge of them, not Rhetoric, I am recommending to the Ladies."[24] In this she differs radically from the *Spectator* because it means that she denies there is a hierarchy of historical genres and that some genres should be banned as disreputable.

Finally, by positing facts rather than rhetoric as central to the historical narrative she hammers in the idea that women's *natural curiosity,*—which was often considered as blameable—is certainly an asset to read and write history:

Neither will she (the reader) be content with knowing that such and such things were done; she must also pry into the Motives by which they were brought about, and as far as is in her Power inform herself whether they were such as deserved Praise, or the contrary: And by this means she will be enabled to judge of Affairs, not by their Success, but by the Intentions of those who conducted them.[25]

The verb "pry" suggests that history must be spied upon to be uncovered and that subsequently all history is somewhat secret.

That Haywood, who had published in her early career several secret histories[26] should support secret history does not come as a surprise. A more delicate matter was to reconcile this sort of writing with a journalistic venture that claimed to be highly moral. This she does in two ways.

The first one, like the *Spectator,* consists in describing the moors and daily histories of her contemporaries, showing what takes place behind the doors of private homes. Most essays contain narratives of the private stories/histories of women trapped in specific situations. And these micro-stories describe the punishment that the heroines implacably met in that patriarchal society if they did not accept the limitations of their conditions as second-rate citizens. Such vignettes are meant to be morally and socially instructive. In this, she follows Livy's moral conception of history.

The second way of reconciling secret history and her moral periodical is to show that the distinction between secret histories and respectable history is irrelevant by intermingling ancient history and secret history. After encouraging her readers to read classical history, the female editor provides them with fragments of seven ancient letters that were supposedly discovered and that were sent to her by a correspondent. These letters are those exchanged by emperor Augustus and Livia when Augustus was courting the latter while she was still married to General Tiberius. The letters reflect the emperor's passion and Livia's reactions to it. As these are incomplete letters, the Female Spectator herself provides her readers with the end of the story (Livia's becoming not only Augustus's mistress but also his wife).

Haywood displays here a primary historical source that shows in the intimate epistolary form as well as in its content, that the private desires and vices of illustrious historical figures are part of the course of history, about which readers should be instructed. Interestingly this leads her to wonder whether censorship should axe scandalous historical narratives.

> OTHERS, on the contrary, may think it better I had suppress'd the whole piece: they will say, perhaps, that when an unwarrantable aim happens to be crown'd with success, the whole event ought rather to be conceal'd than publish'd, lest it should give encouragement to others to attempt the like, and that above all things, the Female Spectator, who sets up for a regulator of her sex's conduct, should not have exhibited a character so fortunately vicious as was that of this roman empress.[27]

Significantly, she argues that moral censorship does not guarantee the writing of good and moral history because first, painting vice can be didactic and, second, the historical representation of corruption cannot corrupt virtuous female readers. Thus, the personna rejects censorship in history and refuses to promote it in her periodical, stating:

> "HISTORY, however, must not be silenced, because matters of fact, which ought not to be imitated, are therein related; nor should the elegant part of mankind be deprived of so agreeable an entertainment as the writings of the ancients afford, because some of them have introduced characters we could wish had never been in the world.

> A WOMAN, whose heart is truly guarded by virtue and religion, will never suffer a vicious example to have any influence over her;"[28]

She thus answers in a very clear way to all those who dismissed the genre of the secret history as a despicable, immoral and unhistorical fictional sort of writing. Like all good history it is entertaining and morally instructive because it is factual and visual. She also mockingly dismisses the then-widespread association between femininity and the writing of secret history by explaining that these letters were sent by a male professional historian specialised in the painstaking study of minute historical evidence, as is reflected by his name: Antiquarius.

At the same time, her epistolary historical narrative ironically debunks the seriousness of the method of professional historians who work from factual, archival and therefore supposedly reliable sources. It is plain to see that the seven letters are fictional and a forgery. Yet, the letters are presented by Antiquarius as being translations of copies of the original Latin letters said to be written by the poet Ovid. As for the translator, Antiquarius reports that it was none other than the late Bishop of Rochester, Francis Atterbury, a great Oxford scholar who had taken side with the ancients in the controversy over the forgery of Phalaris's letters. Neither Ovid, nor Atterbury wrote nor translated these letters. Furthermore, claiming that these letters had been sent by an antiquarian discredits his—and beyond him, all his colleagues'—ability to distinguish truth from fiction.[29] The letters therefore constitute a reminder of the controversies that had flourished since the 1720s and again more recently in 1742 when it was discovered that the correspondence between Cicero and Brutus, that most young gentlemen studied in universities, was a forgery.[30]

The aim of these letters is to show that it is vain to distinguish between historical and fictional texts. And they point out how misogynistic and dishonest it is to claim that fictional history can only be produced by ignorant and scandalous women, especially given that most secret histories were actually written by men.[31]

For Haywood, provided the historical frame, even if parodic and fictitious, entertained readers and prompted them to ponder over the moral and political meaning of the text, the aim of history writing was achieved. She thus warned against associating subhistorical genres with a gender hierarchy, showing that it could easily result in a backlash against male writers who tried to evince them. Subsequently, the letters and the eidolon's comment on them can be read as a clear answer to David Hume's essay on history and women.[32]

Finally, publishing this correspondence between Augustus and Livia confirms that the aim of writing history, and furthermore of writing secret history, is not merely to entertain readers but also to make them ponder over its significance for the present time. And it is there that her conception of history and her publishing history (or histories) in her journal takes on a political meaning.

First of all, she invites female readers to think about women's role in making history. Livia is presented as a very ambitious and manipulative woman ready to sacrifice all rules and people to achieve her personal aims. The obvious conclusion is that feminine values are incompatible with political power and women should not make history this way.

But beneath this rather conservative and facile surface, she also writes a scathing political attack against King George II and his manner of ruling. That Augustus and Livia's love affair is an opposition text is first signalled by the alleged author and translator. The poet Ovid had fallen into disgrace and had been banished by Augustus probably for having witnessed one of his orgies. The letters were therefore produced by one of Augustus's victims. As for the translator, Francis Atterbury had also been a major Jacobite who had gone into exile to France because he had been suspected of plotting to restore the Stuart Pretender. So he too had been a victim of his ruler, namely George II.

Then the topic itself is an indirect and thinly veiled attack against King George that contemporary readers could not miss. In the mid-18th century, George II—whose complete name is George Augustus—was often compared to Augustus, who was responsible for betraying the Roman constitution and for destroying the Republic. Historians depicted him as one who imposed the imperial tyrannical regime, along with a personal form of ruling. Augustus, they recalled, silenced public opinion by making it a capital crime to criticise the ruler.[33] Finally, ancient historians also depicted Augustus as an immoral rake.

In December 1745, for the opposition, Augustus's rule was an accurate mirror image of George's rule. In 1737, George's regime, then represented by the corrupt Prime Minister Robert Walpole, had violated the notion of freedom of expression by passing a law progressively extending censorship to the stage and to the press.[34] In 1745, the new Prime Minister Pulteney thought of extending it even further. In 1745, when Haywood was publishing the *Female Spectator*, George's son, the duke of Cumberland, also named William Augustus, was busy countering the military invasion of the Stuart Young Pretender who had come to reclaim his grandfather's crown. His victory was sealed with savage repression of the Highland Jacobites. Finally, George II, who also ruled over Hanover, was accused of defending the interests of Hanover before those of England. He was criticised for maintaining his German army at the expense of the English people's purse. Worse still, he had behaved like a traitor to the nation when in June 1745, just after the English had been defeated by the French at the battle of Fontenoy, he had deserted England to meet his German mistress Sophie Von Walmoden in Hanover.[35] To have a reformed coquet publish such a historical episode in the *Female Spectator* after explaining to her readers that history is cyclical and that contemporary events were a reflection of the past, could not but be interpreted as a political gesture of opposition to the supposed absolutism of George II's rule.

That this epistolary narrative was perceived by contemporary readers as more than a mere historical amusement for ladies is confirmed by the following statement, which was published, in January 1746—one month after the *Female Spectator* issued the letters of Augustus and Livia—in the most prominent opposition newspaper, *Old England* (led by Lord Chesterfield): "I cannot help congratulating, not only the fair sex, but my own, in having during these degenerate times, in the FEMALE SPECTATOR a polite and elegant advocate for private virtue, the true foundation of that public spirit, which my labours have ever endeavoured to promote."[36]

The allusion to degenerate times and the stress on private virtue and public spirit are characteristic of the vocabulary used by the patriot opposition and show that the authors of *Old England* did identify the *Female Spectator's* oppositional agenda in the historical narrative.

This should incite scholars to reconsider the idea that the historical content of ladies' magazines constituted and was considered to be merely second-rate, recreational forms of didactic writing aimed at merely entertaining leisurely ladies and at selling papers. This historical episode confirms that Haywood's conception of history was much deeper than the blend of facts and parodic fiction suggested. It seems that her ambition was to make as well as to write history.

In the history of the English press, *The Female Spectator* was the first lady's periodical written by a lady. Therefore, its defence of historical fiction as a serious though entertaining venture and of women's ability to write history is significant. It now remains to investigate whether such views were shared by later periodicals written by women.

The Lady's Museum, or the institutionalisation of women's history

Unlike the *Spectator* or the *Female Spectator* each issue of the *Lady's Museum* was a magazine—that is a store of pieces, some literary, others dealing with natural sciences, geography and finally with history. These articles were either extracts from foreign books which Lennox herself had translated and digested, or they were part of her own fictional production. They were published without any direct comment upon them. However, the *Lady's Museum* did retain some features of the Spectatorial essay periodical. Each instalment included an introductory essay written by an anonymous female editor, the Trifler, who gave readers clues about the conception and overall organisation of the periodical. Finally, the choice of themes and Trifler's answers to the correspondents' reactions also provide a limited glimpse of the lifestyle of the correspondents in the 1760s. They consequently contribute to construct a form of social history.

Like the Female Spectator, the Trifler describes herself as a coquet. Yet, unlike the Female Spectator, she is not reformed and she denies that coquetry signals a specifically feminine visual shortcoming. She endeavours to show that on the contrary, coquetry is the sign of a special gift which enables both men and women of exception to participate in the public sphere. In this way, she justifies her journalistic venture as the logical and natural outcome of a desire for fame which she shares with many distinguished men.

> Yet to that laudable principle, in women mistaken for coquetry, we owe the thunder of eloquence in the senate, as well as the glitter of dress in the drawing-room. An animated speech, and a well-chosen silk, are equally the effects of a desire to please, both in the patriot and the beauty: [...] But for this active principle, the statesman would be no politician, and the general no warrior. The desire of fame, or the desire of pleasing, which in my opinion, are synonymous terms, produces application in one and courage in the other. It is the poet's inspiration, the patriot's zeal, the courtier's loyalty, and the orator's eloquence.[37]

She therefore ironically debunks in general terms all the standard arguments about women's flawed vision used to keep women out of the public sphere of print and politics. She indeed contradicts the common reasoning, that claimed that women's coquettery is a sign of their superficiality. Being superficial, women are not only fascinated by the appearances of well-clad persons, to the point of being blind to the latters' more innate moral qualities. But they also wish to dazzle in their turn, so as to be distinguished. In fact, Lennox highlights the ambivalent relationship of women to aesthetics and society's hypocrisy towards it. In a world where women were defined as the "fair sex" but where access to public expression was limited to them, they had little other choice but to rely on being seen in order to draw one's attention.[38] Yet, as is made clear here, coquetterie was a double-edged solution as it fuelled arguments against women's inability to see correctly.

Moreover, curiosity is now presented in the *Lady's Museum* as the power that enabled women to observe things scientifically and therefore to see through the working of nature and made them particularly apt to write history.

> Curiosity is one of the most prevalent, and, when properly applied, one of the most amiable, passions of the human mind; nor can it in any way find a more rational scope for exertion, than in the recollection of historical facts, and a curious inquisition into the wonders of creation [...] Their (Women's) more exalted faculties, not being tied down by wearisome attention to mathematical investigations, metaphysical chimeras, or abstruse scholastic learning, are more at liberty to observe with care, see with perspicuity, and judge without prejudice.[39]

Interestingly, Lennox hammers in this idea by publishing a chapter entitled "Of the study proper for Women" translated from the French essay *L'ami des femmes* (1758). Its author, Boudier de Villemer (his authorship is not mentioned), a moderate reformist[40] acknowledged that "History and natural philosophy are alone sufficient to furnish women with an agreeable kind of study [...]."[41] He even defended women's legitimate right to write history on the grounds that:

> Women have at all times had so great a share in events, and have acted so many different parts, that they may with reason consider our archives as their own; nay, there are many of them who have written memoirs of the several events of which they have been eye-witnesses. Mademoiselle de Montpensier, Madame de Nemours, Madame de Motteville are of the number. Christina de Pisan, [...] has given us the life of that prince; and long before her, the princess Anna Comnenus wrote the history of her own times. We call upon the ladies to assert their rights, and from the study of history to extract useful lessons for the conduct of life.[42]

Through Boudier de Villemer's pen, Lennox clearly denied the spectatorial idea that the faculty of seeing was gendered and that, to paraphrase Steele's definition of natural femininity, there is a sex in sight[43]. Lennox thus lifted all objections to women's capacity to write any kind of history and any historical genre.

But most of all, the title of the magazine highlights the link between femininity, vision and history. In his *Dictionary of the English Language* (1755), Dr. Johnson defined a Museum as "a repository of learned curiosities." The magazine therefore appealed to the intellectual and scientific curiosity of its readers, a curiosity that was a sign of utmost fashion and modernity since in 1759 the British Museum had just opened its doors in Bloomsbury house in London. Now, through its guidebooks the British

Museum presented its collections as a historical narrative of the British possessions.[44]

To conceive the periodical as a museum was therefore to put historical narrative at the heart of its scheme and to associate it with femininity. For it offered a double historical narrative—that of the objects displayed, namely each article, many of which were directly related to history—and that of the collection, whose arrangement as a whole was to provide readers with the author's narrative. Thus, the author of the *Lady's Museum*, by displaying her collection presented herself as an enlightened virtuoso and a historian. At the same time the meaning of this collection was itself to be construed by readers who, by visualising the items of the collection had to make sense of its overall factual content, a task that is also that of the historian.

Furthermore, to associate the magazine with museology signalled Lennox's will to stress the respectability of her vision of history. It is not insignificant that the periodical should be called "the Museum" and not for instance "the Lady's Cabinet of Curiosity." The latter associated history with female private curiosity and prurient topical fiction and was largely considered a scandalous genre. By contrast, the collection gathered by a literary museum was to be an assemblage of public texts disconnecting curiosity from secrecy and on the contrary connecting it with historical worth. Lennox for instance produced the translation of an excerpt from the minutes of Joan of Arc's trial, whose source was the French 16th-century historian Jean Nagerel's *Annales de Normandie* (1580), a rare antiquarian text which was transcribed from the archives of Normandy.[45]

Besides, the periodical's respectability was enhanced by the fact that contemporary readers would associate it with *The Museum,* a successful and prestigious magazine edited by Mark Akenside in 1746–47. The latter clearly vindicated his collection of historical and literary pieces as a decidedly male gathering of rarities for literati. The *Lady's Museum* promised therefore to constitute some equivalent of the institutional knowledge provided by such printed museums,[46] a guarantee of respectability that was still strengthened by its addressing wellborn female readers—ladies—whose taste and intellect it would shape.

The very word *museum* also suggested ways in which the institution could be adapted to ladies. It conjured up two words linked with femininity namely, muse—the museum is the original abode of the muses—and amuse. Implicitly, therefore, the visual display of what would constitute a female collection was to be entertaining and imaginative as well as instructive.

Entertainment, which Lennox, in the tradition of the *Spectator* acknowledged as essential to instruct, was directly supplied by another feature of the museum: the variety of its collection. And variety was also a means for the author to define what she meant by writing history. Interestingly, while Akenside's *Museum* essentially published reviews of history books and serialised original narratives of topical and political contemporary events—such as the 1745 Jacobite Rebellion or the contemporary history of Europe—the *Lady's Museum* hardly mentioned topical subjects. Moreover, it defined history in much broader terms than the narrative of military, political events and facts. The *Lady's Museum* provided a range of different historical genres, from the more prestigious grand political and chronological narrative of national history to the subgenres of biography and memoirs.

The *Lady's Museum* publishes a serialised digest of the history of England from the Roman invasions to the Saxon Heptarchy which Lennox titled "an Essay on the original inhabitants of Great Britain." Despite the social dimension of the title, this narrative, which runs through seven issues (from *LM* 3 to 9), was chronological and provided a sweeping panorama of the political and military manoeuvres of the various original British kings who controlled the country. It conjured up battle scenes as well as the political intrigues and corrupted motifs of the rulers. Finally, it included some social vignettes meant to enliven an otherwise rather austere account of the period. Thus, it combines both political and social history. To show readers the seriousness of her narrative, the editor named some of the historians whose works she used to write about in her digest. The names of Guthrie, the Whig author of a *General History of England from the Invasion of the Romans* [...] *to the late Revolution (1688–89)*, along with the French and Whig historian Rapin (who wrote the successful *Histoire de l'Angleterre* translated into English in 1725) and the Jacobite historian Thomas Carte (whose 4 volumes *General History of England* had been published in 1747) are cited in the text. Last, her instruction was completed by the insertion of such visual elements as a map of Saxon England.

Furthermore, the periodical popularised the genre of art history for the ladies, by printing an original translation of the "Life of Anthony Van Dyck," a chapter which was originally published in Italian in 1672 by the Academician Giovan Bellori in his *Le Vite de Pittori*. The article highlights Van Dyck's contribution to history painting (rather than to portrait painting), a stance which taught readers to grasp this artist's prestigious contribution to the development of the British arts.

Historical variety in the periodical includes the genre of the biography, the prestige of which was on the rise after 1750, which features in the magazine with the account of the life of the famous courtesan from the Italian Renaissance Bianca Capello. It goes along with the genre of private memoirs, which is not a surprise since Lennox had already published several translations of various memoirs.[47]

Moreover, the *Lady's Museum* made it clear that the distinction between history and fiction was unimportant as the periodical's collection interpolates four histories which today would be called stories, starting with Lennox's serialised novel the *History of Sophia and Harriet* and the serialised translation of Madame de Tencin's novel *The History of the Count de*

Comminges.[48] At a time when history and literature were slowly emerging as seperate disciplines, this constitutes some evidence of her will to go against a mainstream discourse on history writing.[49]

Finally, historical variety was one of subjects as well as one of genres. Researchers have highlighted Lennox's inclusion of numerous female historical figures in the magazine, ranging from the English Queen Bodicea to the French warrior Joan of Arch and the Indian princess Padmani, not to mention the French Dutchess of Beaufort and the Roman Vestal Virgins.[50] This historical female focus was then unusual. It contrasts for instance with Charlotte Cowley's *Ladies History of England*, (1780). Though its author claimed to write about women and for women readers, the book did not centre on the achievement of female historical figures more than standard history books of the period.[51] But *The Lady's Museum* is also interesting in that it also narrated the lives and exploits of men, who were ruffians, like Italian Castruccio Castacani or like Lord Ferrers. Lennox thus built up a historical global narrative highlighting the role of both men and women in history and reminding readers that vice and virtue were equally distributed among the two sexes.

The magazine was therefore intended to write a historical narrative where the respective weight and roles of historical genres and genders were rebalanced, which in itself is remarkable. The spirit of this new kind of museum is best reflected by the plates inserted in the magazine. These plates conjured up both fictional characters (two engravings represented scenes from the novels *Harriot and Sophia* and the *Memoirs of the Count de Comminges*), and portraits of true factual historical characters like Gabrielle D'Estrée or of the inhabitants of Ceylon.

One plate featuring a couple of ancient Britons captures quite well the purpose of *The Lady's Museum* and Lennox's conception of history. The plate objectifies the pair of Britons and turns them into oddities and rarities that help construct a national narrative. (Figure 7.1)

First, the engraving reflects both the past customs of the Picts who, men and women alike, painted their skin to impress their enemies and who fought together, thus giving women a public role to play in the construction of British history. Next, it is an assemblage of two original plates published at different times. Indeed the male figure in the picture is a borrowing of a plate published in John Owen's *Compleat History of the Ancient Britons* (1743) in which a single male warrior represented the whole British nation. *The Lady's Museum* completed Owen's illustration with a female warrior, whose graceful female figure is an elegant reworking of a rare engraving of a female Pict drawn by Huguenot Jacques le Moyne de Morgues. The latter was a 16th-century cartographer and painter who accurately sketched the tribes he encountered in Scotland. (Figures 7.2 and 7.3)

The collage gives insights regarding the degree of historical and aesthetic research that had preceded the actual publication of the magazine. For Le Moyne's picture had itself been adapted to become an engraving published in

Figure 7.1 Ancient Britons. The Lady's Museum, vol 1, 1760, p. 192, with the permission of the British Library, London.

Thomas Harriot's popular travel account *Briefe and True Report of the New Found Land of Virginia* (1588). It confirms the editor's will to visually rebalance the part played by men and women in history and to display it visually to readers.[52] The delicacy and the beauty of the couple finally qualifies the idea that ancient Britons, despite their nakedness and their different conceptions of femininity and women's role were more brutish than todays'. They rather recall the original couple—Adam and Eve—from which the whole British race had reportedly sprung.

   Hence, it would be wrong to dismiss *The Lady's Museum* as a mere collection of pleasant and striking easy-to-read digested anecdotes made to amuse ignorant ladies. Examining the journal as a version of a new form of historical narrative, one can see that the imperatives of variety and visual entertainment inherent to a museum were in fact the pretext for Lennox to make several serious points about history writing by women. She hinted that as the purveyor of this collection, translating, digesting, collecting all sorts of historical material was not beyond her intellectual curiosity and grasp. Then she contradicted the idea that women writers could only specialise in

Figure 7.2 An Ancient Britain. A complete and impartial history of the ancient Britons. From the earliest account of time to the end of the reign of King Henry Viii. Faithfully Collected and Compiled from ancient Manuscripts, the best Historians and Antiquaries. By John Owen, Rector of Pickworth in Lincolnshire. Vol.I. 1743. p. 4. Gale Cengage, With the permission of the British Library, London.

subhistorical semi-fictional narratives. She showed that the grand narrative of history could be written by a female pen as well as the history of private individuals. Last, the blend of factual and fictional histories shows that for her, all genres were equally historically valuable provided they were related to some forms of sentimentality:

> If of history, a pleasing relation of the most interesting facts shall be endeavoured at, the movement of the grand machine of government shall indeed be set before our readers, and the influence of each apparent wheel be rendered *visible*: but we shall think it unnecessary to look into every secret spring whereby these wheels were actuated; and shall be dispensed with entering into the never to be discovered causes of the rise and fall of nations now no more, to make room for the more useful knowledge of those movements of the human heart on which depend the happiness or ruin of individuals.[53]

Figure 7.3 Jacques le Moyne de Morgues, *A young daughter of the picts*, c. 1585, watercolour and gouache. (Yale Center for British Art, Paul Mellon Collection).

This definition of history was incidentally retaken by Oliver Goldsmith to justify his *Life of Richard Nash* a year later.[54] It revelas that Lennox considered that the meaning of history was ultimately located in the reader's intellectual and moral ability to decipher and see each particular item as some pebble of the grand narrative of human passions. In this sense, Lennox hinted that cabinets of curiosity and Museums –both male or female oriented—were parts of the same historical narrative and that the *Lady's Museum* was a historical narrative just as valuable as the rarities displayed in Sir Hans Sloanes's collections.

It seems therefore that women writing "lower genres of history" and their mixing factual and fictional history in the press was not—as *The Spectator* suggested—the result of amusement, lack of skill or of some ignorance about history: Lennox was nicknamed Clio, the muse of history and was reputed to be a learned lady; Haywood's parody signals a definite if somewhat facetious knowledge of history and of the contemporary debates about history and its readers. Writing history for women had other motives which prove that they genuinely considered history a serious object of study.

Firstly, Haywood and Lennox maintained that the distinction between recreational, fictional kinds of history and the serious grand narrative of national history did not make sense. For them, all genres contributed in their own ways to shaping a national history, an idea that was to be further confirmed by the success of such historical novels as those of Scott and Thackeray in the 19th century. In this sense, their periodicals made history as much as their historical novels.

Secondly, the definition of history was political, Whig for *The Spectator*, Tory inclining to Patriotism for the *Female Spectator*. Lennox's choice to narrate the Anglo-Saxon period in her magazine was probably not meaningless politically speaking. Across the century, what was at stake was highly serious: it was soft power to further readers' intellectual and political emancipation through historical and factual knowledge.

Last, Haywood and Lennox's indiscriminate use of factual and fictional history in the periodicals constituted a conscious form of resistance to the authorial competition between men and women and to the various limits imposed on women, whether as history writers, as writers of fiction or as historical agents. Part of this resistance was to fight gender prejudices. Haywood and Lennox cleverly circumvented the prejudices against female sight by rehabilitating female vision while remaining within the polite spectatorial tradition that had tried to evince them. By reconciling female vision and historical writing and by resisting the hierarchy of historical genres, the female periodical press made the writing of all kinds of historical pieces a respectable and serious activity for women and promoted the idea that history should be shared by both genders. They thus paved the way for female historians like Catherine Macaulay, who started writing national histories in the 1790s. It seems that the study of historical genres in the periodical press teaches us that Macaulay's history is the sign that women writers widened the scope of female historical writings rather than the sign that they were at last able to write serious history.

Notes

1 D. R. Woolf, *"From Hystories to the historical" Huntington Library Quarterly*, 68, 1–2, (2005), 33–70. Woolf dates it back to the 16th century.
2 Among many others, Paulina Kewes, *"History and its uses. Introduction"*, *Huntington Library Quarterly*, 68, 1–2, (2005), 1–31; Mark Salber Philips, *Society and Sentiment: Genres of Historical Writing in Britain, 1740–1820*, (Princeton: Princeton University Press, 2000); Devoney Looser, *British Women Writers and the Writing of History*, (Baltimore: The John Hopkins University Press, 2000).
3 Woolf, "From Hystories", 667–68.
4 *The Spectator* 420. Ed D. F. Bond, Clarendon P, 1965, 5 vols. It will be referenced *S.* followed by the essay number.
5 *S.* 411: "Our sight is the most perfect and most delightful of all our Senses."
6 *S.* 1.
7 On Livy's popularity in the modern period, Peter Burke, "A Survey of the Popularity of Ancient Historians, 1540–1700", *History and Theory*, 5, 2, (1966), 146–48.
8 *S.* 434.
9 Herodotus, *History*, 4, 110–16.
10 On the visual nature of these genres, *S.* 421.
11 *S.* 433, 4, 23.
12 Nicholas Phillipson, *"Politics and Politeness. Anne and the early Hanoverians"*, in *The Varieties of British Political Thought 1500–1800*. Ed. J. G. A Pocock, G. J. Schochet and L. G. Schwoerer, (Cambridge: Cambridge University Press, 1993), 226–27.
13 *S.* note 1, vol 1, 23.
14 On the criticisms women's political activities raised in Addison and Steele's periodicals, Claire Boulard Jouslin, "'The Paradise of fools': l'opinion publique feminine in *The Freeholder*" *Dix-huitième Siècle* 43 (2011), 469–85.
15 *S.* 420.
16 Mark Glat, "John Locke's historical Sense" *The Review of Politics* 43, 10, (1981) 9. On distancing as a mark of historical narrative, Mark Salber Philips," Histories, Micro, and Literary: Problems of Genre and Distance" *New Literary History* 34, (2003), 217–18.
17 David Hume, *Essays moral and political,* Edimburgh, 1741, 69. For a critical approach to this text, read Gilles Rebel's introduction to *Essais moraux, et politiques*, (Gilles Rebel, ed. Paris: Presses Universitaires de France, 2001).
18 David Hume, *Essays,* 72.
19 *The Female Spectator,* London, 1745. 4 vols. 1, I, 2–3. It will be referenced *FS* followed by the volume, book and page numbers.
20 *FS* 1, I, 6.
21 *FS* 1, I, 6.
22 *FS* 1, X, 243. Reading history even strengthens qualities considered feminine: (3, XV, 160).
23 *FS* 3, XV, 161.
24 *FS* 3, XV, 166.
25 *FS* 3, XV, 161.

26 Rachel Carnell, "Eliza Haywood and the Narratological Tropes of Secret History" *Journal for Early Modern Cultural Studies*, 14, 4, New Approaches to Eliza Haywood: The Political Biography and Beyond, (2014): 101–21.

27 FS, 4, XX, 103–04.

28 *FS*, 4, XX, 104.

29 Thomas Madox's *History and Antiquities of the Exchequer of the Kings of England* (1711), a work which relied on national archives, gave respectability to antiquarian studies.

30 Joseph M Levine, "Et tu Brute? History and Forgery in Eighteenth century England", *in Fakes and Frauds Varieties of Deception in Print and Manuscript*, Robin Myers, M. Harris (eds.), (Winchester: St Paul's Bibliographies, 1989), 71–97.

31 Eve Tavor Bannett, "Secret History: Or, Talebearing Inside and Outside the Secretorie" *The Huntington Library Quarterly*, 68, n°1–2, (2005): 376.

32 For further details on Haywood and Hume, Claire Boulard Jouslin, "'Augustus Caesar to Livia Drusilla': théorie(s) de l'Histoire dans le *Female Spectator*", *Études Épistémè* [En ligne], 17 | (2010), URL: http://journals.openedition.org/episteme/664.

33 Howard Weinbrot, *Augustus Caesar in Augustan England*, (Princeton: Princeton University Press, 1978), 110.

34 The ministerial journal *The Walpole Gazetter* suggested that such Augustan laws should be implemented to punish opposition satirists like Pope. Weinbrot, *Augustus Caesar*, 76.

35 Uriel Dann, *Hanover and Great Britain 1740–1760: Diplomacy and Survival*, (Leicester: Leicester University Press, 1991), and Robert Harris, *A Patriot Press, National Politics in the London Press in the 1740s*, (Oxford: Oxford University Press, 1993), chapters 5 et 6; 187.

36 *Old England* 92. Significantly, *Old England*'s praise was used in advertisements to puff up the next issues of the *Female Spectator*. See *The Wesminster Journal*, 218, Feb 1746.

37 *The Lady's Museum*, London, 3 vol, 1760. References will be shortened to *LM* followed by volume and page numbers. 1, 3.

38 On this ambivalence, Véronique Nahoup Grappe, "La belle femme", in *Histoire des femmes XVIe-XVIIIe siècles* eds. Natalie Zemon Davis et Arlette Farge, Paris: PLon, 1991.

39 *LM* 2, 129.

40 Boudier explicitly condemned women who would emulate female scholars like Anne Daciers or Emilie du Chatelet.

41 *LM* 1, 12.

42 *LM* 1, 13.

43 In *Tatler* 172 (1710), Richard Steele asserted that "there is a Sort of Sex in Souls".

44 Barbara M. Benedict, *Curiosity, a cultural History of Early Modern Inquiry*, (Chicago: University of Chicago Press, 2001), 180.

45 *LM* 3, 212.

46 Along with Akenside's *Museum, The Lady's Museum* launched a new periodical trend, the museum magazine. Over twenty of them which included the word *museum* in their titles were published by 1800 in England. They covered a wide range of topics as is reflected by the following examples: *Museum Rusticum et Commerciale* (1764–1766), *The Medical Museum* (1763), *The Universal Museum* (1767), or *The Evangelical Museum* (1793).

47 Lennox had translated *Memoirs of the Duke of Sully, Memoirs of madame de Maintenon, History of Sir George Warrington*, and *Memoirs of the countess of Berci*.

48 *LM* 2; 3; 4; 5; 6, 7, 8, 9. The two other histories are the 'History of the Princess Padmani,' a translation from Nicolao Manucci's *General History of the Mogul Empire* (1709) which accounted for the life of the legendary Indian Princess Padmani and 'The life of Castruccio Castracani', a rewriting of a biography originally published by Machiavel.
   This is further confirmed by Lennox's relying on Rapin's complete edition which includes the history of Bodicea, rather than on his abridged edition where it did not feature. This is unlikely to be left to chance.
49 On Lennox's constant use of history and fiction in her works, Devoney Looser, *British Women Writers and the Writing of History*, 90.
50 Judith Dorn, "Reading Women Reading History: The Philosophy of Periodical Form in Charlotte Lennox's *The Lady's Museum*," *Historical Reflections* 18, no. 3 (1992), 21.
51 Devoney Looser, *British Women Writers and the Writing of History*, 3–4.
52 This is further confirmed by Lennox's also relying on Rapin's complete edition which includes the history of Bodicea, rather than Rapin's abridged edition where it did not feature. This could not be left to chance.
53 *LM* 2, 131.
54 Salber Philips, "Histories, Micro and Literary", 215.

Bibliography

Primary sources

The Female Spectator, London, 1745. 4 vols.
The Spectator. Ed D. F. Bond, Oxford: Clarendon Press, 1965, 5 vols.
The Lady's Museum, London, 3 vols, 1760.
The Tatler, ed D.F. Bond, Oxford: Clarendon Press, 1987, 3 vols.
The Wesminster Journal, 218, Feb 1746.
Hume, David. Essays, Moral and Political, Edinburgh, 1741.

Secondary sources

Benedict, Barbara M. Curiosity, A Cultural History of Early Modern Inquiry. Chicago: University of Chicago Press, 2001.
Boulard Jouslin, Claire. "'Augustus Caesar to Livia Drusilla': théorie(s) de l'Histoire dans le *Female Spectator*." Études Épistémè [En ligne] 17 | (2010). URL: http://journals.openedition.org/episteme/664.
Burke, Peter. "A Survey of the Popularity of Ancient Historians, 1540–1700." History and Theory, 5, n 2 (1966): 135–152.
Carnell, Rachel. "Eliza Haywood and the Narratological Tropes of Secret History." Journal for Early Modern Cultural Studies 14, n 4, *New Approaches to Eliza Haywood: The Political Biography and Beyond* (Fall 2014): 101–121.
Claire Boulard, Jouslin. "'The Paradise of Fools': l'opinion publique féminine in *The Freeholder.*" Dix-huitième Siècle 43 (2011): 469–485.
Dorn, Judith. "Reading Women Reading History: The Philosophy of Periodical Form in Charlotte Lennox's *The Lady's Museum.*" Historical Reflections 18, n 3 (1992): 7–27.
Glat, Mark. "John Locke's Historical Sense." The Review of Politics 43, 10 (1981): 3–21.
Kewes, Paulina. "*History and Its Uses: Introduction.*" Huntington Library Quarterly 68, n 1–2 (2005): 1–31.

Looser, Devoney. British Women Writers and the Writing of History, Baltimore: The John Hopkins University Press, 2000.

M Levine, Joseph. "tu Brute? History and Forgery in Eighteenth Century England," in Robin Myers, and M. Harris (eds.), Fakes and Frauds Varieties of Deception in Print and Manuscript, 71–97. Winchester: St Paul's Bibliographies, 1989.

Phillipson, Nicholas. *"Politics and Politeness: Anne and the Early Hanoverians,"* in J. G. A. Pocock, G. J. Schochet and L. G. Schwoerer (eds.), The Varieties of British Political Thought 1500–1800, 211–245. Cambridge: Cambridge University Press, 1993.

Rebel, Gilles. Ed and Intr. Essais moraux, et politiques. Paris: Presses Universitaires de France, 2001.

Salber Philips, Mark. Society and Sentiment: Genres of Historical Writing in Britain, 1740–1820. Princeton: Princeton University Press, 2000.

Salber Philips, Mark. "Histories, Micro, and Literary: Problems of Genre and Distance." New Literary History 34 (2003): 211–229.

Tavor Bannett, Eve. "Secret History: Or, Talebearing Inside and Outside the Secretorie." The Huntington Library Quarterly 68, n 1–2 (2005).

Weinbrot, Howard. Augustus Caesar in Augustan England. Princeton: Princeton University Press, 1978.

Woolf, D. R. *"From Hystories to the Historical."* Huntington Library Quarterly 68, 1–2 (2005), 33–70.

8 Court intrigues between public and secret history

Some 18th-century Danish solutions

Sebastian Olden-Jørgensen

Court history, that is the history of royal, princely and ecclesiastical courts especially in Medieval and Early Modern times, is in vogue and has been for quite some time. Over the past generation or so it has grown into a thriving, respectable and very interdisciplinary field that effortlessly has caught the prevalent winds of modern scholarship (gender studies, material culture and so forth). From today's vantage point, it is easy to forget how relatively marginalized a topic the court was from the middle of the 19th to the end of the 20th century. Mainstream historians across the political spectrum simply could not take it seriously because they located the dynamics of history in the "progressive" sectors of society: the state, the nation and the economy. To them, the court was an entertaining but archaic institution of dwindling importance that could be safely left to cultural historians and curators of the collections left behind by the selfsame courts.

In a longer historiographical perspective this contempt for court history seems like a long parenthesis because if we look back to the 18th century, court history was self-evidently an important topic. Suffice it to remind that when Voltaire wrote his great best seller *Le Siècle de Louis XIV* (1751), he included no less than four chapters (out of 39) of "Particularités et anecdotes du Règne de Louis XIV" where court intrigues bulk large.

In the following we shall look at Danish 18th-century historiography and ask how a selection of historians grappled with court history. Did they include it? How did they deal with it? Why and with what success? But first a few words on the genre that is connected to court history par excellence: *anecdotes* or *secret history*.

Secret history

The genre of secret history has a birth certificate in the shape of the editio princeps of Procopius' *Anekdota* by the Roman antiquarian Niccolò Alamanni (1583–1626) in 1623.[1] On the title page Alemanni translated "Anekdota" (literally: unpublished) as "arcana historia", that is "secret history". Procopius (ca. 500–565) was the author of well-known official histories of Emperor Justinian's wars and building projects. In his *Secret History* he told a quite

DOI: 10.4324/9781003331971-12

different story, filled with salacious details, among which pride of place is taken by empress Theodora's stunning promiscuity (censored in the first editions but hinted at) and the "fact" that Justinian was a demon. French and English translations translation appeared a generation later in 1669 and 1674.[2]

The first to theorize about the genre rules of secret history was the French historian Antoine Varillas (1624–1696) in the preface to his *Les Anecdotes de Florence ou l'historie secrete de la maison de Medicis* (written 1664, published 1685).[3] He claimed that ordinary historians who write "public history", even when bound by truth, only were obliged to give plausible explanations while the "writer of anecdotes" like himself was bound to reveal the whole truth that would often be inconvenient or shocking. And this whole truth was not found in public but in the private sphere where rulers revealed their true character and "dominant passion" that in reality turned the wheels of history. This demanded special sources—and Varillas at several points advertised his access to confidential papers in the French Royal Library—but most of all it called for a commitment to seek the true causes of any historical development in individual psychology and to relate all other causes and events to this. As he said in a much quoted passage of the preface:

> The historian nearly always looks at men in public while the writer of anecdotes examines them in private. The one thinks he has done his duty when he has described them as they were on the battlefield or in the bustle of cities, the other tries in every way to open the door to their private quarters. The one regards them during ceremonies, the other during conversation. The one focuses on their actions, the other wants to know their interior life and to be present at their most intimate leisure. In a word, the on only knows of command and authority, the other feeds on all that happens in secret and solitude.[4]

This admittedly could sound as the recipe for "tabloid history" but Varillas was careful to stress that "one ought to suppress anything that is impossible to reveal without offending good manners".[5] For Varillas the dominant passions that determined the course of history could be anything. His main interest, maybe even his dominant passion, was individual psychology and its interplay with fortune, not sex.

However, for all his brilliant reasoning Varillas did not succeed in laying down the literary laws of the genre. The late 17th and early 18th centuries witnessed a flood of secret histories that promised scandalous and revealing insights into the *real* intrigues behind the polished facade of the court.[6] The thrill of this sort of secret history hinged on a claim to tell hitherto unknown or suppressed but true stories based on inside information *and* on the expectation that this true story was all about intimate relationships, often sexual, between people who were mean spirited or incompetent or both. As often as not such secret histories were political pamphlets and the proximity to modern conspiracy theories is often striking. In other words, Varillas was overtaken by the book market where the concept of secret history quickly became a sales trick and a political weapon.

With this commercial logic in mind, it is not difficult to understand why serious historical theorists of the next generation would feel obliged to distance themselves from secret history. When in 1694 the prominent Jesuit father Claude-François Ménestrier (1631–1705) sketched out a typology of history, historical genres and historians, he placed anecdotes and secret history together with "chroniques scandaleuses" under the heading of "Satire" and characterized them as so many "plagues that ought to be banished from the face of the earth because they were usually nothing but fables filled with poison and atrocious calumny".[7] Another popular author, the prolific *philosophe* Nicolas Lenglet Du Fresnoy (1674–1755), only mentioned secret histories "in order to show how little store one should put on them", and he deplored "that in this century there exists a certain craze for producing and reading this sort of libel".[8]

However, it would be wrong to suppose that mainstream historians like Ménestrier and Lenglet Du Fresnoy had no higher ambition than producing bland public history in the sense of Varillas' "public history". Father Ménestrier extolled what he called alternately "figural history" or "reasoned history" and he explained (my emphasis added):

> the political and moral histories of the Greeks and the Romans as well as the majority of the moderns do not limit themselves to describing and elaborating the events but **seek out their most secret springs** and trace their causes by examining their **motives** and circumstances … . This is a reasoned history that does not stop at the rind and the appearance of things but **proceeds to the minds of the protagonists**, reveals the intentions and shows through the outcome of their enterprises the wisdom of their conduct or their poor judgment … . One does not only learn the great and illustrious things done by peoples and sovereigns but at the same time **the springs of their policy and the secrets of their conduct**.[9]

Lenglet Du Fresnoy could not but agree:

> To know history is to know the human beings it consists of; it is to pass sound judgment on them; to study history is to study their **motifs, opinions and passions** in order to penetrate all the **springs, the straight route and the detours**: and also to know all the illusions, they succumb to and the **surprises of their hearts**; in short, it is to learn and to know oneself in others.[10]

These few examples indicates that the boundaries between public or mainstream history and secret history were anything but clear cut and that even if the concept of secret history itself quickly degenerated, the subject matter (intrigues) and the analytical drive (the dynamics of personalities and relationships) was something mainstream history could not and would not do without, especially when dealing with court history. The question was rather: How far could you go?

The question of how far you could go was exasperated by what could be termed the pre-modern paradox of contemporary history: Candor and veracity were indispensable historical virtues, celebrated since antiquity, but they often clashed violently with the respect due to public and private individuals, the lack of which could have potentially threatening results for the historian. The 2nd-century Hellenistic author Lucian first formulated this quandary: Published contemporary history is a contradiction in terms because the impartiality of an author is always compromised by his political and personal loyalties.[11] Or as Sir Walter Raleigh formulated the same problem nearly 1500 years later: "who-so-euer in writing a moderne Historie, shall follow truth too neare the heeles, it may happily strike out his teeth".[12] Therefore truthful published history had to deal with the remote past or foreign countries while published contemporary history on the author's own times and country of necessity was either bland or panegyrical, or both. The obvious solution to this problem was for the contemporary historian to write for future readers. After a couple of generations naked truth could be revealed but not before.[13] A second solution was to publish clandestinely. All authors could hope for the first and take precautions for the preservation of their manuscripts (making several copies, depositing them with friends) while the second was an option only in the more developed parts of Europe. 18th-century Denmark certainly did not belong to these developed parts but had access to them through a well developed book trade and the traveling habits of the elites.

The historian who knew too much: Andreas Hojer

The first Danish historian to deal explicitly with the topic of court history was Andreas Hojer (1690–1739).[14] He descended from a clerical family in the duchy of Slesvig, on the southern fringe of the Danish Monarchy. He studied medicine, moral philosophy, history and natural law in Halle but had to cut short his studies for financial reasons and in 1713 became tutor to the sons of Johan Georg Holstein (1662–1730), a Mecklenburg nobleman in the service of the Danish king Frederick IV. Hojer tried to establish a career in medicine but also published works on natural law and history that gave proof of his intelligence and efficiency but also of a certain outspokenness. Through the good offices of his patron Holstein but undoubtedly also because he caught the eye of Frederick IV (ruled 1699–1730), ever on the lookout for bright and reliable young men, he became a chancery official in 1721 and in 1722 obtained the post as royal historiographer.

As royal historiographer his task was to chronicle the exploits of Frederick IV in the shape of detailed, factual, and rather dry annals of which he completed 11 volumes dealing with the years 1700–1711 before the King's death in 1730 and Hojer's subsequent fall from grace interrupted his work.

After a few years he ingratiated himself with the new king, Christian VI (ruled 1730–46), and in 1734 reassumed a splendid career as civil servant (but not as royal historiographer) and professor of natural law at the University of Copenhagen until his early death in 1739. In the lull between these employments 1730–34 and based on his previous work as royal historiographer he completed a shortened and much more readable version of the whole reign of Frederick IV: *König Friedrich des Vierten glorwürdigstes Leben* (*Most Glorious Life of King Frederick IV*). The text was dedicated to the nine years old crown prince Frederick (ruled 1746–1766) but also intended for publication. This, however, took place only in 1829.[15]

Even if *Most Glorious Life of King Frederick IV* is an example of what Varillas would surely have called public history it is not as insipid as one would expect. King Christian VI had had a strained relationship with his father Frederick IV and in combination with the educational aim (the dedication to Crown Prince Frederick) this probably gave Hojer the leeway to write with rather more candor than one would expect.

Concerning the history of Danish politics in general and the court in particular there was a real elephant in the room: the bigamy of Frederick IV. The King did not limit himself to a series of mistresses but actually married two of them in succession while at the same time being lawfully wed to his Queen Louisa (1667–1721). The last and most important of these morganatic wives was the Danish noblewoman Anna Sophie Reventlow (1693–1743) who met the king at a masquerade in 1711 at the royal castle of Koldinghus in Jutland, eloped with the King the following year and was married to him "to the left hand" (in morganatic marriage). When Queen Louisa died in 1721 the King married Anna Sophie "to the right hand" on the day following the Queen's interment, elevated her to the rank of duchess and eventually crowned her as his queen a month later. These events, provocative in themselves for several reasons, caused a permanent estrangement between members of the royal family and a shuffle in the political elite as friends and relatives of Anna Sophie Reventlow rose to prominence. How did Hojer deal with this? Rather slyly it must be admitted.

When he arrived at the point in the narrative (1711) where The King would meet Anna Sophie Reventlow for the first time, he gave a straightforward if summary account of the events including the information that the young lady's mother opposed the union but that the deceased father's kin favored it because of the great advantages that would accrue to them. Then he concluded with the following words that hover between a disclaimer and a teaser: "The well-known as well as the unknown circumstances and fruits of this course of events will here deliberately be omitted".[16]

Hojer was here indicating three things: First, the love life of King Frederick IV had important political repercussions ("fruits"). Second, that he was well informed about both public ("well known") and secret ("unknown") details. Third, that he would not say more, for reasons that everybody could figure out. In in the end, it turned out that he could and would say more. When he arrived at Chapter 12 on the events of the years 1721–1724, he began with the death of Queen Louise in 1721 but did not limit himself to an external account of the events and the ensuing changes in government.[17] He informed the reader that the decision to marry Anna Sophie Reventlow "to the right hand" originated in the pangs of conscience of the King himself, but that her subsequent coronation was her own idea. This was in fact rather equivocal: Did Hojer mean to exculpate the king for the provocation of her elevation to Queenship—or, on the contrary, to criticize him for being susceptible to her pernicious influence?

Furthermore, Hojer not only listed the subsequent changes in government that rocketed the extended family of the new Queen into prominent positions. He added two trenchant obervations that do not exactly sing the praises of the persons concerned: First he suggested that "many believed that this new party [the Renventlow clan] to some extent spoiled their chances by their own discord and jealousy", of which he proceeds to give several examples. Second "that the King himself was well satisfied with these discordant aims and inclinations and used them to keep himself better informed about their [the Reventlows'] individual weaknesses, errors and secret objectives". To this Hojer adds the following comment: "This is a very old and in itself quite sensible maxim of government, but others with a more perfect understanding of the secrets of his [the King's] cabinet must judge whether at times it did not cost him rather dear".[18] Rhetorically couched in the slightest of reservations Hojer here gives a rather unfavorable picture of the Reventlow clan and portrays the King as the victim of his deficient ability to implement otherwise sound political principles, such as divide and rule.

However, these passages culled from the final version of *Glorious Life of King Frederick IV* are only the tip of the iceberg. Hojer's fair copy of *Glorious Life of King Frederick IV* has been preserved, and at the end of the manuscript he included an earlier, discarded version of Chapter 12.[19] This earlier version is even more outspoken and includes rather blunt character sketches of the queen and all the central political players (but not the King!) that he evidently later excised. The first part of the later discarded political portrait of Queen Anna Sophie must suffice as a sample:

However, nobody played a more prominent part in this than Queen Anna Sophie herself, and in the beginning the world would think that her intelligence and merit were as sublime as her luck. In fact, she was intelligent but incomparably more passionate, and her passions were all extremely violent and did not allow her to reflect properly. Her heart was obstinate and timid and on the slightest occasion anger and fear made her loose her head. She was not fit for well-considered measures, unable to control herself, fickle, rash, irascible and totally inflexible. She quickly forgot her friends and was also effortlessly forgotten by them. She loved the King, but this love was a blazing and turbulent fire that only troubled the worthy monarch even more and made herself incredibly confused.[20]

It is easy to understand why Hojer left out these revealing, indeed outright damning passages. Actually, it is more difficult to explain why he included them in the first place and kept them as an appendix to his fair copy. He evidently fully subscribed to Varillas' maxims of identifying the dominant passions and taking a sharp look at the private persons of the rulers. And just as clearly he did not subscribe to any sharp division between public and secret history. Instead, he struggled to combine the historian's duty to give a full and truthful account with the demands of propriety and tried to include as much as possible on the personal relationships, motives and struggles behind the scenes. But this ambition drove him invariably in the direction of secret history and in the end he had to accept that he had gone too far and opt for a double solution to the dilemma: An official version, destined for print, with as much detail as he thought possible—rather much actually—and an unofficial, unexpurgated manuscript version stored on the shelf of his library. This unexpurgated text is a piece of genuine secret history: entirely unsuitable for his contemporaries and really a bottle message for the future.

The historian who knew too little: Ludvig Holberg

It is intriguing that during the very same years that Hojer composed his *Glorious Life of King Frederick IV* his rival and opposite number in the small Danish Republic of Letters, Ludvig Holberg (1684–1754), wrote and published his three volume *Dannemarks Riges Historie* (*History of Denmark*, 1732–35) covering Danish history from the early Middle Ages to the death of Frederick III in 1670.[21] Holberg was a prolific author and a professor at the University of Copenhagen, but he was not royal historiographer with privileged access to archives and other sources of information as Hojer had been. Holberg's *History of Denmark* was of course dedicated to the King but in all other respects it was a private and commercial enterprise written in the tradition of what Ménestrier had called reasoned history and what contemporary German scholars would call "pragmatic history".[22]

According to Holberg himself his *History of Denmark* stopped in 1670 because he "did not want to write gazettes".[23] What he meant by this was that if the contemporary historian insisted on being "impartial" (Holberg's professed ideal and favorite self-description) he would risk serious trouble from the powers that be as well as from the family and friends of historical protagonists. Contemporary history therefore was necessarily limited to insipid reports of events without proper explanation or assessment of anything or anyone, just as in the contemporary gazettes (newspapers). For this reason, he imply abstained.

Concerning court history and anecdotes Holberg was quite explicit: He loved them and repeatedly lamented the fact that Danish history was nearly devoid of memoires dealing with this type of material.[24] Understandably, he did not hesitate to include it in the few instances where it was available, that is concerning the paramours of Christian IV (ruled 1588–1648) and the intrigues at the court of Frederick III (ruled 1648–1670). He was well aware that not everybody shared his taste but to them he replied, occasioned by Christian IV's paramours:

> If anybody will criticize me for writing about such things that here in the Nordic countries have always remained manuscript anecdotes, then I will answer: (1.) That the history is nearly 100 years old. (2.) That even if it was not that old, it would be no different than other anecdotes and interesting events that are told in all other foreign histories, and one can observe that the greatest rulers sometimes have the most adventures in their marriage and romances. (3.) This history gives a portrait of the great King's frankness and the quality of those times that an historian cannot afford to ignore, especially because their description is both pleasant and useful and more interesting to the reader than the long-winded accounts of many useless ceremonies that normally take up the greater part of our Nordic histories and are the cause that they are read so seldom or not at all. Lastly (4.) it is to be feared that such anecdotes, that commonly are the greatest ornament of histories, shall quite disappear, of which there are several examples especially in this King's history that nowadays for long has been deemed impossible to write because most things – and the most interesting – that once had been collected have either simply disappeared or been so mutilated that you almost have to guess the story.[25]

Ludvig Holberg was a prolific author not only of histories but also of plays, essays, satirical poems, humorous autobiography and much more. One might therefore suspect that his high regard for anecdotes as "the greatest ornament of histories" exceeded the proper limits of the serious historian, at least "here in the Nordic countries" (as he hints). But this was not the case. Holberg's colleague at the university, the professor and Hoje's successor as royal historiographer Hans Gram (1685–1748), whom nobody would accuse of recklessness, quite agreed. When Gram in 1737 gave an assessment of Holberg's *Danish History,* he praised Holberg's style and added:

> Praiseworthy is also Holberg's diligence in seeking out different manuscripts that he regularly refers to, especially in the last two volumes on the Kings Christian IV and Frederick III. He tells the latter King's history in a way that possibly no other of our compatriots would have dared, relating many anecdotes and adducing secrets from the manuscripts. And in this regard the third volume is much to be preferred in comparison to the other two.[26]

Gram criticized Holberg for his slipshod work, for his lack of charity towards his predecessor Arild Huitfeldt (1546–1609), for his humorous style and colloquial language and for his love of trivia and lack of gravity, but *not* for telling anecdotes and secrets.

In other words, Holberg and probably nearly everybody else in the local cultural establishment would have loved to include more details on courtly intrigues and the dalliances of kings but the scarcity of sources hindered them from doing it. For them anecdotes were not the opposite of mainstream history as Varillas would have it but part of it as Ménestrier and Langlet Du Fresnoy suggested. The paradoxical conclusion is that when Holberg's *History of Denmark* today in many ways looks surprisingly modern in its concentration on political matters and its scarcity of anecdotes this does not reflect a serious and modern outlook on the part of Holberg but circumstances beyond his control. He would have loved to include more secret history.

The halfhearted author of secret histories: P.F. Suhm

Holberg was a full-fledged "pragmatic historian" who drew upon anecdotes and secret history but never considered writing secret history proper. One of his young fans, however, the gentleman historian and public intellectual P.F. Suhm (1728–98), did try his hand at real secret history in the Procopian sense when in the summer or autumn of 1771 he began a manuscript called *Hemmelige Efterretninger om de danske Konger efter Souverainiteten* (*Secret Intelligence on the Danish Kings after Absolutism*).[27] The composition was prompted by very special political circumstances.

Since the introduction of absolutism in 1660, Denmark had enjoyed generations of dynastic and political stability but this changed abruptly with the accession of Christian VII in 1766. To say that the young King (born 1749) was weak would be an understatement, modern science diagnoses him as a case of schizophrenia. In the first few years of the reign, his behavior went from frantic and unpredictable to embarrassment and torpor and the political barometer from change to stormy. Eventually, in 1770 the King's German physician Johann Friedrich Struensee (1737–72), in conjunction Queen Caroline Mathilde (1751–1775), who had become his mistress, seized full control of the King. Struensee used his position to introduce a torrent of reforms, some of them enlightened like the abolition of all censorship and torture but all of them headlong and with absolutely no regard for the sentiments or interests of those affected by them. By the summer of 1771, the ensuing political and moral chaos was abundantly clear and Suhm put pen to paper in order to seek a historical explanation for what he called "our present awful condition".[28]

According to Suhm, the Danish Absolutist regime suffered from three fundamental weaknesses:

> The reason for our present awful condition first and foremost lies in the nature of absolute or despotic government itself. It is bound eventually to deteriorate, unless God by means of a perpetual miracle sends only good kings, because in itself it is too great a power to be entrusted to a single human being … . The second reason for our present awful condition is that

all acts of government necessarily age. Initially they are good or at least tolerable because in the beginning one [i.e., the King] has to pay attention and because those who first institute something are also best fitted to maintain it. But at length you grow self-confident and fall asleep on the throne and in office. Because you are born to rule you learn that the subjects must be content with you as you are. Our government was therefore with many changes tolerably well from 1660 to 1750. The third reason for our present awful condition must be sought in the discord between Frederick IV and Louisa and the subsequent marriage with Anna Sophie and the disagreement in the royal family itself.[29]

Recent scholarship has claimed that Suhm's *Secret Intelligence on the Danish Kings after Absolutism* was a "planned and carefully prepared" work but a closer look at the text does not warrant this conclusion.[30] There is no doubt that a splendid piece of secret history could be written if Suhm had followed his own Montesquieu-inspired recipe but he did not. He did two other things instead. The first part of his text consists of a series of portraits of the first five absolute kings (Frederick III to Frederick V) and could well qualify as secret history with its focus on court intrigues and passions as well as on finances. Some of this material is unreliable or outright wrong but all of it is interesting because it represents the unofficial, oral tradition of the Danish elite. It becomes clear how things went "tolerably well from 1660 to 1750" and that the kings did not manage their absolute power very well but not catastrophically badly either (point one and two earlier). But Suhm never explains how the discord of King Frederick IV and Queen Louisa and the King's marriage with Anna Sophie Reventlow in the first decades of the 18th century could have such far-reaching consequences and usher in the political crisis of 1771. In other words, Suhm's political views are expressed but the historical plot falters miserably.

The second part of the text has a quite different character and qualifies as a typical piece of memoire writing. In a strictly chronological sequence, it covers the period from the late 1750s to 1775, when the text abruptly ends with the death of the exiled Queen Caroline Mathilde in Celle in Germany 11 May 1775. It is probably based on Suhm's private diaries[31] and details political intrigues, appointments and falls from grace while at the same time providing short and mostly unfavorable character sketches of the protagonists and a fair share of gossip. Information on romantic liaisons is routinely noted. There are some frank political remarks but no strong agenda, no sustained analysis and no plot line. The text rather peters out than concludes.

It is therefore doubtful that Suhm's *Secret Intelligence on the Danish Kings after Absolutism* should be read as a demonstration of the fatal connection between sex and politics in Absolutism where individuals, not laws, ruled, as has been claimed in recent scholarship.[32] Suhm's point is not the rule of law vs. despotism; his political lesson is simply the dangers inherent in direct rule by individuals, whether in the shape of despotic kings or—in the case of a weak king—in the shape of despotic councilors.[33] Suhm's theoretical solution, derived from Montesquieu, was to "restrict the government" and introduce a parliament of 48 elected persons representing the different estates and provinces of the kingdom. He even sketched out a new constitution and gave it to the conspirators against Struensee, but to no avail.[34]

There can be no doubt that Suhm was a major intellectual of his time and an interesting political thinker. He was also a great antiquarian who contributed to scholarship and published sources. But judged by the *Secret Intelligence on the Danish Kings after Absolutism* he was a poor historian in the sense that he was seemingly unable to compose a coherent and integrated narrative expressing his deepest political and historical convictions. A number of his opinions can be recognized in the text but they are neither consistently formulated nor narratively presented. The text begins as secret history but falters and turns into an uninspired digest of his journal, and it never fulfills its initial promise of tracing the connection between the love life of Frederick IV and the present "awful situation".

Maybe the simple answer to Suhm's puzzling failure to live up to his own ambitions is to understand *Secret Intelligence on the Danish Kings after Absolutism* as a piece of historical self-therapy that was made unnecessary by the turn of events. When the crisis passed with Struensee's downfall 17 January 1772 and his execution 28 April, things quickly returned to normal and the urge to make sense of recent events by means of an historical explanation receded too.

However, Suhm took pains to preserve the text of his *Secret Intelligence on the Danish Kings after Absolutism*. He not only, like Hojer, kept the compromising manuscript in his extensive library, later to be included in the Royal Library. He also lent it, together with other confidential material such as the previously mentioned sketch of a liberal constitution, to his friend and collaborator Rasmus Nyerup (1759–1829) who made a copy of it. This copy was eventually published in 1918, and in the same year Suhm's original manuscript was transferred from the secret and uncatalogued collection of the Royal Library to the public and cataloged part![35]

The would-be author of secret histories: N.D. Riegels

However, one Danish author wanted to have his cake and eat it, that is to write candid contemporary history and publish it: N.D. Riegels (1755–1802), the son of a commoner landowner. A recent biographer has called him "the mad dog of the Enlightenment" and radical he indeed was.[36] His published works are replete with violent diatribes against the clergy and the nobility who in his eyes deceived the kings and bled the country white. He was prolific and published both pamphlets and journals but as a historian Riegels is first and foremost remembered for continuing Holberg's *History of Denmark* with histories, published in the years 1792–1800, of the first three absolutist kings: Christian V (ruled 1670–1699), Fredrick IV (1699–1730) and Christian VI (1730–46).[37]

In all three instances he relied heavily on existing manuscripts by other authors to which he added his own ideological bias, sometimes rather clumsily. His literary output was considerable but his major historical works did not sell well.

The key to Riegels's puzzling literary career lies in the role he played in the palace revolution of 1784. At the previously mentioned coup against Struensee in 1772 power was seized by a group led by the Dowager Queen Juliane Marie (1729–1796), her son the Hereditary Prince Frederick (1753–1805) and their trusted advisor Ove Høegh-Guldberg (1731–1808). The new rulers kept up the facade of absolute rule and their legitimacy was strong because the public much preferred to see the King controlled by his own respectable kin than by a stray German doctor who had children with the Queen. However, the Dowager Queen and her collaborators lived on borrowed time because the moment Crown Prince Frederick (born 1768) came of age their authority would crumble because the Crown Prince would be the natural guardian of his poor father, the schizophrenic Christian VII. This eventually happened on 14 April 1784 at a meeting of the council of state where the 16-year-old Crown Prince simply made his father sign at declaration that transferred power to him.

This palace revolution was the fruit of a carefully prepared conspiracy where Riegels had played a part as double agent in his capacity as tutor to the pages of the Dowager Queen. For this reason the Crown Prince owed Riegels a favor and after some hesitation Riegels knew what he wanted. He asked for the post of royal historiographer with the task of writing the history of the palace revolution of 1784, including its prehistory stretching back not only to the Struensee-affair 1770–1772, but also to the reign of Frederick V (1746–66). For this task, he asked for access to papers in the archives and authority to interview relevant people and demand that they deliver him written accounts. In the end, Riegels was turned down and he was not offered any other position. However, he received a generous yearly pension of 1.200 rixdollar and a longer leash than any other Danish author. Occasionally even he came into conflict with the censorship but in general, he was untouchable.

Thus Riegels's published histories of Christian V, Frederick IV and Christian VI were his plan B. His first and most ardent desire was to write a secret history and do it as a royal historiographer and publish it! This is abundantly clear from the specimen consisting of a preface and the first and smallest part of his planned work that he composed in the early spring of 1786 and sent to Johan Bülow (1751–1828), the Crown Prince's fatherly friend and key advisor. Riegels planned a work in four parts called respectively:

1 *The preparations* (the reign of Frederick V 1746–66)
2 *The secret history of Christian VII* (the early reign of Christian VII including the Struensee-affair, the coup of 1772 and the regime of the Dowager Queen 1766–1780)
3 *The education of the Crown Prince* (from his infancy 1768 to ca 1780)
4 *The history of 14 April 1784* (the preparation and execution of the palace revolution 1781–84).

He only completed drafts of a preface to Crown prince Frederick and parts one and three but these give a very clear idea of his intentions.[38] In the preface Riegels compares himself to Suetonius, Plutarch and Procopius and declares his purpose to be the impartial exposition of historical truth. He also advertised his ambition to become royal historiographer and denounced his personal enemies (the aristocratic Reventlow-party) who would rather give the post "to some needy German".[39]

In *The Preparations* proper (part 1) Riegels showed himself a true disciple of Procopius in the sense that most of the text dwells on the alleged greed, corruption and bad faith of the two dominant statesmen during the reign of Frederick V: A.G. Moltke (1710–1792) and J.H.E. Bernstorff (1712–1772). According to Riegels they deceived the unsuspecting King, "this unforgettable friend of man", ruined the economy, oppressed the farmers and only benefitted themselves and the nobility.[40]

In part 3, *The education of the Crown Prince*, the urge to blame individuals is even stronger and the plot is a conspiracy theory: According to Riegels, after the coup against Struensee the Dowager Queen at first had hoped that the sickly Crown Prince Frederick would perish so that her son, the Hereditary Prince of the same name, would become the direct heir to the throne. When the Crown Prince survived, her next move was to ensure that he would forever remain ignorant and hence dependent on her counsel. For this reason she entrusted his education to indolent and pedantic tutors who would keep him ignorant of all he needed to become a competent ruler. Luckily, a few of the Crown Prince's staff, among them the previously mentioned chamberlain Johan Bülow, thwarted these sinister designs and enlightened the Crown Prince.

As this summary demonstrates Riegels's world is one of many villains and a few good men and women, and the fight for power and riches is merciless. Passion, however, is rather absent in comparison to Hojer, Holberg and Suhm. Ignorance, adulation, cowardice, laziness, not to mention greed, are omnipresent, sex absent. In this sense, Riegel's brand of secret history is closer to the English tradition of politically subversive secret history than the abiding French interest in scandals.[41]

This can only in part be explained with reference to Riegels's intended reader, the Crown Prince, for nothing would prevent him from slandering the more ordinary bad guys with accusations of sexual license and misdemeanor (as Suhm did on a regular basis). But for Riegels it seemed to be all about money and aristocratic and clerical prejudice. This must mirror his own personality and outlook. On one crucial point, Riegels shared the predicament of Holberg: a dearth of sources on courtly intrigues. But even if Holberg saw this type of material as "the ornament of history", it was to him only one element among several, whereas it stood at the center of Riegels's conception of history.

It is unlikely that Riegels's draft chapters ever reached the Crown prince. Johan Bülow made copies of the drafts and carefully read and commented on *The education of the Crown Prince* himself, while he sent *The Preparations* to his friend and confidante Charlotta Dorothea Biehl who provided the text with a series of comments. In both cases, the verdict was rather damning. But who was this woman who could function as Bülow's expert on recent Danish history?

The accomplished secret historian: Charlotta Dorothea Biehl

Charlotta Dorothea Biehl (1731–1788) was a successful Danish author of plays, essays, short stories, translations (*Don Quijote*) and a charming autobiography.[42] She was unmarried, and in 1783 intensified a Platonic relationship with Johan Bülow. Twenty years her junior, he was a gentleman and officer of modest means who, since 1773, had been chamberlain to Crown Prince Frederick. When Biehl and Bülow met she entertained him with a rich store of information on events at court during the last two generations, of which she was well informed through her numerous friends and connections at court.

As mentioned previously, Bülow had gained the confidence of the adolescent Crown Prince, and in the months leading up to the palace revolution of 1784 he tried to prepare his young charge for his future responsibilities. This included moral philosophy, information on the administrative structures and a crash course of recent Danish history. This was where Biehl entered the picture. At the behest of Bülow, she wrote a series of "historical letters" focusing on the relationships between the members of the royal family since Christian VI, between the king and his closest advisors and between royalty and the general public.[43] The letters were ostensibly written for Bülow's eyes only but they make sense only if the real addressee was the Crown Prince. After all, Bülow knew it already from his frequent conversations with Biehl and from his own experience at court, while the Crown Prince was in urgent need of a political and historical education. This hypothesis is confirmed by the fact that after the palace revolution 14 April 1784 Biehl through Bülow received the Crown Prince's "command" to write a history of the palace revolution and was given access to official documents.[44] After she had completed this task, in the summer of 1784 she added letters on Frederick IV and further material on Christian VII, thus completing what she herself called "a sketch of recent Danish history" stretching from 1699 to 1784 and intended for "the true and unadulterated information of **posterity**" (my emphasis added).[45]

Biehl's sketch of recent Danish history is very much a history of the royal family and court intrigues but also includes lucid character sketches, occasional source criticism, moral lessons and discussions of the course of events as well as material on economic, administrative and cultural affairs. The plot is tragic and illustrates how the misguided passions of Frederick IV, his Queen Louisa and his morganatic wife and later Queen, Anna Sophie Reventlow, triggered several generations of dysfunctional royal family life, culminating in the Struensee-affair and the coup of 1772.

Biehl shares a number of the conceptions with Hojer, Suhm and even Riegels. Like Hojer she stressed the passionate and possessive character of Anna Sophie Reventlow but while Hojer for understandable reasons focused on the short term consequences (alienation between the King and his brother and sister, rise to power of the disunited Reventlow clan) she described how the failings of all members of the royal *ménage à trois* emotionally crippled Crown Prince Christian (VI), thus setting the scene for his educational blunders in the next generation (Frederick V).

As mentioned previously, Suhm proposed to trace the present misfortune of Denmark back to "the discord between Frederick IV and Louisa and the subsequent marriage with Anna Sophie", but he never fulfilled his promise. But Biehl did and she did it in a way that occasionally reads like modern probing of childhood traumas, at other times like romantic wallowing in tragic passions, but always a good read. The following sample is from one of the letters on how Frederick IV dealt with the reaction of the Crown Prince Christian (later Christian VI) to the elevation of Anna Sophie Reventlow to Queen in 1721:

> That this step [the coronation of Anna Sophie Reventlow] was very disagreeable to the Crown Prince is easy to understand even if he did not betray it in the least but treated her with all due respect, yet very cold and reserved. She on the other hand at all occasions did everything imaginable to gain his goodwill and so to speak anticipate his wishes. And the King, either to humor her or because he thought that the Prince's gratitude would counter his resentment, supported her endeavors so vigorously that it was impossible for the Crown Prince to obtain the least except through the good offices of his stepmother. But to my mind this was an entirely wrong policy, because the more he was forced to resort to her, the deeper and stronger the idea was impressed upon his heart and daily renewed that his birth had destined him to bestow favors and benefits on her, not to receive them from her. And this constantly fanned the fire of revenge that smoldered in his breast.[46]

Even if the social and cultural context (dynastic court life) and the focus on dominant passions is pre-modern, the underpinning psychology is actually surprisingly modern and much more so than Holberg, Hojer and Riegels.

At the other end of the narrative we find the following portrait that Biehl draws of the young Caroline Mathilde, the unhappy Queen of Christian VII, and her lady-in-waiting Louise von Plessen. The Queen was very attached to Mrs. Pless, as Biehl calls her, and deeply saddened when she was removed as a result of an intrigue.

> The Queen was young and ardent and had intense passions and a heart made to love violently. Had her love been but lukewarm, then Mrs. Pless would never have become so important to her as she was, and her constant

love for Mrs. Pless together with the desire to revenge herself on those who had robbed her of this beloved person would not have laid the foundation for another love [viz. Struensee] that maybe was the cause of her death but surely caused Denmark innumerable sighs and tears. This fury of a lady-in-waiting not only poisoned and embittered the Queen's whole life but made the country miserable. For if the Queen's feelings for the King had not been hindered and transformed into bitterness and contempt then she would probably have loved him with her full warmth and maybe communicated to his soul, yet unpolluted by vices, some of her warmth and thus made him, herself and the whole country happy.[47]

This passage is a good example of Biehl's fluent prose style that in full accordance with the stylistic ideals of the age effortlessly combined historical narrative, character portraits and evaluations of the course of events.

A few pages further on Biehl recounts the following lucid anecdote for which she scrupulously gives the King's valet Nielsen as source:

The King had the whimsical idea that he did not want to enter the bed chamber of the Queen before her maids had left, and he also very much liked to go to bed at eleven o'clock. Accordingly, he usually sent word to the Queen before that time, asking whether she had retired. This Mrs. Pless represented as a great crime and presumption and as a grossness that not even the meanest man would commit, and in order to wean him from such commands the Queen would have to answer that it was not yet convenient. The next evening when the question was asked the answer was that Her Majesty played chess and would not retire until the game was finished. The King waited until it was twelve o'clock and then, presumably thinking that the Queen had gone to bed, entered but found her still playing with Mrs. Pless. With an annoyed and angry face he began walking up and down the floor without saying a word. The game did not end until after one o'clock and the Queen not only said that she wanted another one to get revenge but the King saw Mrs. Pless signaling her approval with a triumphant smile. Then he went out, slammed the door violently and for the first time did not come to the Queen during the following two weeks.[48]

It is abundantly clear from these passages that even if Biehl and Riegels disagreed about most things historical and moral—she accused him of having a "black heart"—they shared a predilection for pointing out villains and pass harsh sentences. In Biehl's case it made Bülow exclaim: "Miss Biehl, your judgement is too harsh, too severe, much too severe".[49]

Even if Biehl herself never used the terms anecdote or secret history to describe her own work the sheer volume of intimate details and intrigue justifies the label. But her "sketch of recent Danish history" is not only an example of secret history because of its subject matter. As evidenced by the quotations earlier, she followed quite closely in the analytical footsteps of

Antoine Varillas when she showed how the dominant passions and personal relationships linked up in a tragic chain of events running through several generations of the royal family and how these events connected to the general political history of Denmark. In this ambition to give a full explanation of the private side of politics, she closely parallels Hojer in his unexpurgated first draft of the chapter on the elevation of Anna Sophie Reventlow in 1721. The reason why she kept all the indiscretions in the text while he had to censure them is simple: Hojer's ambition was to enlighten his contemporaries in print about the events of the recent past, while she wrote for a restricted contemporary audience (Bülow and the Crown Prince)—and for posterity.

Needless to say, Bülow after Biehl's death kept her historical works and saw to it that they were distributed to different public collections together with the previously mentioned annotated draft chapters of Riegel's secret history and scattered memories and journal entries by himself. He even added a note explaining Biehl's authorship and lamenting the fact that he himself, after his retirement in 1793, had wanted to write up a coherent history of his times but had not been able to. In other words, Bülow, like Suhm, had wanted to write history but failed, and like Suhm he saw to it that the relevant manuscripts were not only kept in his library but preserved for posterity.

Conclusion

When Biehl's historical letters and her "sketch of recent Danish history" were eventually published in the 1860s, one could say that everything had gone according to plan: Her texts had been preserved and printed after a sufficient period of time had elapsed. Ironically, in the meantime, things had not only cooled down but moral sensibilities and historical genre boundaries had also changed too. The professional historians of the Victorian and historicist age no longer recognized Biehl's texts as serious history. They classed them as personal memoires and anecdotes in the derogatory sense of the word, and they thought she was a "palace gossip".[50]

A hundred years later, in the 1970s, a more permissive age reveled in exactly those passages that offended their Victorian great grandparents.[51] Surprisingly, contemporary feminist scholarship has followed this wrong track and maintained that Biehl was a writer, not a historian, that she never questioned the veracity of the stories she retailed, that her aim was to write a *chronique scandaleuse*, and that her historical letters are a sort of "history of sexuality under Christian VI, Frederik V and Christian VII", where "problems arise due to imbalance in the relationship between men and women"—all of which is wrong.[52]

The simple truth is that Biehl as well as Hojer, Holberg, Suhm and Riegels were 18th-century historians, reflecting with the mental tools of contemporary moral philosophy and living in a dynastic state where politics were personal and often passionate. Accordingly, they dealt with court history to the best of their ability, maneuvering between the genres of public (or pragmatic) history, *memoires* and secret history. All of them wanted to integrate court history into their historical narrative but with mixed results. Hojer was well informed and wanted to include information on the intrigues at court but was hampered by consideration for his patrons and the constraints of his position. However, he went as far as he could and his determination to include as much secret history as possible must be admired. Holberg would surely have included many more anecdotes, those "ornaments of history", if his sources had allowed it. Suhm set out to write real, subversive secret history but simply failed as an author. Riegels ardently desired to write secret history with ample coverage of court history and a strong political agenda but was frustrated through lack of source material. Biehl could build on a broad basis of oral traditions (like Suhm), inside information (like Hojer) and written sources (like Riegels wanted to) and eventually realized the full potential of the genre of secret history. She was in many ways a true Danish disciple of Varillas, also in matters of style. Through the irony of history, or maybe rather of historiography, her "sketch of modern Danish history" was published in an age that was unable to appreciate her achievement and for all their sympathy with Biehl modern feminists have not fared better. It is about time to give Biehl her rightful place in the canon of Danish 18th-century historiography.

Notes

1 For a comprehensive and most useful review see Brian Cowan, "The History of Secret Histories," *Huntington Library Quarterly* 81, no. 1 (2018): 121–151. A recent Nordic contribution:, Ellen Krefting, "Konger uten klær. Hemmelige historier som eneveldekritisk sjanger", *Arr – Idéhistorisk tidsskrift* vol. 1 (2017): 3–15.
2 Procope de Cesarée, *Histoire secrète*, trad. par L. de M. (Paris: Guillaume de Luyne, 1669); Procopius of Cesarea, *The Secret History of the Court of the Emperor Justinian* (John Barkesdale: London, 1674).
3 I use the excellent modern edition Antoine Varillas, *Les Anecdotes de Florence ou l'historie secrete de la maison de Medicis*, ed. Michel Bouvier (Presses Universitaires de Rennes: Rennes Cedex, 2004); a contemporary English translation: Varillas, *Anekdota eteroūiaka, or, The secret history of the house of Medicis*, transl. Ferrand Spence (R. Bentley and S. Magnes: London, 1686).
4 Varillas, *Les Anecdotes de Florence*, 45.
5 Varillas, *Les Anecdotes de Florence*, 59.
6 Cowan, "The History of Secret Histories" Eve Tavor Bannet, "'Secret History': Or, Talebearing Inside and Outside the Secretorie," *Huntington Library Quarterly* 68, no. 1–2 (2005): 375–396.
7 Claude-François Menestrier, *Les diverses caracteres, des ouvrages historiques avec le plan d'une nouvelle historie de la ville de Lyon* (J. Bapt. and Nicolas de Ville: Lyon, 1694): 108, cf. also 75–76.
8 Nicolas Lenglet Du Fresnoy, *Methode pour etudier l'histoire*, vol. 1 (Jean Musier: Paris, 1713): 324 (ch. 14, § 5). An English translation appeared under the title *A New Method of Studying History* (W. Burton: London, 1728).
9 Ménestrier, *Les diverses caracteres, des ouvrages historiques*, 38–40.
10 Lenglet Du Fresnoy, *Methode pour etudier l'histoire*, 4 (ch. 1).
11 Lucian, *How to Write History*, no. 38–43 (*Loeb* edition, 430), 52–58.

12 Walter Raleigh, *The History of the World* (Walter Burre: London, 1614) (second last page of the preface).
13 For a succinct 18th century discussion see the preface of Saint-Simon, *Mémoires*, vol. 1 (La Pléiade: Paris, 1982), 16–17.
14 Troels G. Jørgensen, *Andreas Hojer jurist og historiker* (Arne Frost Hansens Forlag: Copenhagen, 1961), 17–38, 89–97, 115–127; Caspar Paludan-Müller, "Dansk Historiografie i det 18de Aarhundrede," *Historisk Tidsskrift*, series 5, vol. 4 (1883–84), 1–188, on Hojer 3–35; Ellen Jørgensen, *Historieforskning og Historieskrivning i Danmark indtil Aar 1800* (H. Hagerups Forlag: Copenhagen, 1931), 173–179.
15 Andreas Hojer, *König Friedrich des Vierten glorwürdigstes Leben*, 2 vols. (Wittwe Forchhammer: Tondern, 1829).
16 Hojer, *König Friedrich des Vierten glorwürdigstes Leben*, vol. 1, 241.
17 Hojer, *König Friedrich des Vierten glorwürdigstes Leben*, vol. 2, 40–47.
18 Hojer, *König Friedrich des Vierten glorwürdigstes Leben*, vol. 2, 45–46.
19 The Royal Library Copenhagen, Manuscript Collection, shelf mark: Ledreborg 237 quarto. On the following see Sebastian Olden-Jørgensen, "Dronning Anna Sophies personlighed og politiske indflydelse 1721–30," *Historisk Tidsskrift* 123:1 (2023): 1–16.
20 "Niemand aber spielete in diesem allen ein Größer Spiel, als die Königin Anna Sophie selbst; und anfänglich muste die welt glauben, daß Ihr Verstand und Verdienste eben so sublimes als Ihr Glück sey. Sie hatte in der That auch Verstand, aber unvergleichlich mehr Passions; und diese waren insgesammt im höchsten Grad hefftig, und erlaubten ihr kein rechtes Nachdenken. Ihr Hertz war ein trotzig und verzagt Ding, und brachte sie bey der geringsten Widrigkeit durch zorn oder furcht außer sich. Darüber ward sie zu wohl gefasten Maas Reguln nicht geschickt, unfähig sich selbst zu überwinden, unbeständig, übereylend, auffahrend, und eines gantz unbeugsahmen Sinnes. Ihre Freunde vergaß Sie bald, und war wieder von Ihnen ohne Mühe vergeßen. Sie liebte den König; aber diese Liebe war ein loderndes und so unruhiges Feuer, welches den frommen Monarchen nur mehr plagte und Ihr eigen Gemüth unglaublich irre machte.", Ledreborg 237 quarto, original version of Chapter 12, 37–39 (bound with the rest but separately paginated). This earlier version of Chapter 12 is mentioned in a footnote by Jørgensen, *Historieforskning og Historieskrivning,* 178.
21 For an up-to-date introduction in English see *Ludvig Holberg (1684–1754). Learning and Literature in the Nordic Enlightenment*, eds. Knud Haakonssen and Sebastian Olden-Jørgensen (Routledge: London and New York, 2017). All Holberg's works are available in an excellent digitized edition at http://holbergsskrifter.dk/.
22 Merio Scattola, ""Historia literaria" als "historia pragmatica". Die pragmatische Bedeutung der Geschichtsschreibung im intellektuellen Unternehmen der Gelehrtengeschichte," *Historia literaria. Neuordnung des Wissens im 17. und 18. Jahrhundert*, eds. Frank Grunert and Friedrich Vollhardt, (Akademie Verlag: Berlin, 2007), 37–63Sebastian Olden-Jørgensen, *Ludvig Holberg som pragmatisk historiker. En historiografisk-kritisk undersøgelse* (Museum Tusculanum Press: Copenhagen 2015).
23 Ludvig Holberg, *Dannemarks Riges Historie*, 3 vols. (Copenhagen, 1732–35), vol. 3, fol. 1c v.
24 Holberg, *Dannemarks Riges Historie*, vol. 1, fol. 4 r.; vol. 2, 517–518, 884; vol. 3, fol. b2 v.-b4 v.
25 Holberg, *Dannemarks Riges Historie*, vol. 2, 884.
26 "Laudem meretur Holbergii diligentia in exquirendis variis opusculis Msstis, quæ hinc inde allegavit, præsertim in duobus ultimis, quos descripsit, Regibus Christiano IV. et Friderico III. cujus postremi Regis historiam eo modo enarravit,

quo nemo fortassis alius nostratium fuisset ausus, tot anecdota proferendo and secreta ex Msstis inserendo. Atque hinc tertium Volumen multiplici nomine duobus prioribus præferendum. Contra vero culpari possunt varia." Olden-Jørgensen, *Ludvig Holberg som pragmatisk historiker*, 29, 125.

27 P.Fr. Suhm, *Hemmelige Efterretninger om de danske Konger efter Souverainiteten*, ed. Julius Clausen (H. Hagerups Forlag: Copenhagen 1918).

28 "Vor nærværende slette Tilstand," Suhm, Suhm, *Hemmelige Efterretninger*, 16.

29 Suhm, Suhm, *Hemmelige Efterretninger*, 16–17.

30 Henrik Horstbøll, Ulrik Langen and Frederik Stjernfelt, *Grov Konfækt. Tre vilde år med trykkefrihed. 1770–73*, 2 vols. (Gyldendal: Copenhagen 2020), vol. 1, 448.

31 On several occasions the text is called "Suhm's secret diary" in Horstbøl, Langen and Stjernfelt, *Grov Konfækt*, but the text reads more like a summary of a diary that as day-to-day entries in a real diary.

32 Ellen Krefting, "Konger uten klær. Hemmelige historier som eneveldekritisk sjanger," *Arr – Idéhistorisk tidsskrift*, 2017, vol. 1, 3–15, especially 14.

33 Suhm, *Hemmelige Efterretninger*, 29, 34–35, 39, 42–43, 47, 52.

34 Suhm, *Hemmelige Efterretninger*, 69, 72; Rasmus Nyerup (ed.), *Suhmiana* (S. Poulsens Forlag: Copenhagen 1799), 77–86 (= P.F. Suhm, *Samlede Skrifter* (S. Poulsens Forlag: Copenhagen 1799, vol. 16); cf. Horstbøll, Langen and Stjernfelt, *Grov Konfækt*, vol. 1, 410–414.

35 The editor of Suhm's *Secret Information on the Danish Kings after Absolutism* included no information on the manuscript edited but comparisons show that he used Nyerup's copy (now in the Royal Library, shelf mark NKS 1728 folio) and not Suhm's original (shelf mark NKS 2839 quarto). The information on the transfer of the latter from the inaccessible collections in October 1918 derives from the hand written catalog in the Library's reading room.

36 Morten Petersen, *Oplysningens gale hund – en biografi om Niels Ditlev Riegels* (Aschehoug: Copenhagen 2003); Emil Nicklas Johnsen, *I Klios forgård. Forfatterroller, offentlighet og politisk evaluering i Niels Ditlev Riegels' (1755–1802) historieskriving* (Institutt for filosofi-, idé- og kunsthistorie og klassiske språk, Oslo University: Oslo, 2019) (Ph.D. dissertation).

37 N.D. Riegels, *Forsøg til Femte Christians Historie: som en Indledning til Fierde Friderichs ved Etatsraad Høier* (P.M. Høpffner: Copenhagen 1792); N.D. Riegels, *Udkast til Fierde Friderichs Historie efter Højer*, 2 vols (Christian Frederik Holm: Copenhagen 1795–1800); N.D. Riegels, *Christian den Siettes Levnetsbeskrivelse* (A. Soldins Forlag: Copenhagen 1798).

38 The preface and the first part were published in J.H. Bang (ed.), "Anden Fortsættelse af Meddelelser fra den Bülowske Manuskriptsamling i Sorø Akademis Bibliothek," *Indbydelsesskrift til den offentlige Examen i Sorø Akademi Skole i Juni og Juli 1867* (V. Røhrs Bogtrykkeri: Sorø, 1867): 1–56; the third part was published in Sebastian Olden-Jørgensen (ed.), "Niels Ditlev Riegels: Udkast til Kronprints Frederichs Opdragelses Historie (1786)", *Danske Magazin* 54 (2021): 9–44.

39 Bang, "Anden Fortsættelse af Meddelelser," 15–16.

40 Bang, "Anden Fortsættelse af Meddelelser," 29–30.

41 Martine W. Brownley, "Secret History and Seventeenth-Century Historiography," Rebecca Bullard and Rachel Carnell (eds.), *The Secret History in Literature, 1660–1820* (Cambridge University Press: Cambridge and New York, 2017): 33–45; Allison Stedman, "Secret History in Pre-Revolutionary France," Bullard and Carnell, *The Secret History in Literature*, 205–215.

42 Louis Bobé, "Charlotte Dorothea Biehl," Louis Bobé, *Fra Renaissance til Empire. Kulturhistoriske Afhandlinger* (H. Hagerups Forlag: Copenhagen 1916): 79–95; Charlotta Dorothea Biehl: *Mit ubetydelige Levnets Løb*, ed. Marianne Alenius

(Museum Tusculanum Press: Copenhagen 1986); Marianne Alenius, *Brev til eftertiden. Om Charlotta Dorothea Biehls selvbiografi og andre breve* (Museum Tusculanum Press: Copenhagen 1987); Marianne Alenius and Anne-Marie Mai, "Århundredets brevskriver," Elisabeth Møller Jensen, Eva Hættner Aurelius and Anne-Marie Mai (eds.), *Nordisk kvindelitteraturhistorie 1. I Guds navn 1000–1800* (Rosinante/Munksgaard: Copenhagen 1993): 370–380; Sebastian Olden-Jørgensen, "En fortidshistoriker og en samtidshistoriker. Ludvig Holberg og Charlotta Dorothea Biehl," *temp tidsskrift for historie* 17 (2019): 50–66.

43   Charlotta Dorothea Biehl, "Charlotte Dorothea Biehls historiske Breve," ed. J.H. Bang, *Historisk Tidsskrift*, series 3, vol. 4 (1865–66): 147–494. The most recent edition, *Brev fra Dorothea. Af Charlotte Dorothea Biehls historiske breve*, ed. Svend Cedergreen Bech (Politikens Forlag: Copenhagen 1975), is unreliable.

44   Charlotta Dorothea Biehl, "Regeringsforandringen, fremstillet af Charlotte Dorothea Biehl," ed. Edvard Holm, *Historisk Tidsskrift*, series 3, vol 5 (1866–67): 281–455.

45   Biehl, "Charlotte Dorothea Biehls historiske Breve," 184; Biehl, "Regeringsforandringen," 287.

46   Biehl, "Charlotte Dorothea Biehls historiske Breve," 166.

47   Biehl, "Charlotte Dorothea Biehls historiske Breve," 355.

48   Biehl, "Charlotte Dorothea Biehls historiske Breve," 357.

49   Biehl, "Regeringsforandringen," 287.

50   Paludan-Müller, "Dansk Historiografie i det 18de Aarhundrede," 101.

51   The blurb of the most recent and unsatisfactory edition (Biehl, *Brev fra Dorothea* from 1975) advertises the historical letters as "indiscretions" and stresses their "private, intimate form" (6).

52   Alenius and Mai, "Århundredets brevskriver," 375; Anne-Marie Mai, *Hvor litteraturen finder sted. Fra Guds tid til menneskets tid 1000–1800. Bidrag til dansk litteraturs historie bind 1* (Gyldendal: Copenhagen, 2010): 326–327, 330. One example of Biehl's source criticism: Biehl, "Charlotte Dorothea Biehls historiske Breve," 224, 226–227. The erroneous impression that Biehl concentrated on *chronique scandaleuse* probably stems from the use of the previously mentioned edition from 1975 that left out 45% of the text and concentrated on the saucy passages. Imbalanced relationships between the sexes is no issue in Biehl's historical letters (other than in her autobiography) but misguided passion and dysfunctional relationships are.

Bibliography

Alenius, Marianne, and Anne-Marie Mai. "Århundredets brevskriver," *Nordisk kvindelitteraturhistorie 1. I Guds navn 1000–1800*, edited by Elisabeth Møller Jensen, Eva Hættner Aurelius, and Anne-Marie Mai, 370–380. Rosinante/Munksgaard: Copenhagen, 1993.

Alenius, Marianne. *Brev til eftertiden. Om Charlotta Dorothea Biehls selvbiografi og andre breve*. Copenhagen: Museum Tusculanum Press, 1987.

Bang, J.H. (ed.). "Anden Fortsættelse af Meddelelser fra den Bülowske Manuskriptsamling i Sorø Akademis Bibliothek." *Indbydelsesskrift til den offentlige Examen i Sorø Akademis Skole i Juni og Juli 1867*, 1–56. Sorø: V. Røhrs Bogtrykkeri, 1867.

Bannet, Eve Tavor. "'Secret History': Or, Talebearing Inside and Outside the Secretorie." *Huntington Library Quarterly* 68, no. 1–2 (2005): 375–396.

Biehl, Charlotta Dorothea. "Charlotte Dorothea Biehls historiske Breve," edited by J.H. Bang. *Historisk Tidsskrift*, series 3, 4 (1865–66): 147–494.

Biehl, Charlotta Dorothea. "Regeringsforandringen, fremstillet af Charlotte Dorothea Biehl," edited by Edvard Holm, *Historisk Tidsskrift*, series 3, 5 (1866–67), 281–455.

Biehl, Charlotta Dorothea. *Brev fra Dorothea. Af Charlotte Dorothea Biehls historiske breve*, edited by Svend Cedergreen Bech. Copenhagen: Politikens Forlag, 1975.

Biehl, Charlotta Dorothea. *Mit ubetydelige Levnets Løb*, edited by Marianne Alenius. Copenhagen: Museum Tusculanum Press, 1986.

Bobé, Louis. "Charlotte Dorothea Biehl," in Louis Bobé (ed.), *Fra Renaissance til Empire. Kulturhistoriske Afhandlinger*, 79–95. Copenhagen: H. Hagerups Forlag, 1916.

Brownley, Martine W. "Secret History and Seventeenth-Century Historiography", in Bullard and Carnell (eds.). *The Secret History in Literature*, 33–45.

Bullard, Rebecca and Rachel Carnell (eds.). *The Secret History in Literature, 1660–1820*. Cambridge and New York: Cambridge University Press, 2017.

Cowan, Brian, "The History of Secret Histories." *Huntington Library Quarterly* 81, no. 1 (2018): 121–151.

G. Jørgensen, Troels. *Andreas Hojer jurist og historiker*. Copenhagen: Arne Frost Hansens Forlag, 1961.

Haakonssen, Knud and Sebastian Olden-Jørgensen (eds.). *Ludvig Holberg (1684–1754). Learning and Literature in the Nordic Enlightenment*. Routledge: London and New York, 2017.

Hojer, Andreas. *König Friedrich des Vierten glorwürdigstes Leben*, 2 vols. Tondern: Wittwe Forchhammer, 1829.

Holberg, Ludvig. *Dannemarks Riges Historie*, 3 vols. Copenhagen, 1732–35.

Horstbøll, Henrik, Ulrik Langen, and Frederik Stjernfelt. *Grov Konfækt. Tre vilde år med trykkefrihed. 1770–73*, 2 vols. Copenhagen: Gyldendal, 2020.

Johnsen, Emil Nicklas. *I Klios forgård. Forfatterroller, offentlighet og politisk evaluering i Niels Ditlev Riegels' (1755–1802) historieskriving*. Institutt for filosofi-, idé- og kunsthistorie og klassiske språk. Oslo: Oslo University, 2019 (Ph.D. dissertation).

Jørgensen, Ellen. *Historieforskning og Historieskrivning i Danmark indtil Aar 1800*. Copenhagen: H. Hagerups Forlag, 1931.

Krefting, Ellen. "Konger uten klær. Hemmelige historier som eneveldekritisk sjanger." *Arr – Idéhistorisk tidsskrift* 1 (2017): 3–15.

Lenglet Du Fresnoy, Nicolas. *A New Method of Studying History*. London: W. Burton, 1728.

Lenglet Du Fresnoy, Nicolas. *Methode pour etudier l'histoire*, vol. 1. Paris: Jean Musier, 1713.

Lucian. *How to Write History (Loeb edition, 430)*.

Menestrier, Claude-François. *Les diverses caracteres, des ouvrages historiques avec le plan d'une nouvelle historie de la ville de Lyon*. Lyon: J. Bapt. and Nicolas de Ville, 1694.

Nyerup, Rasmus (ed.). *Suhmiana*. Copenhagen: S. Poulsens Forlag, 1799 (= P.F. Suhm. *Samlede Skrifter*. S. Poulsens Forlag, vol. 16).

Olden-Jørgensen, Sebastian (ed.). "Niels Ditlev Riegels: Udkast til Kronprints Frederichs Opdragelses Historie (1786)." *Danske Magazin* 54 (2021): 9–44.

Olden-Jørgensen, Sebastian. "Dronning Anna Sophies personlighed og politiske indflydelse 1721–30." *Historisk Tidsskrift* 123, 1 (2023): 1–16.

Olden-Jørgensen, Sebastian. "En fortidshistoriker og en samtidshistoriker. Ludvig Holberg og Charlotta Dorothea Biehl." *Temp tidsskrift for historie* 17 (2019): 50–66.

Olden-Jørgensen, Sebastian. *Ludvig Holberg som pragmatisk historiker. En historiografisk-kritisk undersøgelse*. Copenhagen: Museum Tusculanum Press, 2015.

Paludan-Müller, Caspar. "Dansk Historiografie i det 18de Aarhundrede," *Historisk Tidsskrift*, series 5, 4 (1883-84): 1–188.

Petersen, Morten. *Oplysningens gale hund – en biografi om Niels Ditlev Riegels*. Copenhagen: Aschehoug, 2003.

Procope de Cesarée. *Histoire secrète*, trad. par L. de M. Paris: Guillaume de Luyne, 1669.

Procopius of Cesarea. *The Secret History of the Court of the Emperor Justinian*. London: John Barksdale, 1674.

Raleigh, Walter. *The History of the World*. London: Walter Burre, 1614.

Riegels, N.D. *Christian den Siettes Levnetsbeskrivelse*. Copenhagen: A. Soldins Forlag, 1798.

Riegels, N.D. *Forsøg til Femte Christians Historie: som en Indledning til Fierde Friderichs ved Etatsraad Høier*. Copenhagen: P.M. Høpffner, 1792.

Riegels, N.D. *Udkast til Fierde Friderichs Historie efter Højer*, 2 vols. Copenhagen: Christian Frederik Holm, 1795-1800.

Saint-Simon. *Mémoires*, vol. 1. Paris: La Pléiade, 1982.

Scattola, Meri. ""Historia literaria" als "historia pragmatica". Die pragmatische Bedeutung der Geschichtsschreibung im intellektuellen Unternehmen der Gelehrtengeschichte." *Historia literaria. Neuordnung des Wissens im 17. und 18. Jahrhundert*, edited by Frank Grunert and Friedrich Vollhardt. Akademie Verlag: Berlin, 2007, 37–63.

Stedman, Allison. "Secret History in Pre-Revolutionary France", in Bullard and Carnell, *The Secret History in Literature*, 205–215.

Suhm, P.Fr. *Hemmelige Efterretninger om de danske Konger efter Souverainiteten*, ed. Julius Clausen. Copenhagen: H. Hagerups Forlag, 1918.

Varillas, [Antoine]. *Anekdota eteroūiaka, or, The Secret History of the House of Medicis*, transl. Ferrand Spence. London: R. Bentley and S. Magnes, 1686.

Varillas, Antoine. *Les Anecdotes de Florence ou l'historie secrete de la maison de Medicis*, ed. Michel Bouvier. Rennes Cedex: Presses Universitaires de Rennes, 2004.

Part 4

Traveling historical genres

9 Historical transfers

Ludwig Albrecht Gebhardi and the transformations of his late eighteenth-century histories of Denmark and Norway

Håkon Evju

The printer and bookseller Christian Iversen (1748–1827) was apparently not a prey to doubt in January 1776, when he advertised the subscription list for a history in Danish of the kingdoms of Denmark and Norway and the duchies of Schleswig and Holstein. He was convinced that such a work would find buyers, or, as he put it, "lovers of history" willing to "support a venture so beneficial for the fatherland".[1] Signing up for these books would not only provide the reader with the latest, most accurate and comprehensive histories of the kingdoms and duchies under the control of the House of Oldenburg, but would also be an act of patriotism, "helping to bring about" a work that would benefit the common good.[2] It was only natural then, that Iversen promised to print the names and titles of all subscribers in the first volume. He would put their love of country on display.

As Iversen also made clear, the historical works he was advertising were translations, and his appeal to patriotism stands out when seen in relation to the originals. The main part, the histories of the kingdoms of Denmark and Norway, was to be based on a two-volume work written in German by a professor at the Gymnasium in Lüneburg, Ludwig Albrecht Gebhardi (1735–1802). They were not national histories as such, but part of a popular German universal history, printed by Johan Justus Gebauer's publishing house in Halle.[3] This series had itself started out as a translation of an English universal history, edited by the Halle theologian Sigmund Jacob Baumgarten (1706–1757), before criticism of the English original and its German rendition made Gebauer commission new editions by historians such as Gebhardi. It is a truly remarkable example of the exchange and circulation of historical thought in Enlightenment Europe.[4] As Monika Baár has shown, it was not uncommon for histories produced in this series to be translated and transformed into national histories outside the German lands.[5] This happened with histories of Hungary and a range of other principalities and territories as well. The different demands of the two genres, universal history and national history, did not prove prohibitive. However, the particular historical circumstances under which the transformations took place still crucially shaped each of these

DOI: 10.4324/9781003331971-14

intellectual exchanges. In the case of Gebhardi's histories, they were bundled together with a translation of the histories of the duchies of Schleswig and Holstein by the historian Wilhelm Ernst Christiani, a professor in Kiel. They were to be national histories for a composite monarchy, at a point in time when the men in power at the court in Copenhagen were particularly receptive toward attempts to forge a common patriotic identity in the aftermath of the Struensee affair and its inflammatory effects on Danish and Norwegian national sentiments. In order to grasp the dynamics of this transfer, we need to pay close attention to the contexts in which it occurred. Christian Iversen surely knew what he was doing when communicating, not only with possible readers, but with the authorities as well.

This chapter is a study of the transfer and transformations of Gebhardi's histories of Denmark and Norway as they traveled from the German lands to Denmark-Norway in the second half of the eighteenth century. They were released in Danish in considerably revised and enlarged form, in eight volumes between 1777 and 1798, and in a series that also included six volumes on the histories of the duchies.[6] Johan Ernst Heilmann (1735–1800), a clergyman with literary interests living close to Christian Iversen in Odense, translated most of them, but after the publishing venture passed from Iversen to Søren Gyldendal in Copenhagen in 1784, others were brought in to translate as well. Up to now, Gebhardi himself has gone below the radar of German scholars interested in eighteenth-century historiography, and has ended up in the shadow of prominent figures such as Johann Christoph Gatterer (1727–1799) and August Ludwig Schlözer (1735–1809),[7] nor has he received much attention from Danish historians either. The exception is Casper Paludan-Müller, who has provided a brief overview of his translated Danish history.[8] Apart from that, the fact that his work is a translation, written by a foreigner, seems to have been enough to exclude him from further consideration.[9] I shall argue that paying more attention to it offers a way to study the links and gauge the distance between the historical cultures of Denmark-Norway and the German lands. Gebhardi was a mediator who straddled the borders of these worlds. On a general level, the many connections between Denmark and the German lands are well-known, especially from a Danish perspective. Schleswig-Holstein, as well as Copenhagen, functioned as a hub for the flow and exchange of goods, people and ideas.[10] Yet we know little of what this meant for historical writing in the eighteenth century. From a German perspective, it is clear that the university in Göttingen was a center for the study of Eastern and Northern Europe in the eighteenth century.[11] Indeed, the shift from a broad understanding of "Norden", of the North, influenced by the ancients, to a modern distinction between Northern and Eastern Europe owed much to scholars from Göttingen.[12] Nevertheless, what we know of these developments is mostly based on their involvement with the histories and societies of the peoples of Central and Eastern Europe. Their contact and exchanges with Scandinavian scholars, and especially Dano-Norwegian ones, remains somewhat in the dark. The fate of Gebhardi's work offers a chance to shed some new light on this topic.

Ludwig Albrecht Gebhardi and the *Allgemeine Welthistorie*

Gebhardi was born in Lüneburg in the duchy of Braunschweig-Lunebürg. He was the son of Johan Ludwig Levin Gebhardi, a historian, genealogist and professor at the local Gymnasium and Ritterakademie, and received his early education at that institution. Following in his father's footsteps, Gebhardi eventually obtained a position as professor and settled at the Gymnasium in Lüneburg,[13] but before that, he studied at the Georgia Augusta in Göttingen and traveled abroad, staying for four years in Schleswig and Copenhagen as a tutor in a private household,[14] familiarizing himself with the Nordic languages and with Nordic history. As a historian, he published early on a history of the St. Michaelis convent in Lüneburg,[15] and like his father, he also wrote genealogical treatises, publishing a three-volume history of the German hereditary nobility.[16] His most substantial output, however, was devoted to different forms of universal history. In addition to the two volumes on the history of Denmark and Norway, he contributed studies of Hungary, Wallachia, Moldavia, Transylvania, Lithuania, and Prussia.[17] Several of these were translated, not just into Danish, but into Hungarian and Slavic languages as well.[18]

In the sixteenth and seventeenth centuries, universal history, the genre to which Gebhardi's histories were a contribution, had been closely linked to the various European Churches, confessional struggles and theological concerns. In Protestant Northern Europe, the humanist Philip Melanchthon's Latin reworking of Johann Carion's medieval world chronicle provided the model for such historical writing. Melanchthon used the ancient and biblical scheme of Four Monarchies to organize and assign meaning to world events, and for him, history took on the character of the Christian history of salvation. History unfolded according to God's preordained plan and the troubles of Melanchthon's own time, the persecution of Protestants, the position of the Catholic Church, and the threat from the Ottomans, served as a sign for him that the last days were approaching. In the Catholic South, the French bishop and court preacher Jacques-Bénigne Bossuet applied an equally prominent theological framework to universal history toward the end of the seventeenth century in his *Discours sur l'histoire universelle* (1681). Bossuet, who interpreted history as a struggle between God and the Devil, saw the hand of God in the fortunes of the Catholic Church and its secular allies, especially the French monarchy. He wrote history to defend the faith and assert the authority of Scripture.

In the eighteenth century, the varying theological concerns that had marked the writing of universal history became less conspicuous. Historical change could more easily be explicated in terms of causal mechanisms, rather than with reference to some divine plan, and the peoples, empires and geographical areas covered in universal histories were less constrained by Old Testament history and schemes such as that of the Four Monarchies. Historians could more freely integrate perspectives and knowledge accumulated from increasing contacts with the rest of the world. As is well known, Voltaire began his universal history, the *Essai sur les mœurs et l'esprit des nations* (1756), with China and included treatments of India and Persia as well. However, the interpretative pattern he and many other philosophical historians of the eighteenth century applied—one of progress, especially within the arts and sciences—still served to focus his work on Europe. Other forms of eighteenth-century universal histories were, in a sense, more universal and an impetus in this regard came from England,[19] with a large-scale historiographical enterprise that is important for understanding Gebhardi's career as a historian. The English *Universal History* was primarily a commercial venture, initiated by publishers and written by a group of mostly unknown jobbing writers.[20] Conceived as truly universal in scope, both spatially and temporally, it was an extremely sprawling and voluminous compilation, published in sixty-four volumes between 1736 and 1765. The *Universal History* was divided into an ancient and a modern part, and it became something of a historical archive or library. There was no one historical idea behind this venture, which consisted of contributions from so many different authors. At any rate, the *Universal History* clearly satisfied a significant demand for historical instruction in the eighteenth century. Several editions in different formats were released, and the publishers, William Guthrie and John Gray, even oversaw an abridged version. It reached a diverse audience and proved a great success.

Both the *Universal History* and the abridged version published by Guthrie and Gray led to translations and adaptations, both single volumes and full-scale enterprises, in continental Europe.[21] The somewhat low scholarly quality of some of the volumes in the English original seems to have been a concern to several European editors, who equipped their editions with corrections in introductory essays and in footnotes. In Germany, the influential theologian Sigmund Baumgarten at the University of Halle chose to translate, edit and annotate an already annotated Dutch adaptation of the *Universal History* on behalf of Gebauer. Baumgarten's interest in history was apologetic. While he did not impose biblical interpretative patterns on civil history, as many Protestant historians had done before him, he sought to use history to support the authority of Scripture against freethinkers, especially through historical investigations of sacred history.[22] While Baumgarten was editor, he therefore focused his efforts on the ancient part of the universal history. Upon his death, Baumgarten's former student, the theologian Johann Salomo Semler (1725–1791), took over as editor and carried on the project in the spirit of his former teacher.

Baumgarten's and Semler's strategy of improving deficiencies in the English original through critical introductions and emendations in footnotes had been contentious for some time, when the volume on Russia appeared in 1765. At that point, August Ludwig Schlözer, who in 1769 became professor of Russian history and literature at the university in Göttingen, brought things to a head. He wrote a highly critical review in the *Göttingische Anzeigen von gelehrten Sachen* (hereafter: GAS) and questioned the approach of the German *Allgemeine Weltgeschichte*.[23] As subscribers started to withdraw, Semler resigned as editor and the publisher discontinued the series. Gebauer then announced a *Fortsetzung der Allgemeinen Weltgeschichte* with a promise of not just translations, but up-to-date scholarly work, written by German historians. The Northern and Eastern European lands were the areas with which the revived series began. Schlözer seems to have acted as a consultant to Gebauer in this process, and he was hired to write an introduction to Northern history. Johann Christoph Gatterer, professor of history at the University of Göttingen, was likewise involved, agreeing to assist the publisher and use his network, established through his *Historisches Institut*, to help recruit scholars to write the new histories.[24]

Gebhardi was one of the authors who came in at this point for the *Fortsetzung der Allgemeinen Weltgeschichte*. Since Schlözer's proposed introduction appeared late, in 1771, Gebhardi's histories of Denmark and Norway were the first volumes in the new series when they were published in 1768 and 1770. Not surprisingly, given the commercial aspect of this venture, both were also released in a separate edition for those who did not subscribe to the universal history.[25] Gebauer wanted to get the most out of the histories he commissioned. A further indication of this is the fact that an abridged one-volume version was published a few years later, in 1774.[26] At the same time, as Gebhardi made clear, he had revised and improved both editions in order to take into account recent work by contemporary Danish and Norwegian historians.[27] He thus provided a scholarly justification for the proliferation of his Dano-Norwegian histories as well, and this helped establish Gebhardi as an authority on the history of Denmark and Norway in the German lands. The prominent Norwegian historian Gerhard Schøning praised "the learned Professor Gebhardi" already in 1771 as someone who had done a great service by increasing knowledge of Norwegian history abroad.[28]

Gebhardi's German histories of Denmark and Norway

As I have suggested, Gebhardi's German history of Denmark and Norway was very much regnal or national in character, in spite of being part of a universal history. He focused on politics and organized his books into separate sections for the two realms, beginning with the history of Norway until the Union of Kalmar of 1397, then moving to a similar treatment of Denmark during the same period. In practice, he composed two separate regnal histories for this period, held together primarily by the preface and by the fact that they were in the same volume and the same series. This was in line with the compilatory technique that marked the *Universal History* since its inception, and is one reason why it was relatively easy to select particular volumes and convert them into stand-alone works. For the period from the Kalmar-Union of 1397 to the reign of King Frederik V (r. 1748–1766), the matter was, in a sense, even more straight forward for Gebhardi. As the monarchy resided in Copenhagen and Norway was without independent state institutions in the early modern period, he classified this era as part of the history of the Danish realm. For the kind of political history Gebhardi practiced, there simply were very few histories to tell about Norway after the kingdom lost its independence.

In spite of his focus on politics, Gebhardi did try to broaden the thematic scope of his histories. Before his narratives commenced, he offered a survey of the geography of each realm and statistical accounts of their present state. Again, this had been a common way for historians to open 'national' or regnal histories since the seventeenth century.[29] Gebhardi was once again following established conventions. In the 1774 edition, he had enlarged this section and added "historical statistics" as well, an extensive analysis of the forms of government, religion, agriculture, trade, customs and manners of the Norwegians and Danes in ancient times but also with a diachronic perspective highlighting historical change in these areas.[30] Thus, he moved beyond politics and into social, economic and cultural conditions. In so doing, Gebhardi clearly hoped to impart some more general lessons to his readers. As he wrote in his preface to the first volume:

> For the history of Norway, when accounts from Greenland are included, does not solely impart a truthful image of man in his natural state, before the formation of societies and lordships and before the development of arts. It teaches us also with greater certainty and clarity than the histories of many other peoples, in what ways the ancestors of humanity have peopled desolate places, founded societies and republics, and finally overturned and transformed them into monarchies.[31]

Gebhardi tried at this point to emphasize aspects of the history of humanity that the history of Norway was particularly well suited to illuminate. His work was not only relevant for those who wanted to know more about Norway but also for others with other historical interests. He alluded to more abstract and generalized forms of historical writing that in different guises were becoming popular in the eighteenth century, like the *Geschichte der Menschheit* of Isak Iselin, or Scottish conjectural history like that of Adam Ferguson and Lord Kames. Continuing his list of the usefulness and relevance of Norwegian history, he also pointed to more specific mechanisms at work in European history:

> Furthermore, it demonstrates how Christianity in the Middle Ages often was introduced to the pagans with deception, or through the use of violence, and idolatry thus extinguished among them. How the most perfect state gradually by numerous uprisings, civil wars, political tricks, insults and the effects of self-interest has been brought to the most felicitous and best constitution.[32]

Through these remarks, which ended in customary panegyrics of Dano-Norwegian absolutism, Gebhardi demonstrated his familiarity with a kind of philosophical reflection that marked some of the most celebrated works of history during the Enlightenment.[33] Once his narrative commenced, however, such more general and comparative insights were not particularly prominent. At that point, accounting for the course of events and identifying the causal mechanisms that explained historical change, took center stage. Gebhardi focused on getting the facts right, and he seems to have left more general "reasoning" to his readers.

This abstention from philosophical reflection that marked the Lüneburg historian's German histories of Denmark and Norway seems to have been a conscious decision. It was mirrored in the scholarly ideals introduced in the prefaces as well. Since Gebhardi's two volumes were the first to appear after the responsibility of editing the *Allgemeine Weltgeschichte* had moved from Halle to Göttingen, Gebhardi was setting a new standard, one which not only reflected upon himself but also on the new editors. Gatterer wrote prefaces to both of Gebhardi's two volumes,[34] and in the first preface, he emphasized Gebhardi's knowledge of Danish and Norwegian historical scholarship, as well as of contemporary Danish state and society.[35] He mentioned Gebhardi's stay in Copenhagen and sought to bolster his credibility as a witness. Gatterer also underlined Gebhardi's commitment to telling the truth, claiming: "It is possible to write a more eloquent history of Denmark and Norway, but I do not believe even a Dane can write a more truthful one".[36] Accuracy and certainty were more important than rhetoric and oratory. These priorities were endorsed and given a positive spin by reviewers as well, by Schlözer and by another Göttingen professor with an interest in Northern history, Johann Phillip Murray.[37] They were also, not least, in line with Gebhardi's own self-presentation as a historian. In his own preface, he listed a range of different purposes for which historians could write history, before concluding that nothing was more important than striving through historical criticism to tell the truth about the past.[38] Demonstrating his commitment to this ideal, Gebhardi went on to provide a twenty-page introduction to Danish and Norwegian historical scholarship and erudition in the manner of *historia litteraria*. Thus, he sought to further bolster his authority as the author of these histories.[39]

Truth, accuracy and historical criticism were key ideals of many historians working in Göttingen and its hinterlands. The espousal of such values is one reason why some modern scholars have spoken of a Göttingen school of historical writing centered on Schlözer and Gatterer.[40] Gebhardi had studied in Göttingen, became a member of Gatterer's *Historisches Institut,* and eventually contributed heavily to the GAS.[41] He clearly had links and commonalities with the Göttingen historians. Some scholars have been skeptical of such labels, however, stressing the disagreements and different institutional ties that marked the relationship between "members" of this school,[42] and in the case of Gebhardi, neither his broad adherence to the same historiographical tenets as Gatterer and Schlözer, nor his collaboration with them, shielded him from criticism. It is telling that while Gatterer wrote prefaces to Gebhardi's histories, he mainly used these prefaces to publish an otherwise unrelated treatise on the use of historical maps.[43] He kept a certain distance, and criticism of Gebhardi's work appeared in the journal Gatterer edited, *Allgemeine Historische Bibliothek*. A contributing factor in this regard might be that Gebhardi not only was familiar with Nordic history and historical sources but also absorbed some of the scholarly positions of contemporary Nordic historians. What estranged him somewhat from the Göttingen historians might very well have been the same as what endeared him to his Danish and Norwegian colleagues, helping his work gain acceptance in Denmark-Norway.

Dano-Norwegian and German historical exchanges

Gebhardi had befriended the historian, royal archivist and founding father of *Det kongelig danske Selskab for Fædrelandets Historie og Sprog* (Royal Danish Society for the Promotion of Language and Letters), Jacob Langebek (1715–1775),[44] while he was in Copenhagen, and he kept in contact with him. Langebek had a central place in the Dano-Norwegian historical world in the mid-eighteenth century. He had been the protégé of the university professor and royal librarian, archivist and historiographer Hans Gram (1685–1748), and he was heir to an erudite and philologically inclined historical tradition in Denmark-Norway going back to Ole Worm. Langebek devoted his labors to editing and publishing medieval Danish documents and historical treatises, and he was an important interlocutor and patron for the two foremost Dano-Norwegian historians of the 1760s and 1770s, the previously mentioned Gerhard Schøning (1722–1780), who was professor of history and eloquence at Sorø Academy, and his friend and collaborator, the Danish historian Peter Frederik Suhm (1728–1798), later to become royal historiographer. Foreign historians interested in Danish history also sought his advice. He assisted the Swedish historian Sven Lagerbring, and he seems to have played a similar role in the case of Gebhardi, helping him keep abreast of Dano-Norwegian scholarship and introducing him to men like Schøning and Suhm.[45] Gebhardi had sent his manuscript to Langebek before it was printed, and he had received his comments as well as improvements from Schøning and Suhm.

   The two latter historians were of particular importance to Gebhardi, since they, like him, worked on regnal histories of Norway and Denmark.[46] Schøning's unfinished three-volume *Norges Riges Historie* (*History of the Realm of Norway*) was released between 1771 and 1780, while Suhm's fourteen volumes on *Historien af Danmark* (*History of Denmark*) appeared between 1781 and 1828. Given that the two Dano-Norwegian historians were engaged in similar historical endeavors to those of Gebhardi, it might seem surprising that they did not see him as more of a competitor. However, there is much to suggest that, in the event, they saw him as occupied with a different, albeit compatible, historical project. The difference in terms of the size or length of their regnal histories, of Gebhardi's two volumes compared to Schøning and Suhm's seventeen, is just one indication in this regard.

Schøning and Suhm saw the Lüneburg historian as a popularizer of Danish and Norwegian history for a foreign audience. As Schøning explained with reference to Gebhardi, the purpose of the universal history did not allow "the admirable man" to "elaborate or go into details".[47] He had to be brief, while they themselves clearly preferred writing more at length. Furthermore, Schøning and Suhm were convinced of the need to probe the distant prehistorical Nordic past and tackle the many difficult historical issues in that period, before they could commence their regnal narratives. Whereas Gebhardi "did not have the opportunity to go to the most ancient testimonies himself",[48] Schøning and Suhm spent a considerable amount of time in the 1760s and 1770s writing erudite and critical articles and books concerning Old Norse-Icelandic literature and other historical sources relevant for ancient Northern history.[49] Gebhardi read these works and referenced them dutifully. His tone was deferential when he commented on the writings of what he called his "Nordic benefactors".[50]

Another factor that was most likely helpful in the relationship between Gebhardi and Schøning and Suhm was the familiarity of the latter two with the *Allgemeine Weltgeschichte* and the historical worlds of Halle and Göttingen. The ancient part of German universal history was taught at the University of Copenhagen, and the two might have read the compilation when they studied in the Danish capital during the 1740s. They first met later on, in Trondheim in Norway, and their first collaborative work, *Forsøg til Forbedringer i den gamle Danske og Norske Historie* (*Attempts at Improvements in Old Danish and Norwegian History*, 1757), was an attempt to provide a Danish equivalent to the previously mentioned Sigmund Baumgarten's translation of a different English enterprise, a biographical compilation.[51] A few years later, Suhm wrote several long articles commenting on the German version of the English universal history and the work of "the learned Doctor Baumgarten" in the proceedings of *Det Trondhiemske Selskab (The Trondheim Society)*, a precursor to the Royal Norwegian Society of Sciences and Letters, newly founded in Trondheim by Suhm, Schøning and Bishop Johan Ernst Gunnerus.[52] He demonstrated a profound and critical engagement with the venture to which Gebhardi contributed so prolifically a few years later.[53]

It is important that Schøning and Suhm also had links with the new editors of the universal history in Göttingen after Baumgarten died and Semler withdrew. They both became members of Gatterer's *Historisches Institut* and their works, as they appeared in the 1760s and onwards, were followed closely and reviewed in the GAS, most often by Murray.[54] While Suhm and Schøning received a good deal of praise in these reviews,[55] a critical attitude was also discernible, and this emerged even more strongly when August Ludwig Schlözer in 1771 released his historical compilation, *Allgemeine Nordische Geschichte,* as volume 31 of the *Fortsetzung der Allgemeinen Weltgeschichte.* About forty percent of Schlözer's compilation consisted of translated excerpts from Schøning's books and articles. To some extent, this was a mark of recognition and reflected the fact that Schlözer agreed with many of Schøning's conclusions, but he also voiced misgivings in some rather critical footnotes.[56] Schøning responded in the form of a pamphlet, and a rivalry developed that also helps to shed light on the reception of Gebhardi's work and its transfer to Denmark-Norway.[57]

These disagreements between Göttingen historians such as Murray and Schlözer on the one hand, and Schøning and Suhm on the other, were multifaceted, but at the center were questions about historical evidence. The two Dano-Norwegian historians sought to write comprehensive histories that linked the peopling and settlement of the North with the primeval history in the Bible, the story of the confusion of languages and dispersion of the peoples at Babel.[58] In so doing, they drew on a wide range of ancient testimonies, Biblical as well as Classical, but the most important in their eyes were the testimonies found in the Old Norse-Icelandic literary tradition. The Icelandic skald, chieftain and historian Snorri Sturlason's story of the legendary migration of Odin and his band of æsir from Asia to the North was particularly crucial to Schøning and Suhm in this regard, since it suggested that collective memories of the migrations from the East had lingered on among the Northerners themselves, within skaldic poetry, before Snorri recorded them.[59] Reconstructions of the wanderings of early humans toward the North did not need to rely solely on geographical or etymological speculations based on scanty evidence from the Bible or from Classical literature. Schlözer, however, believed that the story about Odin was a fable concocted by Snorri, and he brushed it aside. On a general level, he was critical of the tendency of Scandinavian scholars to accept the historical credibility of so much of the Icelandic sagas. Murray, on his side, displayed a similar skepticism in his reviews of Schøning's work in the GAS.

Gebhardi had accepted the historical reliability of Snorri's story of Odin and incorporated it into his histories of Denmark and Norway. This led to similar objections on the part of reviewers such as Schøning and Suhm. In the GAS, Murray had pointed out Gebhardi's "predilection for the Northern tradition" and expressed grave doubts about his assumptions regarding the most distant Northern past.[60] At best, the foundations on which he built his historical narrative of this period were uncertain. Similarly, Schlözer in the *Allgemeine Deutsche Bibliothek* and the reviewer in Gatterer's *Allgemeine Historische Bibliothek* expressed skepticism about Gebhardi's trust in Icelandic sagas. After all, the saga writers based much of their accounts on oral tradition: "the worst and most impure of all historical sources".[61] Gebhardi had anticipated such objections. In the abridged 1774 version of his Danish and Norwegian history, he included a long preface on the status of Odin, in which he laid out his views on the subject at length.[62] Although Gebhardi did not follow Schøning and Suhm without qualifications—he developed his own account of ancient Northern chronology—by accepting the story of Odin as probable, if not certain, history, he had aligned himself with his Nordic benefactors on this issue regarding the earliest part of his Nordic history.

The transformations of Gebhardi's histories in Denmark

Gebhardi's handling of the evidence and the testimonies that constituted the foundation of his narrative, most likely contributed to a favorable scholarly atmosphere for the transfer of his work to Denmark-Norway. He was broadly in line with the leading Dano-Norwegian historians. It was not, however, historians who initiated the translation of Gebhardi's work into Danish, but the printer and bookseller Christian Iversen, drawing on a network of booksellers across Denmark and Norway. His motive was commercial, as had been the case earlier on with the *Universal History* and the *Allgemeine Weltgeschichte*.[63] Iversen announced the subscription plan in a range of provincial newspapers early in 1776,[64] and he gave several reasons for his initiative. One concerned the timing, and was not related to the work of the Lüneburg historian. Iversen offered the translation of Gebhardi's histories of Denmark and Norway in combination with a translation of the history of the duchies of Schleswig and Holstein, by the professor at the University of Kiel, Wilhelm Ernst Christiani.[65] He believed that the transfer of control of the remaining ducal territories in Schleswig-Holstein to the Danish crown in June 1773 had aroused an interest in the history of the German duchies among the Danish-speaking public.[66] The time was ripe for such a publication.

However, the big idea behind Iversen's historical translation project was clearly to offer an up-to-date, comprehensive historical compilation covering the main constituent realms and principalities belonging to the House of Oldenburg from when they were first settled down to the present. It was only Denmark at this point that, in Ludvig Holberg's three-volume *Danmarks Riges Historie* (*History of the Realm of Denmark*, 1732–35), had a recent history in Danish covering the full stretch of the realm's history. Schøning's history of Norway had not yet got beyond King Harald Fairhair and his unification of the realm toward the end of the ninth century, and no other proper alternatives in Danish existed. Christiani had released the first volume of his history of the duchies, but in German. The product Iversen was offering, then, had few competitors, and the fact that a large part of it had its origins within a genre of historical writing that was universal in scope, rather than regnal or national, was not a problem. Iversen's history of Denmark, Norway and Schleswig-Holstein was also a compilation, albeit on a smaller scale, just like the English *Universal History* and the German *Allgemeine Welthistorie*. In neither case were attempts made to provide an overarching structure or system. The work remained serial in nature.

For the printer and bookseller from Odense, the factor that united the different histories in his compilation was patriotism and devotion to the ruling house. In his call for subscriptions, he sought to appeal to the patriotism of his potential customers. According to Iversen, his translation project was a "useful undertaking for the glory of the fatherland".[67] He most likely intended this as a message not only for the public but also for those in charge at the court in

Copenhagen. The rise and the fall from power of the King's physician, Johan Friedrich Struensee, in 1770 to 1772, had awakened strong national sentiments in Denmark-Norway. It had fueled anti-German sentiments in Copenhagen among Danes and stirred hopes among Norwegians of a more equal treatment of the Norwegian kingdom in the union with Denmark.[68] In the aftermath of the fall of the German physician, the new clique in power at court, led politically by Ove Høegh-Guldberg, the new cabinet secretary to the King, tried in various ways to harness and contain the political energies released by Struensee. Guldberg encouraged a patriotism directed not toward the different component parts of the King's House, but to the King and the state.

The most famous policy that emerged from Guldberg's attempts to forge a common identity for the Oldenburg monarchy was the law of 1776, which reserved positions in the civil service for citizens of the state, barring foreigners, including Germans from outside Schleswig-Holstein. However, Guldberg was also very much interested in using history for patriotic purposes. He was a theologian, a former professor at the Academy in Sorø, and on friendly terms with Langebek, Schøning and Suhm.[69] While he was in power, Guldberg reformed the grammar school system and put lessons in the history of the fatherland on the curriculum. At his request, both Suhm and Ove Malling, a historian and prominent civil servant, wrote patriotic textbooks for use in grammar schools, and the framework for both books was quite explicitly that of the conglomerate state.[70] Against such a background, it seems clear Iversen played his hand well when he appealed to the patriotism of his intended customers and when he prefaced the first volumes with dedications to, and engravings of, the royal family. It is significant that the first volume dedicated to the King was followed by volumes dedicated to Dowager Queen Julianne Marie and her son, hereditary prince Frederik.[71] They were Guldberg's patrons, providing dynastic support and legitimacy for his government. Taken as a whole, the presentation of the translations of Gebhardi's and Christiani's work was that of a work devoted to the House of Oldenburg.

If, however, we focus on what happened to Gebhardi's contribution to the German universal history once it traveled to Denmark-Norway, Iversen's packaging is not the full story. The printer and bookseller from Odense had initially planned a direct translation of Gebhardi's two volumes on Danish and Norwegian history.[72] However, when Gebhardi himself heard of the translation, he intervened, wanting to carry out another, third revision of his work that would include new material unearthed by other historians, most notably by Langebek, Schøning and Suhm. As he himself admitted, in yet another confirmation of the exchanges between the German and Dano-Norwegian historical worlds, he did not want to disappoint his Nordic benefactors.[73] This intervention caused troubles for the translator, Johann Ernst Heilmann, who complained about having to translate on the basis of a mix of printed texts, manuscripts and notes.[74] It did not, however, stop Heilmann from producing a large number of translations at a steady pace. More and less simultaneously, Heilmann delivered two volumes on the history of Norway (1777–78), three on the history Denmark (1780–84) and four on the history of the duchies (1776–1781).

At some point after the last of the volumes translated by Heilmann appeared in 1784, the project seems to have stalled. The publisher Søren Gyldendal in Copenhagen released the remaining parts much later, between 1796 and 1798. At that point, Gebhardi's two original German quarto volumes had grown into eight Danish volumes in the same format, two on the history of Norway and six on the history of Denmark. While the Danish volumes were slimmer than the German originals, the product of the translation process was a considerably expanded work. In particular, the period from the Reformation to the death of Frederick V in 1766 received a more extensive treatment. Iversen also rearranged some of the material. Gebhardi's lengthy literary history of the different resources available for those writing histories of the two realms was deemed less important for Nordic readers, and was not included in the important first volume in the series.[75] It appeared later on, and then, it seems, partly to fill the expected number of sheets of paper.[76] A similar strategic consideration might have lain behind the decision to include the antiquarian and statistical treatises from Gebhardi's abridged 1774-edition at the beginning of the first Danish volume. According to Heilmann, these provided "knowledge worthy of any patriot", and the topics they covered had not hitherto "been covered systematically in any work in Danish".[77] He and Iversen believed that they were offering their readers something new. Both the volumes on Norwegian history and those on Danish history now began with an account of customs and manners and forms of government before and after the coming of Christianity.

The reception of Gebhardi's Danish histories of Denmark and Norway

The fact that Iversen received enough subscriptions to put Heilmann to work suggests that the translation of Gebhardi's and Christiani's work was successful. The subscription list counted 1,271 names and included information about title or profession and place of living. This was a high number by Dano-Norwegian standards[78] and seems to reflect an increased interest in history among the expanding reading public in the eighteenth century. An analysis of the list shows that, for obvious reasons, this translation into Danish did not attract many subscribers from the German-speaking duchies of Schleswig and Holstein. Iversen succeeded, however, in attracting subscribers in Copenhagen and in Denmark and Norway outside the capital, especially in rural Denmark. The latter is noteworthy, since the Dano-Norwegian market for print was heavily skewed toward Copenhagen. Iversen's list of subscribers thus seems to bear the mark of his network of booksellers across Denmark and Norway.

In terms of the social background of his readers, his advances toward the court do not seem to have paid off. The royal family did not sign up to the same extent as they did later on for other publications, such as for the prominent monthly journal *Minerva* (1785–1808). A large number of those who subscribed were civil servants, with the clergy being the largest group. In this regard, the list seems to confirm the conventional view of the Dano-Norwegian public as not really bourgeois in the Habermasian sense. The audience that consumed the journals, pamphlets, and books published in eighteenth- and early nineteenth-century Denmark-Norway was, to a lesser extent than in England and France, made up of men and women outside the orbit of the state.[79] As in the German lands, men with a background from universities or academies dominated the public sphere.[80] At the same time, some nuances seem to be called for. Iversen's subscription list also contained quite a few merchants and others occupied in mercantile professions, and military officers were also prominent. There were even some artisans and a few women of high status, although this is probably no guide to the extent of the female readership of this work, since many women would have read copies purchased by their husbands.

The fact that Iversen managed to convince such a relatively large number of people to subscribe to this translated comprehensive history of the various component parts of the Oldenburg monarchy suggests, once again, that the public expected his historical compilation to be an accessible work, not a work mainly for scholars. Iversen had signaled such intentions in his call for subscriptions, when he appealed to patriots and "lovers of history," and Heilmann confirmed this impression when he explained how the work was meant "not for scholars in particular," but for "good citizens with a desire to read the history of the twin monarchies in one comprehensive and accurate account."[81] One reviewer also seems to have indirectly acknowledged the popular appeal of the project, when he complained that Gebhardi's emendations were not visible in the new Danish text. This would have been useful for "those who make history their main pastime," he argued.[82]

With regard to accessibility and popular appeal, there seem also to have been certain expectations linked specifically to Heilmann. His reputation as a translator, earned through an edition of the poetry of the German philosopher Christian Gellert, was a frequent selling point. In one of the calls for subscriptions, Iversen claimed that "Gebhardi's style would benefit a lot from his translation" so much that German readers with knowledge of Danish would prefer the new edition.[83] While the previously mentioned reviewer was not equally satisfied with how the actual translation turned out,[84] Iversen's comment is interesting when seen in the light of Gebhardi's self-presentation. As we have seen, the Lüneburg historian had stressed time and again his commitment to truth, which he called "the only true goal of any historian,"[85] and had emphasized the need to exercise historical criticism in order to come as close as possible to the truth. On the one hand, he excused the lack of entertainment and eloquence that he believed was a consequence of such critical inquiries, while on the other, he polemicized openly against strategies and techniques designed to broaden the appeal of historical writing, such as capturing the attention of the reader by using rhetoric and embellished language. There was an ambivalence in the way he described his own historical writing that fits well with Iversen's comment that Heilmann gave his histories some rhetorical flourish. Gebhardi knew that many contemporary readers prized historical writing with such qualities and complained about the prevailing literary tastes.[86]

The tension that is evident in the writings of Gebhardi, Heilmann and Iversen had deep roots. It mirrored a split between history as a form of literature, the highest form of *belles lettres*, and history as an erudite and critical endeavor for scholars.[87] During the Renaissance, the admiration of classical eloquence had bestowed great prestige on forms of historical writing closely aligned with rhetoric and inspired by ancient historians such as Livy. In the eighteenth century, the so-called neo-classical narrative was the starting point for many of the most famous French and Scottish historians.[88] It was epitomized by Voltaire, above all in his *Le Siècle de Louis XIV* (1754). Gebhardi, however, was not alone in being skeptical of the historical priorities he found mirrored in work of Voltaire and other historians, in tune with contemporary literary tastes. As we have seen, historians in Göttingen shared this attitude. Gatterer even made a virtue of Gebhardi's prioritizing of truth over eloquence, and Murray made the same point when praising the Lüneburg-historian in his review. Gebhardi may perhaps have been out of step, but in their eyes, his priorities were nevertheless correct.

It is important to note that the qualities that Gebhardi sought to realize in his historical writing were also broadly in keeping with those prized by leading historians in Denmark-Norway, by Gerhard Schøning and Peter Frederik Suhm. The prefaces to their many critical inquiries into the most distant and impenetrable Nordic past from the 1760s and 1770s were full of similar complaints about contemporary literary tastes and the need precisely for historical criticism.[89] Like Gebhardi, they were also conscious of the demand for eloquent and entertaining history, and of their own shortcomings in this regard. This was indeed pointed out to them in reviews.[90] To some extent, Gebhardi was more fortunate than Schøning and Suhm, in that the initial format of the universal history forced him to be brief and comprehensive. He was not allowed to lose himself in erudite and uncertain speculations about the distant past. As a whole, however, the historical ideals and values articulated by Gebhardi, Gatterer, Suhm, and Schøning suggest some broad similarities between the historical cultures of Göttingen, on the one hand, and Sorø and Copenhagen, on the other. They suggest a shared commitment to an erudite, critical form of historical writing that was somewhat in tension with the expectations of their readers, but perhaps not so much as to turn them off. Again, the preponderance of men with an academic background among the reading public, and the fact that many of them were part of the state bureaucracy, probably made potential purchasers more willing to accept historical writing of a more erudite and critical kind. The number of subscribers to Gebhardi's and Christiani's histories certainly suggests as much.

Conclusion

Even if the audience was favorably disposed, the relative popularity of the historical compilation on offer from Iversen, must, as I have argued in this chapter, be understood in the light of other factors as well. The lack of recent histories in Danish covering the full stretch of the history of the Norwegian kingdom and the history of Schleswig-Holstein mattered. There was a niche in the market, which Iversen exploited in a way that was also in tune with attempts by those in power at the court at that time to further a common patriotic identity for the Oldenburg monarchy. Iversen presented the historical compilation he tried to sell as a national history for a conglomerate state. These historical circumstances were crucial for the transfer of Gebhardi's German histories of Denmark and Norway to Denmark-Norway. At the same time, as Monika Baár has emphasized, the component parts of the *Allgemeine Welthistorie* lend themselves to transfers. The transformation of a work such as that of Gebhardi, from a contribution to a universal history, a work for German readers in continental Europe curious about the history of the North, to a national history of Denmark and Norway for Danes and Norwegians was, in a sense, prepared. It was already organized according to realms, and their comprehensiveness and limited length made them well suited to Iversen's historical and commercial enterprise. In the case of Gebhardi, the fact that he had received assistance early on from Schøning and Suhm through Jacob Langebek was also significant. Gebhardi had adopted some of their scholarly positions, and drew on the Old Norse-Icelandic literary tradition when he recounted the early history of the North. In so doing, he got involved in a scholarly rivalry between Göttingen historians such as Schlözer and Gatterer and Dano-Norwegian historian such as Schøning and Suhm. Gebhardi was an important intermediary, negotiating between the historical worlds of Göttingen and Sorø and Copenhagen. The narrative of how his texts developed and traveled helps to shed light on the contacts and exchanges between them. Although the contests could be fierce, these quarrels are also evidence of a shared interest among these historians in the history of the ancient North and of a shared commitment to criticism and questions of historical evidence.

Notes

1 *Kiøbenhavns Kongelig allene priviligerede Adresse-Contoirs med Posten forsendte Efterretninger*, no. 12 (1776), 7.
2 *Kiøbenhavns Adresse-Contoirs Efterretninger,* 7.
3 Ludwig Albrecht Gebhardi, *Fortsetzung der Allgemeinen Welthistorie durch eine Gesellschaft von gelehrten in Teutschland und England ausgefertiget*, vol. 32–33 (Halle: Johann Justinus Gebauer, 1768–1770).
4 Marcus Conrad, *Geschichte(n) und Geschäfte: die Publikation der "Allgemeinen Welthistorie" im Verlag Gebauer in Halle (1744–1814)* (Otto Harrassowitz Verlag, 2010).

5 Monika Baár, "From General History to National History: The Transformation of William Guthrie's and John Gray's A General History of the World (1735–1765) in Continental Europe," in *Cultural Transfer through Translation. The Circulation of Enlightened Thought in Europe by Means of Translation*, ed. Stefanie Stockhorst (New York: Rodopi, 2010), 63–82.

6 Ludwig Albrecht Gebhardi and Wilhelm Ernst Christiani, *Kongerigerne Danmarks og Norges samt Hertugdømmene Slesvigs og Holsteens Historie indtil vore Tider*, 14 vols. (Odense and Copenhagen, 1776–1798). This is the title given on the common title page. All volumes also had an additional title page to indicate their place in the history of the realm (Denmark or Norway) or duchy (Schleswig-Holstein) in question. They were assigned numbers according to their place in this latter ranking. In this article, I will refer to these separate titles and their numbering.

7 Hans Erich Bödeker and Peter Hanns Reill, eds., *Aufklärung und Geschichte: Studien zur deutschen Geschichtswissenschaft im 18. Jahrhundert* (Göttingen: Vandenhoeck & Ruprecht, 1986); Martin Peters, *Altes Reich und Europa: der Historiker, Statistiker und Publizist August Ludwig (v.) Schlözer (1735–1809)* (LIT Verlag Münster, 2003); Martin Gierl, *Geschichte als präzisierte Wissenschaft. Johann Christoph Gatterer und die Historiographie des 18. Jahrhunderts im ganzen Umfang* (Frommann-Holzboog Verlag, 2012).

8 C. Paludan-Müller, "Dansk Historiografi i det 18de Aarhundrede," *Historisk Tidsskrift* 5, no. 4 (1883): 130–36.

9 Gebhardi is largely ignored in Ellen Jørgensen, *Historieforskning og historie-skrivning i Danmark indtil aar 1800*, 2nd ed. (Copenhagen: Gyldendal, 1960); Henrik Horstbøll, "Civilization og nation 1760–1830," in *Historiens historie*, Danmarks historie 10 (Copenhagen: Gyldendal, 1992), 105–97.

10 For some recent contributions emphasizing these connections, see Klaus Bohnen and Sven-Aage Jørgensen, eds., *Der Dänische Gesamtstaat: Kopenhagen – Kiel – Altona* (Tübingen: Niemeyer, 1992); Michael Bregnsbo and Kurt Villads Jensen, *Det danske imperium. Storhed og fald* (Copenhagen: Aschehoug, 2004); Eva Heinzelmann, Stefanie Robl, and Thomas Riis, eds., *Der Dänische Gesamtstaat: ein unterschätztes Weltreich?: The Oldenburg monarchy: an underestimated empire* (Kiel: Ludwig, 2006).

11 Helmut Neubauer, "August Ludwig Schlözer (1735–1809) und die Geschichte Osteuropas", *Jahrbücher für Geschichte Osteuropas* 18/2 (1970), 205–230; Manfred Hildermeier, "Von der Nordischen Geschichte zur Geschichte Osteuropas im Göttinger Horizont", in *Geschichtswissenschaft in Göttingen*, eds. Hartmut Boockmann and Hermann Wellenreuther (Göttingen, 1987), 102–121.

12 Hendriette Kliemann, "Et mångfaldigt begrepp. August Ludwig Schlözers konstruktion av Norden," *Historisk Tidsskrift för Finland* 87, no. 3 (2002): 315–36.

13 Dieter Rüdebusch, *Ritterakademie Lüneburg* (Lüneburg: Landkreis Lüneburg, 2007), 23.

14 Jacob Langebek, *Breve fra Jacob Langebek*, ed. Holger Fr. Rørdam (Copenhagen: Gyldendal, 1895), 374; Ludwig Albrecht Gebhardi, *Kongeriget Norges Historie*, vol. 2 (Odense: Christian Iversen, 1778), XLII; Rasmus Nyerup, "Udsigt over Peter Friderich Suhms Levnet og Skrifter," in Peter Frederik Suhm, *Samlede Skrifter*, vol. 15 (Copenhagen: S. Poulsen, 1798), 151.

15 Ludwig Albrecht Gebhardi, *Historische Nachricht von der Ausreitern des Klosters St. Michael in Lüneburg* (Lüneburg, 1754).

16 Ludwig Albrecht Gebhardi, *Genealogische Geschichte der erblichen Reichstände in Teutschland*, 3 vols. (Halle: Gebauer, 1777–1785).

17 See most notably Ludwig Albrecht Gebhardi, *Geschichte des Reichs Hungarn und der damit verbundenen Staaten*, 3 vols. (Leipzig: Weidemanns Erben und Reich, 1778–1781).

18 Baár, "From General History to National History," 75–80.
19 Georg G. Iggers, Q. Edward Wang, and Supriya Mukherjee, *A Global History of Modern Historiography* (Harlow: Pearson Longman, 2008), 29–30.
20 Guido Abbattista, "The Business of Paternoster Row: Towards a Publishing History of the Universal History (1736–65)," *Publishing History* 17 (1985): 5–50.
21 Guido Abbattista, "The English Universal History: Publishing, Authorship and Historiography in a European Project (1736–1790)," *Storia Della Storiografia* 39 (2001): 100–105.
22 Helmut Zedelmaier, *Der Anfang der Geschichte: Studien zur Ursprungsdebatte im 18. Jahrhundert*, Studien zum achtzehnten Jahrhundert 27 (Hamburg: F. Meiner, 2003), 135–63; David Sorkin, *The Religious Enlightenment. Protestants, Jews, and Catholics from London to Vienna* (Princeton, N.J.: Princeton University Press, 2008), 142–52.
23 Johan van der Zande, "August Ludwig Schlözer and the English Universal History," in *Historikerdialoge: Geschichte, Mythos Und Gedächtnis im Deutsch-Britischen Kulturellen Austausch 1750–2000*, ed. Stefan Berger, Peter Lambert, and Peter Schumann (Göttingen: Vandenhoeck & Ruprecht, 2003), 135–56.
24 Johann Christoph Gatterer, "Vorrede", in Gebhardi, *Fortsetzung der Allgemeinen Welthistorie* (32), 4.
25 Ludwig Albrecht Gebhardi, *Geschichte der Königreiche Dännemark und Norwegen* (Halle: Gebauer, 1770).
26 Ludwig Albrecht Gebhardi, *Die Allgemeine Welthistorie durch eine Gesellschaft von Gelehrten in Teutschland und England ausgefertiget. In einem vollständigen und pragmatischen Auszuge. Neue Historie XIII. Band* (Halle: Gebauer, 1774).
27 Gebhardi, *Geschichte der Königreiche*, 22; Gebhardi, *Die Allgemeine Welthistorie … Neue Historie XIII. Band*, 3–4.
28 Gerhard Schøning, *Norges Riiges Historie*, vol. 1 (Sorø, 1771), unpaginated preface.
29 Lydia Janssen, "Antiquarianism and National History. The Emergence of a New Scholarly Paradigm in Early Modern Historical Studies," *History of European Ideas* 43, no. 8 (2017): 843–56, https://doi.org/10.1080/01916599.2016.1223732.
30 Gebhardi, *Die Allgemeine Welthistorie … Neue Historie XIII. Band*, 1–117, 313–427.
31 Ludwig Albrecht Gebhardi, "Vorrede des Verfassers", in Gebhardi, *Fortsetzung der Allgemeinen Welthistorie* 32, 37. All quotations in this chapter are translated by the author.
32 Gebhardi, "Vorrede des Verfassers", 37.
33 J. G. A. Pocock, *Barbarism and Religion*, vol. 2, *Narratives of Civil Government* (Cambridge: Cambridge University Press, 1999); Karen O'Brien, *Narratives of Enlightenment. Cosmopolitan History from Voltaire to Gibbon* (Cambridge University Press, 1997).
34 Johann Christoph Gatterer, "Vorrede", in Gebhardi, *Fortsetzung der Allgemeinen Welthistorie* 32, 3–16; Johann Christoph Gatterer, "Vorrede", in Gebhardi, *Fortsetzung der Allgemeinen Welthistorie* 33, 3–10.
35 Gatterer, "Vorrede", in Gebhardi, *Fortsetzung der Allgemeinen Welthistorie* 32, 4.
36 Gatterer, "Vorrede", in Gebhardi, *Fortsetzung der Allgemeinen Welthistorie* 32, 4.
37 [August Ludwig Schlözer] Z, "Fortsetzung der Allgemeinen Welthistorie", *Anhang zu dem ersten bis zwölften Bände der Allgemeine Deutsche Bibliothek*, no. 2 (1771), 854; [Johann Phillip Murray], "Halle", *Göttingische Anzeigen von Gelehrten Sachen*, no. 65 (1769): 589.
38 Gebhardi, "Vorrede des Verfassers", 17.
39 Gebhardi, "Vorrede des Verfassers", 17–37.
40 Rudolf Vierhaus, "Die Universität Göttingen und die Anfänge der modernen Geschichtswissenschaft im 18. Jahrhundert," in *Geschichtswissenschaft in Göttingen.*

Eine Vorlesungsreihe, eds. Hartmut Boockmann and Hermann Wellenreuther (Göttingen: Vandenhoeck & Ruprecht, 1987), 9–11.

41 Anne Saada, "Albrecht Von Haller's Contribution to the Göttingische Anzeigen Von Gelehrten Sachen: The Accounting Records," in *Scholars in Action. The Practice of Knowledge and the Figure of the Savant in the 18th Century*, ed. André Holenstein, Hubert Steinke, and Martin Stuber, vol. 1 (Leiden: Brill, 2013), 334.

42 Martin Gierl, "Change of Paradigm as a Squabble between Institutions: The Institute of Historical Sciences, the Society of Sciences, and the Separation of Cultural and Natural Sciences in Göttingen in the Second Half of the Eighteenth Century", in *Scholars in Action*, ed. Holenstein, Steinke, and Stuber, vol. 1, 285–86.

43 To some extent, this can be attributed to Gatterer's desire to distance himself from Baumgarten's and Semler's former habit of mending flawed histories by Means of criticism in prefaces. See the comments in the review of Gebhardi's first volume in *Allgemeine Historische Bibliothek* 8 (1768): 52.

44 Paludan-Müller, "Dansk Historiografi i det 18de Aarhundrede," 87–114; Jørgensen, *Historieforskning og historieskrivning i Danmark indtil aar 1800*, 203–9; Torben Damsholt, "Den nationale magtstat 1560–1760," in *Historiens historie*, Danmarks historie 10 (Copenhagen: Gyldendal, 1992), 68–70.

45 Erik Bollerup, "Lagerbrings Svea Rikes Historia. Tilkomst, utgivning, mottagande", *Scandia* 36 (1970): 298–299.

46 For an English introduction to Schøning's and Suhm's historical projects, see Håkon Evju, *Ancient Constitutions and Modern Monarchy: Historical Writing and Enlightened Reform in Denmark-Norway 1730–1814* (Leiden: Brill, 2019), 91–128.

47 Schøning, *Norges Riiges Historie*, vol. 1, upaginated preface.

48 Schøning, *Norges Riiges Historie*, vol. 1, upaginated preface.

49 For some examples, see Gerhard Schøning, "De gamle Grækers og Romeres rette Begreb og Kundskab om de Nordiske Lande, særdeles om den af dem saa kaldte Scandinavia," *Skrifter, som udi Det Kiøbenhavnske Selskab af Lærdoms og Videnskabers Elskere ere fremlagte og oplæste i Aarene 1761,1762,1763 og 1764* 9 (1765): 151–360; Gerhard Schøning, *Afhandling om de Norskes og endeel andre nordiske Folkes Oprindelse* (Sorø, 1769); Peter Frederik Suhm, *Forsøg til et Udkast af en Historie over Folkenes Oprindelse i Almindelighed som en Indledning til de nordiske Folkes i særdeleshed* (Copenhagen, 1769); Peter Frederik Suhm, *Om de nordiske Folks ældste Oprindelse* (Copenhagen, 1770); Peter Frederik Suhm, *Critisk historie af Danmark udi den hedenske Tid fra Odin til Gorm den Gamle*, 4 vols. (Copenhagen: Berling, 1774–1781).

50 Gebhardi, *Kongeriget Norges Historie*, vol. 2, XLIV.

51 Peter Frederik Suhm and Gerhard Schøning, *Forsøg til Forbedringer i den gamle Danske og Norske Historie* (Copenhagen, 1757), unpaginated preface. The English work in question was *Biographia Britannica, or the Lives of the most eminent Persons of Great Britain and Ireland* (London, 1747–1766), translated into German as Sigmund J. Baumgarten, *Merkwürdige Lebensbeschreibungen berühmter Leuthe grösstentheils aus d. Britann. Biographien genommen*, (Halle, 1754–70). On the circumstances surrounding the Danish adaptation, see Christian Bruun, *Peter Frederik Suhm. 18. oktober 1728–7. september 1798. En levnetsbekrivelse* (Copenhagen: Gad, 1898), 54.

52 Suhm and Schøning, *Forsøg til Forbedringer*, unpaginated preface.

53 Peter Frederik Suhm, "Anmærkninger over Verdens almindelige Historie", in *Samlede Skrifter*, vol. 12 (Copenhagen: S. Poulsen, 1794), 121–432; Peter Frederik Suhm, "Anmærkninger over Verdens almindelige Historie", in *Samlede Skrifter*, vol. 13 (Copenhagen: S. Poulsen, 1794), 41–341; Peter Frederik Suhm, "Anmærkninger over Verdens almindelige Historie", in *Samlede Skrifter*, vol. 14 (Copenhagen: S. Poulsen, 1798), 15–225.

54 See the list in Rasmus Nyerup and Jens Edvard Kraft, *Almindeligt Litteraturlexicon for Danmark, Norge og Island*, vol. 2 (Copenhagen: Gyldendal, 1820), 548–549, 587–89.

55 For a flavor of these mixed reviews, see [Johann Phillip Murray], "Sorøe und Kopenhagen", *Göttingische Anzeigen von Gelehrten Sachen* 1 (1770): 577–84.

56 August Ludwig Schlözer, *Fortsetzung der Allgemeinen Welthistorie durch eine Gesellschaft von gelehrten in Teutschland und England ausgefertiget*, vol. 31 (Halle: Johann Justinus Gebauer, 1771), 4–206; See also Schlözer's criticism of Schøning in his own essay in this compilation, 263–272.

57 [Gerhard Schøning], *Sigurd Sigurdsens Anmærkninger i et Brev til sin Ven over den 31te Deel af algemeine Welt-Historie forfattet af A. L. Schlözer* (Sorø, 1773).

58 For more on Schøning and Suhm's historical project, see Evju, *Ancient Constitutions and Modern Monarchy*, 91–101.

59 Håkon Evju, "Gerhard Schøning som religionshistoriker: Odins rolle i hans historiske forfatterskap", *Teologisk tidsskrift* 12, no. 2 (2023): 126–137.

60 [Murray], "Halle", 591.

61 Anonymous, "2. Fortsetzung der Allgemeinen Welthistorie", *Allgemeine Historische Bibliothek* 8 (1768): 76; Schlözer, "Fortsetzung der Allgemeinen Welthistorie", 854.

62 Gebhardi, *Die Allgemeine Welthistorie ... Neue Historie XIII. Band*, 3–52.

63 Abbattista, "The Business of Paternoster Row"; Conrad, *Geschichte(n) und Geschäfte*.

64 *Kiøbenhavns Adresse-Contoirs Efterretninger*, no. 12 (1776); *Jyske Efterretninger*, no. 15 (1776); *Den Viborgske Samler*, no. 17 (1776); *Trondhiems Kongelige allene priviligerede Adresse-Contoirs Ugentlige Udgivende Efterretninger*, no. 9 (1776).

65 Wilhelm Ernst Christiani, *Geschichte der Herzogthümer Schleswig und Holstein*, 4 vols. (Flensburg and Leipzig, 1775–1779). Only the first volume had appeared when Iversen announced his call for subscriptions.

66 *Kiøbenhavns Adresse-Contoirs Efterretninger*, no. 12 (1776).

67 *Kiøbenhavns Adresse-Contoirs Efterretninger*, no. 12 (1776).

68 Ole Feldbæk, "Fædreland og Indfødesret. 1700-tallets danske identitet," in *Fædreland og modersmål 1536–1789*, ed. Ole Feldbæk, Dansk identitetshistorie 1 (Copenhagen: C. A. Reitzels forlag, 1991); Ole Feldbæk, "'For Norge, Kiæmpers Fødeland'. Norsk kritik og identitet 1770–1773," *Historisk tidsskrift* 73, no. 1 (1994): 23–48.

69 Claus Mechlenborg, "Une créature subalterne. En borgersøns vej til indflydelse under den danske enevælde: Ove Høegh-Guldberg 1731–1772," *Fortid og nutid*, no. 2 (2003): 109–29.

70 Peter Frederik Suhm, *Historien af Danmark, Norge og Holsten udi tvende Udtog til den studerende Ungdoms bedste* (Copenhagen: Lauritz Simmelkiær, 1776); Ove Malling, *Store og gode Handlinger af Danske, Norske og Holstenere* (Copenhagen: Søren Gyldendal, 1777).

71 Gebhardi, *Kongeriget Norges Historie*, vol. 1; Ludwig Albrecht Gebhardi, *Kongeriget Danmarks Historie*, vol. 1 (Odense: Christian Iversen, 1780).

72 Johan Ernst Heilmann, "Til Læseren", in Ludwig Albrecht Gebhardi, *Kongeriget Norges Historie*, vol. 1.

73 Heilmann, "Til Læseren".

74 Heilmann, "Til Læseren".

75 Heilmann, "Til Læseren".

76 Christian Iversen, "Forerindring", in Ludwig Albrecht Gebhardi, *Kongeriget Norges Historie*, vol. 2.

77 Heilmann, "Til Læseren".

78 Iversen claimed that 1,200 subscribers signed up for the original German edition of Christiani's history of the duchies. Other different multi-volume enterprises, however, such as the collected works of Jens Schieldrup Sneedorff (9 vols.) and Peter Frederik Suhm (15 vols.), had 700 and 500 subscribers. A best-selling single-volume work of

political thought, such as Michael Birckner's book *Trykkefriheden og dens Love* on freedom of the press from 1797, supposedly sold 2,000 copies.
79 Thorkild Kjærgaard, "The Rise of Press and Public Opinion in Eighteenth Century Denmark-Norway," *Scandinavian Journal of History* 14, no. 3 (1989): 215–30; See also the discussion in Henrik Horstbøll, "Enevelden, opinion og opposition," *Historie/Jyske Samlinger* XVII (1987): 40–42.
80 This point is made for Germany in Georg G. Iggers, "The European Context of Eighteenth-Century German Enlightenment Historiography," in *Aufklärung Und Geschichte*. ed. Hans Erich Bödeker et al., 225–45; See a similar argument which includes Scandinavia in Kasper Risbjerg Eskildsen, "Den nordeuropæiske oplysning," *Fortid og nutid*, no. 1 (2005): 25–38.
81 *Kiøbenhavns Adresse-Contoirs Efterretninger*, no. 12 (1776); Heilmann, "Til Læseren".
82 *Kiøbenhavnske Nye Efterretninger om lærde Sager*, no. 15 (1779), 229.
83 *Trondhiems Adresse-Contoirs Efterretninger*, no. 30 (1776).
84 The reviewer complained more about accuracy and adherence to the original than about style, see *Kiøbenhavnske Nye Efterretninger om lærde Sager*, no. 15 (1779), 229–234. Gebhardi himself was supposedly happy with Heilmann's translation, see Iversen, "Forerindring."
85 Ludwig Albrecht Gebhardi, "Forfatterens Fortale," in Gebhardi, *Kongeriget Norges Historie*, vol. 2, XLIV.
86 Gebhardi, "Forfatterens Fortale," VII-VIII.
87 Arnaldo Momigliano, "Ancient History and the Antiquarian," *Journal of the Warburg and Courtauld Institutes* 13, no. 3/4 (1950): 285–315; Anthony Grafton, *What Was History? The Art of History in Early Modern Europe* (Cambridge: University Press, 2007).
88 Pocock, *Narratives of Civil Government*.
89 See, for instance, Schøning, *Afhandling om de Norskes Oprindelse*, 4; Schøning, *Norges Riiges Historie*; Suhm, *Critisk historie af Danmark udi den hedenske Tid fra Odin til Gorm den Gamle*, vol. 1, 3–5.
90 *Kiøbenhavnske Efterretninger om lærde Sager*, no. 44 (1769): 727; *Kiøbenhavnske Kongl. Privl. Adressecontoires Kritiske Journal*, no. 46–47 (1772): 369.

Bibliography

Abbattista, Guido. "The Business of Paternoster Row: Towards a Publishing History of the Universal History (1736–65)." *Publishing History* 17 (1985): 5–50.
Abbattista, Guido. "The English Universal History: Publishing, Authorship and Historiography in a European Project (1736–1790)." *Storia Della Storiografia* 39 (2001): 100–105.
Anonymous. "Beslutning af Hr. Professor Gerhard Schønings Afhandling om de Norskes og en Deel andre Nordiske Folkes Oprindelse." *Kiøbenhavnske Efterretninger om lærde Sager*, no. 44 (1769): 717–727.
Anonymous. "2. Fortsetzung der Allgemeinen Welthistorie." *Allgemeine Historische Bibliothek* 8 (1768): 50–81.
Anonymous. "Om Odin og den Hedniske Gudelære og Gudstieneste udi Norden." *Kiøbenhavnske Kongl. Privl. Adressecontoires Kritiske Journal*, no. 46–47 (1772): 361–369.
Baár, Monika. "From General History to National History: The Transformation of William Guthrie's and John Gray's A General History of the World (1735–1765) in Continental Europe." In *Cultural Transfer through Translation. The Circulation of Enlightened Thought in Europe by Means of Translation*, edited by Stefanie Stockhorst, 63–82. New York: Rodopi, 2010.

Bödeker, Hans Erich, & Peter Hanns Reill, eds. *Aufklärung und Geschichte: Studien zur deutschen Geschichtswissenschaft im 18. Jahrhundert.* Göttingen: Vandenhoeck & Ruprecht, 1986.

Bohnen, Klaus, & Sven-Aage Jørgensen, eds. *Der Dänische Gesamtstaat: Kopenhagen – Kiel – Altona.* Tübingen: Niemeyer, 1992.

Bollerup, Erik. "Lagerbrings Svea Rikes Historia. Tilkomst, utgivning, mottagande." *Scandia* 36 (1970): 298–332.

Bregnsbo, Michael, & Kurt Villads Jensen. *Det danske imperium. Storhed og fald.* Copenhagen: Aschehoug, 2004.

Bruun, Christian. *Peter Frederik Suhm. 18. oktober 1728–7. september 1798. En levnetsbekrivelse.* Kjøbenhavn: Gad, 1898.

Conrad, Marcus. *Geschichte(n) und Geschäfte: die Publikation der "Allgemeinen Welthistorie" im Verlag Gebauer in Halle (1744–1814).* Otto Harrassowitz Verlag, 2010.

Damsholt, Torben. "Den nationale magtstat 1560–1760." In *Historiens historie.* Danmarks historie 10. Copenhagen: Gyldendal, 1992.

Den Viborgske Samler, no. 17 (1776).

Eskildsen, Kasper Risbjerg. "Den nordeuropæiske oplysning." *Fortid og nutid,* no. 1 (2005): 25–38.

Evju, Håkon. *Ancient Constitutions and Modern Monarchy: Historical Writing and Enlightened Reform in Denmark-Norway 1730–1814.* Leiden: Brill, 2019.

Evju, Håkon. "Gerhard Schøning som religionshistoriker: Odins rolle i hans historiske forfatterskap." *Teologisk tidsskrift* 12, no. 2 (2023): 126–137.

Feldbæk, Ole. "Fædreland og Indfødesret. 1700-tallets danske identitet." In *Fædreland og modersmål 1536–1789,* edited by Ole Feldbæk. Dansk identitetshistorie 1. Copenhagen: C. A. Reitzels forlag, 1991.

Feldbæk, Ole. "'For Norge, Kiæmpers Fødeland'. Norsk kritik og identitet 1770–1773." *(Norsk) Historisk tidsskrift* 73, no. 1 (1994): 23–48.

Gatterer, Johann Christoph. "Vorrede". In Ludwig Albrecht Gebhardi (ed.), *Fortsetzung der Allgemeinen Welthistorie durch eine Gesellschaft von gelehrten in Teutschland und England ausgefertiget,* vol. 32-33. Halle: Johann Justinus Gebauer, 1768–1770.

Gebhardi, Ludwig Albrecht. *Die Allgemeine Welthistorie durch eine Gesellschaft von Gelehrten in Teutschland und England ausgefertiget. In einem vollständigen und pragmatischen Auszuge. Neue Historie XIII. Band.* Halle: Johann Justinus Gebauer, 1774.

Gebhardi, Ludwig Albrecht. "Forfatterens Fortale." In *Kongeriget Norges Historie,* vol. 2. Odense: Christian Iversens Forlag, 1778.

Gebhardi, Ludwig Albrecht. *Fortsetzung der Allgemeinen Welthistorie durch eine Gesellschaft von gelehrten in Teutschland und England ausgefertiget,* vol. 32–33. Halle: Gebauer, 1768–1770.

Gebhardi, Ludwig Albrecht. *Genealogische Geschichte der erblichen Reichstände in Teutschland,* 3 vols. Halle: Gebauer, 1777–1785.

Gebhardi, Ludwig Albrecht. *Geschichte der Königreiche Dännemark und Norwegen.* Halle: Gebauer, 1770.

Gebhardi, Ludwig Albrecht. *Geschichte des Reichs Hungarn und der damit verbundenen Staaten,* 3 vols. Leipzig: Weidemanns Erben und Reich, 1778–1781.

Gebhardi, Ludwig Albrecht. *Historische Nachricht von der Ausreitern des Klosters St. Michael in Lüneburg.* Lüneburg, 1754.

Gebhardi, Ludwig Albrecht. *Kongeriget Danmarks Historie.* Translated by Johan Ernst Heilmann. 6 vols. Kongerigerne Danmarks og Norges samt Hertugdømmerne Slesvigs og Holsteens Historie. Odense: Christian Iversens Forlag/Copenhagen: Gyldendal, 1780–1798.

Gebhardi, Ludwig Albrecht. *Kongeriget Norges Historie.* Translated by Johan Ernst Heilmann. 2 vols. Kongerigerne Danmarks og Norges samt Hertugdømmerne Slesvigs og Holsteens Historie. Odense: Christian Iversens Forlag, 1777–1778.
Gebhardi, Ludwig Albrecht, & Wilhelm Ernst Christiani. *Kongerigerne Danmarks og Norges samt Hertugdømmene Slesvigs og Holsteens Historie indtil vore Tider.* Translated by Johan Ernst Heilmann. 14 vols. Odense: Christian Iversens Forlag/ Copenhagen: Gyldendal, 1777–1798.
Gierl, Martin. *Change of Paradigm as a Squabble between Institutions: The Institute of Historical Sciences, the Society of Sciences, and the Separation of Cultural and Natural Sciences in Göttingen in the Second Half of the Eighteenth Century.* Brill, 2013.
Gierl, Martin. *Geschichte als präzisierte Wissenschaft. Johann Christoph Gatterer und die Historiographie des 18. Jahrhunderts im ganzen Umfang.* Frommann-Holzboog Verlag, 2012.
Grafton, Anthony. *What Was History? The Art of History in Early Modern Europe.* Cambridge: Cambridge University Press, 2007.
Heilmann, Johan Ernst. "Til Læseren," in Ludwig Albrecht Gebhardi (ed.), *Kongeriget Norges Historie*, vol. 1. Odense: Christian Iversens Forlag, 1777.
Heinzelmann, Eva, Stefanie Robl, & Thomas Riis, eds. *Der Dänische Gesamtstaat: ein unterschätztes Weltreich?: The Oldenburg monarchy: an underestimated empire.* Kiel: Ludwig, 2006.
Horstbøll, Henrik. "Civilization og nation 1760–1830." In *Historiens historie*, 105–197. Danmarks historie 10. Copenhagen: Gyldendal, 1992.
Horstbøll, Henrik. "Enevelden, opinion og opposition." *Historie/Jyske Samlinger* XVII (1987): 35–53.
Iggers, Georg G. "The European Context of Eighteenth-Century German Enlightenment Historiography." In *Aufklärung Und Geschichte. Studien Zur Deutschen Geschichtswissenschaft Im 18. Jahrhundert*, edited by Hans Erich Bödeker, Georg G. Iggers, Jonathan B. Knudsen, & Peter Hanns Reill, 225–245. Göttingen: Vandenhoeck & Ruprecht, 1992.
Iggers, Georg G., Q. Edward Wang, & Supriya Mukherjee. *A Global History of Modern Historiography.* Harlow: Pearson Longman, 2008.
Iversen, Christian. "Forerindring," in Ludwig Albrecht Gebhardi (ed.), *Kongeriget Norges Historie*, vol. 2. Odense: Christian Iversens Forlag, 1778.
Janssen, Lydia. "Antiquarianism and National History. The Emergence of a New Scholarly Paradigm in Early Modern Historical Studies." *History of European Ideas* 43, no. 8 (2017): 843–856. 10.1080/01916599.2016.1223732.
Jyske Efterretninger, no. 15 (1776).
Jørgensen, Ellen. *Historieforskning og historieskrivning i Danmark indtil aar 1800.* 2nd ed. Copenhagen: Gyldendal, 1960.
Kiøbenhavnske Nye Efterretninger om lærde Sager, no. 15 (1779).
Kiøbenhavns Kongelig allene priviligerede Adresse-Contoirs med Posten forsendte Efterretninger, no. 12 (1776).
Kjærgaard, Thorkild. "The Rise of Press and Public Opinion in Eighteenth Century Denmark-Norway." *Scandinavian Journal of History* 14, no. 3 (1989): 215–230.
Kliemann, Hendriette. "Et mångfaldigt begrepp. August Ludwig Schlözers konstruktion av Norden." *Historisk Tidsskrift för Finland* 87, no. 3 (2002): 315–336.
Langebek, Jacob. *Breve fra Jacob Langebek*, Edited by Holger Fr. Rørdam. Copenhagen: Gyldendal, 1895.
Malling, Ove. *Store og gode Handlinger af Danske, Norske og Holstenere.* Copenhagen: Gyldendal, 1777.
Mechlenborg, Claus. "Une créature subalterne. En borgersøns vej til indflydelse under den danske enevælde: Ove Høegh-Guldberg 1731–1772." *Fortid og nutid*, no. 2 (2003): 109–129.

Momigliano, Arnaldo. "Ancient History and the Antiquarian." *Journal of the Warburg and Courtauld Institutes* 13, no. 3/4 (1950): 285–315.

Murray, Johann Phillip. "Soröe und Kopenhagen." *Göttingische Anzeigen von Gelehrten Sachen* 1, no. 66 (1770): 577–584.

Murray, Johann Phillip, "Halle." *Göttingische Anzeigen von Gelehrten Sachen* 1, no. 65 (1769): 588–597.

Neubauer, Helmut. "August Ludwig Schlözer (1735–1809) und die Geschichte Osteuropas." *Jahrbücher für Geschichte Osteuropas* 18/2 (1970): 205–230

Nyerup, Rasmus. "Udsigt over Peter Friderich Suhms Levnet og Skrifter." In *Udsigt over Peter Friderich Suhms Levnet og Skrifter. Tilligemed Valg af hans lærde Brevvexling*, 135–494. Copenhagen: S. Paulsens Forlag, 1798.

Nyerup, Rasmus, & Jens Edvard Kraft. *Almindeligt Litteraturlexicon for Danmark, Norge og Island*. 2 vols. Copenhagen: Gyldendal, 1820.

O'Brien, Karen. *Narratives of Enlightenment. Cosmopolitan History from Voltaire to Gibbon*. Cambridge University Press, 1997.

Paludan-Müller, C. "Dansk Historiografi i det 18de Aarhundrede." *(Dansk) Historisk Tidsskrift* 5, no. 4 (1883): 1–188.

Peters, Martin. *Altes Reich und Europa: der Historiker, Statistiker und Publizist August Ludwig (v.) Schlözer (1735–1809)*. LIT Verlag Münster, 2003.

Pocock, J. G. A. *Narratives of Civil Government*. Barbarism and Religion 2. Cambridge: Cambridge University Press, 1999.

Rüdebusch, Dieter. *Ritterakademie Lüneburg*. Lüneburg: Landkreis Lüneburg, 2007.

Saada, Anne. "Albrecht Von Haller's Contribution to the Göttingische Anzeigen Von Gelehrten Sachen: The Accounting Records." In *Scholars in Action. The Practice of Knowledge and the Figure of the Savant in the 18th Century*, edited by André Holenstein, Hubert Steinke, and Martin Stuber, 1:319–338. Leiden: Brill, 2013.

Schlözer, August Ludwig Z. "Fortsetzung der Allgemeinen Welthistorie." *Anhang zu dem ersten bis zwölften Bände der Allgemeine Deutsche Bibliothek*, no. 2 (1771): 850–854.

Schlözer, August Ludwig. *Fortsetzung der Allgemeinen Welthistorie durch eine Gesellschaft von gelehrten in Teutschland und England ausgefertiget*, vol. 31. Halle: Johann Justinus Gebauer, 1771.

Schøning, Gerhard. *Afhandling om de Norskes og endeel andre nordiske Folkes Oprindelse*. Sorø, 1769.

Schøning, Gerhard. "De gamle Grækers og Romeres rette Begreb og Kundskab om de Nordiske Lande, særdeles om den af dem saa kaldte Scandinavia." *Skrifter, som udi Det Kiøbenhavnske Selskab af Lærdoms og Videnskabers Elskere ere fremlagte og oplæste i Aarene 1761,1762,1763 og 1764* 9, (1765): 151–360.

Schøning, Gerhard. *Norges Riiges Historie*. 3 vols. Sorø and Copenhagen, 1771–1781.

Schøning, Gerhard. *Sigurd Sigurdsens Anmærkninger i et Brev til sin Ven over den 31te Deel af algemeine Welt-Historie forfattet af A. L. Schlözer*. Sorø, 1773.

Sorkin, David. *The Religious Enlightenment. Protestants, Jews, and Catholics from London to Vienna*. Princeton, N.J.: Princeton University Press, 2008.

Suhm, Peter Frederik. *Critisk historie af Danmark udi den hedenske Tid fra Odin til Gorm den Gamle*. 4 vols. Copenhagen: Berling, 1774m1781.

Suhm, Peter Frederik. *Forsøg til et Udkast af en Historie over Folkenes Oprindelse i Almindelighed som en Indledning til de nordiske Folkes i særdeleshed*. Copenhagen, 1769.

Suhm, Peter Frederik. *Historien af Danmark, Norge og Holsten udi tvende Udtog til den studerende Ungdoms bedste*. Copenhagen, 1776.

Suhm, Peter Frederik. *Om de nordiske Folks ældste Oprindelse*. Copenhagen, 1770.

Suhm, Peter Frederik, & Gerhard Schøning. *Forsøg til Forbedringer i den gamle Danske og Norske Historie*. Copenhagen, 1757.

Trondhiems Kongelige allene priviligerede Adresse-Contoirs Ugentlige Udgivende Efterretninger, no. 9 (1776).

Vierhaus, Rudolf. "Die Universität Göttingen und die Anfänge der modernen Geschichtswissenschaft im 18. Jahrhundert." In *Geschichtswissenschaft in Göttingen. Ein Vorlesungsreihe*, 9–29. Göttingen˸: Vandenhoeck & Ruprecht, 1987.

Zande, Johan van der. "August Ludwig Schlözer and the English Universal History." In *Historikerdialoge: Geschichte, Mythos Und Gedächtnis Deutsch- Britischen Kulturellen Austausch 1750–2000*, edited by Stefan Berger, Peter Lambert, and Peter Schumann, 135–156. Göttingen: Vandenhoeck & Ruprecht, 2003.

Zedelmaier, Helmut. *Der Anfang der Geschichte: Studien zur Ursprungsdebatte im 18. Jahrhundert*. Studien zum achtzehnten Jahrhundert 27. Hamburg: F. Meiner, 2003.

10 "For no other cause than the lack of writers"

Travel knowledge and the preservation of memory

Anne Helness

> One of the most admirable and greatest things our times has seen has been the discovery of the many and so varied lands of this globe of the Earth, that were not known even to our ancient forefathers.[1]

In the wake of ships carrying merchants and seaman around the globe, early modern Europeans needed new ways of conceptualising the world that incorporated changing paradigms of world trade and communication. Thus, the period gave rise to new genres[2] one of which was the travel collection, which appeared in sixteenth-century Venice in response to this new historical situation.[3] In this chapter, I will discuss early modern collections of travel writing as a genre of historical writing. The first travel collection relating to the changing paradigm, was the *Navigationi et viaggi* (1550–1559), collected, edited, translated, and compiled by a Venetian humanist, Giovanni Battista Ramusio (1478–1557). Ramusio did not only present a novel conception of the physical world, but he also had an unprecedented way of organising the material that constituted a 'new "world history" or 'history on a world-scale"' to borrow the terminology of Sanjay Subrahmanyam.[4] In the last part of this chapter, I will argue that the empirical material and the editorial commentary combine in forming a historical genre drawing on the Ramusian prototype to illustrate my argument; here I will rely on terminology developed by Helge Jordheim on genre in historical texts.[5] In the first sections I will focus on the *Navigationi and Viaggi* itself and its various contexts of knowledge. In all sections, I will connect this to genre.

Collecting knowledge about the world: A wide-ranging cultural and social practice

> I doubt that, with the length of time, the memory of such a great and notable undertaking could be lost, I [still] thought it was a praiseworthy thing to collect and put together (as best I could) some travel letters written by various [Portuguese captains] on this subject [i.e., their discoveries in Asia].[6]

DOI: 10.4324/9781003331971-15

Early modern intellectuals were collectors of knowledge of the inhabitable and natural world in many forms and formats[7]: cabinets, gardens, books – all usually with a natural and/or geographical-historical component. One such form was the travel collection organised as a compilation. I will argue that such compilations may be viewed as a genre of knowledge-producing histories. It is reasonable to assume that when Francis Bacon (1561–1626) divided history into multiple categories in *The Advancement of Learning* (1605), he was expressing a view of history that already was legion. One such category was

> history manifoldly mixed, and that is History of Cosmography [i.e., geography]: being compounded of natural history, in respect of the regions themselves; of history civil, in respect of the habitations, regiments, and manners of the peoples; and the mathematics, in respect of the climate and configurations towards the heavens.[8]

In other words, early modern thinkers did not have the strict division that we have today. History, therefore, included geography, which comprised both natural and civil history on the one hand, and the Ptolemaic astronomically based geography on the other hand. The *Navigationi et viaggi* complies principally with the first two, only touching upon the last. Both geography and history, thus broadly understood, were major interests among Ramusio and his circle of friends. They all collected more than just texts to understand the new physical globe they inhabited: plants to be cultivated in their gardens, maps and globes, ancient coins, medallions, and inscriptions, as well as artifacts to be poured over in their studies. They collected accounts of the world outside their culturally and geographically known ecumene. Situated in Venice, they had unique access to a variety of knowledge material arriving in the city through both official and unofficial channels, of which Ramusio, who spent a lifetime in the Venetian chancellery, made ready use.

Carolyn Miller has argued that genres should be understood rhetorically as social actions.[9] Not only the publishing compilations of travel but also the practice of collecting, translating, editing, and compiling them should be viewed as social actions included in the cultural practice in which Ramusio and his circle of friends engaged. At times these practices overlapped and merged as when Ramusio included descriptions and illustrations of plants and fish independently of travellers' accounts, or when Fracastoro in a letter to Ramusio discusses the rhubarb Ramusio had sent him to plant in his garden, while Ramusio writes of the plant in the *Navigationi et viaggi*.[10] The collecting practices were an important part of humanist activities, and they were undertaken to make sense of the past and its relation to the present, as well as making sense of the wider world. Following Alastair Fowler, I maintain that texts within travel compilations, as well as the collecting practices in which humanists engaged, should be understood as overlapping and adjacent activities connected through the notion of family resemblances.

Fowler, transferring Ludwig Wittgenstein's notion of family resemblances in language games to literary kinds (i.e., genres in early modern parlance), argues convincingly that such resemblances make various overlapping and adjacent genres understandable to readers.[11] Equally, the various social actions of knowledge-collecting activities of Ramusio and his friends become understandable viewed in this way. Returning to the travel collection, the many kinds of text and discourses found here share a family resemblance ensuring that they make sense to readers, both individually and collectively. The compilation may thus be understood as a genre consisting of a collection of a variety of kinds of texts, making travel literature a 'genre of genres',[12] an apt label as early modern travel writing 'embraced a bewildering diverse range of material',[13] covering anything from ballads to ambassadorial reports if it related to a country outside one's own. Such family resemblances between the various genres and sub-genres also enables me to argue that a collection of travel-related texts describing the world outside the Mediterranean ecumene comprise a genre of historical writing. Before moving on to discuss the early modern renewal of knowledge and its implication for the early modern genres of history, I will present Ramusio's own compilation.

The *Navigationi et viaggi* was published in Venice in three volumes between 1550 and 1559. Each volume focuses upon a certain part of the world associated with an area of interest to different commercial powers. Volume one (1550, 1554) is concerned with the Portuguese economic sphere of interest.[14] It provides readers with accounts relating to the entire African coastline, the Red Sea, then moves around India, and on to the Spice Islands before finally reaching Japan; it also includes the circumnavigation of Ferdinand Magellan (1480–1521) and Amerigo Vespucci's (1451–1512) travels for the Portuguese king. This volume consists of thirty-seven accounts and thirteen texts authored by Ramusio. The second volume (posthumous, 1559),[15] is concerned with Venetian interests, providing readers with accounts of the East (China and Persia), besides accounts of the north and north-east (Norway, Muscovy, Hungary, Poland). It consists of nineteen accounts (of which six were added posthumously) and six texts authored by Ramusio, as well as publisher Tommaso Giunti's (1494–1566) preface to the readers.[16] The third volume (1556)[17] is concerned with Spanish interests and focuses on the discoveries of Peru and Mexico, the Caribbean and the north-eastern part of the American continent discovered by the French and English. It consists of twenty-six accounts and five texts that may or may not have been authored by Ramusio. Marica Milanesi argues that only the first *discorso* (the dedication to Fracastoro) was written by Ramusio himself, and she speculates that the other four *discorsi* were added either by his son or by Giunti.[18]

Each volume is a compilation of texts belonging to a variety of genres: travel accounts, peripluses, ambassadorial reports, histories, natural histories,[19] discussions, letters, dedications, treatises, and so on, all treating matters which may be categorised under the umbrella of geography and history (or Bacon's History of Cosmography).[20] Ramusio does not focus solely on contemporary and near-contemporary material. In the first volume, especially, he also includes several ancient accounts, often alternating between ancient and contemporary material thereby ignoring their chronological order. Interspersed between accounts are his own *discorsi* (discussions), in which he usually discussed new knowledge in relation to ancient knowledge or highlighted the knowledge presented. Thus, the two serve to bolster and confirm each other.

The other texts authored by Ramusio are varied in kind. His first dedication to Girolamo Fracastoro (1479–1553) is rather traditional, in the second and third, however, also to Fracastoro, he discussed geographical problems inherited from antiquity. Following the second dedication Ramusio used Marco Polo's account as a jumping point to allow him to discuss rhubarb, the various place names mentioned by Polo in addition to the role of Venice in Constantinople in the decades following the fourth crusade (1204). He authored a treatise on the history of the spice trade, a short text on fisheries in the North Atlantic, and was co-author with Fracastoro on a treatise on the annual flooding of the Nile. As these examples show, a travel compilation included much more than merely accounts by travellers of their sojourn in other parts of the world. Its aim was, to paraphrase the publisher, to provide the public with something useful and enlightening that would make ancient accounts of the world obsolete.[21]

While Ramusio was given due credit for his work posthumously by Giunti, the *Navigationi et viaggi* should tentatively also be understood as the result of the cultural practice of collecting in which he and his friends partook: Andrea Navagero (1483–1529) collected travel accounts in the late 1520 s when he represented the Venetian state in Spain – accounts which he (and later his heirs) turned over to Ramusio who had them published (1534–1536) and then republished as part of the third volume; Pietro Bembo (1470–1547) included the discoveries of Vasco da Gama (1469–1524), Christopher Columbus (1451–1506) and Magellan in the *Historia Veneta* (1552) basing this part on material provided by Ramusio.[22] Both were close friends of Ramusio, as was Fracastoro, who included the discoveries of America in his poetic study of syphilis and discussed travel accounts in his correspondence with Ramusio.[23]

Renewal of knowledge

These [accounts] are truly worthy of being read by scholars, because they will see the country towards that line [i.e., equator], which ancient sages claimed was scorched by the sun and without habitation, is very green and very pleasant and inhabited by infinite peoples.[24]

... [then] it would not have been necessary to read neither Ptolemy nor Strabo nor Pliny nor any other of the ancient writers concerning matters of geography.[25]

Ramusio's *Navigationi et viaggi* was never intended only for scholarly use, he planned it as a valuable tool for princes and their advisors. In a Venetian context, this meant trade and trade relations, as well as political and diplomatic relations. In this capacity, the *Navigationi et viaggi* may be viewed as a type of 'advice to princes' usually written as straight-forward traditional histories of the affairs of men or towns (i.e., Bacon's 'history civil') or as chronologies of world history.[26] Early modern practices of collecting knowledge of various sorts on the other hand often belonged to the category of 'natural history'. In connection with the *Navigationi et viaggi* Ramusio aimed at critically scrutinising knowledge handed down from earlier periods, a very worthy aim according to him, as illustrated in the first of the previous quotes where he comments upon mistakes made by the ancients concerning the habitability of the world.[27]

While Ramusio was not the first to compile travel accounts in the Veneto, his importance lies in the structural difference between *Navigationi et viaggi* and earlier compilations. In his first dedication to Fracastoro, Ramusio explicitly stated that his intention was to correct outdated knowledge, in particular maps based on the tables in Ptolemy's *Geography* (2nd cent. AD) by presenting readers with new 'discoveries' made by the Portuguese.[28] Geographical knowledge had undergone a radical renewal since the Latin West had rediscovered ancient works of geography in the fifteenth century. A hundred years before Ramusio, Florentine humanists with connections to the maritime world provided, based on their reading of ancient geographers, a theoretical foundation for the exploration done by Iberian sailors.[29] Ramusio's project included not only the 'New World' 'discovered' by Christopher Columbus – news of which had been extensively published – but also the forgotten ancient world rediscovered by Vasco da Gama. News of such rediscoveries circulated in letters and diplomatic reports, but detailed accounts, and not least correct maps, of this forgotten world were lacking.[30] This lacuna was what Ramusio set out to correct.

> [U]pon studying the geographical tables of Africa and India found in Ptolemy, [finding] that they were very inadequate when compared with new knowledge of these areas, he has judged that it would be dear and probably useful to the world if he put together the narratives of the writers of our time who have been in the previously mentioned parts of the world and have spoken a little about it.[31]

Thus, Ramusio utilised practical experience to support bookish knowledge besides correcting truth assumptions transmitted from the past. Up to date information about the world would be pleasing to scholars, but more so to princes: 'To them more than to any other belongs knowledge of the secrets and particularities of this said part of the world and all the regional sites, provinces and cities in these, and the dependencies that one or another of the rulers and people that live there'.[32] In other words, Ramusio points to a practical relevance for the princes of Europe. Ramusio emphasised this utility value in his final note 'To readers' in the first volume (1554 edition), stating that he 'has chosen to include in his own volume what he found of pertinent information about the most notable lands, rivers, mountains, cities, and coastlines' in the *Decades* of the Portuguese historian João de Barros (1496–1570), but had excluded 'what Barros has written on the wars with the people of India *as it is not profitable*'.[33] Ramusio here took the stand of an economic geographer: wars were not profitable, news of foreign lands though could be turned into profits. According to Ramusio a true historian should focus on bringing forth new knowledge of the human and natural worlds to the benefit of scholars as well as other interested parties. Gonzalo Fernández de Oviedo y Valdés' (1478–1557) descriptions of animals, birds, fishes, trees, grasses, flowers, and fruits were in Ramusio's view the 'truly interesting things'. They were to be accompanied by four hundred drawings, but to Ramusio's chagrin, only the original *Sommario* (1526) was published. Ramusio included a few images and descriptions of such things elsewhere.[34]

That Ramusio was more concerned with nature than culture should be understood within a Venetian mercantile context. Not only would the *Navigationi et viaggi* provide interested readers with reliable knowledge of the world outside of Europe which could be commercially viable and politically interesting, thus satisfying merchants and princes, such accounts – in so far as the writer was capable of pinpointing where on the globe cities and regions were – would contribute to updating the latitudinal tables found in Ptolemy, thus also satisfying intellectual desires. Ramusio collaborated with the most outstanding cartographer of his time, Giacomo Gastaldi (c. 1500–1566), to produce maps for his own compilation. Gastaldi was also commissioned to produce maps for the Venetian Ducal palace, a commission handled by Ramusio as part of his professional duties.[35] A correct global representation would thereby be valuable and useful to both scholars and princes as well as merchants.[36]

As mentioned, the difference between the *Navigationi et viaggi* of Ramusio and earlier compilations lies in the formal structure of the work. Whereas earlier compilations were structured chronologically, Ramusio chose a different approach. He ordered his material spatially according to the political and commercial realities of his day, namely worldwide trade along oceanic routes rather than land routes. When Ramusio claimed that his intention was to correct Ptolemy this may be understood literally,[37] in which case Ramusio's intention is solely to correct the science of geography. Or it may be understood much more radically, as Milanesi has convincingly argued, namely, that his intention was to provide readers with a totally new conception of the world, a conception in line with a new global reality. This also tallies with Giunti's statement (see the second quotation earlier) that reading Ramusio made ancient writers obsolete.[38] Only such a reading of Ramusio's project enables me to view the travel compilation as a genre of historical writing making Ramusio 'the first historian of the age of discovery'.[39]

Trade in the Indian Ocean was known to the Romans, but Europeans had lost contact with this ocean after the fall of the Roman Empire. When the Portuguese rounded Africa at the turn of the sixteenth century, they reconnected European merchants directly with this trade. And it is precisely this and other oceanic trade routes linking various parts of the world together that was Ramusio's new understanding of the ecumene. Rather than writing a geographical treatise, Ramusio chose instead to present his readers with a history of discoveries, or maybe even a history of how he had reached this conclusion presenting all the arguments in the form of accounts of travellers' first-hand experience of the world. He chose to include Magellan's circumnavigation (1519–1522) in a volume otherwise mainly dedicated to Portuguese discoveries, thereby proving that oceans surrounded all landmasses, rather than the other way around, thus demonstrating to readers that the Ptolemaic world picture had become obsolete.

The travel compilation with its motley collection of texts and genres combined to present those in the need to know with new knowledge as well as either confirming or correcting ancient knowledge. The enlargement of the ecumene brought about by what has been dubbed the first globalisation happened at a time when Venice was both a dominant power in the spice trade and a major centre of print and information.[40] As such Venice was an 'involved witness' to the previously mentioned shift to an 'oceanic-centred economy',[41] making the need for new knowledge paramount. Central in the dissemination were printers, humanists, 'cartographers, geographers and compilers of travel collections', and atlases in Venice, Basel, London, Antwerp, all participating in the translation of knowledge (*translatio studii*) and, with the exception of Basel, all these cities were ports.[42] Ramusio was to include works or extracts from works that, although written earlier in the sixteenth century, had not yet been published elsewhere, such as Duarte Barbosa's *Book*, Tomé Pires's *Suma Oriental*, and Leo Africanus's *History of Africa*, thus enhancing its newsworthiness.

Ramusio's division of the world into homogenous areas of human occupation that surrounded the oceans was without precedent, but natural for a Venetian whose state viewed itself as a *stato del mar*.[43] After the Treaty of Tordesillas (1494) Spanish interests were confined to the west, Portuguese interests to the south and east, thus covering the first and third volume. Belonging to a major trading republic Ramusio included Venetians as protagonists on the world stage to the north and east in his second volume. Familiar with Herodotus (5th cent. BC) Ramusio divided Asia into two parts: one of silk reached by land, and one of spices reached by sea.[44] Thus, *Navigationi et viaggi* – the first example of a new genre answering the change from a telluric and Mediterranean paradigm to an oceanic and Atlantic paradigm – became an example of Baconian history of cosmography. Ramusio's new vision embraced both the physical world as well as being a record of human action in the age of discovery.[45]

Geography and history: Preservation of the memory of knowledge

> It is truly astonishing to ponder the great change and alteration that the coming of the Goths and other barbarians in Italy caused throughout the Roman Empire, the fact is that these populations extinguished all arts, all sciences and all traffics and merchandise that was carried out in different parts of the world: and [it was] almost like the darkness of a dark night lasting 400 years and more, so that some did not dare to leave his native country and go elsewhere, while before the coming of said barbarians when the Roman empire flourished, it was certainly possible to sail all over the East Indies by sea; and this voyage was so popular and famous and as known as it is at present due to the navigation of the Portuguese. And that this was true is clearly shown by what Strabo writes, which was in the time of Augustus and Tiberius ...[46]

Ramusio's 'Discourse on the spice trade', which was the penultimate text in the 1550 edition of the first volume, opens with this lamentation of lost knowledge. Lost or forgotten knowledge was a theme he addressed several times in connection with his own task. The early modern period inherited two traditions of geographic learning from Antiquity: the first mathematical, experimental, and locative (Ptolemy) and the second anthropocentric, descriptive, and historical (Strabo, Pliny, and others). Through these two basic approaches sixteenth-century humanists 'sought to describe and understand their world'.[47] Ramusio refers to all or most of the important figures from both traditions though he focused on the second. I have already discussed his reworking of the Ptolemaic worldview. In this section, I will address the Straboan and Plinian tradition, which Francis Bacon half a century later would include in his concept of the history of cosmography.[48]

Excellent humanist that he was, Ramusio, treated his sources with great respect always seeking the most authentic version of a text for translation and editing.[49] But he went further, comparing ancient and modern sources, so that he could present readers with the most correct up-to-date knowledge. In the process, readers were treated to both modern and ancient accounts, as well as ancient writers of geographical learning (Strabo, Pomponius Mela (1st cent.), Solinus (3rd cent.), Pliny (23–79) to mention the most important) thereby demonstrating Ramusio' considerable knowledge in ancient geography. Intermixed with these accounts were Ramusio's own *discorsi* to help guide readers. In this way Ramusio allowed readers to follow his implicit argument that the present world required a completely new interpretive image – an image Ramusio presented through a radically new way of ordering his material.

Ramusio's own commentaries – his *discorsi* – consist of dedications and discussions of topics of interest in the various accounts such as points of geography (old and new) as well as matters of interest to international commerce. Milanesi, followed by Romain Descendre and Fiona Lejosne, argue that Ramusio drew on ancient and modern knowledge in order both to correct and verify what could be known about the world.[50] And it is precisely at this point that geography and history intersect. The past functions as a corroborating witness to the present, contrary to François Hartog's view in which the past ('the old regime of historicity') functions as a series of *exempla* for the *magistra vitae*. In this 'old regime', the present and the future would never go beyond the past, even if they did not repeat it. Ramusio, however, understood perfectly well that the future would go beyond his new image of a terraqueous globe and would thus belong to Hartog's modern regime of historicity.[51]

In his discussion of the first globalisation, Sanjay Subrahmanyam argues that historical writing consists of a variety of genres that to a certain degree correspond to Hartog's 'modes of historicity', and Hartog's modern regime can already be seen in the new historical writing emerging in the sixteenth century. Subrahmanyam associates this with what he calls 'a major and significant transformation in general historiographical practice'.[52] He argues that the sixteenth century was 'an explosive conjunctural moment in relation to the changing conventions of history-writing' due to 'the rise to prominence of the innovative form of "world history"'.[53] What happened was that writers of history began to conceive their projects as 'history-writing on a world scale'.[54] In other words, sixteenth-century thinkers found new ways of conceptualising the changed paradigm, which resulted in the invention of new historical genres.[55] What Subrahmanyam is pointing out is that historically and geographically inclined writers conceived of their subject matter in terms of a global vision rather than local. Thus, there is a change in spatial scale.

When this new concept of history emerged it was often in conjunction with geographical and cartographical material, and as Subrahmanyam points out 'some of this work is by translators ... or compilers like ... Giovanni Battista Ramusio'.[56] Although Subrahmanyam includes Ramusio here he also points out that Ramusio's 'multivolume compendium ... was to serve as a staple for historians', and goes on to discuss such writers.[57] It is therefore somewhat ambiguous whether Subrahmanyam includes Ramusio among the new historians or not. I am arguing that Ramusio's *Navigationi et viaggi* should be counted as a proper example of Subrahmanyam's new form of writing history on a world scale. In my opinion, this innovative form of history appeared in the mid-sixteenth century when Ramusio presented his readers with a wholly new and unprecedented conception of the world where the individual landmasses – construed as homogenous areas of human occupation – were connected by oceans constructed as social spaces.[58] The structure of *Navigationi et viaggi* is innovative and the three volumes of the work constitute a world history. Earlier compilations of travels lacked this dimension. Thus, they are better regarded as chronicles, rather than globalising histories of the world.

Broadly speaking, early modern compilations belong to two types of discourse, an empirical and descriptive discourse focusing on particulars of the external world wherein people act, and a historical and argumentative discourse presenting the editor-humanist's interpretation of the new knowledge provided. This last takes the form of dedications, introductions, commentary – that inform readers of the editorial project as well helping them understand the significance of the knowledge provided. In general, there was an emphasis on disseminating useful data,[59] and these compilations would become important sources for debates on humanity and society central to later philosophers.[60] The early humanist collector-editors were historians, not only armchair travellers or dilettante geographers and cosmographers.

From the point of view of the order of knowledge, Ramusio referred to geographical learning as science (*scienze*) rather than history (*istoria*), and he regretted the fact that he was compelled to present readers with unpolished texts but insisted that it was necessary as no historian had yet produced a history of the Portuguese in Asia. He hoped that someone would use them as source material: 'And when some gentle spirit in the future would feel the urge to write this history in an orderly fashion, they can use these writings in some part, even if they are crude and inordinate'.[61] João de Barros would be such a 'gentle spirit', but, as mentioned, Ramusio did not have access to his *Décadas de Asia* (published 1552, written in the 1520s) when the first volume was published in 1550. Ramusio rectified this in the second edition of 1554 in which he added extracts from this text.[62]

The third volume of *Navigationi et viaggi*, consisting mainly of Spanish material in addition to some material on the French in the north of the continent, was published in 1556. Here he included a shortened version of Pietro Martire d'Anghiera's (1457–1526) *Decades of the New World* (1516), Oviedo's *Sumario de la history natural de las Indias* (1526) and his *Historia general y natural de Las Indias* (1535), as well as two short texts on the conquest of Peru, most of which had been translated into Italian and published anonymously in Venice in 1534–36. The first two texts had been picked up by Navagero in Spain, and maybe translated, but most certainly edited by Ramusio, while the pamphlets concerning Peru had most certainly been translated by him.[63] Both Barros and Oviedo complied with Ramusio's ideal of a historian, a learned man who was able to integrate the history of his nation's discoveries with the natural history of the area. Oviedo modelled himself and his work upon Pliny, one of Ramusio's ancient authorities. Ramusio lashed out at Spanish chroniclers for not supplying readers with an informed and knowledgeable history that would be useful to the learned and other interested parties, as may be deduced from his comment upon Spanish chroniclers of the conquest of America:

Of which wars all the Spanish historians of these times have laboured and are continually struggling to write with extreme diligence, noting that in the battles of Salinas, Chupas, Quito, Guarina, Xaquixaguana there were such and such captains, standard bearers and *adelantadi*,[64] with the names of all the Spanish soldiers, both on horseback and on foot, and in which city of Spain each of them were born, a vain and ridiculous thing; of the truly [interesting] natural things mentioned above [i.e., items of flora and fauna] they pass briefly [over], except inasmuch as they cannot help but mention them in passing.[65]

Ramusio considered such detailed descriptions of every participant to be vain and ridiculous. A truly informed history in Ramusio's mind was thus a work which introduced readers to new knowledge about the global physical world, something chronicles did not do. Thus, one could say that for Ramusio the genre of history referred more to the intention than to the text itself. Early modern genre distinctions were more fluid than we often think of genres today, and history referred to a genre that could appear in a variety of expressions. The important fact was that it presented particular and empirical knowledge of the world, rather than universal knowledge. During the early modern period history became detached from rhetoric while increasingly attracting the attention of princes and their advisors.[66] While traditionally having been more engaged with past *res gestae* of political history, *storia* had always also included the more anthropocentric approach of geography that early modern humanists inherited from Herodotus and Strabo describing places, people, and nature in which they travelled. Thus, *historia* included a broad range of truthful experience-based knowledge, as did *scienzia*.[67]

Ramusio saw it as his task to preserve the memory of these discoveries – which he terms 'the most admirable and greatest thing that our times has seen'[68] – and sought the most up-to-date and correct geographical information that he could lay his hands on to preserve for posterity:

I doubt that, with the length of time, the memory of such a great and notable undertaking could be lost, I [still] thought it was a praiseworthy thing to collect and put together (as best I could) some travel letters written by various [Portuguese captains] on this subject [i.e., Portuguese discoveries in Asia].[69]

At the time Ramusio printed these texts there did not yet exist any Portuguese history of their discoveries.[70] And it is here that history and geography intersect in Ramusio: preserving the memory of such events in spite of the prohibitions to print imposed by Portuguese kings was of paramount importance, a prohibition of which Ramusio was highly critical.[71] Similarly, it was by relying on information found in Strabo and Pliny that he could demonstrate that the Romans were well acquainted with Southeast Asia and the Spice Islands since they regularly traded with these areas,[72] knowledge that had been lost after the 'barbarian invasions': 'the arrival of the Goths and other barbarians in Italy ... extinguished ... all the sciences (*scienze*)'.[73] – Here is a good example of how Ramusio tended to use the word *scienzia* as was common in his day, imbuing it with a much broader meaning than we do today, namely knowledge pure and simple. As shown previously, Ramusio saw it as his calling to ensure that memories of contemporary discoveries should not get lost, as had happened so often before: '[I]nfinite countries discovered by different captains, at different times, which, as there is no memory of them, rest in eternal oblivion, no different from what they were in the past'.[74] And even worse, Portuguese captains have discovered multiple islands 'who are nameless and unknown, and for no other cause than the lack of writers'.[75] So, he collected and published travel and travel-related accounts and related texts following the strict standards of humanism in the process, always seeking the most correct version because no memory of these events also meant that knowledge of them would be lost forever.

Understanding the travel compilation as a genre of historical writing

Herodotus of Halicarnassus, his *Researches* are here set down to preserve the memory of the past by putting on record the astonishing achievements both of our own and of other peoples; and more particularly, to show how they came into conflict.[76]

'Historie without geographie like a dead carcass has neither life nor motion at all ... geographie without historie hath life and motion, but at random, and unstable'.[77]

Having discussed the compilation itself, its contents, and the geographical and historical knowledge-preserving project of Ramusio, it is time to return the question of genre. Not only should early modern genres be understood as social actions participating in language games following Miller and Fowler, genre should also be understood as something texts participate in, rather than belong to according to John Frow who argues that texts use or perform genres.[78] This view resembles that of Helge Jordheim when he argues that understanding genres historically means to understand the 'genre field' in which genres take part. Genre fields are where 'genre conventions' and 'genre intensions' meet in 'genre negotiations'. On the one hand, he defines genre negotiations as the way genres unfold within a genre field both synchronically and diachronically in relation to other genres. On the other hand, one also needs to understand how the text one is studying relates to other texts and genres that lie before and after it in time.[79] What has been defined as travel literature may be said to constitute one such (composite) genre field.[80] And it is within this genre of genres that the genre negotiations take place.

Early sixteenth-century travel literature consists of a great variety of material from ships' logs to journals and letters to the reports of merchants, spies, and diplomats; accounts of exploration, pilgrimage, and colonial conquest and administration; narratives of shipwreck and captivity.[81] All these different kinds of travel-related texts (different genres in modern terminology) come together in the fields of both geography and history. Each kind of text is imbued with conventions and intentions related to its particular kind both on a synchronic and a diachronic time scale thus complicating notions of the travel compilation as an early modern genre of historical writing.

Along a synchronic scale (a lateral historical section) covering roughly the first half of the sixteenth century one finds earlier Venetian compilations that are purely chronologically ordered, as well as cosmographies printed else-where,[82] maps, geographical treatises, natural histories, routiers, etc. – the list goes on and on. The same list is part of these same fields viewed diachronically (a longitudinal historical section) going back at least to Herodotus.

In Antiquity, there were two main types of travel accounts, the *periplus* (concerned with coastal navigation) and the *periegesis* (meaning a travelogue or a geographical survey). In medieval times one distinguished between *peregrinatio* (pilgrim's guides falling under the field of theology), travel *regimina* (collections of hygiene and dietary advice for travellers both on land and at sea probably falling under medicine), and *navigationes* (secular travels) as well;[83] also medieval trade or merchant manuals which first appeared in the fourteenth century are part of the longitudinal section.[84] All these earlier kinds are continued in the early modern period, though the emphasis now was on accounts covered by the rubric *navigationes* including both the ancient types (*periegesis* and *periplus*). Justin Stagl divides early modern travel writing into three types: compilations, cosmographies, and statistical surveys that developed in three different cities: Venice, Basel, Paris. To these he adds the new *ars apodemica* producing advice to travellers.[85] Belonging to the last half of the sixteenth century is yet another kind: the atlas, which was first developed in Antwerp.

Stagl argues that it was due to Herodotus that the term *historia* became a general term 'for antiquarian historical-ethnographic research and by extension for empirical research in general'.[86] In other words, the meaning of the term broadened as it no longer strictly belonged to the field of rhetoric. I have quoted Herodotus at the beginning of this section. Various editions will translate these opening lines slightly differently: '*Histories*' rather than '*Researches*' (which is what the term actually means in Greek), or 'great and marvellous deeds' rather than 'astonishing achievements'. And 'great and marvellous deeds' is precisely what Ramusio sought to preserve the memory of, as discussed earlier.[87] Ramusio was well-known among his contemporaries for his excellent skills in Greek as well as in Latin, and he would, thus, know that *historia* referred to knowledge of changeable phenomena, while *epistème* referred to knowledge of the unchanging order of the *kósmos*, terms which were translated into Latin as *historia* and *scientia* respectively. Both these terms acquired a much broader and not always exclusive sense in early modern times, and they referred to a much broader range of knowledge than they do today.[88]

Prose genres such as geography and history were not clearly demarcated in Antiquity, and both genres need to be understood as inclusive after the model of Herodotus who was to provide 'the literary model as well as exemplifying how such an undertaking could be used to rewrite a new world'.[89] Ramusio was well acquainted with the Greek historian and drew on him as an authoritative source.[90]

Geography and history were so closely connected that for example Strabo not only wrote *Geography* but also *History*. From the existing fragments of the latter, it is not clear what the difference was between these two (distinct?) fields of knowledge.[91] Also medieval historians would include geographical knowledge as an integral part of their histories, and although titles seldom reflect this they usually acknowledged the tight connection between these two fields.[92] A quarter of a century after Ramusio, Richard Hakluyt (1553–1606) maintained that 'Geographie and Chronologie (which I may call the Sunne and the Moone, the right eye and the left of history)' were both necessary in order to put the 'torne and scattered limmes' of historical knowledge back together.[93] Thus, there existed a notion not only of a close connection between the two but that geography and history together comprised all knowledge of the natural world as experienced by men – as also shown by the second of the initial quotes in this section. While the English expressed this sentiment and the connection between history and geography explicitly, it was implicit in Ramusio.

While his favourite ancient geographer Strabo focused on presenting the Greek and Roman ecumene, Ramusio's conception of the ecumene embraced the entire globe, a conception he developed over three pages in his final dedication to Fracastoro, concluding that it was not reasonable to believe that God had created a world that was not everywhere inhabited and available to human traffic:

> For it is not reasonable to believe that the maker of so beautiful and perfect a work as are the heavens, the sun, and the moon, made with so much stupendous and marvellous order, would want the sun to illuminate only a particle of this globe they call earth, the rest of its course over the seas, snows and ice be in vain ...[94]

Thus, Ramusio dismissed geographical science that had been handed down through the ages. He thanked God for living in an age when the other parts of the world had been (re)discovered and were thus again open to European commerce.[95]

Ramusio's organising principle of the seas where ships sailed from port to port was a parallel to ancient historians' and geographers' understanding of the world as a series of 'nodal points' separated by space and connected through itineraries.[96] He was not only concerned with correcting maps based on Ptolemy, but in accordance with the anthropocentric tradition of geography, he was just as much if not more interested in the ethnographic and natural history of these lands, as well as their commercial potential. As discussed previously, this accords with a reading of these volumes as presenting readers with a completely new vision of a global earth. The *Navigationi et viaggi* is a history of what led up to this new vision. Even though the compilation as such was not a new genre, Ramusio's use of it to promote his vision of a changed globe was new.

Concluding remarks

I have argued that early modern travel compilations constitute a historical genre, using the *Navigationi et viaggi* of Giovanni Battista Ramusio as an example. The editors of such compilations viewed their works as contributions to the history of knowledge of the natural and physical world – in the eyes of Ramusio and his friends the most commendable pursuit of men. The heirs to Ramusio's compiling practice were the English compilers later in the century, namely Richard Hakluyt, who modelled himself on Ramusio, and following him, Samuel Purchas (1575–1626). Both explicitly claimed they were concerned with *peregrinationis historia*, and they insisted that history and geography were two sides of the same coin, a connection Ramusio took for granted. The travel compilation was one type of history being told in early modern times. Its aims, however, varied. None of Ramusio's intellectual heirs engaged with presenting a new world picture. They did arrange material according to continents but relied on a chronological order. They had in common that they all addressed political and mercantile authorities (as well as scholars), and they all contributed to presenting new knowledge to their readers.

In Ramusio's case, a humanist armchair geographer with a concern for the loss of cultural memory ended up inventing a new genre, a new kind of historical writing in the early modern period. Compilations of travel accounts had been published in the Veneto prior to Ramusio, but these were straightforwardly chronological in structure. Ramusio was the first to structure such writing spatially rather than temporally while using old knowledge to verify new. By dedicating each volume to separate areas of the globe and connecting them to discoveries made by or in the name of a specific mercantile power, Ramusio's spatially oriented compilation became histories of the mercantile expansion of three early modern powers: the Kingdom of Portugal, the Republic of Venice, and Imperial Spain. At the same time, he produced the first history of a global world in the age of discovery supplying his readers with a new social vision of an interconnected terraqueous globe.

Early modern times were a period of unrest religiously and politically but also a period when the existing world picture centred upon Christendom and a millennia-old ecumene, no longer sufficed. The first globalisation required new conceptions of the world. During the past fifty years the Western world picture has been steadily challenged and studying how earlier times met such paradigmatic challenges could provide inspiration and useful insights for our present regime of historicity. Also, the use of travel literature as source material points to the potential of other types of sources than those which have typically concerned intellectual history. The so-called age of discovery constituted Ramusio's contemporary historical setting. He found sources that enabled him to meet the challenges posed by his time and solve them conceptually, and in doing so he invented a new genre of historical writing.

Notes

1 Giovanni Battista Ramusio and Marica Milanesi, eds., *Navigazioni e viaggi* (Torino: Giulio Enaudi editore, 1978–1988), vol. I: 599 ('Discorso sopra alcune lettere e navigazioni fatte per li capitani dell'armate delli serenissimi re de Portogallo verso le Indie orientali'). 'Una delle piú mirabili e gran cose che l'età nostra abbia veduto, è stato il discoprir di tanti e cosí varii paesi di questo globo della terra, che mai per lo adrieto gli antichi nostri avean saputo'. This is the modern six-volume edition edited by Marica Milanesi. All citations and references will be to this edition. All quotations are translated by the author unless otherwise stated. The modern version has two volumes for each of the original three volumes.

2 William Boelhower, 'Three Early Modern Genres: A Microhistorical Approach to "World Literature"', *Atlantic Studies* 16, no. 1 (2019): 21–37, https://doi.org/10.1080/14788810.2017.1349064. The other two being utopia and *naufragium* (shipwreck narrative).

3 Tim Youngs, *The Cambridge Introduction to Travel Writing* (New York: Cambridge University Press, 2014), chap. 1.

4 Sanjay Subrahmanyam, 'On World Historians in the Sixteenth Century', *Representations*, no. 91 (2005): 26–57.

5 Kristin Asdal et al., *Tekst og historie: å lese tekster historisk* (Oslo: Universitetsforlaget, 2008), chap. 6. The book is a collaboration by several authors who have each been responsible for various chapters. Helge Jordheim has been the main author of the chapter on genres.

6 Ramusio and Milanesi, *Navigazioni e viaggi*, vol. I: 599 ('Discorso sopra alcune lettere e navigazioni fatte per li capitani dell'armate delli serenissimi re di Portogallo verso le Indie orientali'). '[D]ubitando che, con la lunghezza di tempo, la memoria di cosí grande e notabil impresa si potesse perdere, ho pensato esser laudevol cosa il raccogliere e metter insieme (meglio che si è potuto) alcune lettere di viaggi scritti per diversi sopra questa materia ...'

7 For a discussion of the importance of form in early modern knowledge construction, see Anne Eriksen and Ellen Krefting, 'Formens makt og materialitet: Om studiet av kunnskapens former i katekismer og skipslogger', *Slagmark: Videnshistorie*, no. 81 (2020): 31–49.

8 'The Advancement of Learning' in Francis Bacon, *The Major Works*, ed. Brian Vickers, Oxford World's Classics (Oxford: Oxford University Press, 2002), 183; for a discussion of the use of the terms 'cosmography' and 'geography', see Marica Milanesi, 'Geography and Cosmography in Italy from XV to XVII Century', *Memorie Della Società Astronomica Italiana/ Journal of the Italian Astronomical Society* 65, no. 2 Atti del Convegno 'La cultura astronomica e geografica in Italia dal XV al XVII secolo', Roma, 29–30 ottobre 1992 (1994): 443–68.

9 Carolyn R. Miller, 'Genre as Social Action', *Quarterly Journal of Speech*, no. 70 (1984): 151–67.

10 Ramusio and Milanesi, *Navigazioni e viaggi*, vol. II: 779 (betel leaves), III: 62 (rhubarb), 877–885 (fishes); Francesco Lorenzini, Girolamo Ruscelli, and Dionigi Atanagi, *Lettere Di XIII Huomini Illustri: Nelle Quale Sono Due Libri Di Diuersi Altri Auttori, et Il Fiore Di Quante Belle Lettere, Che Fin'hora Si Sono Uedute: Con Molte Del Bembo, Del Nauagero, Del Fracastoro, Del Manutio, & Di Altri Famosi Auttori Non Piu Date in Luce*, [24], 768 p. (In Venetia: Per Francesco Lorenzini da Turino, 1560), 737–738 (letter from Fracastoro to Ramusio dated March 18, *s.a.*).

11 Alastair Fowler, *Kinds of Literature: An Introduction to the Theory of Genres and Modes* (Oxford: Clarendon Press, 1982), 40–44.

12 Joan-Pau Rubiés, 'Travel Writing as a Genre: Facts, Fictions and the Invention of a Scientific Discourse in Early Modern Europe', *Journeys: The International Journal of Travel and Travel Writing* 1, no. 1 (2000): 6.

13 Carl Thompson, *Travel Writing* (London: Routledge, 2011), 11 and 19 for examples.

14 This would be volumes I and II of the modern edition, see note 1.

15 This would be volumes III and IV of the modern edition, see note 1.

16 Ramusio and Milanesi, *Navigazioni e viaggi*, vol. III: 3–5 (Giunti to the readers). It was much delayed due to a fire in the printer's workshop.

17 This would be volumes V and VI of the modern edition, see note 1.

18 Marica Milanesi, *Tolomeo Sostituito: Studi Di Storia Delle Conoscenze Geographiche Nel XVI Secolo*, Studi e Richerche Sul Territorio (Milano: Edizioni Unicopli, 1984), 58–60.

19 I am aware that the label 'natural history' first appeared in the 1540s, although these early modern histories built on ancient models, such as Pliny, Aristotles and Theophrastos. Brian W. Ogilvie, 'Natural History, Ethics, and Physico-Theology', in *Historia: Empiricism and Erudition in Early Modern Europe*, ed. Gianna Pomata and Nancy G. Siraisi (Cambridge, Massachusetts: The MIT Press, 2005), 75.

20 The modern organisation of knowledge into distinct specialised fields does not comply with that of the early modern period when both geography and history could overlap considerably.

21 Ramusio and Milanesi, *Navigazioni e viaggi*, vol. I: 8 (Giunti to the readers). For the quotation, see note 25.

22 *Libro primo delle Indie occidentali* and *Libro secondo delle Indie occidentali* (1534) are always bound together, sometimes also *Libro ulitimo del summario delle Indie occidentali* (1536) is included. Pietro Bembo and Robert W. Ulery, *History of Venice* (Cambridge, Mass.; London: Harvard University Press, 2007), vol. II: bk. 4: 1–14; see Andrea Del Ben, *Giovanni Battista Ramusio: Cancelliere e Umanist, Con l'edizione Di Quarantacinque Lettere a Pietro Bembo (Ms. Ambrosiano D 335 INF)* (Bagnaria: Edizioni Goliardiche, 2005) for Ramusio's letters to Bembo; for letter from Bembo, see the four volumes of his collected letters: Pietro Bembo, *Lettere*, ed. Ernesto Travi, 4 vols, Collezione di opere inedite o rare (La Commissione, 1987–1993).

23 The letters from Fracastoro are found in Lorenzini, Ruscelli, and Atanagi, *Lettere Di XIII Huomini Illustri,* 706–746.

24 Ramusio and Milanesi, *Navigazioni e viaggi*, vol. I: 469 ('Discorso sopra il libro di M. Alvise da Ca' da Mosto'). 'Le quali veramente sono degne di esser lette dagli studiosi, perciochè vederanno il paese verso detta linea, il qual gli antichi savi affermavano che era abbruciato dal sole e senza abitazioni, esser verdissimo e amenissimo e da infinite genti abitato'.

25 Ramusio and Milanesi, vol. I: 8 (Giunti to the readers). '... non avesse fatto più di bisogno leggere né Tolomeo né Strabone né Plinio né alcun altro degli antichi scrittori intorno alle cose de geografia'.

26 See e.g. Nicholas Popper, *Walter Ralegh's 'History of the World' and the Historical Culture of the Late Renaissance* (London: University of Chicago Press, 2014); Anthony Grafton, *What Was History? The Art of History in Early Modern Europe* (Cambridge: Cambridge University Press, 2007).

27 For a discussion of the habitability of the world in Venice at the time of Ramusio, see John M. Headley, 'The Sixteenth-Century Venetian Celebration of the Earth's Total Habitability: The Issue of the Fully Habitable World for Renaissance Europe', *Journal of World History* 8, no. 1 (1997): 1–27.

28 I am well aware that the use of the word 'discovery' is contested for its Eurocentric imperialistic connotations. I am using it in the sense that Europeans acquired new knowledge about the world that they had not known before or knowledge that had been lost after the fall of the Roman Empire; in that sense, most of the world were 'new worlds.

29 Margaret Small, *Framing the World: Classical Influences on Sixteenth-Century Geographical Thought* (Boydell & Brewer, 2020); Denis E. Cosgrove, *Apollo's Eye: A Cartographic Genealogy of the Earth in the Western Imagination*, A Johns Hopkins Paperback (Baltimore, Md.: Johns Hopkins University Press, 2003), 104–110.

30 Both the Portuguese and the Spaniards sought to control the circulation and dissemination of maps that were created because of their discoveries.

31 Ramusio and Milanesi, *Navigazioni e viaggi*, vol. I: 4–5 (First dedication to Fracastoro). '[V]edendo, e considerando le tavole della Geografia di Tolomeo, dove si descrive l'Africa, e la India esser molto imperfette, rispetto all gran cognitione che si ha oggi di quelle regioni, ho stimato dover esser caro, e forse non poco utile al mondo il mettere insieme la narrationi de gli scrittori de' nostri tempi, che sono stati nelle sopradette parti del mondo, e di quelle han parlato minutamente'.

32 Ramusio and Milanesi, vol. I: 5 (First dedication to Fracastoro). 'Ai quali piú che ad alcuno altro appartiene il saper i secreti e particolarità della detta parte del mondo e tutti i siti delle regioni, provincie e città di quella, e le dependenzie che hanno l'uno e dall'altro i signori e popoli che vi abitano'.

33 Ramusio and Milanesi, II: 1043 ('Alli lettori') (my emphasis). '[A]bbiamo scelto e fatto elezione delle cose pertinenti alla intelligenzia delli piú notabli paesi, fiumi, monti, città e colfi delli mari orientali e occidentali, avendo lasciato adietro quanto per lui è referito delle guerre fatte con quelli popoli dell'Indie, come cose alli desiderosi di maggior intelligenza dei poco profitto'.

34 In the first volume: betel leaves (II: 779); in the second volume: rhubarb (III: 362); in the third volume: various fishes and marine animals (VI: 883–885).

35 Fiona Lejosne, *Écrire Le Monde Depuis Venise Au XVIe Siècle: Giovanni Battista Ramusio et Les Navigationi et Viaggi* (Genève: Droz, 2021), chap. 7 (especially pp. 516–534).

36 George Bruner Parks, *Richard Hakluyt and the English Voyages* (New York: Frederick Ungar Publishing, 1961), 158, 159. Purchas was later to make a notation that Hakluyt's *Principall Navigations* had saved the East India Company 20,000 £.

37 R. A. Skelton, 'Preface', in *Navigationi et Viaggi*, vol. I (Amsterdam: Theatrum Orbis Terrarum, 1970), v–xvi.

38 Milanesi, *Tolomeo Sostituito*, 58–60; Ramusio and Milanesi, *Navigazioni e viaggi*, vol. III: 8 (Giunti to the readers).

39 Ramusio and Milanesi, *Navigazioni e viaggi*, vol. I: xxi (Milanesi's introduction); Subrahmanyam, 'On World Historians in the Sixteenth Century', 28.

40 Peter Burke, 'Early Modern Venice as a Center of Information and Communication', in *Venice Reconsidered: The History and Civilization of an Italian City-State, 1297–1797*, ed. John Martin and Dennis Romano (Baltimore: The Johns Hopkins University Press, 2000), 389–419; Filippo de Vivo, *Information and Communication in Venice: Rethinking Early Modern Politics* (Oxford: Oxford University Press, 2007).

41 Boelhower, 'Three Early Modern Genres', 21.

42 Boelhower, 23.

43 Ramusio and Milanesi, *Navigazioni e viaggi*, vol. 1: xvi; Anne Helness, 'Et tidligmoderne politisk verdensbilde: Ramusio, Venezia og havet', *Arr – idéhistorisk tidsskrift: Havet*, no. 3-4 (2018): 75–91.

44 Milanesi, *Tolomeo Sostituito*, 43.

45 For a discussion of early modern understandings of *historia*, see Gianna Pomata and Nancy G. Siraisi, 'Introduction', in *Historia: Empiricism and Erudition in Early Modern Europe*, ed. Gianna Pomata and Nancy G. Siraisi (Cambridge, Massachusetts: The MIT Press, 2005), 1–38.

46   Ramusio and Milanesi, *Navigazioni e viaggi*, vol. II: 967 ('Discorso sopra ... le spezierie ...'). 'Maravigliosa cosa veramente è a pensare la gran mutazione e alterazione che fece in tutto l'impero romano la venuta de' Goti e altri barbari in Italia, conciosiacosaché tali populazioni estinguessero tutte l'arti, tutte le scienzie e tutti i traffichi e mercanzie che in diverse parti del mondo si facevano: e durarono per 400 anni e piú quasi come le tenebre d'una oscura notte, sí che alcun non ardiva di partirsi del suo paese natio e andar altrove, dove che avanti la venuta di detti barbari, quando fioriva l'imperio romano, in tutte l'Indie orientali per mare sicuramente si poteva navigare; ed era cosí frequentato e celebre questo viaggio e conosciuto come egli è al presente per la navigazion dei Portoghesi. E che questo fusse il vero, chiaramente lo dimostra quel che scrive Strabone, che fu nel tempo d'Augusto e di Tiberio ...'

47   For a detailed presentation of these two approaches, see Matthew McLean, *The Cosmographia of Sebastian Münster: Describing the World in the Reformation* (Aldershot: Ashgate, 2007), chap. 2. The quote is on page 47.

48   See Francis Bacon, 'The Advancement of Learning', in *The Major Works*, ed. Brian Vickers, Oxford World's Classics (Oxford: Oxford University Press, 2002), 120–299.

49   Fabio Romanini, *'Se fussero più ordinate, e meglio scritte ...' Giovanni Battista Ramusio correttore ed editore delle Navigationi et viaggi* (Roma: Viella, 2007).

50   Marica Milanesi, '"Come dicono gl'isorici antichi ...": Nearco come fonte nelle *Navigazioni* di Giovanni Battista Ramusio (1550–1559)', *Geographia Antiqua* XXII (2013): 6975; Romain Descendre and Fiona Lejosne, 'Giovanni Battista Ramusio et la "Conférence" Des Récits: Anciens et Modernes dans les "Navigationi et Viaggi"', in *Le Présent Fabriqué*, À paraître aux Éditions Classiques Garnier (Garnier, 2019).

51   François Hartog, 'Time, History and the Writing of History: The Order of Time', in *History-Making: The Intellectual and Social Formation of a Discipline*, ed. Rolf Torstendahl and Irmline Veit-Brause, Proceedings of an International Conference, Uppsala, September 1994, Konferenser 37 (Stockholm: Kungl. Vitterhets Historie ooc Antikvitets Akademien, 1996), 97, Hartog's concept of historicity points to modes of structuring time (past, present, future) within different 'regime of historicity'; Ramusio and Milanesi, *Navigazioni e viaggi*, vol. V: xxii.

52   Subrahmanyam, 'On World Historians in the Sixteenth Century', 28.

53   Subrahmanyam, 28.

54   Subrahmanyam, 28.

55   Boelhower, 'Three Early Modern Genres'.

56   Subrahmanyam, 'On World Historians in the Sixteenth Century', 36.

57   Subrahmanyam, 43.

58   Subrahmanyam, 36, 28; on Ramusio's project, see Milanesi, *Tolomeo Sostituito*, 41, 42, 44–45; Ramusio and Milanesi, *Navigazioni e viaggi*, vol. 1: xvi, xxx–xxxi, xxxiv–xxxv; for the construction of oceans as social spaces, see Philip E. Steinberg, *The Social Construction of the Ocean*, Cambridge Studies in International Relations 78 (Cambridge: Cambridge University Press, 2001).

59   Thompson, *Travel Writing*, 20.

60   For a discussion of this point, see Jaś Elsner and Joan-Pau Rubiés, 'Introduction', in *Voyages and Visions: Towards a Cultural History of Travel* (London: Reaktion Books, 1999), 4; as well as Joan-Pau Rubiés, 'Travel Writing and Humanistic Culture: A Blunted Impact?', *Journal of Modern History* 10, no. 1–2 (2006): 131–68.

61   Ramusio and Milanesi, *Navigazioni e viaggi*, vol. I: 599 ('Discorso sopra alcune lettere e navigazioni fatte per li capitani dell'armate delli serenissimi re di Portogallo verso le Indie orientali'). 'E quando a qualche gentil spirito nell'avenire venisse voglia di scriver questa istoria ordinatamente, potria servirsi in qualche parte di queste tal scritture, ancor che siano rozze e inordinate'.

62 For a short discussion of Portuguese attempts to control information see Donald F. Lach, *Asia in the Making of Europe, Volume I: The Century of Discovery. Book 1.*, ACLS Humanities ebook (Chicago: University of Chicago Press, 2008), 151–154, https://hdl.handle.net/2027/heb03149.

63 George B. Parks, 'Ramusio's Literary History', *Studies in Philology* 52, no. 2 (1955): 136–137; Ramusio and Milanesi, *Navigazioni e viaggi*, vol. V: 21–22; Lejosne, *Écrire Le Monde Depuis Venise Au XVIe Siècle: Giovanni Battista Ramusio et Les Navigationi et Viaggi*, 173–174.

64 *OED s.v.* An *adelantado* was 'a military leader with the authority to explore, colonise, and govern new territories for the Spanish crown'.

65 Ramusio and Milanesi, *Navigazioni e viaggi*, vol. V: 10 (Dedication to Fracastoro in the third volume). 'Delle quali guerre tutti gl'istorici spagnuoli di questi tempi s'hanno affaticato e affaticano di scrivere con un'estrema diligenza, notando ch ne' fatti d'arme di Salinas, Chupas, Quito, Guarina, Xaquixaguana v'erano i tali e tali capitani, alfieri e adelantadi, co' nomi di tutti i soldati spagnuoli, sí da cavallo come da piedi, e in qual città di Spagna ciascun di lor nacquero, cosa vana e ridicolosa; delle cose naturali veramente sopradette se ne passano brevemente, se non in quanto non possono far di meno di non nominarle alle fiate'.

66 Popper, *Walter Ralegh's 'History of the World' and the Historical Culture of the Late Renaissance*, chap. 1.

67 Joan-Pau Rubiés, 'From the "History of Travayle" to the History of Travel Collections: The Rise of an Early Modern Genre', in *Richard Hakluyt and Travel Writing in Early Modern Europe*, ed. Daniel Carey and Claire Jowitt, Hakluyt Society Extra Series 47 (Aldershot: Ashgate; For the Hakluyt Society, 2012), 26; Pomata and Siraisi, 'Introduction', 4; Gianna Pomata, '*Praxis Historialis*: The Uses of *Historia* in Early Modern Medicine', in *Historia: Empiricism and Erudition in Early Modern Europe*, ed. Gianna Pomata and Nancy G. Siraisi (Cambridge, Massachusetts: The MIT Press, 2005), 109; see also Anthony Grafton, 'The Identities of History in Early Modern Europe: Prelude to a Study of the *Artes Historicae*', in *Historia: Empiricism and Erudition in Early Modern Europe*, ed. Gianna Pomata and Nancy G. Siraisi (Cambridge, Massachusetts: The MIT Press, 2005), 41–74.

68 Ramusio and Milanesi, *Navigazioni e viaggi*, vol. I: 599 (see note 1 for the full quotation).

69 Ramusio and Milanesi, vol. I: 599 ('Discorso sopra alcune lettere e navigazioni fatte per li capitani dell'armate delli serenissimi re di Portogallo verso le Indie orientali') (see note 6 for the full quotation in the original).

70 See Milanesi's introduction to these texts: 'Navigazioni portoghesi verso le Indie orientali', Ramusio and Milanesi, vol. I: 596–597.

71 Lach, *Asia in the Making of Europe, Vol. I Bk. 1*, 151–154.

72 For modern discussions of contact between Rome and the East, see Lach, 12–19; Raoul McLaughlin, *The Roman Empire and the Indian Ocean: Rome's Dealings with the Ancient Kingdoms of India, Africa and Arabia* (Barnsley: Pen & Sword Military, 2014).

73 Ramusio and Milanesi, *Navigazioni e viaggi*, vol. II: 967. '[L]a venuta de' Goti e altri barbari in Italia, ... estingussero ... tutte le scienze'.

74 Ramusio and Milanesi, vol. I: 600 ('Discorso sopra alcune lettere e navigazioni fatte per li capitani dell'armate delli serenissimi re di Portogallo verso le Indie orientali'). '[I]nfiniti paesi discoperti per diversi capitani, in diversi tempi, li quali per non esserne memoria, restano in eterna oblivione, non altramente che erano il passato'.

75 Ramusio and Milanesi, vol. I: 600 ('Discorso sopra alcune lettere ...'). '[C]he sono senza nome e incognite, e non per altra causa se non per manacamento di scrittori'.

76 Donald Kelley translates *historie* with 'inquiries', see Herodotus, *The Histories*, ed. Andrew Robert Burn, trans. Aubrey De Sélincourt, Rev. ed., repr, Penguin Classics (Harmondsworth: Penguin Books, 1984), bk. 1: 1; Donald R. Kelley, *Faces of History: Historical Inquiry from Herodotus to Herder* (New Haven: Yale University Press, 1998), 2.

77 Peter Haylyn (1599–1622), *Microcosmus* (1621) quoted in Katherine Clarke, *Between Geography and History: Hellenistic Constructions of the Roman World*, Oxford Classical Monographs (Oxford: Clarendon Press, 1999), 4.

78 John Frow, *Genre*, The New Critical Idiom (London: Routledge, 2006), 125. He borrows this view from Jacques Derrida.

79 Asdal et al., *Tekst og historie*, 185. The book is a collaboration between seven different authors who are mutually responsible for every chapter, although they each have a main responsibility for separate chapters, thus Helge Jordheim on genres.

80 A composite genre field would be akin to Rubiés' notion of travel literature as a 'genre of genres'. What the genres have in common is that they 'share travel as their essential condition of production'. Rubiés, 'Travel Writing as a Genre', 6.

81 Thompson, *Travel Writing*, 19.

82 Justin Stagl, *A History of Curiosity: The Theory of Travel, 1550–1800* (London: Routledge, 2006), 56; the most famous cosmography was that of Sebastian Münster, first published in 1544, see McLean, *The Cosmographia of Sebastian Münster*. In cosmographies geographical and ethnographical knowledge was more systematically ordered than in compilations, as the information was taken out of its original textual context.

83 Stagl, *A History of Curiosity*, 53–56.

84 Michel Mollat du Jourdin, *Les Explorateur Du XIIIe Au XVIe Siècle: Premiers Regards Sur Des Mondes Nouveaux* (Paris: Éditions du CTHS, 2005), 31.

85 Stagl, *A History of Curiosity*, chap. 2.

86 Stagl, 36; Clarke, *Between Geography and History*, 57.

87 See notes 1, 6 and 63.

88 Cf. Gianna Pomata and Nancy G. Siraisi, eds., *Historia: Empiricism and Erudition in Early Modern Europe* (Cambridge, Massachusetts: The MIT Press, 2005).

89 Clarke, *Between Geography and History*, 338, 339; for the use of Herodotus in the early modern period, see also Achille Olivieri, *Erodoto nel Rinascimento: l'umano e la storia*, L'eredità dell'antico 8 (Roma: L'Erma di Bretschneider, 2004).

90 Ramusio and Milanesi, *Navigazioni e viaggi*, vol. 2: 398, 399 (discussing the annual flooding of the Nile), 3: 23, 486 (discussing the credibility of travellers), 4: 16, 18, 328, 444, 503 (comparing with other sources).

91 Clarke, *Between Geography and History*, 2 n. 2.

92 A. H. Merrills, *History and Geography in Late Antiquity*, Cambridge Studies in Medieval Life and Thought: Fourth Series (Cambridge: Cambridge University Press, 2005), 1–3, 6–7, https://doi.org/10.1017/CBO9780511496370.

93 Richard Hakluyt, 'A Preface to the Reader as Touching the Principall Voyages and Discourses in This First Part', in *The Principal Nauigations, Voyages, Traffiques and Discoueries of the English Nation* (London: George Bishop, Ralph Newberie, and Robert Barker, 1599), vol. I: fol. sig. *4ʳ.

94 Ramusio and Milanesi, *Navigazioni e viaggi*, vol. V: 8 (Dedication to Fracastoro, third volume). 'Percioché ragionevolmente non è da credere che il fattore di così bella e perfetta fabrica come sono i cieli, il sole e la luna, non abbia voluto che, essendo ella fatta con tanto stupendo e maraviglioso ordine, il sole non illumine se non una particella di questo globo oche chiamano terra, e il resto del suo corso sia in vano sopra mari, nevi e ghiacci ...' See also page 6 where he argues against Plato.

95 Ramusio and Milanesi, V: 6–7 (Dedication to Fracastoro, third volume). 'E veramente noi siamo, oltra gl'infiniti doni concessine da Iddio, obligati grandemente a sua divina Maestà di questo sopra tutti gli altri uomini stati nei secoli passati, che a' nostri tempi si sia scoperta questa nuova parte del mondo, della quale in cosí lungo spazio di tempo no se n'è avuta notizia ...'

96 Merrills, *History and Geography in Late Antiquity*, 10.

Bibliography

Asdal, Kristin, Kjell Lars Berge, Karen Gammelgaard, Trygve Riiser Gundersen, Helge Jordheim, Tore Rem, & Johan L. Tønnesson. *Tekst og historie: å lese tekster historisk*. Oslo: Universitetsforlaget, 2008.

Bacon, Francis. "The Advancement of Learning." In *The Major Works,*edited by Brian Vickers, 120–299. Oxford World's Classics. Oxford: Oxford University Press 2002.

Bacon, Francis. *The Major Works*. Edited by Brian Vickers. Oxford World's Classics.xford: Oxford University Press, 2002.

Bembo, Pietro. *Lettere*. Edited by Ernesto Travi. 4 vols. Collezione di opere inedite o rare. La Commissione, 1987–1993.

Bembo, Pietro, & Robert W. Ulery. *History of Venice*. 4 vols. Cambridge, Mass.; London: Harvard University Press, 2007.

Boelhower, William. "Three Early Modern Genres: A Microhistorical Approach to "World Literature." *Atlantic Studies* 16, no. 1 (2019): 21–37. 10.1080/14788810.2017. 1349064.

Burke, Peter. "Early Modern Venice as a Center of Information and Communication." In *Venice Reconsidered: The History and Civilization of an Italian City-State, 1297–1797*, edited by John Martin & Dennis Romano, 389–419. Baltimore: The Johns Hopkins University Press, 2000.

Clarke, Katherine. *Between Geography and History: Hellenistic Constructions of the Roman World*. Oxford Classical Monographs. Oxford: Clarendon Press, 1999.

Cosgrove, Denis E. *Apollo's Eye: A Cartographic Genealogy of the Earth in the Western Imagination*. A Johns Hopkins Paperback.Baltimore, Md.: Johns Hopkins University Press, 2003.

Del Ben, Andrea. *Giovanni Battista Ramusio: Cancelliere e Umanist, Con l'edizione Di Quarantacinque Lettere a Pietro Bembo (Ms. Ambrosiano D 335 INF)*. Bagnaria: Edizioni Goliardiche, 2005.

Descendre, Romain, & Fiona Lejosne. "Giovanni Battista Ramusio e la "Conférence" des récits: Anciens et Modernes dans les "Navigationi et Viaggi." In *Le Présent Fabriqué*. À paraître aux Éditions Classiques Garnier. Garnier, 2019.

Elsner, Jaś, & Joan-Pau Rubiés. "Introduction'. In *Voyages and Visions: Towards a Cultural History of Travel*, 1–56. London: Reaktion Books, 1999.

Eriksen, Anne, & Ellen Krefting. "Formens makt og materialitet: Om studiet av kunnskapens former i katekismer og skipslogger." *Slagmark: Videnshistorie*, no. 81 (2020): 31–49.

Fowler, Alastair. *Kinds of Literature: An Introduction to the Theory of Genres and Modes*. Oxford: Clarendon Press, 1982.

Frow, John. *Genre*. The New Critical Idiom. London: Routledge, 2006.

Grafton, Anthony. "The Identities of History in Early Modern Europe: Prelude to a Study of the *Artes Historicae*." In *Historia: Empiricism and Erudition in Early Modern Europe*, edited by Gianna Pomata and Nancy G. Siraisi, 41–74. Cambridge, Massachusetts: The MIT Press, 2005.

Grafton, Anthony. *What Was History? The Art of History in Early Modern Europe*. Cambridge: Cambridge University Press, 2007.

Hakluyt, Richard. "A Preface to the Reader as Touching the Principal Voyages and Discourses in This First Part." In *The Principal Nauigations, Voyages, Traffiques and Discoueries of the English Nation*. London: George Bishop, Ralph Newberie, and Robert Barker, 1599.

Hartog, François. "Time, History and the Writing of History: The Order of Time." In *History-Making: The Intellectual and Social Formation of a Discipline*, edited by Rolf Torstendahl and Irmline Veit-Brause, 95–113. Proceedings of an International Conference, Uppsala, September 1994, Konferenser 37. Stockholm: Kungl. Vitterhets Historie ooc Antikvitets Akademien, 1996.

Headley, John M. "The Sixteenth-Century Venetian Celebration of the Earth's Total Habitability: The Issue of the Fully Habitable World for Renaissance Europe." *Journal of World History* 8, no. 1 (1997): 1–27.

Helness, Anne. "Et tidligmoderne politisk verdensbilde: Ramusio, Venezia og havet." *Arr – idéhistorisk tidsskrift: Havet*, no. 3–4 (2018): 75–91.

Herodotus. *The Histories*, edited by Andrew Robert Burn. Translated by Aubrey De Sélincourt. Rev. ed., Repr. Penguin Classics. Harmondsworth: Penguin Books, 1984.

Kelley, Donald R. *Faces of History: Historical Inquiry from Herodotus to Herder*. New Haven: Yale University Press, 1998.

Lach, Donald F. *Asia in the Making of Europe, Volume I: The Century of Discovery. Book 1*. ACLS Humanities ebook. Chicago: University of Chicago Press, 2008. https://hdl.handle.net/2027/heb03149.

Lejosne, Fiona. *Écrire le monde depuis Venise au XVIe siècle: Giovanni Battista Ramusio et les Navigationi et Viaggi*. Genève: Droz, 2021.

Lorenzini, Francesco, Girolamo Ruscelli, & Dionigi Atanagi. *Lettere Di XIII Huomini Illustri: Nelle Quale Sono Due Libri Di Diuersi Altri Auttori, et Il Fiore Di Quante Belle Lettere, Che Fin'hora Si Sono Uedute: Con Molte Del Bembo, Del Nauagero, Del Fracastoro, Del Manutio, & Di Altri Famosi Auttori Non Piu Date in Luce*. [24], 768 p. In Venetia: Per Francesco Lorenzini da Turino, 1560.

McLaughlin, Raoul. *The Roman Empire and the Indian Ocean: Rome's Dealings with the Ancient Kingdoms of India, Africa and Arabia*. Barnsley: Pen & Sword Military, 2014.

McLean, Matthew. *The Cosmographia of Sebastian Münster: Describing the World in the Reformation*. Aldershot: Ashgate, 2007.

Merrills, A. H. *History and Geography in Late Antiquity*. Cambridge Studies in Medieval Life and Thought: Fourth Series. Cambridge: Cambridge University Press, 2005. 10.1017/CBO9780511496370.

Milanesi, Marica. *Tolomeo Sostituito: Studi di storia delle conoscenze geographiche nel XVI secolo*. Studi e richerche sul territorio. Milano: Edizioni Unicopli, 1984.

Milanesi, Marica. "'Come dicono gl'isorici antichi ...': Nearco come fonte nelle *Navigazioni* di Giovanni Battista Ramusio (1550–1559)'. *Geographia Antiqua* XXII (2013): 69–75.

Milanesi, Marica. "Geography and Cosmography in Italy from XV to XVII Century." *Memorie Della Società Astronomica Italiana/ Journal of the Italian Astronomical Society* 65, no. 2 Atti del Convegno 'La cultura astronomica e geografica in Italia dal XV al XVII secolo', Roma, 29–30 ottobre 1992 (1994): 443–468.

Miller, Carolyn R. "Genre as Social Action." *Quarterly Journal of Speech*, no. 70 (1984): 151–167.

Mollat du Jourdin, Michel. *Les Explorateur du XIIIe au XVIe Siècle: Premiers regards sur des Mondes Nouveaux*. Paris: Éditions du CTHS, 2005.

Ogilvie, Brian W. "Natural History, Ethics, and Physico-Theology." In *Historia: Empiricism and Erudition in Early Modern Europe*, edited by Gianna Pomata and Nancy G. Siraisi, 75–103. Cambridge, Massachusetts: The MIT Press, 2005.

Olivieri, Achille. *Erodoto nel Rinascimento: l'umano e la storia*. L'eredità dell'antico 8. Roma: L'Erma di Bretschneider, 2004.

Parks, George B. "Ramusio's Literary History." *Studies in Philology* 52, no. 2 (1955): 127–148.

Parks, George Bruner. *Richard Hakluyt and the English Voyages*. New York: Frederick Ungar Publishing, 1961.

Pomata, Gianna. "*Praxis Historialis*: The Uses of *Historia* in Early Modern Medicine." In *Historia: Empiricism and Erudition in Early Modern Europe*, edited by Gianna Pomata and Nancy G. Siraisi, 105–146. Cambridge, Massachusetts: The MIT Press, 2005.

Pomata, Gianna, & Nancy G. Siraisi, eds. *Historia: Empiricism and Erudition in Early Modern Europe*. Cambridge, Massachusetts: The MIT Press, 2005.

Pomata, Gianna, & Nancy G. Siraisi. "Introduction." In *Historia: Empiricism and Erudition in Early Modern Europe*, edited by Gianna Pomata, and Nancy G. Siraisi, 1–38. Cambridge, Massachusetts: The MIT Press, 2005.

Popper, Nicholas. *Walter Ralegh's 'History of the World' and the Historical Culture of the Late Renaissance*. London: University of Chicago Press, 2014.

Ramusio, Giovanni Battista, & Marica Milanesi, eds. *Navigazioni e viaggi*. 6 vols. Torino: Giulio Enaudi editore, 1978–1988.

Romanini, Fabio. *'Se fussero più ordinate, e meglio scritte ...' Giovanni Battista Ramusio correttore ed editore delle Navigationi et viaggi*. Roma: Viella, 2007.

Rubiés, Joan-Pau. "From the "History of Travayle" to the History of Travel Collections: The Rise of an Early Modern Genre." In *Richard Hakluyt and Travel Writing in Early Modern Europe*, edited by Daniel Carey and Claire Jowitt, 25–41. Hakluyt Society Extra Series 47. Aldershot: Ashgate; For the Hakluyt Society, 2012.

Rubiés, Joan-Pau. "Travel Writing and Humanistic Culture: A Blunted Impact?" *Journal of Modern History* 10, no. 1–2 (2006): 131–168.

Rubiés, Joan-Pau. "Travel Writing as a Genre: Facts, Fictions and the Invention of a Scientific Discourse in Early Modern Europe." *Journeys: The International Journal of Travel and Travel Writing* 1, no. 1 (2000): 5–35.

Skelton, R. A. "Preface." In *Navigationi et Viaggi*, I: v–xvi. Amsterdam: Theatrum Orbis Terrarum, 1970.

Small, Margaret. *Framing the World: Classical Influences on Sixteenth-Century Geographical Thought*. Boydell & Brewer, 2020.

Stagl, Justin. *A History of Curiosity: The Theory of Travel, 1550–1800*. London: Routledge, 2006.

Steinberg, Philip E. *The Social Construction of the Ocean*. Cambridge Studies in International Relations 78. Cambridge: Cambridge University Press, 2001.

Subrahmanyam, Sanjay. "On World Historians in the Sixteenth Century." *Representations*, no. 91 (2005): 26–57.

Thompson, Carl. *Travel Writing*. London: Routledge, 2011.

Vivo, Filippo de. *Information and Communication in Venice: Rethinking Early Modern Politics*. Oxford: Oxford University Press, 2007.

Youngs, Tim. *The Cambridge Introduction to Travel Writing*. New York: Cambridge University Press, 2014.

11 Histories from Barbary

Empirical and imperial aspirations in an eighteenth-century history

Svein Atle Skålevåg

Historiography in the eighteenth century was not unaffected by European expansion. At the university of Göttingen a preoccupation with the Orient was an important part of the emergence of new approaches to history in the second half of that century.[1] August Schlözer, a prominent historian at Göttingen, wrote what has been considered "the first real history of the Maghreb", when he published *Summarische Geschichte von Nord-Afrika* in 1775. This little book, written for students, provided a brief overview over the many "revolutions" that had been felt in the northern regions of Africa. But the author himself was defensive from the fact that it had not been possible for him to base such a story on a critical work with the sources.[2] Which at least goes to show that historical information about Maghreb, North-Africa or Barbary *was* available for a European at the time that Schlözer wrote his book. It was available in travel writings, in diplomatic correspondence and in topographical literature – as well as in rare Arabic manuscripts. In the following years more historical literature would be produced about Barbary.

The subject for this chapter is one of those later histories from Barbary: *The history of the Moroccan Emperor Mohamed Ben Abdallah* [*Den Marokanske Kajser Mohamed Ben Abdallah's Historie*], written by Georg Høst (1734–1794), in Danish, and published in Copenhagen in 1791.[3] It is noteworthy for being a book-length history of a sovereign from a state in Barbary, narrating the life of the emperor who had died only a year prior to the book's publication. It is also notable for the way that it boasts its reliance on archival sources. The book followed up an earlier work by the same author, *Relations from Marokos and Fès,* that was published in 1779 [*Efterretninger om Marókos og Fes*], which was a description of the domains of the emperor written in the topographical tradition.[4] That book had been immediately published in German as well as in Danish and may well have been the best available description of a country that was not easily available for travelers. Høst's second book, *The History of the Moroccan Emperor*, seems to have been less read, and it was not translated to another language until a French translation appeared in the late 1990s.

By writing the life of a recently deceased ruler, Høst chose a genre that was structured as a pure chronological narrative. What I am interested in figuring out here is why Høst chose biography as a genre for conveying further

DOI: 10.4324/9781003331971-16

knowledge about Morocco, after his successful topography about the lands of the emperor that was both translated and plagiarized. This choice needs to be understood in the epistemic context that Høst found himself in, and it may also illuminate some emerging developments in late eighteenth century historiography. *The History of the Moroccan Emperor*, published some fifteen years after Schlözer's *History of North-Africa*, indicates a shift away from genres where the historical narrative was not subsumed under a spatially conceived body of knowledge (as in topography), towards history understood as *a* genre for communicating knowledge.

Genre as community

The historian of science Gianni Pomata understands genre as shared and standardized "textual formats". By the fact that they are shared they are also inherently social: by contributing to a genre, one means to join a community.[5] To understand the genre of the book about the Moroccan emperor we need to ask what kind of community the author wanted to join in writing the book, and how that choice shaped its content.

Changes in historiography in the late eighteenth century seem associated with the emergence of a new community: The community of professional historians. "Our" historian, Georg Høst, seems to have been more concerned with other communities, such as the community of orientalists or of civil servants. We may consequently classify Høst's writings as belonging to the genre of orientalism. The orientalists combined the philologist's interest for language with the antiquarians' interest in material remains of the past, and the historians' interest for the revolutions of the past. Høst's interest in all these things and more was expressed in his first book about Morocco. But *The History of the Moroccan Emperor* shows a narrower interest, that seems to be contained by the possibilities of one specific source of evidence, which is the archive. A chronological narrative based on archival work, and in a historiographical situation that was changing at this time – in this case, and in this context it may seem as fruitful to see history as *a* genre, as to look for what genre of history it represents.

Barbary as a space

Høst's biography of the Moroccan emperor would never have been written if it were not for diplomatic events forty years prior to its publication, at the very beginning of the reign of its protagonist, that in turn led to the author spending several years in the domains of the emperor. These events implied diplomatic negotiations between the Moroccan and the Danish courts, as well as the establishment in the 1760s of a Danish chartered trade company that traded with goods from Morocco. The Danish Africa company was led by a board in Copenhagen, it hired European traders based in Morocco, and it also sent some Danes to work for them there. Georg Høst came to Morocco in 1760 as a young clerk for this company and stayed there for eight years. Those years shaped his interest in Morocco, and he collected a lot of material that would later become *Relations from Marokos and Fès,* as well as making the acquaintance of the emperor who would become the subject of his second book.

The term Morocco was in the mid-eighteenth century a European name for the city today known as Marrakech, hence the title of Høst's first book. Occasionally he spells it "Meraksch", which is closer to the local pronunciation (current and in the epoch), which serves to underline Høst's claim to local knowledge of the place.[6] The city at the feet of the Atlas Mountains was understood to be the capital of a distinct kingdom comprising the southern parts of the territory of modern Morocco. The northern parts, including the Mediterranean coast and the Rif mountains, were known under the name of the kingdom of Fes. Gradually, the name Morocco came to refer regularly to the entire empire.

The dominions of the emperor belonged to the larger region of Barbary. This was not a very specific geographical designation in the eighteenth century. It referred to the southern shores of the Mediterranean, roughly from Tripoli to the straits of Gibraltar, with a focus on the ports in this region and their hinterlands.[7] It can be understood as less of a territory, than a network of places, or an idea even. It was associated with "barbarians", though eighteenth-century commentators disagreed whether there was an etymological connection between Barbary and Barbarians. But when a historian such as Edward Gibbon, in *Decline and fall of the Roman Empire,* referred to the emperor as a Barbarian, it was certainly not just a geographical reference.[8] Høst also uses the adjective "barbaric" in the pejorative sense, but only rarely. One of these rare examples relates to a description of diplomatic negotiations as "barbaric negotiation". In this case "barbaric" has little to do with geography.[9] On a different occasion he characterizes the actions of Sidi Muhammad as "less barbaric" than one might expect.[10]

Barbary was also associated with Islam and notably with corsairs who for centuries engaged in hostilities towards ships of European origin, as European ships engaged in hostilities towards ships originating from Barbary. An important part of these hostilities was the taking of captives to be returned for ransoms.[11] Due to the corsairs, a large number of sailors on European ships had some first-hand experience from the region. Through church and government, a considerable effort was made to raise money for ransoms and negotiate the release of such captives, and this activity also contributed to keeping these places on the mental map of many Europeans.

The westernmost parts of this vague region were the domains of the rulers of the Alawi dynasty, though their hold of corsair ports such as Tangiers and Salé was tenuous. They were referred to as the *sherifs,* as they claimed descendance from the Prophet. Høst refers to the government as "the government of the sherifs". More commonly they were referred to as the emperors of Morocco and Fes. The title of emperor was customary in the diplomatic language, and its usage seems to say something about the geopolitical power struggles at the time. Høst suggests with some hesitation that this language originated in an agreement between the Moroccan and the French sovereign to address each other as emperors.[12] Gibbon refers to "the barbarian whom we condescend to style the emperor of Morocco", indicating that the title fitted the man badly, and Schlözer stated outright that he found it ridiculous to address the sovereign of a people he considered "anthropomorpha" or "half-men" in such way.[13]

The strong association of pirates and the geographical term Barbary is evident in the title of a book from the mid-eighteenth century, *A compleat [sic] history of the piratical states of Barbary*. Still, the emperor's tenuous hold on the Corsair ports made it debatable whether his domains were part of Barbary. Though the book just mentioned included the Moroccan domain in Barbary, as did Schlözer, the French diplomat-historian Louis Chenier did not.[14]

There had been diplomatic relations between the sovereigns of Morocco, Fès and Meknes and those of England, France and Spain for a very long time. But as Sidi Muhammad, son of Abd Allah, rose to power in the 1750s, following a long period of internal unrest, the diplomatic relations with European powers multiplied.[15] Sidi Muhammad initiated many peace initiatives directed towards European powers, similar to the ottoman "capitulations".[16] In 1765 he also founded a new city, Essaouira, on the Atlantic coast, to be a node for trade with Europe. These rapprochements seem to have been motivated partly by Sidi Muhammad's need for military equipment and partly by the military and economic competition between the many European powers: the European states needed to be sheltered from the corsairs of Barbary to be able to promote the international trade of their subjects.[17] Hence the rapprochement was as much related to the European competition, as to any eternal hostility between Christian Europe and Muslim Africa.

Among the first of Sidi Muhammad's new European partners were the government of King Frederick V of Denmark, who signed a treaty with Sidi Muhammad in 1754 (with later revisions).[18] A Danish consul was consequently placed in Morocco, a Danish trading station was established in Safi (later moved to Essaouira), and the Danish African Company was created. As part of the agreement, the Danish crown was to pay an annual tribute to the Moroccan sovereign, and Danish merchants were to do tax farming in the port cities of Safi and Salé. The Danish sources from the eighteenth century, including Georg Høst, repeats time and again that there was a special relationship between the two governments and that their treaty was the first of the long line of treaties with European powers that Sidi Muhammad negotiated. Høst has Sidi Muhammad proclaim (to the Danish consul in an audience): "I will never forget that the king of Denmark was the first who made peace with me; it is he who has led the other European princes to me".[19] It may be hard to imagine that the emperor uttered these exact words, but it seems feasible enough that he expressed something along these lines in this specific context, as there are many signs that he aimed to play the Europeans against each other.

These events are dealt with both in Høst's *Efterretninger*, and in his *History of the Moroccan Emperor*. He indicates that the Danes were misled by their interlocutors in this affair because the Danes had insufficient information about the land they were encountering.[20] This perceived lack of information and knowledge was the immediate backdrop for Høst's histories from Barbary, and in this way, his histories were both a product from and a response to the events in the 1750s. It explains both why Høst felt he had the necessary knowledge, and why there was a felt need for his knowledge.

Some outlines of the history of this loose geographical area, and of the western parts more particularly, were well known to educated Europeans. In ancient times parts of the area had been roman provinces, and they were hence known from Roman sources. This is significant because of the importance roman history held as a reference point for European historiography. Barbary held historiographical importance because it had been part of Rome. The Muslim conquest and the succession of dynasties following were also well described in European literature. What the scholars of the last third of the eighteenth century found lacking, were sources to the modern history of this region, the period when it came to be seen as the home of a number of "piratical states".

Georg Høst: An agent of empire and of knowledge

Georg Høst was the son of a Lutheran pastor and had studied for a theology degree in Copenhagen in the 1750s.[21] A suitable calling as a pastor seems not to have been available, and so he took a position with the Danish African company as a "kommis" (agent) and traveled to Morocco in 1760. He stayed there until 1767, when the company was dissolved (after having lost a lot of money). He learned both written and oral Arabic in Morocco, and on several occasions, Høst functioned as an interpreter for the consul. In this capacity, he met the emperor, Sidi Muhammad, who seemed to have favored him. In 1766, when Sidi Muhammad transferred the European trade to the newly founded port of Essaouira, Høst temporarily became vice-consul, representing the Danish king in Essaouira, while the consul, Barisien, remained in Safi. According to Høst himself, this promotion happened following the wishes of the emperor Sidi Muhammad.[22] At this stage Høst started to collect information about Morocco.

Høst himself writes little about what the work as a clerk in Morocco actually consisted of, and for whom he worked. He was attached to a *factory*, where a few factors were engaged by the company direction in Copenhagen. A consul was appointed by the king in Copenhagen. But the distinction between royal diplomacy and private commerce are not very clear, and apparently the young man performed services for both the royal consul and the company. We can assume that he was not only serving as an interpreter, but also that lot of material goods passed through his hands, literally. The work of a merchant demanded a feel for different qualities, and a mind for value judgements. The eye for valuable objects that Høst developed in the factories is notable also in his History of the Moroccan emperor, as the pages are full of detailed listings of the gifts given and gifts received, constituting a veritable catalog of matters of exchange.

Harold Cook has argued that the scientific revolution in the sixteenth and seventeenth centuries arose at least in part from commercial culture and its reliance on "careful descriptive information about objects". The novelty of these descriptions was that they were not soaked in metaphysical meanings, they were the fruit of a desire for superficiality. These descriptions in turn relied on corporeal interaction with the world: "the new philosophy arose not from disembodied minds but from the passions and interests of mind and body united".[23] Similarly, it is fair to assume that Høst's experience of evaluating the qualities of goods, as well as his experiences as an interpreter, shaped his approach to historical sources.

When the Danish company was dissolved, Høst got a new appointment as secretary in the colonial administration in Danish West India (St. Thomas). Here he married the daughter of the governor, and upon the latter's death, Høst was promoted to temporary governor. He returned to Denmark in 1776 and lived there with no position for a few years before he took a position as a secretary with the department of foreign affairs (1780). According to his son, Jens Kragh Høst, this engagement was the result of boredom, but we may also assume that pecuniary needs played a role, as it does not seem that Høst's finances were in very good shape, and he had by this time a family to support.[24]

In these years Høst became a scholar. In the years of leisurely activity in Denmark, he organized his notes into the description of Morocco, that he circulated in his circles before publishing it as a book in 1779. He went on to write the history of the Moroccan sultan Muhammad b. Abd Allah, as well as his successor Mulay Yazid. The latter book has not survived.[25] Høst also worked on a history of Algiers which he did not finish before his death. It was also in the 1770s that Høst made contact with the orientalist community in Denmark and Germany, most notably Carsten Niebuhr.

Niebuhr was the sole survivor of the Danish Arabia expedition in the 1760s, which had taken him to Yemen, India and Persia.[26] The famous scientific expedition had been initiated by professor David Michaelis in Göttingen, August Schlözers mentor, and sponsored by count Johann Hartwig Bernstorff, who was in charge of the foreign affairs of the Danish king. Though Niebuhr was originally hired as a junior member and a cartographer of the expedition, he developed a broad interest in all things relating to the lands he passed through, and he later published two books from his travels. In the 1770s, he was back in Denmark working on the edition of his own travel descriptions (published 1774–78), and he encouraged Høst to work on his own oriental book.

Maybe the friendship with Niebuhr explains the fact that Høst's *Efterretninger* bear the marks of the research program that originated with Michaelis in Göttingen and that informed Niebuhr's scientific travel to Arabia. Michaelis' project was, in Peter Hans Reill's words, to improve understanding of the "religious and social milieu in which the Old and New

Testaments were composed".[27] To achieve this, Michaelis convinced the Danish government to send the expedition to Yemen, equipped with a long list of questions to be elucidated.[28] There are numerous passages in Høst's first book where he confronts observations in Morocco with readings of the Bible. As for example when he describes the way of building houses in Morocco and adds in a footnote: "When one observes this carefully, then the 19th verse of the 5th chapter of Luke easier to understand, where it says ..."[29] And he goes on to add five additional passages that he finds clarified by the same observation. But in *The History of the Moroccan Emperor* there is no longer any references to the Bible.

Høst's career gives indications of his position in the social hierarchy of his time. He was the son of a pastor, fresh out of theology studies when he left Denmark for Morocco. By all accounts, what motivated him was the need of an income. Being efficient in this job would probably not be enough to rise in the hierarchy. It took a direct intervention of the Moroccan emperor for Høst to be promoted to vice-consul, and then only for a brief period.[30] Also, at St. Thomas his promotion as governor was only temporary, due to an unexpected death. In comparison, the first Danish consul in Morocco, Andreas Æreboe, was the son of a jurist who had traveled abroad in service of the king. Johann Friedrich Barisien who succeeded Æreboe, was the son of a court architect but he also held the title of *cancelliråd* before being appointed consul, i.e., he was already a man of rank. In 1784, Georg Høst received the title *etatsraad*, an honorary title awarded to public servants. It is possible that the publication of the description of Morocco helped Høst in earning this title and becoming a man of rank. The author's social position may also be relevant for our understanding of Høst as a historian: Among historians, there was also a hierarchy, with the antiquarians by many considered a lesser form of knowledge, and philosophical history as a more noble form of knowledge. Høst's form of historical knowledge may be situated between these forms, as a middle form of historical knowledge, appropriate for a man of his social standing.

History in literary descriptions of Barbary

For an eighteenth-century reader, for example anyone planning to engage in trade or diplomacy with the emperor, a variety of literature was available in several European languages that provided information of past and present Moroccan society. The dominant genres were stories by former captives or slaves, correspondence from diplomats and topographical descriptions, but there were also a few narratives of political events available.

The Europeans who traveled in Morocco until the mid-eighteenth century were mostly there involuntarily, as the result of the activities of the corsairs. Most of the available travel writings were consequently written by former captives. These narratives came to form a distinct genre in European literature (captive narratives).[31] A Norwegian example of this is the sea captain Diderich's *Sandfærdig fortællelse om de christnes ynkværdig slaverie udi Barbariet.*[32] The stories of the former slaves were often met with skepticism by contemporary commentators.[33] Part of the reason was the common suspicion that these people may have "turned" Muslim during captivity, and that these authors therefore had an overly strong self interest in communicating a specific narrative.

A second source of information was correspondence from people who visited the area, in a capacity of diplomatic envoys or trade. This correspondence could be circulated in closed networks, but in some cases, it was also published. An example of this is *Letters from Barbary, France, Spain, Portugal etc* by the English officer Alexander Jardine, that was published anonymously in London in 1788 and in German translation in 1790. This literature erases the borders between published and private literature, as also exemplified by a letter from a Swedish diplomat in Morocco that was published in the Swedish periodical *Samlaren* in 1773, and then translated and included in Schlözer's own periodical *Briefwechsel meist historischen and politischen inhalts.*[34]

A third genre of literature, which is highly relevant here, is topographical description. These books catered to the eighteenth-century thirst for observations, and would contain descriptions of geography, population, culture, nature, etc.[35] They were written with at least some first-hand experience. They were "histories" in the meaning the word had when speaking of "natural history", that is that they contained the results of observations. But they were also "histories" in that they contained chronologically organized narratives of past events. There is a fluent border between these two meanings of history in this literary landscape.

Høst's own *Efterretninger om Marokos og Fes is* a prime example of topographical descriptions of Morocco. In this book, he communicated information of commercial as well as military relevance. For the potential traveler he provided information on distances and water holes in the land. For the would-be invader he provided information on fortifications of the Moroccan cities. For the naturalist he provided information on animal life. For the orientalist and the culturally curious he provided information on food, dress, music and much more.

A few years later, a French book with a somewhat similar origin story was published in Paris, as *Recherches historiques sur les Maures et Histoire de l'Empire de Maroc* (1787).[36] His book seems to have become a reference work on Morocco, and it was referred to by no lesser historian than Edward Gibbon.[37] The author, Louis (de) Chenier, was a former French consul who resided in Morocco in the 1760s. The title of the book is reminiscent of Høst's: Both *Efterretninger* (In the German translation: *nachrichten*) and *Recherches* suggest information that is uncovered through an active search, and it is here offered as material for others to use. It stands in contrast to "History" (which is also used in titles by both authors), that indicates something more finished, more polished, and maybe more ambitious.

The title of Chenier's book suggest that this is really two books, *Researches in the history of the moors* (vol 1 and 2), and a *history* of the Moroccan empire (vol 3). Only the third volume was translated to English (though published as two volumes). The translator interestingly gave as the reason for this choice that the first two volumes did not offer any new information. The long title of the English translation also indicates a text of a dual nature: *The Present State of the Empire of Morocco* but also *The History of the Dynasties since Edris* and not least *The Character, Conduct and Views, Political and Commercial of the Reigning Emperor*. The "reigning emperor" was none other than Sidi Mohammad, and the last part of the book is dedicated to trade and politics under his reign.

Chenier's book is more self-consciously a history book than any of Høst's books, and he also owes more to a philosophical tradition. He compares the history of the Moroccan empire with that of ancient Rome, and finds the former less edifying than the latter. Where the history of Rome presented an oscillation between *grandeur* et *médiocrité,* the history of the moors seems to be more monotonous – cycles of changes of equal valor. He was in line with developments in Enlightenment historiography when he devoted place to the changing *mœurs, usages* and *façons de penser,* as well as to dynastic politics.[38] One chapter (VII, French edition)) deals with commercial relations between the European nations and the empire of Morocco, another characteristically enlightened subject for historical investigation. The author identifies "the spirit of industry" in Europe as the driving force behind increasing trade. He also reflects on the forces operating in history: "although it be true that similar causes will produce similar effects, we must not always judge of the future by the past; the smallest difference of circumstances, either in the times, or the characters of those men who head insurrections, will change the state of things, and decide on the destiny of nations". (347)

Høst's *Efterretninger* subsumed the historical under the topographical. *Recherches* subsumed the topographical under an overarching chronological organization. His first two volumes represent his 'studies' of the history of ancient Mauritania, the Arab conquest and the Muslim states in Spain. The third volume treats Morocco in a more restricted sense, and is organized thematically. Only after treating the cities, the ports, the rivers, the climate, the inhabitants, the religion, the government, etc. (ch 1 – 3) does the author treat the dynasties since the establishment of Fes in the eighth century. The reign of Muhammad b. Abd Allah, is also organized in thematical chapters covering the emperor's positions on trade, the state administration, domestic policy, and "revolutions" during his reign.[39] This organization is chosen, writes the author, in order to highlight "les moeurs" – the customs of the country and their "way of thinking". (*façon de penser*).[40] It allows for the inclusion of subjects that are not so easily included in a coherent narrative. For example, he describes several invasions of locusts that ravaged the country and created famine, in 1778 and 1780.[41] These natural disasters fits into Chenier's chapter "Events" during the reign of Sidi Muhammad, but are not mentioned at all by Høst. This is probably a reflection of the fact that Chenier lived in Morocco himself at the times of these ravages and had seen them first-hand. Høst was by then living in Copenhagen, working on his history, and the locusts seem to have left no traces in the archives of Copenhagen. Both *Efterretninger* and *Recherches* claimed epistemic authority from the fact that the author had lived in the country he described. Høst claimed already on the title page that the information he communicated was "collected in these countries". The translator of the English version of Chenier's book emphasized the same point: "To give authenticity to a performance which would describe this particular people, it is necessary that the writer should have been himself a witness of the facts he relates".[42]

Høst's first book and Chenier's multi-volume work both shows how topographical descriptions typically contained history, often in the form of one of several narrative chapters, integrated in the synchronous descriptions. For some of these authors, "history" implied empirical knowledge in a broad sense. The history book, following a stricter chronological organization, was a less common genre in this literary landscape. There are actually very few European histories about Morocco from before the mid-century. An exception is *Histoire du regne de Moulei Ismael*, written by Dominique Busnot, published 1714. Busnot was a member of a religious order who traveled to Morocco to negotiate the release of French captives. From the turn of the century, there is the much more scholarly *Histoire de l'Afrique et de l'Espagne sur la domination des arabes* by Denis Dominique Cardonne (1765). Cardonne was a diplomate and translator spent many of his early years in Constantinople. His History covered the ancient and medieval history of Northern Africa and Spain and was based on sources in the Royal Library in Paris. It did not venture into the terrain of "modern" history, where Høst went with his second book.

It should be mentioned that history was also produced in Morocco in Arabic at the time, though not familiar to European authors. Abu al-Qasim b. Ahmad al-Zayyani, a courtier in the service of both Sidi Muhammad and his successors composed several historical texts. Abu al-Qasim is mentioned in Høst's History of the Moroccan emperor, but then as a secretary, not as a historian.[43] His historical works was unknown in Europe until a French translation appeared in the late nineteenth century.

The History of the Moroccan Emperor

The History of the Moroccan Emperor delivers a consistent narrative, with no inserted topical chapters. It contains no discussions of the ethnic makeup of the population, the wildlife of its territories or religious mores or culinary traditions. All these topics had been discussed in *Efterretninger*. Instead, the new book is event-oriented, based on archival sources, strictly chronologically organized. Through the text, the relevant year is indicated on the top of each page, facilitating the *use* of the book but also its character as a chronicle.

The final five pages of the book consist of an assessment of the character of the emperor.

The intention of the narrative is to shed light on the character of the protagonist. His actions are consistently at the center of the narrative, and these actions are treated as expressions of his character. He is at times represented as a despot, but his despotic acts are always portrayed as goal oriented: He does what he must do to maintain power. There is no psychological development in the protagonist during his life. From the beginning to the end, love of money (avarice) is his most defining character trait. This is admittedly something of a cultural trope, a trait of an oriental despot. On the other hand, it goes against the orientalist tropes when Høst insists that the emperor did not have a desire for cruelty, though he could be tough when it was required of him ("his purpose was not so much to revenge himself, as to infuse fear in others").[44] His occasional use of harsh punishment is considered rational. At a more general level also, the emperor is described as a rational actor, working within the constraints of his culture.[45] This in contrast to his father, the former emperor, who, though he plays a minor role in Høst's book, is characterized as a tyrannical and cruel person.[46]

To some degree this portrait seems to have been written *against* received opinions of what oriental subjects were like. This is a tendency that Høst shares with other writers, such as Chenier and Laugier de Tassy, who all had experience from being there, and all wrote more nuanced representations of the orient than the ones thar could be found in e.g., captive narratives.

The portrait of the emperor's character constitutes the frame of the book. The events that fill it are concentrated on the interactions between Sidi Muhammad's court and the various European courts. We read about interactions with the grand duchy of Tuscany, the emperor in Vienna, the republics of Genova, of Venice, the Netherlands and of Ragusa (Dubrovnic), the French, Swedish, Danish, English, Spanish, Portuguese kingdoms, as well as the Russian empire, the north American republic, and the kingdom of Sicily. Most of these powers had consuls in Morocco or sent occasional ambassadors to the emperor. Most of them also took part in exchanges or redemption of captives or slaves. They signed treaties with him, once or repeatedly, and they paid tributes to him and received gifts from him.

The person-oriented approach is an organizing principle as much as it is a historiographical genre. The book explains Moroccan politics by following the reign of one ruler from his birth to his death. Only in the very last pages does the author explicitly say something about the protagonist's character. This way of organizing a historical narrative was common in Høst's time: A narrative of the significant events of a reign, followed by a brief assessment of the ruler's character. Concluding a history with an assessment of the ruler was something of a literary convention. This was, e.g., how Ludvig Holberg organized his *Dannemarks riges historie* (1732–35). It was how Georg Høst organized most of the historical information in his first Morocco book, *Efterretninger*. And it was how Voltaire concluded his history of Charles XII of Sweden. Chenier also has a chapter on the "character of the reigning emperor".[47] It is plausible that the model for this approach was Plutarch.

The heuristic premise is that the acts of the protagonist, described in the bulk of the book, reveal the character of the man. And further that it is important to understand this character for those who want to navigate these waters. Here lies the utility of the exercise, and in this sense, Høst's book may be read as an example of useful history. Even though the main character in this case is dead, it is implied that an understanding of his character is useful to understand other players from his culture.

The History of the Moroccan Emperor is equipped with footnotes, though not in abundance. In the footnotes, the author occasionally points to the sources he has used in composing his history, but (more often) he uses them to signal disagreement with other available sources – they are there to correct the record, not to document. On the very first page, Høst uses a footnote to signal disagreement with Chenier as to the exact year of birth of Sidi Muhammad. There are also some footnotes were the author comments his own text, as when he expresses regrets that he has so little information about the early years of his protagonist's life.[48]

In *Efterretninger*, Høst was more interested in kinds of people and customs, than in actual individuals, though there were exceptions. In a chapter, about the Jews in Morocco, he discussed the role of the so-called Court Jews, and in passing he gave a characteristic of Samuel Sumbel and his relation to the emperor: Sumbel, he wrote, is «a man of noteworthy wit and intelligence, and a perfect Moroccan courtier; he is a dangerous enemy, but no powerful friend, as the king believes, that he will not take anyone's side if not for money. The king cannot do without him, but engages him for all the most important business, though he watches over him, and he often plucks his feathers".[49] Sumbel was instrumental in the negotiations between the Danish and the Moroccan court in the 1750s, and as such he plays an important role in the narrative in *The History of the Moroccan Emperor*. But there he is just introduced briefly as "the well-known Jew Samuel Sumbel". A description of his character similar to this is not to be found there.

Efterretninger also gave some glimpses into Høst's life in Morocco, and his encounters with Moroccans. Some of these related to the emperor and hence this book revealed aspects of the emperor's personality or private life that are not dealt with in *The History of the Moroccan Emperor*. One example is a passage where Høst discusses music in Morocco.[50] In a footnote he relates an episode where he had played the *clavesin* for the emperor: "Once, when I played the Clavesin for him, on an instrument which the king of Denmark had given him as a gift, he told me that this music was overly artificial, but not natural, and that it would be better to play it with one finger (which he instantly tried to do) (...)"[51] Høst adds that he thereafter avoided "the honor" of playing for the emperor. The reason he gives is not the emperor's lack of enthusiasm but the fact that the instrument was posed directly on the ground and therefore was most uncomfortable to play on.

This footnote renders the encounter between the clerk/secretary/translator and the emperor with some intimate details. The detail gives it a character of authenticity – it feels immediately true. Did it have the same effect on the eighteenth-century reader? Was that one reason for including it? This and similar scenes give an impression of the relationship between the two. It also gives an impression of the personality of the emperor, that we never see in this way in *The History of the Moroccan Emperor*. Furthermore, it makes the author of the book a character in the same book.

Also in *The History of the Moroccan Emperor* Høst appears in the text in a footnote referring to his arrival in Morocco (p. 25), in another couple of footnotes to inform that he had indeed been an eyewitness to the related events (pp. 41 and 72) and he appears in the text, describing his promotion to vice-consul (pp. 41 and 53). These mentions are briefer than those in *Efterretninger*.

The absences of these kinds of details, about the protagonist as well as the author, may be regarded as genre specific features. The format of a chronologically organized history seems to have given Høst less room for details about the cultural situation from which the books arose.

The nature of historical knowledge

Efterretninger had, from the author's declaration, been based on information "collected in the country" and was therefore to be trusted. *The History of the Moroccan Emperor*, on the other hand, was based on archives far away from the country and was *therefore* to be trusted. The archives give the narrative its "due authenticity".[52]

The reliance on archival sources must have seen as a necessity, as much as a virtue. Whereas a narration of the "old" history, which Høst had offered in *Efterretninger*, could be based on available literature, there were no precedent for a history as recent as the reign of Sidi Muhammad. Hence, *The History of the Moroccan Emperor* was not primarily based on information collected in the field, nor on literature in the library, but on documents that the author, by royal permission, dug out of the archive of the Department for Foreign Affairs in Copenhagen.

In the royal archives, Høst found two kinds of sources. First, there was a series of consular reports, bringing news from Morocco to the government in Copenhagen. These are the sources that Høst himself mentions in his preface, as giving his narrative its authenticity. The second category of documents is the original correspondence between the governments of Morocco and Denmark. These documents were of a different kind from the reports: rather than talking about events, they were part of these events. They were written by persons who were not only witnessing history but was performing it. On many occasions Høst quotes entire letters from the Moroccan emperor to his Danish equivalent. These letters are not mentioned in the preface (where he mentions the consular reports), but the author seems to be aware that they may give more direct access to the protagonist of his history, than do the consular reports. These sources are often translated, from a variety of languages, and inserted in the text, thereby being made available for the reader.

An example can illustrate the use of these sources: In 1756, in one of the frequent conflicts between Morocco and Great Britain, Sidi Muhammad sent a letter to the English. This letter was read out loud in French in front of all the Christian merchants and then handed over to the English envoy. Copies of the letter may also have been distributed, as it seems that a copy was available to Høst in Copenhagen in the 1790s. Høst quotes the entire letter (in Danish translation) and even comments on the choice of words in the letter: According to him, in 1791, there can be no doubt that Muhammad, in 1756, had dictated most of the letter himself, since it is "full of features that completely reveals his [i.e., Muhammad's] character".[53] But Høst also identifies the voice of the translator, Samuel Sumbel, in the letter. These remarks reveal that Høst had the letter before him, and that he was attentive to different voices in the text. In these observations, Høst clearly drew on his own experiences as he had met both men in question. As mentioned, Sumbel is a significant character in Høst's History of the Moroccan emperor. His close association with the Danish affairs in Morocco was recognized by paying him an annual Danish pension.[54] What is significant is that Høst uses this document not only as a source to events but as a source to understanding the character of the actors.

It is worth noting that Høst never interprets the Danish letters to the Moroccan court in a similar way. Never does he distinguish the voice of, e.g., count Bernstorff, by all accounts the real hand behind the Danish foreign policy, in the letters signed by king Frederik.

Høst's reliance on the Danish archive means that the events that emerge as important in Sidi Muhammad's reign are the events that seemed important for the diplomatic community in Morocco at the time. The critical questions that this situation might have given occasion to is never raised by Høst. It leads to conspicuous omissions in his narrative, when read in light of other narratives of Morocco.

This emphasis on documents does not mean that Høst disregarded neither existing literature or hear-say. The latter is e.g., the case when he tells a story of a Jew, Ben Isso, who had both his hands cut off, as a response to fraud. The emperor ordered a random bystander to do the cutting.[55] This happened in 1762, when Høst was living in the country, but there is no indication that he was himself a witness to this.

Nor does the emphasis on documents mean that Høst does not invent. Occasionally he does follow the old convention of using direct speech also in scenes where he cannot possibly have had any eyewitness reports. One example is the already mentioned story about Ben Isso, where Høst has the emperor proclaim: "You scoundrel will now have what you deserve, not for the money you owe me, because your brothers, the other Jews, will repay me until the last shilling, but because your whole life you have deceived Moors,

Christians and Jews".[56] It is very unlikely that these words were ever uttered by the emperor.

Power and knowledge in a preface

The bulk of the well 300 pages of *The History of the Moroccan Emperor* consists of a narrative of the many power struggles the protagonist was involved in during his life time. A concern with the history of powerful people had of course for very long been characteristic of history as a genre. In this case, as in many contemporary histories, the concern with power also put its stamp on the paratext. The book opens with a dedication and continues with a preface. Then follows a list of subscribers, before it embarks on the chronological narrative.

The book is dedicated is to Andreas Petrus Count Bernstorff, the King's minister of foreign affairs. He was the nephew of another count Bernstorff, Johann Hartwig who had been foreign minister at the time when Høst lived in Morocco, who had played a key role in the establishment of the Danish African Company, and who was also a discrete presence in *The History of the Moroccan Emperor*. The younger Bernstorff rose to power under the protection of his uncle, but the two "reigns" were separated by the revolutionary period of Struensee-rule. By this very dedication the text is situated within the power relations contemporaneous with the publication. But through the relationship of the two counts, this web of power extends back to what is here historical time, the time of the elder count Bernstorff and Sidi Muhammad.

The preface that follows the dedications consists of two parts, the first of which also addresses a question of power. The question Høst raises for discussion, before a word is read about the Moroccan emperor is: What can the reason (*aarsag*) be, that causes these people willingly to be deprived (*berøve*) of all their belongings, to expose their throat to the knife, to kiss their own chains, to adore their executioner?[57] The question about power and freedom, posed in 1791, seems to be in tune with political concerns in Europe at the time, where so many were concerned with the freedom of man. But it also seems to raise an issue of cultural difference, as Høst's concern is to understand why "these people" are so little bothered by renouncing their freedoms. The explanation he gives of this puzzling willingness to submission has three elements: 1) the "enthusiasm" that the Muslims demonstrate for their prophet and his descendants (among whom are to be found the Moroccan sovereigns); 2) the doctrine of predestination that is part of their religion; 3) the upbringing, ignorance, and poverty of the Moroccan subjects ("they are used to being repressed".)

This first part of the preface is the most visible sign that Høst is also interested in the kind of philosophical historiography of his time. We may perhaps read it as an effort to write himself into the community of philosophically inclined historians.

But the second part of the preface points to a different community, and therefore also indicates a different genre. Here Høst reproduces a letter that he received after the publication of *Efterretninger*. It was written by professor Olaus Gerhardus Tychsen of Rostock, a famous expert on Arabic and Syriac philology. In the letter, Tychsen speaks of a set of plaster casts of Cufic coins that Høst had sent him via Niebuhr, and which had also been reproduced in *Efterretninger*. Tychsen here suggests interpretations of the inscriptions of these coins. This part of the preface is a statement that Høst aspires to be a part of the orientalist community, with its penchant for antiquarianism. And that even when writing a history of people with power he was as interested in the empirical evidence of things.

Conclusion

Georg Høst must be considered a minor historian if we judge him by the criteria of posterior fame or impact on subsequent historiography. It was never his profession to write history, and there are no indications in his writing that he considered himself as a "historian". His history of the Moroccan emperor is largely unknown among historians of Danish historiography. Yet, a consideration of his work is instructive for understanding the genres of history writing in the eighteenth century.

With his two books on Moroccan affairs from the 1770s and 90s, the former clerk Georg Høst gave his contributions to the general knowledge of the orient. Orientalism may be regarded as a genre, that is a shared format for production and dissemination of knowledge, that also supported a community, the orientalists. It was a heterogeneous genre, but its basic structure was a map. It could be *considered* history, if we by that understand a general systematic description, as did the natural historians. But it also *contained* history, if we take the word history in a second meaning, as a narrative of a sequence of significant events. With his second book on Moroccan affairs, however, Høst made a move in the direction of a different format. This was not a book with narrative history in it, but a "history book", where history no longer refers to mapping, but to events.

Furthermore, in addition to the question of the structure of the text, there was a shift in evidentiary basis: Where the first book claimed an epistemic authority from the author having had personal experience in the landscape that he maps, the second claims authority from having been in the archives, and thence constructing a narrative from authentic documents.

This shift may have been motivated by practical circumstances, namely by the fact that Høst had already delivered a map, both literally and figuratively, in his first book, and that what remained was to narrate recent affairs. But I have also wanted to suggest that this shift on the micro-scale is in tune with shifts on a grander scale in the history of historiography, a shift towards an understanding of history as a narrative of human events that acquires its authority from the archive.

August Schlözer, in his *Summarische Geschichte,* could only regret that it was not possible for him at that point in time to perform the necessary critical work on the sources on the history of North Africa. Georg Høst took upon him a more modest task; not to work through all available sources but to stay true to his archive.

Notes

1 Suzanne L. Marchand, *German Orientalism in the Age of Empire: religion, race, and scholarship,* Publications of the German Historical Institute, (Washington, D.C.; Cambridge; New York: German Historical Institute; Cambridge University Press, 2009).

2 August Ludwig Schlözer, *Summarische geschichte von Nord-Afrika nemntlich von Maroko, Algier, Tunis und Tripoli* (Göttingen: Johann Christian Dietrich, 1775), Vorrede, unpaginated.

3 Georg Høst, *Den Marokanske Kajser Mohamed ben Abdallah's historie* (Kiøbenhavn: Nicolaus Møller og Søn, 1791). The many alternative spellings of Arabic names may cause some confusion. I will in this chapter spell the name of the emperor Sidi Muhammad b. Abd Allah, which seems most common in the literature today.

4 The *Efterretninger* is discussed more in length in Svein Atle Skålevåg, "Truths from Morocco: Knowledge Production and Danish-Moroccan Encounters in the Eighteenth Century", *Itinerario* 47, no. 1 (2023), https://doi.org/10.1017/S01 65115323000074.

5 Gianna Pomata, "Observation rising: Birth of an epistemic genre, 1500–1600", in *Histories of scientific observation*, ed. Lorraine Daston and Elizabeth Lunbeck (Chicago, Ill.: University of Chicago Press, 2011), 48.

6 Georg Høst, *Efterretninger om Marókos og Fes, samlede der i Landene fra 1760 til 1768* (Kiøbenhavn: N. Møller, 1779), 70.

7 For a discussion of the geographical concepts of the region in the eighteenth century, see Ann Thomson, *Barbary and enlightenment: European attitudes towards the Maghreb in the 18th century*, Brill's studies in intellectual history, (Leiden: Brill, 1987).

8 Gibbon, *The decline and fall of the roman empire*, ch I, part III https://gutenberg.org/files/25717/25717-h/25717-h.htm.

9 Georg Høst, *Den Marokanske kajser Mohamed ben Abdallah's historie* (Kiøbenhavn: Nicolaus Møller og Søn, 1791), 54. Høst also characterizes Sidi Mohammed's son as having a "barbaric character" due to the unmotivated killing of a number of people (p 74) Another place he holds that Sidi Mohammed was not so much of a "barbaric despot" (314) In our time it is often claimed that the name Barbarian derives from Berber. Jamil M. Abun-Nasr, *A history of the Maghrib in the Islamic period* (Cambridge: Cambridge University Press, 1987), 2. Colley follows Abun-Nasr. Linda Colley, *Captives: Britain, empire and the world, 1600–1850* (London: Jonathan Cape, 2002), 44.

10 Høst, *Den Marokanske Kajser* 314.

11 Se e.g., Colley, *Captives: Britain, empire and the world, 1600–1850*; Mario Klarer, ed., *Piracy and captivity in the Mediterranean: 1550–1810*, 1st. ed. (London: Routledge, 2019).

12 Høst, *Den Marokanske Kajser* 228–230. He further refers to a negotiation in 1781 in which the French tried to convince the Moroccans to address the king of France as Sultan, which they refused.

13 Schlözer, *Summarische geschichte* 92. See also August Ludwig Schlözer, *Briefwechsel meist historischen und politischen Inhalts*, vol. XVIII (Göttingen, 1778), 353.

14 Louis Chenier, *The present state of the Empire of Morocco its animals, products, climate, soil, cities, ports, provinces, coins, weights and measures with the language, religion, laws, manners, customs and character of the moors; the history of the dynastis since Edris; the naval force and commerce of Morocco; and the character, conduct and views, political and comercial of the reigning emperor.*, 2 vols., vol. II (London: G.G.J. and J. Robinson, 1788), 352. Schlözer, *Summarische geschichte* 2.
15 James A. O. C. Brown, *Crossing the strait: Morocco, Gibraltar and Great Britain in the 18th and 19th centuries*, Brill eBook titles, (Leiden; Boston: Leiden; Boston: Brill, 2012). Bernard Lugan, *Histoire du Maroc. Des origines a nos jours* (Paris: Ellipses, 2011), 194.
16 Maurits H. van den Boogert, *The capitulations and the Ottoman legal system: qadis, consuls, and beratlıs in the 18th century*, v. 21 (Leiden; Boston: Brill, 2005).
17 Chenier writes that what motivated the Europeans was not to increase trade with Morocco, but a "growth of maritime power". Chenier, *the Empire of Morocco*, II, 353.
18 The history of the Dano-Moroccan relationship is described in J.L. Rasmussen, *Det under kong Frederik den Femte opprettede Danske Afrikanske Kompagnies Historie* (Kiøbenhavn: Andreas Seidelin, 1818); Emil Madsen, "De vigtigste af danske foretagne Rejser og Forskning i Afrika", *Geografisk tidsskrift* 22 (1913), https://tidsskrift.dk/index.php/geografisktidsskrift/article/view/36824/70849; C. F. Wandel, "Danmark og Barbareskerne 1746–1845", ed. C. F. Wandel (København, 1919); H. de Castries, "Le Danemark et le Maroc, 1750–1767", *Hesperis* 6 (1926). There exists also an eyewitness account of the events leading up to the treaty, written in rhyme: Wilh Fr Ravn, *Kort Underretning om det maroccanske slaverie i aarene 1751, 1752 og 1753, dagviis forfattet paa værs* (Kbh.1754).
19 Høst, *Den Marokanske Kajser* 92. See also a letter from the emperor from 1775, quoted same place, p 171.
20 Høst, *Efterretninger*, 58.
21 The biographical details are from Jens Kragh Høst, "Georg Høst", *Clio: et Bidrag til læsning for den fædrelandske histories yndere. Bd. 1, 1–3 Hft* 1, no. 2 (1813 [1821]).
22 Høst, *Den Marokanske kajser* 53.
23 Harold John Cook, *Matters of exchange: commerce, medicine, and science in the Dutch Golden Age* (New Haven, Conn.; London: Yale University Press, 2007).
24 Jens Kragh Høst, "Georg Høst", *Clio: et Bidrag til Læsning for den fædrelandske Histories Yndere. Bd. 1, 1–3 Hft* 1, no. 2 (1813 [1821]).
25 All the copies of this work were destroyed in a fire. Jens Kragh Høst, Clio. 1821, vol 1, no 2,
26 Lawrence J. Baack, *Undying Curiosity: Carsten Niebuhr and The Royal Danish Expedition to Arabia 1761–1767* (Stuttgart: Stuttgart: Franz Steiner Verlag, 2014).
27 Peter Hanns Reill, *The German enlightenment and the rise of historicism* (Berkeley: University of California Press, 1975).
28 Baack, *Undying Curiosity*.
29 "Naar man nøie betragter dette, saa bliver 19 vers af Lucæ 5 Cap lettere at forstaa, hvor det heder ..." Høst, *Efterretninger*, 248.
30 Several authors claims erroneously that Høst was a consul. E.g. Castries, "Le Danemark et le Maroc", 344.
31 Klarer, *Piracy and captivity*; Mario Klarer, ed., *Mediterranean Slavery and World Literature: Captivity Genres from Cervantes to Rousseau* (Milton: Milton: Routledge, 2020).
32 See Skålevåg, "Truths from Morocco: Knowledge Production and Danish-Moroccan Encounters in the Eighteenth Century".

33 See e.g., Louis de Chenier, *Recherches Historiques sur les maures et Histoire de l'empire de Maroc*, 3 vols., (Paris1787), vol 1, p. 4.
34 Schlözer, *Briefwechsel*, XVIII, 342–57.
35 Lorraine Daston, "Observation and Enlightenment", in *Scholars in action*, ed. Steinke and Stuber Holenstein, History of Science and Medicine Library (Brill, 2013).
36 Louis de Chenier, *Recherches historiques sur les Maures et histoire de l'Empire de Maroc*, 3 vols., vol. 1 (1787).
37 Gibbon, *The decline and fall of the roman empire*, ch LI, part IV, note 152 https://gutenberg.org/files/25717/25717-h/25717-h.htm
38 Chenier, *Recherches historiques*, 1, 7.
39 Revolution was in the eighteenth century a frequently utilized term for political upheavals of all kinds. Jürgen Osterhammel, *Unfabling the East: the Enlightenment's encounter with Asia* (Princeton; Oxford: Princeton University Press, 2018), 265.
40 Chenier, *Recherches historiques,* Vol 1, Discours preliminaire, p. 7.
41 Chenier, *The Empire of Morocco*, II, 333–36; Chenier, *Recherches Historiques* 3, 495–99. A situation of famine in 1750 is described by Diderich in his dialogue on slavery. Lars Diderich, *Sandfærdig Fortællelse om de Christnes ynkværdig Slaverie udi Barbariet, i sær hos den Maroccanske Keyser* (Kiøbenhavn: Trykt paa Autors egen Bekostning, 1756), 144.
42 Chenier, *The Empire of Morocco*, II. See also Chenier's dedication in the first volume of the French edition.
43 Høst, *Den Marokanske Kajser* 303.
44 "Hans øjemeed var ikke så meget at hævne sig, som at indjage andre skræk". Høst, *Den Marokanske Kajser* 30.
45 See page 332: "as a Despot he was constrained to an occasional show of severity, without which he woud have been seen as afraid and would have been unable to sustain his hold on the throne" ("han var, som Despot, nød til undertiden at vise Strænghed, uden hvilken han var bleven anseet som bange og ikke kunne soutenere sig paa Tronen")
46 See e.g., Høst, *Den Marokanske Kajser* 23.
47 Chenier, *The Empire of Morocco*, vol II, ch VI.
48 Høst, *Den Marokanske Kajser* 3.
49 "en Mand af besyndelig vittighed og forstand, og en perfect marokansk hofmand; en farlig fjende, men ingen Mægtig Ven, siden kongen troer, at han ikke tager nogens Parti, uden for Penge. Kongen kan ikke undvære ham, men bruger ham til de allervigtigste sager, dog har han et vaagent Øie over ham, og plukker ofte hans Fiere", Høst, *Efterretninger*, 137.
50 Høst shows a considerable interest in music. The book includes drawings of musical instruments (table 31) and also note sheets (table 32).
51 Høst, *Efterretninger,* 246.
52 Høst, *Den Marokanske kajser,* preface.
53 "(...) det er fuldt af Træk, der fuldkomen røber hans character", Høst, *Den Marokanske Kajser* 21.
54 See *Den Marokanske kajser* 6, 21, 46–48, 51, 98, 186, 210–11, 42. The information about the pension is from Louis Bobé, "Familien Sumbel fra Marokko og dens Forbindelser med Danmark", *Tidsskrift for jødisk historie og literatur* 1, no. 1 (1917): 40. The Sumbel family retained close connection to Denmark. Samuel's son Joseph visited in the 1780s, to lay claim on his father's assets there. His son Samuel later settled in Copenhagen where he died in 1831.
55 Høst, *Den Marokanske kajser* 30.
56 "Du Skjelm skal nu faae din fortjente Løn, ikke for de Penges Skyld, som jeg har tilgode hos dig; thi dem skal dine Brødre, de andre Jøder, betale indtil sidste

Skilling, men fordi du din hele Livs-Tid har bedraget Maurer, Christne og Jøder", Høst, *Den Marokanske Kajser* 30–31.
57 "Hvad kan dog være Aarsag til, at disse Folk godvilligen lade sig berøve alt det de eje, at de selv, saa at sige, række Struben til Kniven, kysse deres lænker, og tilbede deres Bøddel?", Høst, *Den Marokanske Kajser* preface (unpaginated).

Bibliography

Abun-Nasr, Jamil M. *A History of the Maghrib in the Islamic Period.* Cambridge: Cambridge University Press, 1987.
Bobé, Louis. "Familien Sumbel Fra Marokko Og Dens Forbindelser Med Danmark." *Tidsskrift for jødisk historie og literatur* 1, no. 1 (1917): 37–50.
Boogert, Maurits H. van den. *The Capitulations and the Ottoman Legal System: Qadis, Consuls, and Beratlıs in the 18th Century.* Leiden: Boston: Brill, 2005.
Brown, James A. O. C. *Crossing the Strait: Morocco, Gibraltar and Great Britain in the 18th and 19th Centuries.* Brill Ebook Titles. Leiden: Boston: Leiden; Boston: Brill, 2012.
Baack, Lawrence J. *Undying Curiosity: Carsten Niebuhr and the Royal Danish Expedition to Arabia 1761–1767.* Stuttgart: Stuttgart: Franz Steiner Verlag, 2014.
Castries, H. de. "Le Danemark Et Le Maroc, 1750–1767." *Hesperis* 6 (1926): 327–351.
Chenier, Louis. *The Present State of the Empire of Morocco Its Animals, Products, Climate, Soil, Cities, Ports, Provinces, Coins, Weights and Measures with the Language, Religion, Laws, Manners, Customs and Character of the Moors; the History of the Dynastis since Edris; the Naval Force and Commerce of Morocco; and the Character, Conduct and Views, Political and Comercial of the Reigning Emperor.* 2 vols. Vol. II, London: G.G.J. and J. Robinson, 1788.
Chenier, Louis de. *Recherches Historiques Sur Les Maures Et Histoire De L'empire De Maroc.* 3 vols. Vol. 1, 1787.
Colley, Linda. *Captives: Britain, Empire and the World, 1600–1850.* London: Jonathan Cape, 2002.
Cook, Harold John. *Matters of Exchange: Commerce, Medicine, and Science in the Dutch Golden Age.* New Haven, Conn.; London: Yale University Press, 2007. Table of contents only http://www.loc.gov/catdir/toc/ecip0619/2006026973.html.
Daston, Lorraine. "Observation and Enlightenment." In *Scholars in Action*, edited bySteinke and Stuber Holenstein. History of Science and Medicine Library, 657–677: Brill, 2013.
Diderich, Lars. *Sandfærdig Fortællelse Om De Christnes Ynkværdig Slaverie Udi Barbariet, I Sær Hos Den Maroccanske Keyser, Med Noget Angaaende Folkets Religion, Regierings-Form, Skikke Og Leve-Maade, Etc. Forfattet for Enhver Christen, Som Et Opbyggeligt Speyl, Ved En Samtale Imellem Theophilum Og Timotheum, Hvorudi Den Første Fremstiller Den Historiske Sandhed, Hvilken Timotheus Bruger Til Gudfrygtigheds Opbyggelse.* Kiøbenhavn: Trykt paa Autors egen Bekostning, 1756.
Høst, Georg. *Den Marokanske Kajser Mohamed Ben Abdallah's Historie.* Kiøbenhavn: Nicolaus Møller og Søn, 1791.
Høst, Georg. *Efterretninger Om Marókos Og Fes, Samlede Der I Landene Fra 1760 Til 1768.* Kiøbenhavn: N. Møller, 1779.
Høst, Jens Kragh. "Georg Høst." *Clio: et Bidrag til Læsning for den fædrelandske Histories Yndere. Bd. 1, 1–3 Hft* 1, no. 2 (1813 [1821]): 14.
Klarer, Mario, ed. *Mediterranean Slavery and World Literature: Captivity Genres from Cervantes to Rousseau.* 1 ed, Routledge Interdisciplinary Perspectives on Literature. Milton: Milton: Routledge, 2020.

Klarer, Mario, ed. *Piracy and Captivity in the Mediterranean: 1550–1810*. 1st. ed. London: Routledge, 2019.

Lugan, Bernard. *Histoire Du Maroc. Des Origines a Nos Jours*. Paris: Ellipses, 2011.

Madsen, Emil. "De Vigtigste Af Danske Foretagne Rejser Og Forskning I Afrika." *Geografisk tidsskrift* 22 (1913): 121–129. https://tidsskrift.dk/index.php/geografisktidsskrift/article/view/36824/70849.

Marchand, Suzanne L. *German Orientalism in the Age of Empire: Religion, Race, and Scholarship*. Publications of the German Historical Institute. Washington, D.C.; Cambridge; New York: German Historical Institute; Cambridge University Press, 2009.

Osterhammel, Jürgen. *Unfabling the East: The Enlightenment's Encounter with Asia*. Princeton; Oxford: Princeton University Press, 2018.

Pomata, Gianna. "Observation Rising: Birth of an Epistemic Genre, 1500–1600." In *Histories of Scientific Observation*, edited by Lorraine Daston, and Elizabeth Lunbeck, 45–80. Chicago, Ill.: University of Chicago Press, 2011.

Rasmussen, J.L. *Det under Kong Frederik Den Femte Opprettede Danske Afrikanske Kompagnies Historie*. Kiøbenhavn: Andreas Seidelin, 1818.

Reill, Peter Hanns. *The German Enlightenment and the Rise of Historicism*. Berkeley: University of California Press, 1975.

Schlözer, August Ludwig. *Briefwechsel Meist Historischen Und Politischen Inhalts*. Vol. XVIII: Göttingen, 1778.

Schlözer, August Ludwig. *Summarische Geschichte Von Nord-Afrika Nemntlich Von Maroko, Algier, Tunis Und Tripoli*. Göttingen: Johann Christian Dietrich, 1775.

Skålevåg, Svein Atle. "Truths from Morocco: Knowledge Production and Danish-Moroccan Encounters in the Eighteenth Century." *Itinerario* 47, no. 1 (2023): 24–39. 10.1017/S0165115323000074.

Thomson, Ann. *Barbary and Enlightenment: European Attitudes Towards the Maghreb in the 18th Century*. Brill's Studies in Intellectual History. Leiden: Brill, 1987.

Wandel, C. F. "Danmark Og Barbareskerne 1746–1845." edited by C. F. Wandel. København, 1919.

12 Between Vico and the Virgin

Images and genres of history in Lorenzo Boturini's *Idea de una nueva historia general de América septentrional*

John Ødemark

We find that the principle of these origins, both of language and of letters, lies in the fact that the *first Gentile peoples, by a demonstrated necessity of nature, were poets who spoke in poetic characters*. This discovery, which is the master-key of this Science, has cost us the persistent research of almost all our literary life, because with our civilized natures we cannot at all imagine and can understand only by great toil the poetic nature of these men. The poetic characters of which we speak were certain imaginative genera (images for the most part of animate substances, of gods or heroes, formed by their imagination), to which they reduced all the species or all the particulars to each genus; exactly as the fables of human times, such as those of late comedy, are intelligible genera reasoned out by moral philosophy, from which the comic poets form imaginative genera (for the best ideas of the various human types are nothing but that) which are the persons of the comedies. These divine or heroic characters were true fables or myths, and their allegories are found to contain meanings not analogical but univocal, not philosophical but historical, of the people of Greece of those times.

(Vico 1968: §34)

Introduction: Why did Boturini's history fail?

In 1746, the Milanese traveller Lorenzo Boturini, published *Idea de una nueva historia general de América septentrional* in Madrid. Boturini based his historical *Idea*—or outline—upon a collection of Mesoamerican manuscripts gathered in New Spain, which he called his *museo historico indiano* (Boturini 1746; Boturini 1974; hereinafter *Idea*). The *Idea de una nueva historia general de America septentrional* was an outline of a more comprehensive *Historia General,* which Boturini aimed to write. Initially, he also received royal support and was even appointed as *Coronista e historiador en los reinos de Indias.* However, he was only able to write the first volume of this larger work, before he died in 1755.

Boturini was a knight of the Holy Roman Empire, and lord of Torre and Hono in Sondrio in Lombardy. After studying law, he wanted to take a seat in the senate in Milan, but the Polish war of succession forced him to travel. In Spain, he made the acquaintance of a descendant of the house of Moctezuma, who needed legal assistance with some business in New Spain.

DOI: 10.4324/9781003331971-17

Boturini accepted the task, and in 1736 he was established in Mexico City. After eight years, however, he was expelled and sent to Spain for having entered the dependency without the required authorisation and for collecting funds for the coronation of the image of Virgin of Guadalupe; the image that miraculously had stuck to the cape of Juan Diego after a series of apparitions.

According to tradition, Guadalupe had appeared several times to Juan Diego and affectionately spoke to him in his native Nahuatl as *Juantzin* (a reverential form of "Juan") and *noxocoyouh*, "my youngest child" (Burkhart 1997: 202). In the earliest published account of the apparitions (from 1648), this was said to have occurred in December 1531 (ten years after Cortes' conquest of Tenochtitlan). The divine intention behind the address to Juan Diego was that the Virgin wanted a sanctuary built in her honour on the Tepeyac hill; the very place where the apparitions occurred. At first, Juan de Zumárraga, the Franciscan who served as New Spain's first bishop, refused to comply. He demanded a sign of verification. When this was provided, however, he changed his mind: In his cape Juan Diego brought "Castilian flowers", not only growing out of season (in December), but on the rocky hilltop of Tepeyac; a place inhospitable to anything but cactus. Before the eyes of the hitherto incredulous bishop, the "youngest child" of the mother of God unfolded the cloak with the flowers in it, and in a miraculous way her image presented itself upon the fabric, and without any intervention of human hands, the apparitions left an enduring visual trace on Juan Diego's cape (Nebel 1995; Wolf 1958).

This, then, was the image that Boturini wanted to crown, and he even received permission from Rome to coronate the image at his own expense (in a letter dated 11 July 1740). Along with the letter came instructions for the coronation ceremony and a drawing of the coat of arms of the Council of St. Peters, and that of Count Alexander Sforza Palavicino, the "founder of the pious work" of coronation.[1] Boturini was required to furnish the crowned image with the coat of arms of the Count and the Council of St. Peters (Glass 1979: 9, 13–14).[2] Because of the illicit proceedings with Rome and the unauthorised fundraising, Boturini was incarcerated and expelled. On the way to Spain, his ship was boarded by English pirates outside Gibraltar, and the few pieces that Boturini had been able to bring with him from his collection of Mesoamerican sources were lost. In Spain, he presented the manuscript of his *Idea* to the Council of the Indies, and in December 1745, the Council licensed the publication of the work, which subsequently was published by the printer Juan de Zuñiga, and in 1746, he published the *Idea de una nueva historia general de America septentrional* (Léon-Portilla in Boturini 1974).

Boturini based this outline of a new history upon his *museo historico indiano*, a vast collection of manuscripts had assembled in New Spain. The Boturini collection has been called the first Mexican museum, and in the *Handbook of Middle American Indians*, John B. Glass even asserts that it was "the most important such collection for Mexican Ethnohistory ever assembled" (Bernal 1966: 320, Glass 1975: 473, my emphasis).[3] In addition to the part Boturini played in the history of Mesoamerican collecting, he also played a remarkable role in the history of the early reception of G. Vico's *New Science,* published in different editions from 1725 to 1744. Boturini quoted extensively from Vico, but never identified him as his source, and consequently was accused both of "translating" the NS (Ødemark 2011). Vico has been called "the true father of the concept of culture" (Berlin 2000, see also Berlin 1990), the "rehabilitator" and discoverer of myth (Mali 1992), a producer of philosophy of images and signs that escaped Western, logocentric semiotics (Trabant 2003), as well as the inventor of historicism (Mali 1992)—just to name a few discoveries in the human sciences attributed to Vico. In short, Vico has been seen as "the forerunner, the sage who grasped and expressed many truths of the future" (Mali 1992: 1).

In this chapter, I will challenge this historiographical metanarrative that sees Boturini's historical work as an "effect" of Vico's discovery or invention of a modern historical and cultural consciousness. The (slim) Boturini reception has pinpointed how the influence from Vico enabled Boturini to recognise and praise Mesoamerican historiography and script (Ødemark 2011). Even the decolonial scholar W. Mignolo assumes the metanarrative of historiographical breakthrough in Boturini. He makes Vico the main agent behind Boturini's recognition of the history of "the other". Hence, the decolonial take on historiographical maturity and the development of cultural tolerance in this case is premised on the standard narrative of a historiographical modernity developed in early modern Europe. This is paradoxical, since, as K. Davis observes in the case of Koselleck's ideas of modernity and historiographical maturity, such ideas of periodisation and temporality

> cannot be separated from the contemporaneous and interrelated discourses of "world order" such as anthropology and Orientalism, which defined Europe's others in precisely the terms Koselleck applies to the Middle Ages, and which in effect it extends (Davis 2012).

In the following, I will combine the technique of close *reading* and the scale of *microhistory* to challenge the model of influence mostly applied to explain (away) Boturini's historiographical work—even by decolonial and revisionist historians like Mignolo and J. Cañizares-Esguerra. Pace Mignolo, Cañizares largely disassociates Boturini's history from the new science—or, at least, from a "correct" reading of the historical "paradigm" of the philosopher from Naples. I will be concerned with the relation between Vico's historical "paradigm" (Cañizares) and Boturini's praise of Mesoamerican script and historiography (Mignolo). Does the "influence" from Vico explain this praise of the history of the "other", as both humanists and decolonial scholars like Mignolo appears to assume?—Or did they simply share a historiographical paradigm, as totalising approaches pinpointing "mentality", "culture" or "period" perhaps would presuppose? Or did other genres of historiography and knowledge practices—like the collecting practices of antiquarianism and the attempt to document the apparitions of Guadalupe for Rome—also impact Boturini's history and the recognition of Mesoamerican images and sources this was premised on?

In the first section (I), I will give more detail on the reception of Boturini. Next (II), I will examine the different knowledge practices and genres involved in Boturini's attempt to historicise Guadalupe. Finally (III), I will examine how Vico's philosophy of history enters Boturini's text—and how the two differs when it comes to the value of gentile history—and its visual sources.

I

Vico as the source of Boturni's recognition of Mesoamerican history

In the *Estetic Recognition of Ancient Amerindian Art*, G. Kubler devotes a few pages to the Boturini. The art historian Kubler is concerned with what he calls the aesthetic recognition of ancient Amerindian art; Europe's recognition, from 1492 onwards, of art in indigenous America. Such recognition takes "art" as its object, and thus assumes the relevancy of the category of "art" for indigenous America—as well as the early modern Europeans who first described indigenous Americas for European readers (Kubler 1991). Boturini, Kubler concludes, "marks the continuing vacuum in Spanish America between the teachers of the Indians and their exploiters" (ibid: 87).

Perhaps the most surprising act of "aesthetic recognition" in Boturini, is his citation of the passage in the *Iliad* where Homer reads the story of the past on the shield Vulcan crafted for Achilles (*Iliad* 18: 478–608). Boturini thus invokes what is certainly the most influential instance of ekphrasis in the Western literary tradition to figure out his own attempt to write the history of the indigenous peoples of Mesoamerica. To establish a place for himself as a historian *and* legitimise the use of indigenous pictorial sources for history, he constructs a bold comparison:

> If Homer describes on the Shield of Achilles, [...] the histories [las Historias] of ancient times [... .] why could not I read on the shields [los escudos] of the Indians [*Indios*] the stories of the two ages, the obscure and the fabulous?

> Que si Homero describe en el Escudo de Aquiles, [...] las Historias de los tiempos antepasados [...], por què no podrè yo en los Escudos de los Indios leer las Historias de los tiempos Obscuros, y Fabuloso? (Boturini 1974: 84, my translation)

Boturini, then, references Homer to assert that these historical periods can be studied using indigenous images as sources. Accordingly, the "recognition" as it is worked out here, is not so much "aesthetic" as it is *historiographical;* it primarily concerns the value of what Boturini calls "shields" as sources of certain historical periods. If Homer could use images as sources for histories of the past, why should Boturini be forbidden to use indigenous writings and images as sources? The focus here, then, is on the production of historical knowledge—not the aesthetic appreciation of images. Moreover, we also observe that a division of historical times is involved in the comparison; the Homeric equivalences apparently only apply to what is called the "obscure" and "fabulous age" of history.

This historical scheme also organised the disposition of *Idea*, which was divided into three ages. In the section of the text that accounts for the disposition ("Orden de escribir esta historia"), Boturini states that "following the renowned idea of division of time that the Egyptians thought, I have partitioned the Indian History in three ages: The first, that of the Gods, the second, that of the heroes, the third, that of men" (Siguiendo la idèa de la cèlebre división de los tiempos, que enseñaron los Egypcios, he repartido la Historia Indiana en tres Edades: La primera. la de las Dioses, La segunda, la de los Heroes: La tercera, la de los hombres") (Idea: 7). Hence, an Egyptian manner of partitioning historical time furnishes the grid for the division of Mexican time. This, Boturini adds, is the same as the scheme Varro used, but the Roman historian called the three ages "Obscuro, Fabuloso, e historico" (ibid). Thus, this twofold nomenclature will organise the idea of a new history of *America septentrional*. Indeed, this manner of dividing historical time was commonplace in early modern historiography, but Boturini had claimed the two first ages as his own. Since the time before the historical age has not been the object of "any other pen", it has become "exclusively mine", he claims (*por no haver entrado en poder de alguna otra Pluma, viene a ser privativamente mia*) (Idea: 140) Vico had also invested much in this framework, and he had added a set of semiotic criteria to the traditional tripartite division of time and made it the basis of what he called his ideal universal history, which began with hieroglyphs and gods. Vico, however, restricted the application of this periodisation to pagan nations and gentile history.

Boturini quoted extensively from Vico in *Idea*, but never identified him as his source, and subsequently he was accused of "translating" Vico by Spanish intellectuals. At the time of Boturini's death in 1755, his historiographical project had been fiercely debated in Madrid for almost ten years. One reason for this was that he was charged of being, in the words of the Jesuit and courtier Andrés Marcos Buriell, a

mere translator of Juan Bautista Vico, a Neapolitan who in the 25th year of this century printed an idea of a science and a law of nature and of nations against Grotius, Puffendorf and Selden, which I have here but have been unable to read [es mero traductor de Juan Bautista Vico, napolitano, que el año de 25 de este siglo imprimió una idea de una ciencia y Derecho natural y de Gentes contra Grocio, Puffendorf y Seldeno, al qual tengo aquí pero no he podido leer].

Andrés Marcos Buriell to Gregorio Mayans 30 July 1746, Mayans y Siscar 1972 and 2002)[4]

The origin of, and evidence for, the charges against Boturini were rather banal: Boturini's annotated edition of the 1725 edition of the *New Science* had come into the hands of Blas Antonio Nassarre, the chief librarian at the Royal Library in Madrid, who subsequently turned against Boturini:

> Nassarre has the book by Vico, and it is the same one that Señor Boturini made use of and it contains the paragraphs, underlined by his hand, which he put into Castilian in the Idea of the history of the Indies [*Nassarre tiene el libro de Vico i es el mismo libro que tuvo i manejó el Sr. Boturini con los párrafos que, rayados de su mano, puso en castellano en la Idea de la historia de Indias*] (M. Martínez Pingarrón to G. Mayans, 14 february 1750)

The scholarly literature on Boturini mostly repeats the eighteenth-century claim of "translating Vico", not as an accusation but as an explanation of his "recognition" of the image and culture of the Amerindian "other". Kubler is a case in point. In the section of Boturini, he simply excerpted seven "time defying ideas" taken from Vico:

> Human nature is variable;
> makers know more than observers;
> natural and human sciences differ;
> each society has a pervasive pattern;
> history requires knowledge of all arts;
> art is relative to society;
> changing expressions allow new discovery.
>
> (Kubler 1991: 88)

Holding these philosophical ideas, then, is the reason why Boturini is inserted in the strange "vacuum" between "teachers and exploiters" of the indigenous peoples of America.

The ideas in question, however, are all cited from I. Berlin—and from a section where he summarises Vico's philosophy. The ideas here referenced by Kubler express some of the most basic assumptions of the modern human sciences. Berlin credits Vico with these notions, and concomitantly also asserts that Vico

> is the true father of the modern concept of culture and of what one might call cultural pluralism, according to which each authentic culture has its own unique vision, its own scale of values (Berlin 1990: 59–60).

The philosophical source of Boturini's aesthetic recognition of "Amerindian art" is, so is the claim, to be found in Vico's discovery or invention of culture as a distinct domain one must approach with a specific set of methods.

While Boturini's work mainly has been stored in the archive, the book he underlined and annotated, Vico's *New Science*—primarily in its 1744 edition, which Boturini never read—would eventually become one of the canonised works of the human sciences.[5] Apparently, it was the "father of culture" that was "translated" in Spain and used to interpret history from indigenous America in 1746—only two years after the publication of the last edition of the *New Science*.

People without writing are people without history

Many commentators have contested the casting of Vico in the role of the "precursor", and what P. Burke has called "the Vico myth", which he further describes as "a stylised interpretation of his career in dramatic terms—a tragicomedy of errors or misunderstandings which is put right in the end, although too late for the hero" (Burke 1985: 1). As we have seen, even the decolonial Latin-Americanist W. Mignolo turns to the "Vico myth" and a rather conventional" narrative about the history of historiography when dealing with Boturini's *Idea*. In the *Darker side of the Renaissance*, he sees it as the very first construal of Amerindian writing and history that breaks with colonial Spanish understandings of non-alphabetic Amerindian writing as a source for history. Mignolo maintains, that the colonisation of the Americas was also an encounter between civilisations whose systems of representations, and the semiotic networks that these were based upon, were entirely different. The European book-culture confronted the Andean *quipus* and Mesoamerican script based upon complex relations between pictography and oral tradition. The mutual implication of letters and historiography in European thought led to a semiotic colonisation of indigenous systems of representation; and created an image of the Amerindians as primitives who "lacked letters, did not have history, and had painted books dictated by the devil" (1992: 303). Boturini, however, "realised that alphabetic writing was not a necessary condition for writing history, despite the fact that sixteenth-century scholars had difficulty understanding this" (Mignolo 1995: 162). Thus, Boturini represents an escape from the "trap of the Renaissance celebration of alphabetic writing" (Mignolo 1995). This was the historiographical "trap" Spanish observers of the Americas been caught in, or formed for themselves, and which hinged history upon alphabetic writing.

Mignolo underscores the role of Vico in the recognition of histories using pictographic writing: "Boturini read Vico" and this

> allowed him to see in Mexican writing what missionaries of the first century failed to see: the Amerindian's magnificent and exemplary [...] ways of writing history, which could be positively compared—according to Boturini,—with the most celebrated histories written anywhere in the world (ibid: 149).

To demonstrate this Vico-inspired praise of historiographic otherness, Mignolo quotes the first paragraph from the section in *Idea* where Boturini lists four reasons for the "Excelencias de la historia de la Nueva España". These are,

> Firstly, because it is the most eloquent of all that have to date been discovered, since there are four ways of committing noteworthy matters to public memory: first by means of Figures, Symbols, Characters and Hieroglyphs, each of which contain a sea of wisdom as we shall see shortly. Secondly, by means of multicoloured knots, which are called quipu in the Peruvian language and *nepohualtzin* in the language of our Indians [i.e., those in central Mexico, (Mignolo's comment)]. Thirdly, in poems full of exquisite metaphors and noble conceits. Fourthly and lastly, after the Spanish Conquest, in manuscripts written in Indian and Castilian; some on local paper, others on European, by which we have come to know the peculiarities of their civil life (Boturini cited and translated ibid: 149–50).

It is apparently the influence from Vico that explains the Milanese's praise of Amerindian historiography and historical cultures—and his liberation from the Eurocentric construal of alphabetic writing as a semiotic pre-requisite for having a history. Mignolo here assumes a rather conventional model of intellectual influence and the emergence of historical consciousness. The decolonial scholar repeats the metanarrative previously presented by scholars like Kubler and Berlin about a rupture with the European tradition.

The cultural historian A. Grafton maintains that Mignolo disregards the intellectual context of early modern European antiquarianism and historiography when dealing with what are "after all European texts" (Grafton 2001).[6] Hence, texts such as Boturini's and those of the friars and chroniclers governed by the intellectual paradigm Boturini (supposedly) broke with, must be seen in relation to the idioms and language games of which they formed a part. That, however, also implies not seeing such text along a line of historical liberation, as decontextualised performances of tolerance and cross-cultural recognition of the history of "the other"—applying the same metahistorical grid as conventional stories about how renaissance clearings in the medieval darkness prepared the way for enlightenment (cf. Davis 2012).

Jorge Cañizares-Esguerra, a revisionist historian of the Hispanic world and the wider Atlantic, cites Grafton, and further argues against Mignolo's view of the European disregard for indigenous documents, noting that "sixteenth-century chroniclers and historians went out of their way to retrieve the information stored in Amerindian sources", even if they often regarded these as primitive (2001: 5). Contrary to Mignolo and Kubler, moreover, Cañizares largely disassociates Boturini's history from the new science—or, at least, from a "correct" reading of it, and of Vico's "intention".

> Although he lifted this entire historiographical paradigm from Vico without acknowledgment, Boturini in fact, stood Vico on his head. [...]

Vico had sought to demonstrate that the histories and chronologies of the Chaldeans, the Phoenicians, and particularly the Egyptians were untrustworthy. For Vico, hieroglyphs were the product of poetic, primitive minds, and the Bible was the only reliable continuous historical record. Paradoxically, Boturini used Vico to give Mesoamerican sources a historiographical status similar to that enjoyed by the Bible. [...] It is clear that Boturini misunderstood Vico's intention. Unlike Vico, for example, Boturini thought highly of hieroglyphic writing. He took the German Jesuit Athanasius Kircher to task for having declared that Mexican hieroglyphs were manifestations of "rustic minds", an idea with which Vico would have agreed wholeheartedly (2001: 139–140).

Although the conclusion differs, Cañizares' way of conceiving the relation between Vico and Boturini is still assuming the model of influence, but now (*pace* Kubler and Mignolo) the departure from Vico's "paradigm" is the condition for the praise of Mesoamerican script and history. As Cañizares' observes, there are important differences between Vico's and Boturini's views on "hieroglyphs" and pictorial writing as historical sources. But are these differences only explainable in terms of a "misreading"? Is the "paradigm" still the same when the "intention" behind the original is inverted? In other words, does Boturini still remain inside the paradigm of the NS even after this revolt? "Paradigm" here appears to refer to something like a tool, an instrument that one can choose to lift or not to lift: Boturini was not confined to this "paradigm" the phrasing further implies that Boturini was external to the "paradigm" that he grabbed, or even "stole". Thus, Vico's historical paradigm turns out to be a historically contingent method practiced in *Idea*, not a shared and comprehensive pattern that describes the "style of reasoning" of a particular epistemic culture.

Grafton and Cañizares turned to the work of the Italian philosopher and historian G. Cantelli to counter the "Vico myth" as this had appeared in Mignolo's decolonial story of a rupture (1986; 1990). Cantelli pointed to the identity of fables and hieroglyphs in Vico's philosophy of history; and that that constellation was a staple in Neo-Platonic thought. The identity of fable and hieroglyph was commonplace, also bolstered by printing practices, such as publishing the fables of Aesop bound with the *Hieroglyphics* of Horapollo (Boas in Horapollo 1950). Accordingly, the fable-hieroglyph "unit" formed a part of a wider intellectual paradigm in European antiquarianism and historiography with ample places for visual and material sources.

I shall explore how Boturini uses this "paradigm" for different purposes in my last section. Firstly, however, I will focus on Boturini's work with the history of the Virgin of Guadalupe, and the many genres and knowledge practices applied to this. Strangely, neither Mignolo nor Cañizares' give much attention to Boturini's work with the apparitions on Tepeyac. As we shall see, there was ample place for the recognition of the image and the historiography from Mesoamerica in this religious discourse on history.

II

The Boturini collection as the basis for historiography

The circumstances around the production of Boturini's *Idea* were unusual already before the accusation was levelled by the circles around the Royal Library; the Milanese collector and author wanted to base his history upon the sources in his collection, but he had to proceed to compose it without them. This was because the collection had been confiscated by an order of the viceroy of New Spain, dated January 31, 1743. Later in the same year Boturini was deported from New Spain while the *museo* remained in custody at the Royal Treasury (*Caxa Real*) in Mexico City (Glass 1975:473). Boturini constantly struggled to get his museum back. While still in New Spain, he had complained to the Viceroy about the confiscation in the terms that closely resembles those he will use in the book published in Madrid,

> Your Excellency could give me no greater torment than to take out of my hands the historical archive that has cost me seven years of hard work, many sicknesses, and a large amount of money.
> No podia V. E. darme mayor tormento que el Apartar de mis manos el Archivo Histórico, que me há costado siete años de pesadaísimos trauajos, muchas enfermedades, y cantidad crecida de dinero.
> (Boturini cited and translated in Glass 1981: 92)

Soon after arriving in Spain in 1744, Boturini addressed the king in a *memorial* where he begged him to intervene on his behalf with the authorities in New Spain to secure the collection. Boturini now worried that the humidity in the royal treasury where the collection was stored could ruin "the manuscripts and maps since these were very old and of a fragile material" ("*los Manuscritos y Mapas por ser antiquísimos y de material debil*"). In the same *memorial* he also described this fragile materiality of the manuscripts; the pieces in the museum consisted of "paper of metl [*maguey*], silk or palm leafs, and animal hides ("*papel de Metl, Palma o Gusano y en Pieles de Animales*") (Torre Revello 1936: 13). By underlining this fragile materiality of the texts, Boturini also pinpoints their material "otherness" and "authenticity". Thus, if Boturini's museum was in the main a *museo cartaceo*, all his papers were not of the "ordinary" European kind, as some of his opponents in Spain claimed. Boturini never managed to retrieve his *museo historico indiano*, but it served as the basis for the *Idea* that he published in Spain.

I shall now turn to how Boturini construed the relation between the *museo* and the historical text by examining the paratextual framing devices of the 1746 publication. How are the "voices" of the Amerindians producers of these texts given a place in this textual framework? And how does the author/collector position himself towards the "cultural" object which he placed at the feet of the King?

The full title of the first part of Boturini's 1746 publication was

Idea of a New General History of Northern America founded upon copious material of figures, symbols, characters and hieroglyphs, songs and manuscripts by Indian Authors recently discovered.

Idea de una nueva historia general de América septentrional fundada sobre material copioso de figuras, symbolos, caractères y geroglificos, cantares y manuscritos de autores indios últimamente descubiertos

Already in the title, Boturini thus states that the *museo historico indiano* should serve as the "foundation" for the general history outlined in *Idea*, and that the "copious material" consisted of the sources "recently discovered" by himself during his stay in New Spain. The second part of the publication was an extensive catalogue of the *museo* with a separate title page. Here Boturini writes that

the following literary treasure [...] can serve to order and write the general history of the New World, based upon indisputable monuments of the Indians themselves.

el siguiente Tesoro Literario [...] puede servir para ordenar, y escribir la historia general de aquel Nuevo Mundo, fundado en Monumentos indisputables de los mismos Indios.

(ibid)

On the one hand, the items in the collection are located in a specific "cultural" zone; the authors are the Indians (cf. "*manuscritos de autores indios*"), and this "cultural identity" is "indisputable", Boturini states on the first page of the catalogue. Besides, we can assume that the native authors are the *producers* of what Boturini calls a "literary treasure". Accordingly, the *museo* has a literary quality as well as containing historical information. This is then testimony of the literary and poetic competence of the native authors. But Boturini also presents the authentic "monuments of the Indians themselves" as his personal possession. We see this clearly further down the title page of the catalogue-section, where he adds the following description of how he assembled his museum:

Catalogue of the Indian historical museum of the gentleman Lorenzo Boturini Benaduci, Lord of Torre and of Hono, who arrived in New Spain in February of the year 1736, and with persistent efforts, and immense expenses from his own purse, gathered, in different provinces, the following literary treasure.

Catalogo del museo historico indiano del Cavallero Lorenzo Boturini Benaduci, Señor de la Torre y de Hono, Quien llegó a la Nueva España por Febrero del año 1736. y à porfiadas diligencias, è inmensos gastos de su bolsa juntò, en diferentes Provincias, el siguiente Tesoro Literario.

(ibid)

At this textual border between *Idea* and the *Catalogo*, the history and its "foundation", Boturini frames "his" collection in an economic idiom; it has been made a possession because of hard work accompanied by huge monetary expenses. In the introduction to the catalogue section (coming immediately after the title page), Boturini, extending the economic metaphor, claims that the collection is his only "estate" *(hacienda)* in New Spain. Moreover, this literary *hacienda* is so valuable that he is unwilling to exchange it for other, more mundane treasures. If the museum is a personal possession, and as such part of a private economy, it has also entered an economic sphere that transcends a mere monetary economy:

> This is the only estate I have in the Indies, and so precious [is it] that I will not exchange it for gold and silver, for diamonds and pearls.
>
> Esta es la unica Hacienda, que tengo en Indias, y tan preciosa, que no la trocàra por oro, y plata, por diamantes, y perlas.
>
> (ibid.)

Thus, the collection is so valuable that it cannot be traded back into the economy within which it was in play when it was established as symbolic capital it has crossed into the sphere of a cultural and scientific economy. This rhetorical marking of the importance of the collection can be seen as an example of antiquarian hyperbole, postulating a "possession" beyond comparison. Obviously, this praise also reflects upon the collector himself and his connoisseurship (cf. Findlen 1994; Ødemark 2011).

The *museo historico indiano* was also a part of an economy of knowledge. This as well can be understood from the way Boturini attempts to classify and organise the different parts of his text. The catalogue has a separate pagination and a new preface. *Idea* runs from page 1 to 167, while a section consisting of seven pages without pagination interrupt the historical outline and introduces the catalogue. Here Boturini on ninety-six pages (i.e., 1–96), lists, classifies, and excerpts the material contained in the *museo,* his "literary treasure" and "historical archive". Hence, we have two *separate* textual units, differentiated by textual borders inside the physical unity of the book. Nevertheless, whereas there is an internal division, it is evident that Boturini intended a well-defined relation between the two parts. After all, these parts belong to the same architectonically conceived structure, for the historical *Idea,* a historical narrative, was *"funded"* upon the *"copious material"* contained in the museum. Consequently, the museum will also provide the basis for a text performing a historical narrative. We have here a historiographical poetics articulated with an architectural metaphor where the construction of the architectonics was planned in several stages with the collection as the corner stone.

1 *Museo*/foundation: already collected but confiscated in New Spain and kept in the Royal Treasury

2 *Idea*/outline: referring to the information and literature of the embargoed museum, but also forward to the

3 *Historia general*, which when finished will deliver the "novelties" and have the "utility" promised by Boturini in the last section of the 1746 publication.

We could compare the textual grid of the "idea"/"*fundada*" with what de Certau calls the "split structure" of the historical text (Carrard 1992: 159). With this term, de Certeau refers to "the page's division between a primary text and footnotes usually set in smaller prints" (ibid). The footnotes function as links to the "archive" consulted by the historian, and by inscribing this relation on the page the historical text both *differentiates* itself from other genres (fiction) and establishes reference to the "real events" that the documents in the archive are supposed to be testimony of. Thus, we could say that both *difference* (with respect to other textual grids presenting other kinds of reality posits) and *reference* (one aspect of this historical difference) is accomplished through this constitutive gesture of historical poetics.

In the case of Boturini's 1746 publication, however, we not only have a "split page" but also a "split volume", where the historical narrative performed in the *Idea* was based upon sources the *museo* listed in the catalogue. Nevertheless, the textual division between the historical outline and the catalogue serves a similar function in Boturini's poetics of knowledge; it furnishes at the same time both the real reference of the text and its historical authority.

The paratextual framing of sacred and gentile history

In the dedication to Philip V, the first Bourbon king of Spain, Boturini states that another authority had ordained his passage to the New World. "Divine Providence", he says, "transferred me *per ambages, & judicia maxima* from other European courts to that of Your Majesty and destined me to the Indies in the year 1735." ("*La Divina Providencia me trasladó* per ambages, & judicia maxima *de otras cortes de Europa a la de V.M. y destinó por el año 1735 a las Indias*") (ibid). Thus, the agency behind Boturini's transfer to the Indies—and between the Habsburg court in Vienna and the Bourbon court in Madrid—is Divine Providence herself.

Boturini further explains that two projects of historiography were born almost simultaneously, immediately after his arrival in New Spain. The first concerned the Virgin of Guadalupe, the second the history of the "gentiles". Here is his own metahistorical account of the origins of his work:

I felt stimulated by a superior and tender desire, which led me to investigate the prodigious miracle of the apparitions of Our Lady Patron of Guadalupe. In these circumstances, I found that the histories about them were founded only on tradition, without anyone knowing where or into whose hands the monuments of such an extraordinary portent had come to rest. The history of the gentility itself was about to expire, and this also called for a person who could bring it out of the tomb of oblivion.

me sentì estimulado de un superior tierno impulso para investigar el prodigioso milagro de las Apariciones de Nuestra Patrona de Gudalupe; en cuya occasion hallè la Historia de ellas fundada en la sola tradicion, sin que se supiesse en donde, ni en qué manos parassen los Monumentos de tan peregrino Portento. La misma Historia de la Gentildad, que estaba para expirar, clamaba por Sugeto, que la sacasse de el tumolo del olvidio (1746: "Señor").

The passage from the first to the second project of historiography was apparently smooth. Almost in the same breath as he voices his admiration for the Virgin, Boturini adds the history of the "gentiles" to his historiographical repertoire. According to Boturini's metahistorical account in the dedication text, he conceived of the two histories almost simultaneously, and as two parts of a complex whole, and based upon the same set of sources; the Mesoamerican *pinturas* he compared to the shield of Achilles.

His visual self-presentation in another paratext, the authors' portrait inserted at the beginning of his 1746 publication, is consistent with this framing of two histories that are separate but also related since both are based upon his collection. (Figure 12.1)

The author is depicted inside a medallion. On its frame, Boturini's pedigree is inscribed; he is a knight of the Holy Roman Empire and Lord of Turrret et Hono. Below the medallion, we find his coat of arms. Hence, the author demonstrates his nobility by visual means from European culture, like the "shields" he referred to in the comparison between himself and Homer.

Inside the frames of the medallion, two visual artefacts from New Spain are depicted. The action in the image is played out in between these two. Under Boturini's right hand, we have a Mexican calendar wheel, furnished with an explanatory text in Spanish, "*siglo de los americanos*". This Mexican device for counting time lies in the shadow of the author's right hand. In his left hand, Boturini holds an image of the Virgin of Guadalupe; in his right hand, a pen. While gazing out from the book, Boturini uses the tip of his pen to unfold the image of the Virgin, making Guadalupe touch the calendar wheel. The image of Guadalupe thus appears to be what the author most of all wants to show the reader of his new "idea" of history.

The *siglo de los americanos* is a pre-Hispanic calendar wheel representing the eighteenth months of the Nahua annual cycle (Cañizares 2001: 275). This object then was an instrument used in counting and accounting for time before the coming of the Spaniards. In the light that emanates from the image of the Virgin (Boturini's face and the image of Guadalupe are the two main sources of light inside the medallion) it is in fact possible to glimpse sequences of Mexican calendar signs just below the serpent who serves as the outer frame of the calendar. On top of the calendar wheel—between the words

Figure 12.1 Portrait of Boturini.

"*siglo*" and "*de los Americanos*" and above the sign *tochtli* ("rabbit")—one sees the contours of the head of a serpent that coils around the calendar, forming its external boundary.

Boturini has taken this image from the Neapolitan travel-writer Giovanni Francisco Gemmeli Careri's *Giro del mondo*.[7] Gemmeli Careri had visited New Spain around the turn of the century and had furnished the volume with several illustration. He had also treated the calendar and its hieroglyphs. In the chapter dealing with this, he says that he will account for "The months, year and century of the Mexicans with their hieroglyphs" (*Meses, año, y siglo de los mexicanos con sus jerogligicos*) (Gemelli Careri 1976: 46). The linkage between the calendar, its temporal units and the hieroglyphs representing them had thus been made in the work that furnished Boturini with images and pictorial references in a situation where he lacked his collection. In the first paragraph of the chapter, Gemelli Careri praises the astuteness of the makers of the Mexican calendar signs and asserts that the hieroglyphs were functional equivalents of letters:

> Due to the lack of letters the ingenious Mexican used figures and hieroglyphs to signify corporal things with a form, and for the rest, other characters proper [to them], and in this mode they signified for the good of posterity all the things that had succeeded.
>
> A falta de letras usaron los ingenios mexicanos figuras y jeroglíficos para significar las cosas corpóreas que tienen figura; y para las restantes otros caracteres propios, y de ese modo señalaban, para bien de la posterioridad todas las cosas sucedidas.
>
> (ibid)

Letters were not in use, a fact that is described as a "lack", but all past events could nevertheless be represented ("they signified for the good of posterity all the things that had succeeded"). Hence, there can be a history written with visual sign that can serve as an instruction to posterity. The Neapolitan antiquarian Matteo Egizio, who served as a ghost-writer for Gemelli Careri, was also a friend of Vico (Stone 1997: 77–83). However, this recognition of the script and historiography of the other, exemplified by Gemmelli Careri, can—as we shall see in more detail in the last section of this chapter - hardly be regarded as referring to an influence from Vico.

The virgin and the signs of Mesoamerican history

"Stimulated by a superior and tender desire" for the Virgin, Boturini began to search native manuscripts and paintings for testimony that could corroborate what until now had been an undocumented tradition, and he found it, or so he thought. In a passage in the catalogue section of the 1746 publication where Boturini lists all the sources in his *museo*, he identifies one of the documents he considers to be contemporary with the apparitions. In his description of the portentous event and the proof for it, he claims that the Virgin "imitated" the manner the natives had of writing history. Thus, she not only spoke Nahuatl, but she also used Mexican script to communicate. Boturini describes the document now referred to as the *Lienzo de Tlaxcalla* in the following way:

> The map that I cited in Section 31, n. 2 by which it is proved that the Indian authors left memories of the Most Holy Lady, and that they historicized her apparitions in paintings in accordance with the style of their nation; and that the Sovereign Virgin, imitating the uses and customs of the Empire as to their way of historicizing, wanted to paint herself on the Ayatl of Juan Diego. With this painted testimony, the Indians were so satisfied that they took great care to serve her all the time.

> El mapa que citè en el §.31, n.2 por el qual se prueba, que los Autores Indios dexaron memorias de la Santissima Señora, è historiaron sus Apariciones con Pinturas, según el estilo de su Nación; y que la Virgen Sober[an]a, imitando tambien los usos, y costumbres del Imperio, por lo que toca al modo de historiar, quiso pintarse en el Ayatl de Juan Diego, de cuyo Testimonio pintado quedaron tan satisfechos los indios, que se esmeraron siempre en servirla (Catalogo: 92).[8]

The *Lienzo de Tlaxcala* was a post-Hispanic object which depicted the Virgin along with the incarnated logos as an infant. Other European subjects also appeared inside the representational space of the document, which is clearly influenced by European motifs and manners of representation, and thus must be considered a "hybrid" both with reference to the conceptual and semiotic organisation of the text (cf. Gruzinski 1993: 22).[9] In Boturini's understanding, this "hybridity" implicates what we could call a scene both of semiotic and historiographical recognition—paralleling the *storia* enacted in the authors' self-portrait. Boturini's claim for the value of the *Lienzo de Tlaxcala* as historical proof that can supplement tradition is thus intrinsically linked to a notion of a mutual and felicitous translation or "accommodation" between the Virgin and indigenous Mexicans, resulting in an enduring cult of the mother of God in Mexico ("With this painted testimony, the Indians were so satisfied that they took great care to serve her all the time"). The *Lienzo de Tlaxcala* is consequently evidence of two things vital for Boturini:

i [memory and history] Indian authors had produced testimony that contained "memories" of the apparitions. These memories were "historicised" by native authors who used paintings and the other semiotic means at their disposal to inscribe them ("it is proved that the Indian authors left memories of the Most Holy Lady, and that they historicised her

apparitions in paintings in accordance with the style of their nation").
Consequently, paintings and other non-alphabetic signs are vehicles
capable of carrying memories over to historical discourse, i.e., there can
be a pictographic historiography.

ii [accommodation and cult] Furthermore, the *lienzo* proves that the Virgin
"imitated" the Mexican system of representation ("the Sovereign Virgin,
imitating the uses and customs of the Empire as to their way of
historicising, wanted to paint herself on the *Ayatl* of Juan Diego").
The very style and the manner of historicising of the "nation" (that later
was used to historicise her apparitions by the Indians) was already used
by the divine agent herself in her original apparition—which thus
constituted a kind of inter-semiotic translation. In return for her
"accommodation" to the Mexican signs, the Virgin received continuous
veneration.

Consequently, the images here function both as a medium for history and
as a contact zone between the human and the divine where it had showed its
efficacy in maintaining the vitality of the cult—the latter a vital criterion for
the coronation of an image.

The praise of Mesoamerican history and the criteria for coronation

Boturini had made inquiries about whether it was possible to crown an image
outside of Italy, and if so, what were the requirements and protocols for
doing it?(Glass 1979: 13 and 1981: 75).[10] Even if, "the coronation of an image
of an apparition is not as serious an ecclesiastical act as the confirmation of
an apparition or the canonisation of a saint", the Council of St. Peter's had
established a protocol for the coronation ceremony, as well as criteria for
which images could be given such an honour (Glass 1981:75, n. 2). The
criteria are listed in the so-called *Instructio coronationis,* which explains that
the image should be "no less" ("non minus"):

    i vetustate, quam
    ii populi concursu ac
    iii miraculorum frecuencia, celebrem.
       (Cited in [Anon] *Sacerdote de la Compania de Jesus,* (1897; Vol. 2, 53))

The first criteria (concerning the age or the antiquity of the image)
already creates a demand for historical and antiquarian documentation.
While this criterion is strictly historical (as it only concerns the age of the
image) the two next are—increasingly—theological and "functional": In
addition to having a certain age, the image must be shown to be a vital
force in popular piety. Accordingly, this religious function in the present
must also be documented. These criteria, then, were the institutionalised

protocols that Boturini had to apply if he wanted to write the history of the image of Guadalupe.

I have already cited the passage from *Idea* that Mignolo used to argue for a Vico-influenced break with the tradition of denying history to people without alphabetic writing. Boturini, we remember, claimed "that this history not only can compete with the most celebrated in the world but exceed them" ("que no sólo puede competir esta historia con las mas célebres del orbe, sino excederlas"). As Mignolo observed, there is an intrinsic relation between history and semiotics in Boturini's praise.

> Firstly, because it is the most eloquent of all that have to date been discovered, since there are four ways of committing noteworthy matters to public memory: first by means of Figures, Symbols, Characters and Hieroglyphs, each of which contain a sea of wisdom as we shall see shortly. Secondly, by means of multicoloured knots, which are called quipu in the Peruvian language and *nepohualtzin* in the language of our Indians. Thirdly, in poems full of exquisite metaphors and noble conceits. Fourthly and lastly, after the Spanish Conquest, in manuscripts written in Indian and Castilian; some on local paper, others on European, by which we have come to know the peculiarities of their civil life (Boturini in Mignolo 1995: 149–50).

The cited passage, however, also appears in an earlier work by Boturini. The text is known as *Margarita Mexicana.* Boturini also called it his *Prólogo Galeato* ("helmeted prologue")—a genre designation referencing a combative preface defending the coming work (Matute 1976: 18, Burrus 1984: 34). An examination of *Margarita Mexicana* shows that Boturini's admiration of indigenous script and historiography is intrinsically related to the issue of supplementing the tradition of the Virgin's apparitions with historical documentation. Firstly, I shall now reinsert the passage cited by Mignolo in the textual environment from which the citation is extracted in Idea. Secondly, I shall compare it to a prior and almost identical passage in *Margarita Mexicana* also dealing with Mesoamerican history and writing.

The section praising indigenous historiography is the first section in Idea after the author's self-portrait i.e., after the author and the artis have shown us visually how Guadalupe is put in contact with Mexican time. The introductory part of the first paragraph continues with a description of the *museo*, which, Boturini says, contains "such copiousness of material that was not found by the other historians" ("*tanta copia de material que no hallaron los demás historiadores*") (Idea: 2). In the last clause of the paragraph (Idea: 6–7), Boturini returns to the *museo* and its contents before he presents in the next paragraph—more precisely a part of it entitled "*Orden de escribir esta historia*"—the tripartite division of historical time he will use as his principle of periodisation. Furthermore, he also treats his *museo* both in the clause preceding the passage Mignolo cites and in the final clause of the paragraph where it belongs.

We could say that the descriptions of Boturini's "own" *museo*, what he calls his property and only *hacienda*, is the context of the expression of admiration for the collected documents and sources; they are culturally other but also the collector's own property (cf. Ødemark 2011). In this part of the text, then, Boturini authorises his historical work with reference to the *museo* and the difference this collection makes compared to the material earlier chroniclers had to work with. This brief examination of the immediate textual environment of the passage suffices to show that the praise of Mesoamerican historiography and writing in *Idea* was intrinsically linked to the *museo*.

Margarita Mexicana was written in New Spain before Boturini's expulsion and is consequently prior to Idea, and the rhetorical situation in which Boturini struggled to get back his *museo* and be accepted as a royal historian in Spain. The passage Mignolo put so much weight upon, as the place for a rupture with tradition, thus has a religious prehistory; it was used to communicate with Rome about the apparition and the image of Guafalupe. In this unpublished manuscript,[11] Boturini applies the same grid to organise indigenous forms of writing and historiography. In *Margarita Mexicana*, however, the passage is presented as the first "funda-ment" in a series of thirty-one that shall document the apparitions of the Virgin (Burrus 1984: 34–35).

Boturini presents his first *fundamentum* under the heading "*Ab elegantia et fide Historiae Indiae*" (ibid: 34). Here then, the "quality" and trustworthiness of Mexican systems of representations is presented as the first "fundament" for establishing the truth of the apparition; this section of the *Margarita Mexicana* will later be incorporated into *Idea*.

After the caption, Boturini continues with four (numbered) paragraphs listing the same semiotic classes of historical sources and indigenous historiography as in the passage from *Idea* cited by Mignolo:

"De filis Indiorum historicis, quae peruani Quipus et Mexicani Nepohualtzin appellant",
  "De Indiorum poetarum cantices, sive prosodis",
  "De figures Indiorum Historicis"
  "De characteribus Indiorum Chronologicis"
                                        (Boturini cited in Matute 1976: 19).

Without doubt, this is an earlier version of the passage upon which Mignolo bases his narrative of a break with the Eurocentric tradition of seeing the alphabet as a prerequisite for history. The order in which the semiotic classes of the evidence are listed is different, but the classes themselves, and thus the principle organising them, remain roughly the same. We see the similarity clearly if we reorganise the order of presentation:

Idea	*Margarita Mexicana*
• Firstly, it is the most eloquent [facunda] of all [histories] that to this day have been discovered, since it has four modes of committing noteworthy matters to public memory:	
• First with figures, *symbols, characters and hieroglyphs, which envelop a sea of erudition* [...].	De figures Indiorum Historicis, De characteribus Indiorum Chronologicis
• Secondly, in knots of various colours, which in the language of the Peruvians is called quipu, and in the one of our Indians Nepohualtzin:	De filis Indiorum historicis, quae peruani Quipus et Mexicani Nepohualtzin appellant,
• Thirdly, in songs of exquisite *metaphors and elevated concepts*:	De Indiorum poetarum cantices, sive prosodis,

If the aim was to obtain permission to coronate the image of the Virgin, fulfil the requirements of the *Instructio coronationis*, Boturini must have had a Roman recipient in mind. Boturini consequently had to persuade the addressee in Rome about the worthiness of the Mexican Virgin, and as we know, he succeeded in doing this. This success at the centre of the catholic world indicates that we should be wary of construing Boturini's views of historiography and Mesoamerican sources as a fundamental break with the "European" tradition.

As noted earlier, Cañizares' observed that there are important differences between Vico's and Boturini's view on "hieroglyphs" as historical sources. In contrast to Mignolo, he claims that the departure from Vico's "paradigm" is the condition for Boturini's praise of Mesoamerican script and history. Actually, there seems to be ampler space for Mesoamerican script and "gentile hieroglyphs" in the religious history Boturini started to write for Rome, than in Vico's "new science". In the last section, I will examine the extent to which Vico and Boturini can be said to share a paradigm, but to be able to do this we must grasp that Vico's philosophy of history only applies to "gentile history".

III

Reading the history of images from the first age

Vico is brought into contact with the Mexican material at an early place in *Idea* where Boturni cites what Vico called "the first civil metaphor". This was the metaphor "in which Jove, identified with the Sky, would write his laws in lightning and promulgate them in thunder". Because of the fear early men felt towards thundering Jove and the shame they experienced when copulating in the open, men returned to sedentary life, first in the caves, and subsequently in more elaborated dwellings. Though he quoted widely from the New

Science of 1725, Boturini never named and cited Vico explicitly. At one place in Idea, however, he cites the Neapolitan scholar but only vaguely attributes the quoted text to an "Italian poet".

The text taken from the "Italian poet" is linked to the story of the manifestation of the law of Providence in Mexico. At this place in the text, Vico's philosophy of history is brought into contact with new empirical material from the new world. The Mexican deity Tezcatlipoca is the Mexican manifestation of Providence, while Tlaloc promulgates the new law in the "first age" of gentile history:

> And even if the Indians of the second and third age held this idol [Tlaloc] as the God of Rain, those of the first, nevertheless revered him as the promulgator of Providence, thinking that she wrote the laws with lightning and published them with thunder, which is the same as was said of Jove in an elegant metaphor by an Italian poet.
> *Ne la primera etade*
> *Gli Eroi leggevan le leggi in petto a Giove.*
> Y aunque los Indios de la segunda y tercera Edad tuvieron à este Idolo [Tlaloc] por Dios de la lluvia, no obstante, los de la primera le reverenciaron como Pregonero de la Providencia, pensando que ella escribia las leyes con los rayos, y las publicaba con los truenos, que es lo mismo, que de Júpiter dixo con elegante metafora un Poeta Italiano.
> *Ne la primera etade*
> *Gli Eroi leggevan le leggi in petto a Giove.*
>
> (*Idea:* 13, italics in the original)

As we shall see in more detail later, the "local" Mexican deity Tlaloc here fulfils the universal historical function of the "first civil metaphor" already described in Vico. We note that it is important for Boturini that Tlaloc has had different functions and significances in the different historical ages; he was not a mere "god of rain" in the first age. Moreover, Tlaloc, or his "effigy", is also a part of Boturini's collection. To supplement the lack of his own image, Boturini again turns to Gemmeli Careri's publication on New Spain:

> TLALOC, whose effigy I have in my Archive, a copy of which is provided in Doctor Francisco Gemmeli Careri's history of the *Giro del Mundo vol. 6. pag. 83.* is Hieroglyph of the Second Deity, and almost Minister of Divine Providence.
> TLALOC, cuya efigie tengo en mi Archivo; y de quien trae la copia en su Historia del *Giro del Mundo* el Doctor Francisco Gemmeli Careri tom. 6. *pag. 83* es Geroglifico de la Segunda Deidad, y casi Ministro de la Divina Providencia (Idea: 12).

Since Boturini did not have access to his *museo*, Tlaloc enters the text by way of the reference to an image in *Giro del mondo*. (Figure 12.2)

Figure 12.2 Image of Tlaloc from *Giro del mundo*.

The illustration in the travelogue, however, is itself a copy of an "effigy" Boturini had "in his archive". This reference to an illustration in the work of another Italian traveller underscores that the coming description and explication of the "hieroglyph Tlaloc" will be about an object forming a part of Boturini's "hacienda" in New Spain. Thus, this passage also functions as a reference to the Boturini collection, and reminds the reader that the *museo* is the best source of Mexican history:

[O]n the mentioned print one sees Tlaloc crowned with feather diadems, which should be white and green. In the right hand he holds a bolt of lightning, and in the left, a shield adorned with many other feathers of a sky-blue colour. These three colours symbolized the following: white; those first children that will be born innocent within perfection of matrimony; green, the propagation of their lineages; and sky blue, the care they took in keeping religion pure and providing regular sacrifices to the gods.

[E]n dicha estampa se vè à Tlaloc coronado con diademas de plumas, que deben ser blancas, y verdes, teniendo en la mano derecha una Centella, y en la siniestra una Rodela, hermoseada de otras muchas plumas de color celes[te]; en cuyos tres colores symbolizaban, en el blanco, aquellos primeros hijos, que candidos havian de nacer en la hermosura de los matrimonios; en el verde, la propagacion de sus linages; y en el celeste, el cuidado, que se les encargaba de mantener pura la Religion, y constantes los sacrificios para con los Dioses.

(ibid.)

Boturini not only supplements Gemmeli Careri's black-and-white illustration with the colours of the feather-diadem on Tlaloc's crown, but he also deciphers their symbolic meaning. Gemmeli Careri had written that Tlaloc represented "rain and abundance" (Gemelli Careri 1976: 59–60). Boturini adds an ekphrasis that first takes the illustration in *Giro del mondo,* the cited "copy", as its object. However, he also adds visual information from observations made of his own "effigy", the original material image, to explain the imagery of Tlaloc—the colours lacking in Gemmeli Careri's black and white print.

Historicising the fable-hieroglyph paradigm

As I noted in the introduction, G. Cantelli pointed to the identity of fables and hieroglyphs in Vico's philosophy of history as a part of a broader, and older, paradigm:

That literature which, from the Italian Renaissance down through the whole of the seventeenth century, saw in the images of the gods a figurative language, analogous or almost completely similar to Egyptian hieroglyphics, is practically unlimited. [...] Here Egyptian hieroglyphics and pagan fables (images and statues of the gods) are considered as parts of a single symbolic mode of expression, parts that oftentimes are not even distinct, since myths, even the Greek myths, are treated as direct derivations from Egyptian hieroglyphics, the allegorical significance of which they conserve even if in a corrupted form (Cantelli: 57–58).

Boturini certainly construed his visual material, like the effigy of Tlaloc, within this paradigm. He extracts a fable from the Tlaloc-hieroglyph. The tale is about marriage, one of Vico's three human common senses; customs that all societies share (cf. later). Intriguingly, it turns out that one reference of a detail of the image of Tlaloc is a fable from Ovid's *Metamorphosis*. The green colour on Tlaloc's crown indicates a particular story, for "with this [colour] they alluded to the fable of Daphne ("*Y en esto aludian a la Fabula de Daphne*") (Idea: 12). In Ovid, Daphne is a chaste woman who wanders around in the woods to avoid male sexuality. Chased by Apollo, she is transformed into a laurel three when the god is about to rape her—thus preserving her chastity by changing shape (Battistini in Vico 1990, vol, 2: 1843, n. 2). Unable to consummate his desire, the son of Jupiter, now turns the laurel crown into the symbol of triumph, which was used to honour Roman heroes on their way to Capitol.

Vico had interpreted this fable in the *New Science* of 1725 [12] (Vico 1990). The attempted rape is here a civilising act; Daphne, Vico infers, is "[t]he poetic character of women who sleeps nefarious" (1725: §289). Daphne represents female sexuality unbound by the (patriarchal) rules of marriage; she is conceived as a "wild animal" whose nomadic life is ended by Apollo's attempted rape, culminating in Daphne's transformation into a laurel three. Apollo's act is thus construed as the domestication of female sexuality in marriage, an institution that in its turn guarantees legitimate offspring—and, as Boturini read into the green on Tlaloc's crown, the further propagation of legitimate lineages, property, and inheritance. Thus, Daphne and the laurel is not only a sign of a local (Roman) custom, but of one of the three human common senses and customs of humanity that functions as a precondition for all social life.

According to Boturini, all the colours on Tlaloc's crown. represent social institutions: matrimony, the propagation of the lineage, i.e., family, property, and religion. Boturini's exposition of the iconological implication of the colours on Tlaloc's crown is thus a silent citation of Vico's notion of the three human common senses that serve as the precondition for social life. Thus, the "unit" of hieroglyph and fable, visual and verbal symbols, that Cantelli commented upon, are further articulated with a historical anthropology that traces the emergence of the "three common senses of mankind" among "gentile nations".

firstly, that Providence exists; secondly, that certain children are bred by certain women with whom they share a least the principles of a common religion, in order that they be brought up by fathers and mothers in a single spirit and in conformity with the laws and religions amidst which they were born; and thirdly, that the dead should be buried (1725: § 10).

The three human common senses guarantee a kind of "cross-cultural" understanding. They constitute customs all societies have in common, since they serve as the precondition for social life.[13] In turn, these common senses are all a consequence of the "first civil metaphor", the perception of Jove on the sky, communicating angrily with lightning and thunder, i.e., the primordial drama Boturini transported to Mexico when he claimed Tlaloc as "the promulgator of Providence" who "wrote the laws with lightening and published them with thunder, which is the same as was said of Jove in an elegant metaphor by an Italian poet" (cf. earlier):

> Of all the children of the Sky, Jove was imagined to be the father and king of all the gods. Hence he was the origin of idolatry and divination, i.e., the science of auspices, because of the mode in which, as demonstrated above, he was the first god to be born in the Greek imagination. And, as our principles of poetry tell us, idolatry and divination were twin daughters born of that first civil metaphor in which Jove, identified with the Sky, would write his laws in lightning and promulgate them in thunder. From this metaphor came the first poetic civil sentiment in which the sublime and popular were united, more wonderful, than anything to which poetry later gave birth: "in the first age/the heroes read the laws on Jove's breasts" (1725: §411)

From the first civil metaphor, then, both the human common senses that constituted society—cross-culturally—and idolatry emerge. In Vico's own wording, "idolatry and divination were twin daughters born of that first civil metaphor". Idolatry was regularly seen as a subclass of superstition in early modern European theology, while divination was a further subclass of idolatry (Clark 2002: 120). It follows that this is the history of a society that comes into being through idolatry, of a religious other defined in contrast to the Christian logos.

The history of idolatry

A. Battistini claimes that G. J. Vossius treatment of the trope *antonomasia* in the latter's monumental history of idolatry (*De theologia gentilli et physiologia Christiana: sive de origine et progressu idolatria*) was a model for Vico's poetic character, i.e., the concrete universals that served "primitive" men after the deluge as general concepts—like Jove, or in Boturini's version, Tlaloc (Battistini 2004: 186). Voss used this trope to explain the rhetorical and mental characteristic of idolatry. He took *antonomasia* to be a figure of speech where a concrete thing represented an abstract idea.

Vico's poetic character did some of the same work, it was a concrete and sensory universal, which served "primitive" men after the deluge—at a stage where abstract thought had not evolved (or re-evolved)—as their first general concepts.[14]

In line with this, Vico regarded hieroglyphs as primitive men's cognitive responses to events that they were unable to comprehend. Due to the absence of abstract thought in what Vico called the "childhood of the world", the gods and hieroglyphs of the early men who lived outside the space where God intervened directly were personified and animated as deities representing the necessities of life. One example (from the *NS* of 1744) captures his way of processing information from different historical and ethnographical zones and transforming them into stages in what Vico called the *storia ideale eterna*. The example is taken from a section of the text where Vico treats the "language of the gods"—i.e., the hieroglyphs of the first age, which is also the class to which Boturini's Tlaloc-hieroglyph belongs. Here Greeks, Romans, Amerindians, and Egyptians are all turned into instances of "the same":

> [T]here can be no doubt that among the Latins Varro occupied himself with the language of the gods, for he had the diligence to collect thirty thousand of their names, which would have sufficed for a copious divine vocabulary, with which the peoples of Latium might express all their human needs, which in those simple and frugal times must have been few indeed, being only the things that were necessary to life. The Greeks had gods to the number of thirty thousand, for they made a deity of every stone, spring, brook, plant, and offshore rock. [... .]. *Just so [appunto come]* the American Indians [americani] *make [fanno]* a god of everything that exceeds [supera] their limited understanding. *Thus [talchè]* the divine fables of the Greeks and Latins must have been *the first true hieroglyphs, or sacred or divine characters, corresponding to those of the Egyptians.*
>
> (1744: §437; my italics)

In this dense passage, Vico undertakes a comparison of world-historical scope. The cited text begins in the past, with Greek and Roman polytheism. Rather abruptly—in the clause beginning with "just so"—he then turns to his present-day America and assimilates this into the same historical stage with the manner of creating the gods as the criteria of periodisation. This obviously erases the historical and cultural difference between the Greco-Roman past and the ethnographic present of the *americani* (although the verbs in this clause are in the present tense and thus retain traces of a certain difference). The concluding clause, beginning with "thus" (signalling continuity of subject and a coming conclusion), returns to the Mediterranean past, adds the Egyptians, and reaches a form of "trans-cultural" conclusion that applies to all the times and places that have furnished ethnographic and historical evidence for the proposition put forward here. The fables of the gods from "classical antiquity" and the hieroglyphs of the Egyptians are equated. In the last instance, these semiotic forms are about "the same" (gods who represent basic human needs) and they signify their basic socio-economic referent in the same way (hieroglyphically).

The common trait that makes these huge leaps in historical time possible is the identification of fables with hieroglyphs but added to this is the association of "primitiveness" and "idolatry". This, then, is not "primitiveness'" defined entirely in historical terms; it is influenced by theological concerns. This is evident if we turn to an earlier assimilation of Amerindian "culture" in Vico. Already in *The Constancy of the Jurist* (a part of the *Diritto universale* [1721]), Vico had quoted the Jesuit J. Acosta on the topic of how "[t]he sublimity of the fables proceeds agreeably from prejudices carried on from infancy". Here, Vico writes that '[t]he Peruvians, a most illiterate people [*stupidissima gens*], admitted that whatever exceeded the average size, like an immense river, a mountain, a tree, as Acosta narrates in the *Historia*, were believed to be gods" (Vico 1936: 374: 372; cf. Ødemark, 2011).[15]

Concluding remarks

In this chapter, I have demonstrated that Boturini's attempt to document and historicise the image and apparition of the Virgin of Guadalupe certainly had an impact upon Boturini's "recognition"—and praise!—of Mesoamerican historiography. Hence, we can conclude that the canonical history of human science and historical modernity, called upon by humanist and decolonial scholars alike, cannot explain the details of Boturini's historiographical encounters with Mesoamerican images and texts. Neither Mignolo nor Cañizares' give much attention to Boturini's writings on Guadalupe. This could be seen as a repression of the medieval historiographical practices—practices that had to be "othered" to stage the narrative of the early modern origin of historical consciousness (cf. Davis 2012 cited earlier).

Cañizares' asserted that there are important differences between Vico's and Boturini's views on "hieroglyphs" and pictorial writing as historical sources. In the last section earlier, I have shown that there is a certain paradigm, in the sense of a shared manner of poetically stitching together visual and verbal evidence, that constitute the unit of investigation of Vico and Boturini. Vico did not invent this unit, however, he took it from tradition and converted it into the *explanandum* of his *New Science,* linking it with his notion of human common senses and an idea of a uniform development of history among idolatrous nations, but thus also distinctly separating sacred and secular history—i.e., the very histories that Boturini put in touch in the portrait at the entrance to his 1746 publication.

Even if Boturini (as Cañizares rightly observes) associates a different historical and cultural value with hieroglyphs, he deploys the notion of a historical progression of common senses to explain material like "his" image of Tlaloc, but not the image of the Virgin. Nevertheless, Boturini does not construe Mesoamerican writing as the semiotic and cognitive means of a *stupidissima gens.* On the contrary, he praises it because "hieroglyphs", like Tlaloc, "envelop a sea of erudition". This refusal could be related to the "double" references of the collector's talk about the collection; every statement of the value of Mesoamerican sources and images also refers to the symbolic value of Boturini's own "museum" as a "possession". Placing Mesoamerican "culture" in a primitive and idolatrous zone would thus also imply a devaluation of the *museo* (Ødemark 2011).

Notes

1 Sforza Palavicino had also established a legate to fund them. This legate, however, would not support coronations outside Italy.
2 Complying with the ceremonial protocol of Rome would have caused the image of Guadalupe, a particularly potent symbol of Creole identity, to be marked with foreign signs as a result of a project instigated by a foreigner (Brading 2001, Gruzinski 2001, Florescano 1994, Wolf 1979).
3 The comprehensiveness of Boturini's museum can be illustrated by the huge percentage of the items in the census of "ethnohistorical" sources made for the *Handbook of Middle American Indians* that once formed part of the Boturini collection. "The pictorial manuscripts in the census that were in the Boturini collection amount to 21%, or one out of every five [Boturini owned around 160 of these]. Boturini also owned 12.5% of the recorded Techaloyan manuscripts, 12% of the Testerian manuscripts, and 39% of the Central Mexican prose manuscripts (Glass 1975: 483). In addition to these "ethnohistorical" sources, Boturini also collected a considerable number of historical sources pertaining to other aspects of Mexican history, not least ecclesiastical history, which were not counted in this "ethnohistorical" context.
4 Buriell wrote this to the Valencian intellectual Gregorio Mayans y Siscar in 1746, the year Idea was published. This and all other letters referred to are from the collected correspondences of Mayans y Siscar. I will just refer to the date, and the name of the sender and recipient in the following. The *Epistolario* has been digitalised and is easily searchable
5 In addition to the so-called first *New Science,* from 1725, which Burriel referred to, Vico published extended versions of the *New Science* in 1730 and 1744. Furthermore, an "essay of a new science" had been presented already in 1721, in the second part of the *Diritto Universale.*
6 For instance: "Any full account of Europeans' efforts to assess, describe, and analyse Mexican codices will have to set them in the wider context Cantelli has laid out—and compare them with the same intellectual efforts to deal with the traditions of other "barbarian" nations, like the ancient Egyptians and Chaldeans. This story may provide some intriguing parallels to Mignolo's. It may partly confirm his thesis—one that he develops in what amounts to a dialogue with Jacques Derrida—that Western intellectual, from the Renaissance to the present, have characteristically seen alphabetic writing as the only true form, and codices as the only true books. But the story will have a complexity his lacks, and will suggest a new range of historical questions in its own right: for example, why do the early modern intellectuals who knew something from Greek descriptions about the forms of Egyptian language and scribal culture seem not to have used these as a model for thinking about Indian images and wise men" (Grafton 2001: 91–92).
7 If we compare the two images, we find that the Italian inscription "*Secolo Mexicano*" is placed in the same position as the Spanish translation in Boturini,

"*Siglo de los Americanos*". This phrase is in both cases divided into two by the head of the serpent. We also observe that this division is made just above the glyph representing *tochtli* (which, as we shall see, in the "character" 7 Rabbit Boturini claims "reminds us" of the equinox that took place at the time of the crucifixion).

8 *Idea* and the added catalogue over the museum have separated pagination. When referring to the catalogue I indicate this in the manner done here.

9 It was probably painted between 1550 and 1564 at the request of the Viceroy don Louis de Velasco (and thus slightly later than the tradition placed the apparitions). The map celebrated the role of the Tlaxcaltec, native allies of Cortés, in the conquest of Mexico, and thus had a clear political agenda (Gruzinski 1993: 22).

10 In a letter to a Jesuit in Rome, Father Domingo Torrani, dated July 18, 1738 (Glass 1979: 13 and 1981: 75).

11 Parts of it are, however, transcribed and published in Burrus (1984) and Matute (1976). I use these transcriptions as sources for my discussion.

12 When quoting from the NS, I refer to the different edition by the year of publication, e.g., 1725. The references to these works will be to paragraphs – not pages. It should be noted that the paragraphs have been furnished by later editors and thus did not form part of the manuscripts that Vico saw printed.

13 In the wording of L. Pompa, "Bayle had argued that it would be impossible to understand the history of societies which had no beliefs in common. Vico accepted this claim but was therefore concerned to show that there could be no societies with no beliefs in common, since all was based upon religion. This position is fortified by his further claim that there could be no societies without the institution of marriage and burial of the dead" (Pompa in Vico 2002 (1725): 9, n. 2).

14 Vico himself relates the heroic or poetic character to antonomasia in the following passage from *Diritto universale*: "Ingenious children, because they do not understand the substances of things, describe them by the attributes which fall under their senses. From this ingenuity comes not only emphatic epithets, but also the trite epithets of the poets, and those illustrations which now seem dull to us, in which Homer abounds. ANTANOMASIA: WHENCE HEROIC CHARACT-ERS. From this same source comes antonomasia. In large part, heroic characters were shaped by antonomasia. The fact that all strong men are called Hercules sheds great light on the matters that we are discussing uniform ideas" (Vico 2005: 77)

15 The source seems to be a passage from the fifth chapter of Acosta's *Historia natural y moral* where he treats Mexican and Andean idolatry: 'Porq[ue] en la mayor parte de su adoració[n] y ydolatria se ocupaba en ydolos, y no en las mismas cosas naturales, aunque a los ydolos se atribuyan estos efectos naturales, como de llover, y del Ganado, de la Guerra, de la generación, como los griegos y latinos pusieron también ydolos de Febo, y de Mercurio, y de Júpiter, y de Minerva, y de Marte'" (Acosta 1590: 310).

Bibliography

Anon. [un sacerdote de la Compañia de Jesús.] *Historia de la aparición de la SMA. Virgen María de Guadalupe en México desde el año de MDXXXI al de MDCCCXCV por un sacerdote de la Compañia de Jesús*, vol. 2. 1897. http://www.cervantesvirtual. com/servlet/SirveObras/03691736455715784332268/index.htm

Acosta, J. D. *Historia natural y moral de las Indias*. Impresso en Seuilla, en casa de Iuan de Leon, 1590.

Battistini, A. *Vico tra antichi e moderni*. Bologna: Il mulino, 2004.

Berlin, I. *The Crooked Timber of Humanity: Chapters in the History of Ideas*. London: Murray, 1990.

Berlin, I. *Three Critics of the Enlightenment: Vico, Herder and Haman.* Princeton: Princeton University Press, 2000.

Bernal, I. "The National Museum of Anthropology of Mexico." *Current Anthropology* 7(1966): 320–326.

Boturini Benaduci, L. *Idea de una nueva historia general de América septentrional fundada sobre material copioso de figuras, símbolos, caracteres y jeroglíficos, cantares y manuscritos de autores indios últimamente descubiertos.* Madrid: La imprenta de Juan de Zúñiga, 1746.

Boturini Benaduci, L. *Idea de una nueva historia general de la América Septentrional.* Mexico D. F., Editorial Porrúa, 1974.

Brading, D. A. *Mexican Phoenix: Our Lady of Guadalupe: Image and Tradition across Five Centuries.* Cambridge: Cambridge University Press, 2001.

Burke, P. *Vico.* Oxford: Oxford University Press, 1985.

Burkhart, L. M. "The Cult of the Virgin of Guadalupe in Mexico," in G. H. Gossen and M. Lèon-Portilla (eds.), *South and Mesoamerican Spirituality. From the Cult of the Feathered Serpent to the Theology of Liberation.* New York, Crossroad Publishing Company, 1997.

Burrus, E. J. *Juan Diego and Other Native Benefactors in the Light of Boturini's Research,* Washington, D.C.: Centre for Applied Research in the Apostolate, 1984.

Cañizares-Esguerra, J. *How to Write the History of the New World: Histories, Epistemologies, and Identities in the Eighteenth-Century Atlantic World.* Stanford: Stanford University Press, 2001.

Cantelli, G. "Myth and Language in Vico," in G. D. P. V. Tagliacozzo (ed.), *Giambattista Vico's Science of Humanity.* Baltimore & London: The John Hopkins Press, 1976.

Cantelli, G. *Mente corpo linguaggio.* Firenze: Sansoni, 1986.

Cantelli, G. *Gestualita e mito: i due caratteri distintivi della lingua originaria secondo Vico. Bolletino del Centro di studi vichiani.* Anno XX, 1990.

Carrard, P. *Poetics of the New History: French Historical Discourse from Braudel to Chartier.* Baltimore, Md.: Johns Hopkins University Press, 1992.

Clark, S. "Witchcraft and Magic in Early Modern Culture." in B. Ankarloo et al. (ed.), *Witchcraft and Magic in Europe, vol 4: The Period of the Witch Trials.* Philadelphia: University of Philadelphia Press, 2002.

Davis, K. *Periodization and Sovereignty. How Ideas of Feudalism and Secularization Govern the Politics of Time.* Pennsylvania: Penn University Press, 2012.

Findlen, P. *Possessing Nature: Museums, Collecting, and Scientific Culture in Early Modern Italy.* Berkeley & London: University of California Press, 1994.

Florescano, E. *Memory, Myth, and Time in Mexico: From the Aztecs to Independence.* Austin: University of Texas Press, 1994.

García Ayluardo C. "Historias de papel: los archivos en México," in E. Florescano (ed.), *El patrimonio nacional de México, II.* México D.F.: Fondo de cultura económica, 1997.

Gemelli Careri, G. F. *Viaje a la Nueva España.* México D.F.: UNAM, 1976.

Glass, J. B. "The Boturini Collection," in H. F. Cline (ed.), *Handbook of Middle American Indians,* Vol. 15. Austin, University of Texas Press, 1975.

Glass, J. B. *The Boturini Collection and Text of the Legal Proceedings in Mexico, 1742–1743.* Lincoln Center, Mass.: Conemex Associates, 1979.

Glass, J. B. *The Boturini Collection: The Legal Proceedings and the Basic Inventories, 1742–1745.* Lincoln, Mass.: Conmex Associates, 1981.

Grafton, A. "The Rest vs. the West," in A. Grafton (ed.), *Bring Out Your Dead: The Past as Revelation.* Cambridge, Massachusetts & London: Harvard University Press, 2001.

Gruzinski, S. *The Conquest of Mexico: The Incorporation of Indian Societies Into the Western World, 16th–18th Centuries.* Cambridge: Polity Press, 1993.

Gruzinski, S. *Images at War: Mexico from Columbus to Blade Runner (1492–2019)*. Durham: Duke University Press, 2001.

Horapollo *The Hieroglyphics of Horapollo*. New York: Pantheon Books for Bollingen Foundation, 1950.

Kubler, G. *Esthetic Recognition of Ancient Amerindian Art*. New Haven & London: Yale University Press, 1991.

Mali, J. *The Rehabilitation of Myth: Vico's "New Science"*. Cambridge: Cambridge University Press, 1992.

Matute, A. *Lorenzo Boturini y el pensamiento histórico de Vico*. México D. F.: Universidad Nacional Autónoma de México, Instituto de Investigaciones Históricas, 1976.

Mayans Y Siscar, G. *Mayans y Buriell. Epistolario II*. Valencia: Publicaciones del Ayuntamiento de Oliva, 1972.

Mayans Y Siscar, G. *Obras Completas, Epistolario, Bibliografía*. Madrid: Digibis, 2002. Also on: http://bv2.gva.es/i18n/corpus/unidad.cmd?idUnidad=20000&idCorpus= 20000&posicion=1#gr11

Mignolo, W. D. "On the Colonization of Amerindian Languages and Memories: Renaissance Theories of Writing and the Discontinuity of the Classical Tradition." *Comparative Studies in Society and History* 34 (1992): 301–330.

Mignolo, W. D. *The Darker Side of the Renaissance: Literacy, Territoriality, and Colonization*. Ann Arbor, Mich.: The University of Michigan Press, 1995.

Nebel, R. *Santa María Tonantzin, Virgen de Guadalupe: continuidad y transformación religiosa en México*. México D. F.: Fondo de Cultura Económica, 1995.

Ødemark, J. "Genealogies and Analogies of 'Culture' in the History of Cultural Translation – on Boturini's Translation of Tlaloc and Vico in *Idea of a New General History of Northern America*." *Bulletin of Latin American Research*: 2011: 10.1111/ j.1470-9856.2010.00482.x

Stone, H. S *Vico's Cultural History. The Production and Transmission of Ideas in Naples 1685–1750*. Leiden: Brill, 1997.

Torre Revello, J. "Documentos Relativos a D. Lorenzo Boturini." *Boletín del Archivo General de la Nación*. Mexico D.F., 1936

Trabant, J. *Vico's New Science of Ancient Signs. A study of Sematology*. New York & London: Routledge, 2003.

Vico, G. *"Il diritto universale,"* in F. Nicolini (ed.), *Scrittori d'Italia*, vol. 1-3. Bari, Laterza & Figli, 1936 [1719-1721].

Vico, G. *The New Science of Giambattista Vico*. Ithaca & London: Cornell University Press, 1968 [1744].

Vico, G. *Vico opere,vol. 1–2*, A. Battistini (ed.). Milano: Mondatori Editori, 1990.

Vico, G. *"Principi di una scienza nuova intorno alla natura delle nazioni per la quale si ritrovano i principi de altro sistema del diritto naturale delle genti,"* in A. Battistini (ed.), *Vico opere vol. 2*. Milano: Arnoldo Mondadori Editori, 1990 [1725].

Vico, G. *The First New Science*. Cambridge: Cambridge University Press, 2002 [1725].

Vico, G. "On the Constancy of the Jurisprudent." *New Vico Studies* 23 (2005 [1721])

Wolf, E. R. "The Virgin of Guadalupe: A Mexican National Symbol." *The Journal of American Folklore* 71, no. 279 (1958) (Jan.- Mar., 1958): 34–39.

Part 5

Afterword

Afterword

Some reflections on genre in early modern histories

Daniel Woolf

Historiographically, the years between 1450 and 1800 in Europe might be summarized as the period during which many of the modern genres of historical representation were born, and the adequacy of inherited ones proved wanting in an era of novelty, social change and widening experience. Some of these older genres ultimately proved unable to "keep up" and eventually became the literary equivalent of endangered species.[1] As a prime example one might cite the conventional, annalistically-based chronicle that had served historical writers so well for centuries, and that gradually became the carcass on which would feed newer forms of historical writing such as humanist biography and prose history, and historically-informed dramas such as Shakespeare's.[2] Authors, printers, publishers and especially readers were faced with a bewildering range of works using the word "history" in their titles—not all of which dealt with the past.[3] Some older classical models were revived and adapted to new purpose, while most of the models of historical writing that had flourished through the medieval millennium either gradually fell into desuetude or were transformed so extensively as to be unrecognizable.

Mark Salber Phillips observes in this volume that "Like dog breeds, the progress of the genres has been marked by proliferation leading to new identities". It is not merely the case that new genres of historical representation were added during the early modern centuries (including the late eighteenth-century dramatic tableaux explored by Ina Louisa Stovner, a cross between theater and painting designed to preserve a particular moment for the historical record). Older genres faded, and those that survived from the Middle Ages were themselves transformed to the degree that one may well ask whether it even makes sense to group so many disparate works under the same name. Let us, again, take as one example the "chronicle" which, as mentioned earlier, in 1500 still denoted the dominant medieval form of historical writing; by 1800 the word was well on its way to being associated with one of the genres that its early modern printed specimens had spawned, the newspaper, "today" rather than "last year" now being the temporal unit for which readers sought information (the name lingers on in newspapers and organizational publications such as the *Chronicle of Higher Education* that many North American academics read daily). "Annals" could denote both the chronological organizational structure within

DOI: 10.4324/9781003331971-19

chronicles, but the word also a denoted a respected form of humanist political or ecclesiastical history (William Camden's *Annales* of the reign of Elizabeth I comes to mind, the model for which was Tacitus' *Annales*, or Cesare Baronio's *Annales Ecclesiastici*) and which might or might not follow a strict year-by year pattern. ("*Annales*" lives on, too, in academic journals such as the prestigious periodical founded in 1929 by Marc Bloch and Lucien Febvre). The annalistic form as a means to record mundane and seemingly trivial events did not vanish entirely—manuscript examples can be found in local and family archives.[4] A year-by-year organizational scheme remained useful to those writing epitomes, handbooks, chronologies, almanacs and the myriad specimens of informational *vade mecum*. But as a living, publishable genre, the chronicle increasingly seemed an archaism, derided by humanist historians for credulity and poor style, its vernacular urban sub-genre satirized by the likes of Thomas Nashe as the detritus of "lay chronigraphers, that write of nothing but of mayors and sheriefs, and the dere yere, and the great frost".[5] Indeed, as an umbrella category, the chronicle is a perfect illustration of the view that genres are only truly identifiable as such when they are alluded to, quoted from, stylized and even parodied in other genres.[6]

In contrast to the annalistic chronicle, "Universal history", among the most ancient and protean of genres with roots as far back as a lost history by Ephorus (fourth century BC) survived and thrived, now with a confessional-ideological aspect occasioned by the splintering of Christianity. But by the time Göttingen scholars such as J.C. Gatterer (whose interest in the emerging "ancillary disciplines" of history such as diplomatic did not inhibit his taking a larger view of the *nexus rerum universalis*) penned their own entries, the universal history had re-transformed once again, and to such a degree that it would be difficult to say that this was the same genre envisaged by sixteenth-century writers such as Johannes Sleidan or Johann Carion,[7] never mind that of the many medieval and ancient histories and chronicles aspiring to "universal" coverage.[8] The indirect ancestor of today's Global or World History, and even the currently fashionable "Big" History (which really is "universal" in a literal sense),[9] universal history eventually ceased to be the mainly religiously framed, theologically-heavy polemical genre it had become between Lutheran Sleidan and Gallican Bossuet.[10] It evolved into the more comprehensive, secular work of the sort written by the English compilers of the *Universal History*,[11] Johann Andreas Fabricius' *Abriss einer allgemeinen Historie der Gelehrsamkeit* (tr: "*Outline of a General History of Scholarship*", 1752–54), or the German Johan Ludwig Levin Gebhardi's *Allgemeine Welthistorie* (studied here by Håkon Evju), the last a work that itself underwent further transformations as it was adapted for northern readers by Scandinavian translators.

Universal history had a close cousin in ecclesiastical history. Often equated somewhat inaccurately with the broader category of "sacred history" (the holy counterpart of "profane" or sometimes "civil" history) of which it was really a sub-branch, ecclesiastical history originated with Eusebius and Julius Africanus and was practiced subsequently by the likes of Sozomen and Bede, and thence through the Middle Ages.[12] As a late antique genre without classical precedent, it was "imperfectly grafted onto secular history and the history of nations". Ecclesiastical history, taken strictly as the history of the Christian church, fractured along confessional lines in the early sixteenth century and spawned sub-genres such as both Catholic and Protestant martyrologies, and greater attention to matters of truth and evidence as one side tried to steal a march on the other. But despite the disappearance of consensus, and of a concurrent increase in historical skepticism,[13] the "chronogeographic grip" of its parent category, sacred history, remained formidable as a constraint on thought about the past, and about matters of time, evidence and periodization, through and beyond the Enlightenment.[14] Its best known early modern examples include Bossuet's 1681 *Discours sur l'histoire universelle*, a hybrid mixture of universal history, theology and sacred history in an Augustinian mode, which was reissued many times in the nineteenth century, and through such works as this, and colonial examples such as Cotton Mather's protonationalist *Magnalia Christi Americana* (1702) sacred history endured as a grand category or super-genre.[15]

Hagiography, the microhistorical counterpart to ecclesiastical history, too survived, though under the greater scrutiny imposed by a rising tide of incredulity toward the miraculous, combined with a desire to provide naturalist explanations for seemingly abnormal events. But it required buttressing through the efforts of critical scholars, the Bollandists through the *Acta Sanctorum*. The *gesta* (which dealt with secular rulers but also overlapped with both ecclesiastical history and hagiography in its coverage of prelates' dual roles as princes and priests) evolved into the classically crafted "Lives and Reigns" genre that memorialized Renaissance rulers. The celebratory tone of both, replete with *gloire et piété*, thrives today in such unlikely remote descendants as the modern corporate history, with its apotheosis of far-seeing and noble founders. The money-changers really have taken over this one-time temple.[16]

*

With the exception of the nineteenth century, which built the professional codes and apparatus (history departments, graduate schools, national archives, academic journals) that rule over Clio's domain today, no period in the history of history has been more transformative than that between 1450 and 1800. The historiographical universe was vastly more complex, multi-faceted and multi-genred by the end of the period than it had been at the start, and this complexity was accompanied by, and indeed driven by, a high degree of social, intellectual and cultural disorder. The reasons for this are themselves multiple, and no single cause can be singled out for primacy. The printing press made more copies of books, new and old, available, but it did not on its own create new genres since authors could simply have added new specimens of the medieval chronicle, and indeed they did so right through the sixteenth century. Humanism is justly credited with re-introducing ancient poetics and classical models from which early modern historians could draw, and an attendance to accuracy in textual rendition, but without print the "neoclassical" history would have had a limited audience. Increased literacy, the child of both these parents, created a much greater market for all sorts of works, historical among them, as did social stratification, with a middling sort of reader soon no longer content with limited choice. This in turn inspired the creation of further vehicles for the dissemination of historical information such as the periodical essay, discussed here by Claire Boulard Jouslin, and the "small historical writings" of Niels Ditlev Riegels, examined by Emil Nicklas Johnsen, which were often written with a satirical or moral purpose; both played a critical role in expanding history's penetration of a wider public sphere.

One cannot ignore a host of intellectual and epistemological developments from humanism to reformed theology. Skepticism and doubt, stimulated by religious conflict and changes in the understanding of the workings of nature, undoubtedly played a part in genre-change, even if this has been overstated. When combined with social and educational differentiation, disbelief had the effect of pushing oral forms of historical discourse, and local, popular beliefs about the past, into the margins, displacing them within learned culture with the written and printed. (Though exceptions such as James Macpherson's pseudo-Ossianic poems could still excite interest in the new, sentimental reader of the eighteenth century.)[17] The most notable late seventeenth-century example of historical skepticism (though not pyrrhonism), the Protestant Pierre Bayle's *Dictionnaire historique et critique* (first published in1697) was itself part of an emerging genre, the historical encyclopedia or dictionary, and was intended initially to correct errors in other such works such as the much-circulated and translated *Le Grand Dictionnaire historique* (first edition 1674) by the Catholic priest Louis Moréri.[18]

There can be little doubt that pure politics affected history also. Previously an occasional tool of the aristocracy and nascent central monarchies in the Middle Ages, became more decisively a vehicle for the establishment and maintenance of state power and pride. Officially sanctioned secular histories had not enjoyed a great deal of prominence in medieval Europe (at least in comparison, say, with China's elaborate Tang Dynasty-established Historiographical Office). There were some late medieval exceptions such those produced by Aragonese and Catalan kings and, at a slightly greater remove, the chronicles of Saint-Denis and their successor, the *Grandes Chroniques de France*),[19] but the genre had surged in the Renaissance as rulers grasped with Orwellian clarity the immense power to be derived from control over perceptions of the past. Italian city-states and national monarchies alike paid prestigious humanist scholars and, ultimately lesser professional writers such as the somewhat unsavory, and factually cavalier, satirist and biographer Gregorio Leti of Milan to provide panegyrical accounts of their regimes (it seems likely that in some cases, such individuals were paid *not* to write about them).[20] Official history's dark twin was the scurrilous "secret history" that leaked lascivious details of the private lives of the high and mighty into the public sphere. This was an early modern revival of an older genre whose late antique archetype was Procopius' salacious *Anekdota.*[21] Both reader tastes and epistemic authority could wax and wane: "court history", something of a hybrid between official histories of kingdoms and secret histories, traversing the concourse between the private and the public spheres, was well regarded through the eighteenth century but would lose favor by the mid-nineteenth (though studies of royal and imperial courts have enjoyed something of a comeback in recent decades, as Sebastian Olden Jørgensen reminds us in his chapter).

Reactions to works of princely propaganda were eventually also engendered in a kind of dialectical chain reaction as historical controversy, once rare, became for the first time a defining feature of historiography, with *ad hominem* charges of bias and partiality furnishing polemicists with a blunt cudgel with which to smite erring foes.[22] Not merely new specimens of history but entirely novel forms of it occupied both European courts and the public sphere; and dissent from orthodox master narratives, initially found primarily in religious dispute, had by the mid-eighteenth century begun to address perceived deficiencies in the social and political order, in the hands of philosophes and exiles. This particular politicization and polemicization illustrates especially well what Carolyn Miller has called (and Anne Eriksen has taken up in her chapter herein) the phenomenon of "genre as social action", whereby new forms of writing were invented to meet real-life "exigence".[23] Intellectual and epistemological values such as "impartiality", the early modern counterpart to modern notions of "objectivity", rubbed uncomfortably against the reality of a religiously and politically divided Europe whose regimes and their critics alike saw the past as a useful cudgel. Finally, the widening of European horizons both east and west had a profound effect, not merely because historians had to explain the existence of native peoples previously unimagined, but because it exposed Europeans to the very different forms of historicity practiced by so-called savage or barbarian peoples in Latin America,[24] and by very ancient traditions of historical writing practiced in both South and East Asia; this influenced historical thought in Europe and occasioned mixed, Creole genres of history in the colonies.

It would be a fool's errand to assign primacy to any single one of these factors; together, however, they overdetermined both the blooming, buzzing confusion of genres and the efforts of scholars, bibliographers and booksellers to reduce this to some sort of order. Michel Foucault's *The Order of Things* found in the seventeenth and eighteenth centuries an episteme that was "classical" in the sense of ordering and differentiating the phenomenal world. That included imposing order on the past and the forms used to represent it. Analogies with our own time risk oversimplification and cast limited light on the past, but the earliest centuries of the printed word saw some of the frenetic energy and creative chaos that has marked the first three decades of the internet. In both cases, the availability of knowledge expanded, and the means of distributing it exploded. Issues of censorship, power and credibility have been important in both periods, as have decisions around how to impose rules and principles. In the early modern era, governments and churches struggled in vain to hold back the tide of unapproved works through various agencies of censorship, while they used historians to create positive narratives of their own origins. Nowadays the task is mainly one of sorting unverified nonsense from truth in the ocean of material available on the web, though we know all too well that censorship still exists whether through the direct involvement of authoritarian regimes or the risk of "cancellation" by the extremes of left and right.

If one prefers a slightly less contemporary comparison, the business of knowledge and information in the early modern centuries can be regarded as a kind of epistemic and generic Wild West, initially with few rules and little enforcement, gradually settling into a tamer phase by the eighteenth century, with academies and literary critics the town marshals of the republic of letters. As a field of enquiry and a form of literary writing, history was no exception. The nineteenth century would prove important in the development of *method* (in an empirical, research-oriented sense early modern users of that term such as Jean Bodin would not have recognized) and in the final taming, disciplining and "desublimating" of history into its modern academically-dominated profession with rules, institutions and informal codes of conduct. The transition to industrial-level printing in the nineteenth-century would turn the expanded early modern readership of history for the first time into a mass market.[25] While much of the work of multiplying and creating new modes of historical representation was done by Renaissance and subsequent authors, it has continued down to our time. Nietzsche was not wrong in commenting on the sterility of mainstream historical works (and especially the thinking behind them), which he famously reduced to three, monumental, antiquarian and critical, at the end of the nineteenth century, but he neglected the notable experimentation that still occurred, for instance in his friend Jacob Burckhardt's plotless, impressionistic representation of the *Civilization of the Renaissance* in Italy, Henry Adams's nostalgic *Mont Saint Michel and Chartres*, or, earlier, Chateaubriand's mixture of the private and public in his *Mémoires d'outre-tombe*, and what Bonnie G. Smith has termed, in the case of Germaine de Staël, a "narcotic road to the past".[26] In the past hundred years still others have appeared such as microhistory, and we appear to be in a new state of disorder, a combination of the digital environment and the influences of both postmodernism and postcolonialism.

*

As the chapters in this book show, early modern genres remained fluid and permeable. Authors and their books pushed back against the efforts of cataloguers and authors of *ars historica* to impose rules; classical guidelines were increasingly honored in the breach rather than the observance, even in the face of a conscious return to classicism in the late seventeenth century.[27]

Form and content were often in tension as both Europeans and settler cultures struggled to find ways to write history that was up to Renaissance levels of eloquence, increasing degrees of erudition and the expectations of an audience that, apart from aristocratic, gentle and merchant/craftsman readers, now increasingly included women, whose own contributions as authors to the genres of history have been underrated.[28] J.G.A. Pocock's mammoth study of Gibbon's *Decline and Fall of the Roman Empire* brilliantly demonstrated how Enlightenment-era authors continually had to make compromises that undercut genre-rules in order to integrate material that "belonged" in other genres. What sort of thing was Giannone's *Dell'istoria civile del regno di Napoli* (1723), or, two generations later, Möser's 1768 *Osnabrückische Geschichte*? Was Gibbon's book a work of civil history or ecclesiastical, given the attention it paid to the role of Christianity? Did Mosheim's *Ecclesiastical History* (a major source for Gibbon) really have much in common with its same-named medieval antecedents? And where did Voltaire's *Siècle de Louis XIV* figure, an early example of the new *histoire des moeurs* or cultural history that was no more limited to the life of its titular king than, two centuries later, Fernand Braudel's *La Mediterranée* would be confined to that of Philip II.

Conjectural history, devoted to triangulating human social progress in the absence of direct evidence, through comparison with ancient sources and contemporary missionary and travel literature, entered the field in the eighteenth century, as also did works that were manifestly historical but not so-styled by their authors. These included Vico's *Scienza Nuova*, an initially neglected masterpiece silently used (we would now say plagiarized, but such borrowing was more freely practiced in earlier ages) in the antiquary and historian Lorenzo Boturini's *Idea de una nueva historia general de America septentrional*, well before Vico's "rediscovery" by Herder and Michelet.[29] As "polite and commercial" values displaced martial and religious ones in the eighteenth century, and major trading companies such as the Dutch East India Company and its British counterpart became major instruments of colonial expansion, histories of commerce and trade also appeared, such as Schlözer's 1758 *Essay on the General History of Trade and of Seafaring in the Most Ancient Times* (written during his Swedish sojourn). Sometimes, as with Raynal's multi-authored *Histoire philosophique des deux Indes*, these entered the lists against the depredations of colonialism.[30] One could argue, in fact, that the very need to subvert canons of genre in the name of exigency proved a creative force that operated to prevent history from entirely falling into that very torpor that so badly vexed Nietzsche.

Given all this, one might well ask what exactly *is* a "genre" when one is speaking of writing (or other forms of representation) about the past? It is common to think of "history" *tout court* as constituting a single genre, but that won't really do. If one is at all concerned with matters of form, language and content, to say nothing of scope, then this is a gross misuse of the term—about as helpful as grouping all manners of prose fiction writing together as "novels". While we can credit our early modern predecessors with greatly expanding the types of history written, to say nothing of their numbers, we can also admire their ultimately quixotic efforts to preserve a sense of *historia* as constituting a unified and orderly genre with clearly distinguishable sub-branches. In fact, the very attempts by *ars historica* authors or *trattatisti* from Francesco Patrizzi, Jean Bodin, Sebastián Fox-Morcillo and Henri de la Popelinière, through Francis Bacon, G.J. Vossius and Agostino Mascardi, all the way to Nicolas Lenglet Dufresnoy,[31] did exactly the opposite of what those authors intended. It established that *historia* was profoundly heteroglossic; that its meaning was perpetually malleable; and that its sub-categories could be sliced and diced in various ways depending on chronological scope, subject and narrative organization. Inheritors as they were of classical definitions, these would-be lawgivers sought to include the study of the natural world within history's embrace—not unreasonably given its original, Herodotean sense of "inquiry", "research" or "investigation". Natural history museums are a modern artifact of that usage, as are the medical "histories" that doctors record concerning their patients. The historical approaches to geological and biological change of Cuvier, Lyell and Darwin would reinforce the notion of nature as something to be studied along temporal lines, though most modern biologists or geologists would not self-identify primarily as "natural historians". And we haven't yet mentioned manifestly fictional or only loosely verisimilar "histories" such as the chapbook "pleasant histories" or *Bibliothèque bleue* titles that circulated in England and France,[32] or early novels considered "histories" of a fictional sort, such as Henry Fielding's *Tom Jones* or the Jesuit José Francisco de Isla's *Historia del famoso predicador fray Gerundio de Campazas, alias Zotes.*

The authors of the *ars historica* had always had to wear multiple hats, as classifiers of historical texts, critics of past and recent writers of history, debunkers of myth, clarifiers of periodization, chronology and biblical history, digesters of historical knowledge and excavators of useful lessons from the past. It was a highly adaptable genre in its own right, and successfully self-transformed over the course of three centuries, its first, Renaissance phase peaking with the publication of the 1579 compendium entitled *Artis Historicae Penus*. Its late seventeenth- and eighteenth-century practitioners from René Rapin and Pierre Le Moyne to Peter Whalley and Joseph Priestley reflected the interests of readers in shifting the emphasis of the genre away from classification and method (in that word Renaissance, primarily pedagogical or "how to study" sense) and more heavily toward its other features: conjecture and speculation (or what first Voltaire and later Hegel, in their strikingly different ways, called "philosophy of history"); the instruction of future leaders in the lessons of history as in the case of Bolingbroke's famous *Letters*; and judgment of the literary and scholarly merits of histories old and new.[33] But in the end the *ars historica* finally ran out of steam in the early eighteenth century primarily because the impossibility of covering all the forms of history in a way that reflected the complexities and size of the print universe had finally become inescapable. A leading indicator of this may be found in the multiplication of terms generated to label variants and sub-variants: for instance la Popelinière's *histoire accomplie* or "perfect history" or Vossius' *historia justa* (a sub-category of "civil history" virtually identical to what Vossius termed "memoriae" or history proper, but with philosophic consideration of "causes" added in).[34]

In sum, by 1700 there simply existed a much more complicated knowledge-universe, and a more diverse readership, than had been the case in the mid-sixteenth century when specimens of historical writing were also considerably more limited and the historical works of the ancients dominated. While some contributions to the genre such as the Oxford praelector Degory Wheare's 1623 *De Ratione et Methodo Legendi Historias* (a work spun off from this first Camden Professor's lectures on the minor Roman historian Lucius Florus), endured in reprints and translations into the next century, the old task of sorting and sifting histories into self-contained genres was increasingly a thankless dead end, "the incoherence at the heart of [which] matched the incoherence in historians' practice", Anthony Grafton has remarked. By 1766 at the latest, the *ars historica* itself was just as dead.[35] The need to keep knowledge as a whole—vastly expanded into the grand category of "erudition" embracing both the human/moral and natural worlds—did not go away, of course, but newer genres such as the *historia literaria*, along with countless encyclopedias, periodicals and emerging scholarly journals, now took up the task.[36]

Building on theories first outlined by Mikhail Bakhtin, John Frow has remarked that the novel is "more like a fusion of other genres than a genre in its own right" while pointing also to the intertextuality of genres: they are constituted in relation to one another.[37] For "novel" we can substitute "history" and conclude that it is best regarded not as a distinctive, enclosed genre with subdivisions or sub-genres but rather as a boundary-less and non-delimited set of types of work, in oral, written, material or visual form, concerning the past (another term the singularity of which is now in doubt as we pluralize everything including "pasts", "modernities" and "truths") in all its manifestations. This helps to make sense of what early modern Europeans—and eventually non-Europeans, who by the end of the nineteenth century would embrace Western modes of historicity either through colonization or voluntary adoption—thought they were doing when writing, telling, singing, painting or performing what they deemed to be true stories about the past. In fact, although we speak of genres having originated in governing texts such as Aristotle's *Poetics*, no early modern writer to my knowledge actually used the word "genre" to describe historical work, and it was not current in a literary sense before the late eighteenth century. Derived, as this book's co-editors note, from the Latin *genus*, "genre" appears as early as the 1549 edition of Robert Estienne's *Dictionnaire françoislatin* and Randle Cotgrave's 1611 *A Dictionarie of the French and English* Tongues, but in neither of these cases was the term applied to literary works; it simply denoted a "sort" or "kind".[38]

Formal use of "genre" as a key term to classify art, music and literature—including history—is a modern, not an early modern, invention.

That does not, of course, prevent us from using the word and the concept it signifies to make sense of past historical representation, or any other aesthetic endeavor. But Aristotle's hiving off of history from poetry was not especially useful even in his own day when, apart from the fourth-century successors of Herodotus and Thucydides (many, like Ephorus, long since lost), there were likely still extant the works of the Atthidographers, horographers and logographers, especially among the last group Hecataeus of Miletus in whose work geography and history blended in ways that subsequent writers (for most of whom Hecataeus was known only through fragments) would find useful. In fact, many of the earliest European historical authors were unconcerned by boundaries either between works organized by place vs time, an indifference that frequently extended to the marches between fact and fiction, despite the more determined efforts of Thucydides and others to erect a wall between the two.[39] That has also been true of other societies that first engaged with the non-mythical past, including those of East and Southeast Asia and pre-Mughal India and Sri Lanka.[40]

If we abandon the use of genre to enclose "history" in the broadest sense, then it becomes possible, as in this volume, to talk of genres, and sub-genres, within the set of all historical works, that exhibit certain common features. But the commonality of those features is as much in the eye of the reader as the author: we see early modern works in different relations to one another than do those who wrote or read them at the time. As Anne Helness argues in her chapter, a case can be made for deeming the compilations of travel accounts, such as Giovanni Battista Ramusio's *Navigationi et viaggi*, that began to appear in the sixteenth century, as constituting a distinct historical genre (in their peculiar combination of "empirical" material and editorial comment), though perhaps not one that contemporaries would have recognized as such. So, arguably, could "histories of the orient" of the sort written by the Danish civil servant Georg Høst (who, Svein Atle Skålevåg reminds us in his chapter, never self-identified as a historian). These flourished in the eighteenth century, increasing knowledge of the pasts of exotic realms at the same time that they helped to create the Orientalist discourse from which both West and East now struggle to extricate themselves. Indeed, the chapters of this book, *in toto*, demonstrate that historical works can fit into multiple genres at the same time: the category of "pragmatic history" (more an approach to the uses of the past than a genre in its own right) appears in the present book within chapters ostensibly on different topics. Genre is as much a consequence of historiographical *purpose* as it is of aesthetic or subject-matter decisions. I shall return to this point in the following.

But perhaps these combinations and re-combinations of works into different groupings are best regarded as over-lapping sub-sets of works rather than as formal, self-contained genres. It was all very well for early modern theorists—the *ars historica* authors among them but also various writers announcing their intent in prologues and dedications—to declare rules for this or that type of history, but in practice, it rarely worked out. Renaissance English writers insisted, well into the seventeenth century, that *history* was exclusively a narrative that was neither an old chronicle (archaic form, written by Catholics, credulous, and in bad prose, according to its humanist critics) nor a new antiquarian work. "Chorography" (a word loosely related, in its denotation of local descriptions with historical content, to the Greek horography) was a classification borrowed very loosely from antiquity to embrace the kind of itinerant antiquarian study that became popular in the late sixteenth century, as authors such as William Camden explicitly disavowed the title of historian while paradoxically writing works such as the *Britannia* (1586) a book that, from our point of view, was manifestly a work of historical scholarship, even without a narrative/chronological spine.[41] In this, Camden was reflecting the Renaissance division between history and erudition that Arnaldo Momigliano would not fully bridge till the eighteenth century, with writers such as Francis Bacon regarding antiquities as the mere "vestiges or "remnants" of time.[42] Camden's later-life *Annales*, by contrast, was announced as a history, but even then with hedges and narrowings of scope; Camden defended his choice of model by associating the *Annales* not only with ancient greats such as Polybius but with the contemporary French work he had been commissioned to combat, Jacques-Auguste de Thou's *Historiarum sui temporis*. De Thou's work itself was a recent addition to the growing genre, dating back to Commynes and Guicciardini, of "contemporary history", composed by participants in or close observers of recent events, and concerned as much with the present as the past, anticipating eighteenth-century pragmatic history. And among Camden's other writings, his survey of Westminster Abbey monuments with which Angus Vine's chapter commences, was something else again—a *sui generis* composition without as yet a sub-genre to which it could comfortably be assigned. Meanwhile in contemporary France, as the work of George Huppert, Donald R. Kelley and others has demonstrated, like-minded scholars such as Etienne Pasquier used more neutral terms (in his case *Recherches*) to permit open-ended exploration of his country's past.[43] Within a century or so after, these vestiges and fragments of pastness were certainly seen as belonging firmly within the historian's sphere—Gibbon, Momigliano tells us, successfully bridging the triad of erudite, philosophic and civil history. But even then there remained countervailing efforts to distinguish between substance and style, researcher and writer: Voltaire's distinction between the ideal, discerning *historien* and the useful but merely assistive *historiographe*, a researcher or compiler, is a well-known but scarcely unique expression of this sentiment. Hume might have respected Catharine Macaulay's herculean account of seventeenth-century history despite their political differences, but he had little patience for the time she spent digging up materials, while across the channel so prominent a mind as Jean d'Alembert similarly saw erudition as at best a first step on the road to philosophic history.[44]

By the eighteenth century, if not sooner, the discomfiture of efforts to classify was evident in the labors of cataloguers, both librarians who had to decide where to shelve particular titles (hampered further of course by the fact that in books as in other spheres of human activity, size matters) and the auction sale organizers who wrestled with the designation of works of ecclesiastical history under "history" or "divinity"—and this despite the efforts of European historians to raise historical narrative up to the marks of elegance and gravitas set by Thucydides and Tacitus. The problems were apparent as early as the pioneering work of library science, Gabriel Naudé's 1627 *Advice on Establishing a Library*, which firmly endorsed arrangement by subject, and included history as a primary division alongside medicine, jurisprudence, theology, philosophy, mathematics and "humanities". Naudé gives little counsel on subdivisions within these subjects beyond suggesting that "the most universal and ancient always take precedence", and he stuck works of primarily religious history, such as the protestant *Magdeburg Centuries* with theological and polemical "works of the most learned and famous heretics".[45] By this time, too, history had even overflowed the confines of verbal representation to become not just one, but *the* hegemonic form of painting (see Mark Salber Phillips' chapter), and it found visual and tactile representation in monuments, ruins, virtuoso cabinets and collections of exotica such as Lorenzo Boturini's confiscated *Museo historico indiano*, the subject of John Ødemark's chapter.

The assorted different types of historical representation that emerged from early modern Europe can, in short, be called genres only in a relatively loose sense. Yet, "loose sense" does not mean "no sense". Genre remains a useful concept if we accept the following cautions going in: 1) that it is more often than not a retrospectively imposed grouping of a set of "similar" instances of historical writing—Aristotle and even the *ars historica* writers were writing as much descriptively and retrospectively as they were prescriptively and prospectively; and 2) that "similar" can be defined along multiple different dimensions including but not limited to the ten sketched very tentatively in the following:

- Subject: e.g., human, non-human
- Language: (e.g., "the English history play" "the Latin chronicle")
- Form: e.g., verse, prose, iconic (for instance Mesoamerican history paintings), analogic
- Chronotopical context: common time and place or creation; or alternately creation in comparable situations but different times and places
- Primary axis of arrangement: chronological/geographical/alphabetical/ genealogical
- Scope: focused or comprehensive; individual or collective
- Scale: biographical, local, national, regional, global, universal
- medium: graphical (manuscript and print), material (sculpture, architecture, painting, tapestry), performative (ballad, drama [including history plays], oral tradition and the *tableaux* featured in Ina Louise Stovner's essay in the present volume)

- social purpose/motive (or to use Carolyn R. Miller's terms, "exigence" or "the action it is used to accomplish"):[46] polemical; pragmatic; situational; satirical; commercial; informational and educational
- Verisimilitude or mimetic quality: novels; secret histories, romances vs "real" history so-called and so on.

There is no space here to explicate further these dimensions, and rhetoricians and literary theorists could doubtless add others to the list. The point is simply that any work that purported to represent the past between 1500 and 1800 (and before and after those years) can be analyzed and categorized differently depending on which of these criteria we prioritize and in what order. The compilers who worked from other historians' writings rather than practicing their own erudition, such as Ludvig Holberg, could not have cared less what "genre" their sources fell into so long as they were by creditable authors and provided clear information—though they likely had preferences as to the sorts of history they owned, as Holberg's lack of ecclesiastical history in his own library, recounted here by Thomas Ewen Daltveit Slettebø, suggests. In the very act of compiling, a task as unappreciated by the eighteenth century as chronicling had become a century or so earlier, such authors were obliged to prioritize the story that they wished to tell, and their own resulting works formed yet another (loose) genre; as Slettebø observes, derision simply made them innovate and adapt, "re-branding their role and refashioning their image". Others similarly borrowed from genres ostensibly at some distance: consider, from Eriksen's chapter, the mid-eighteenth century Danish vicar Christian Grawe's "poem with footnotes", an erudite parish history that built on a relatively recent tradition of combining verse and scholarship, something the Englishman Michael Drayton had done, in combination with the philologist and lawyer John Selden in the early seventeenth-century poetical chorography, *Poly-Olbion*.[47]

*

Throughout the period covered by this book, new genres of historical representation came into vogue, and older ones suffered and fell out of favor, just as the chronicle had done earlier—casualties as much of social as intellectual snobbery. The increasing social stratification of the reading population, and the emergence of the "public sphere", ensured that there was a history book for every type of reader, and a type of reader for nearly every book. Although the marketplace and the self-interest of publishers and printers could and did spell success or failure for individual authors (such as N.D. Riegels, the "mad dog" radical Dane and would-be "secret history" purveyor in Olden Jørgensen's and Johnsen's chapters) it did little to prune the bookshelves of entire forms. Unlike the discredited medieval chronicle—no longer a living "genre" but an artifact or "source",[48] disdain from academicians and critics rarely occasioned the complete disappearance of a new genre of history. If "history" had ever been a single genre of the sort described by

Aristotle (something doubtful even in his own time), the early modern centuries had fragmented and re-fragmented it in all the ways, and more, that this collection of essays has illustrated. We late-modern/post-modern scholars wrestle with challenges to the foundations of knowledge, with massive changes to its location and representation, and with the continuing fission of historiographic fields into ever smaller subfields, the literary outputs of which constitute even newer genres. We should sympathize with the anxieties of our early modern predecessors facing similar quandaries.

Notes

1 Nor is Europe unique in this regard during the same centuries. In much of India, for instance, "no single genre was allotted to history writing", while China maintained through the Ming and Qing dynasties a system of highly formalized genres for the organization and classification of writings about the past: see respectively Velcheru Narayana Rao, David D. Shulman, and Sanjay Subrahmanyam, *Textures of Time: Writing History in South India 1600-1800* (Delhi: Permanent Black, 2001), p. 4 (for quotation); Harbans Mukhia, *Historians and Historiography During the Reign of Akbar* (New Delhi: Vikas, 1976); On-cho Ng and Q. Edward Wang, *Mirroring the Past: The Writing and Use of History in Imperial China* (Honolulu: University of Hawaii Press, 2005).

2 D.R. Woolf, "Genre into Artifact: the Decline of the English Chronicle in the Sixteenth Century", *Sixteenth Century Journal* 19.3 (1988), 321–54. See also further in the present chapter.

3 See especially Gianna Pomata and Nancy G. Siraisi (eds), *Historia: Empiricism and Erudition in Early Modern Europe* (Cambridge, MA: MIT Press, 2005); Arno Seifert, *Cognitio Historica: Die Geschichte als Namengeberin der frühneuzeitlichen Empirie* (Berlin: Duncker und Humblot (1976); Anthony Grafton, *What was History? The Art of History in Early Modern Europe* (Cambridge: Cambridge University Press, 2007).

4 For English examples see D.R. Woolf, *Reading History in Early Modern England* (Cambridge: Cambridge University Press, 2000), 57–78.

5 *Works of Thomas Nashe*, ed. R.B. McKerrow (London: Bullen, 1904), I: 194.

6 John Frow, *Genre* (London: Routledge, 2005), 44–45.

7 Karen Skovgaard-Petersen, "Carion's chronicle in sixteenth century Danish historiography", *Symbolae Osloenses*, 73.1 (2010), 158–167; Alexandra Kess, *Johann Sleidan and the Protestant Vision of History* (Aldershot: Ashgate, 2008); on the universal history as a source of advice in statecraft, see Uwe Neddermeyer, "Darümb sollen die historien billich fürsten warden sein un genennet warden: Universalhistorische Werke als Ratgeber der Fürsten im Mittelalter und in der frühen Neuzeit", in Chantal Grell, Werner Paravicini, and Jürgen Voss (eds), *Les princes et l'histoire du XIVe au XVIIIe siècle* (Bonn: Bouvier, 1998), 67–108.

8 J.M. Alonso-Núñez, *The Idea of Universal History in Greece from Herodotus to the Age of Augustus* (Amsterdam: J.C. Gieben, 2002); Michele Campopiano and Henry Bainton (eds), *Universal Chronicles in the High Middle Ages* (Woodbridge, Suffolk, UK: York Medieval Press, 2017); Raoul Mortley, *The Idea of Universal History from Hellenistic Philosophy to Early Christian Historiography* (Lewiston, NY: Edwin Mellen, 1996); Andrew Fear and Peter Liddell (eds), *Historiae Mundi* (London: Duckworth, 2010); Hall Bjørnstad, Anne Régent-Susini, and Helge Jordheim (eds), *Universal History and the Making of the Global* (London: Routledge, 2017).

9 David Christian, *Maps of Time: an Introduction to Big History* (Berkeley: University of California Press, 2005); Fred Spier, *Big History and the Future of Humanity* (Chichester, UK and Malden, MA: Wiley-Blackwell, 2010); Ian Hesketh, A History of Big History (Cambridge: Cambridge University Press, 2023), forthcoming.

10 The degree of secularization should not be overstated: writers of *Weltgeschichte* from Gatterer to Ranke did not abandon the Christian assumptions that had first given rise to the genre in the Middle Ages, and confessional interests, Protestant and Catholic, were never far from the surface; perhaps de-theologization, though ungainly, is a more accurate term.

11 Guido Abbattista, "The Business of Pater-Noster Row: Towards a Publishing History of the *Universal History* (1736–1765) *Publishing History* 17 (1985): 5–50; Tamara Griggs, "Universal History from Counter-Reformation to Enlightenment", *Modern Intellectual History*, 4.2 (2007): 219–247.

12 A comprehensive survey of ecclesiastical history from late antiquity to the seventeenth century may be found in Peter Meinhold, *Geschichte der Kirchlichen Historiographie*, 2 vols (Freiburg and Munich: Verlag Karl Alber, 1967)For sacred history during the Renaissance, and the degree to which it overlapped with other genres such as national and regional history, see Katherine van Liere, Simon Ditchfield and Howard Louthan (eds), *Sacred History: Uses of the Christian Past in the Renaissance World* (Oxford: Oxford University Press, 2012).

13 The impact of historical skepticism, especially in its more extreme forms such as Pyrrhonism, may have been over-rated, or at least used as to much of a catch-all explanation of intellectual, including historiographic change in this period. In contrast to classic studies such as Richard H. Popkin's *The History of Skepticism from Erasmus to Spinoza* (Berkeley: University of California Press, 1979), see Dmitri Levitin, *The Kingdom of Darkness: Bayle, Newton, and the emancipation of the European mind from philosophy* (Cambridge: Cambridge University Press, 2022), 16, 229.

14 Daniel Lord Smail, "Genealogy, Ontology, and the Narrative Arc of Origins", *French Historical Studies* 34.1 (2011): 21–35, at 25; idem, "In the Grip of Sacred History", *American Historical Review* 110 (2005): 1337–1361.

15 J.-B. Bossuet, *Discourse on Universal History*, trans. E. Forster and ed. Orest Ranum (Chicago: University of Chicago Press, 1976). As Ranum points out in his introduction (p xviii) to this edition, Bossuet's choice of "discourse" rather than "history" freed Bossuet "from the tyranny of conventions established for the genre of universal history". For examples of nineteenth- and early twentieth-century affirmations of sacred history, defying geological and evolutionary science, see Smail, "Grip of Sacred History", 1347–48. For Mather's work, and its complexity, see most recently Jerome McGann, "From Cultural Memory to Living Word: On Mather's *Magnalia*", New Literary History 50.2 (2019), 171–95.

16 Agnès Delahaye et al, "The Genre of Corporate History", *Journal of Organizational Change Management* 22.1 (2009): 27–48, at p. 36.

17 Anne Eriksen, "Entangled Genealogies: History and the Notion of Tradition", *Ethnologia Europaea* 46.2 (2016), 91–105, 98. On the sentimental reader see Mark Salber Phillips, *Society and Sentiment: Genres of Historical Writing in Britain, 1740–1820* (Princeton: Princeton University Press, 2000).

18 Levitin, *Kingdom of Darkness*, 244.

19 Peter Linehan, *History and the Historians of Medieval Spain* (Oxford: Oxford University Press, 1993); Jaume Aurell, *Authoring the Past: History, Autobiography and Politics in Medieval Catalonia* (Chicago: University of Chicago Press, 2012); Richard L. Kagan, *Clio & the Crown: the Politics of History in Medieval and Early Modern Spain* (Baltimore: Johns Hopkins University Press, 2009); Gabrielle

Spiegel, *The Chronicle Tradition of Saint-Denis: a Survey* (Brookline, MA: Classical Folia editions, 1978); Antoine Brix, "Aux origines des Grandes Chroniques de France: Nouveaux regards sur un succès littéraire", *Revue historique* 694 (2020), 3–39, which questions the degree to which the Grandes Chroniques reflected royal intervention and promotion.

20 See Ranum, *Artisans of Glory*; Cecil H. Clough, "Federico da Montefeltro's Concept and Use of History", in Grell, Paravicini and Voss (eds), *Les princes et l'histoire*, 297–325; Eric Cochrane, *Historians and Historiography in the Italian Renaissance* (Chicago: University of Chicago Press, 1981); Gary Ianziti, *Humanistic Historiography under the Sforzas: Politics and Propaganda in Fifteenth-Century Milan* (Oxford: Clarendon Press, 1988) and idem, *Writing History in Renaissance Italy: Leonardo Bruni and the Uses of the Past* (Cambridge, MA: Harvard University Press, 2012); Karen Skovgaard-Petersen, *Historiography at the Court of Christian IV (1588–1648): Studies in the Latin Histories of Denmark by Johannes Pontanus and Johannes Meursius* (Copenhagen: Museum Tusculanum Press, 2002).

21 Peter Burke, *Secret history and historical consciousness from the Renaissance to Romanticism* (Brighton: Edward Everett Root, 2016); Rebecca Bullard and Rachel Carnell (eds), *The Secret history in Literature 1660–1820* (Cambridge: Cambridge University Press, 2017); cf. Brian Cowan's extensive review essay on these volumes, "The History of Secret Histories", *Huntington Library Quarterly* 81.1 (2018), 121–51.

22 Joseph H. Preston, "English Ecclesiastical Historians and the Problem of Bias, 1559–1742", *Journal of the History of Ideas* 32.2 (1971);

23 Carolyn R. Miller, "Genre as Social Action", *Quarterly Journal of Speech*, 70 (1984):151 –167.

24 A subject to which I cannot do justice here, but see such useful works as Jose Cañizares-Esguerra, *How to Write the History of the New World: Histories, Epistemologies, and Identities in the Eighteenth-century Atlantic World* (Stanford, CA: Stanford University Press, 2001).

25 Hayden White, "The Politics of Historical Interpretation: Discipline and De-Sublimation", *Critical Inquiry* 9.1 (1982), 113–37. The literature on the professionalization of history throughout Europe and the Americas (and beyond) in the nineteenth century is too vast to list here.

26 Bonnie G. Smith, *The Gender of History: Men, Women, and Historical Practice* (Cambridge, MA: Harvard University Press, 1998), 14–36. Women as both readers and writers of history—across many genres—in early modern Europe is a subject that received relatively little attention till the 1990s but which has flourished in the past quarter-century; and an important genre not considered in the present volume is that of "histories of women", often by male authors at first but with greater female authorship (including the likes of Mary Hays and Jane Austen, to give only British examples) near the end of the period.

27 Philip Hicks, *Neoclassical History and English Culture from Clarendon to Hume* (Basingstoke: Palgrave, 1996); Orest Ranum, *Artisans of Glory: Writers and Historical Thought in Seventeenth-Century France* (Chapel Hill, NC: University of North Carolina Press, 1980); W.H. Evans, *L'historien Mézeray et la conception de l'histoire en France au XVIIe siècle* (Paris: J. Gamber, 1930); Blandine Barret-Kriegel, *Les historiens et la monarchie*, 4 vols (Paris: Presses universitaires de France, 1988); Chantal Grell and Catherine Volpihac-Auger (eds) *Nicolas Fréret, légende et verité* (Oxford: Voltaire Foundation, 1994).

28 See in addition to Smith, *The Gender of History*, the following: Charlotte Woodford, *Nuns as Historians in Early Modern Germany* (Oxford: Oxford University Press, 2002); K.J.P. Lowe, *Nuns' Chronicles and Convent Culture in Renaissance and*

Counter-Reformation Italy (Cambridge: Cambridge University Press, 2003); Kate Davies, *Catharine Macaulay and Mercy Otis Warren: the revolutionary Atlantic and the politics of gender* (Oxford: Oxford University Press, 2005);
29 *The New Science of Giambattista Vico*, trans. T.G. Bergin and M.H. Fisch, revised edition (Ithaca, NY: Cornell University Press, 1968); Lorenzo Boturini, *Idea of a New General History of North America: an Account of Colonial Mexico*, ed. S. Poole (Norman, OK: University of Oklahoma Press, 2015).
30 Sankar Muthu, *Enlightenment against Empire* (Princeton: Princeton University Press, 2003); Antonella Alimento and Aris della Fontana (eds) *Histories of Trade as Histories of Civilization* (Cham, Switzerland: Palgrave, 2021).
31 Jean Bodin, *Method for the Easy Comprehension of History*, trans. B. Reynolds (New York: Columbia University Press, 1945; repr. New York: Octagon, 1966); Sebastián Fox-Morcillo, *De historiae institutione dialogus* (Paris: Martin Iuuenem, 1557); Henri Lancelot Voisin, sieur de la Popelinière, *L'histoire des histoires avec l'idée de l'Histoire accomplie* (Paris: Jean Houzé, 1599); Agostino Mascardi, *Dell'arte historica* [1636] (Florence: F. Le Monnier, 1859); N. Lenglet Dufresnoy, *Méthode pour étudier l'histoire* (Paris: Antoine Urbain Coustelier, 1713). On the Renaissance and seventeenth-century *Ars historica* see, in addition to Grafton, *What was History?* the following: Antonio Cortijo Ocaña, *Teoría de la historia y teoría política en Sebastián Fox Morcillo* (Seville: Universidad de Alcalá de Henares, 1999) (published dissertation, including an edition of Fox-Morcillo's work); Girolamo Cotroneo, I trattatisti dell'ars historica (Naples: Giannini, 1971); Nicholas Wickenden, *G.J. Vossius and the Humanist Conception of History* (Assen, Netherlands: Van Gorcum, 1993).
32 Margaret Spufford, *Small Books and Pleasant Histories: Popular Fiction and Its Readership in Seventeenth-Century England* (Cambridge: Cambridge University Press, 1985); Robert Mandrou, *De la culture populaire aux XVIIe et XVIIIe siècle; la Bibliothèque bleue de Troyes* (Paris: Stock, 1964).
33 René Rapin, *Instructions pour l'histoire* (Paris: Sébastien Mabre-Cramoist, 1677); Pierre Le Moyne, *Of the Art Both of Writing & Judging of History with Reflections Upon Ancient as Well as Modern* (London: R. Sare and J. Hindmarsh, 1695); Peter Whalley, *An Essay on the Manner of Writing History* [1746], ed. K. Stewart (Los Angeles: Augustan Reprint Society/Clark Memorial Library, 1960); Joseph Priestley, *Lectures on History and General Policy* (Birmingham: J. Johnson, 1788); Henry St John, Viscount Bolingbroke, *Letters on the Study and Use of History* [1738], new edition (London: T. Cadell, 1779).
34 Wickenden, *G.J. Vossius*, 80–82.
35 Grafton, *What was History*, 189, 229; J.H.M. Salmon, "Precept, Example, and Truth: Degory Wheare and the Ars Historica", in Donald R. Kelley and David H. Sacks (eds), *The Historical Imagination in Early Modern Britain: History, Rhetoric, and Fiction, 1500–1800* (Cambridge: Cambridge University Press, 1997), 11–36.
36 Chad Wellmon, *Organizing Enlightenment: information overload and the invention of the modern research university* (Baltimore: Johns Hopkins University Press, 2015), 53–65.
37 Frow, *Genre*, 44.
38 *Dictionnaires des 16e et 17e s*, online, s.v. "genre" accessed 2023.01.24. In English, it was first applied in a cultural sense to art rather than literature in 1770, in a letter from Charles Jenner to David Garrick: OED, s.v. "genre" accessed 2023.01.24
39 See for instance Matthew Fox, *Roman Historical Myths: the Regal Period in Augustan Literature* (Oxford: Clarendon Press, 1996); Emily Baragwanath and Mathieu de Bakker (eds), *Myth, truth, and narrative in Herodotus* (Oxford: Oxford University Press, 2012); R.E. Asher, *National Myths in Renaissance France* (Edinburgh: Edinburgh University Press, 1993);

40 E.g. Michael Aung-Thwin, *Myth and history in the historiography of early Burma* (Athens, OH: Ohio University Center for International Studies, 1998); Robert Campany (ed.), *A Garden of Marvels: tales of wonder from early medieval China* (Honolulu: University of Hawaii Press, 2015); Taro Sakamoto, *The Six National Histories of Japan* (Vancouver: UBC Press, 2011); Romila Thapar, *The Past Before Us: Historical Traditions of Early North India* (Cambridge, MA: Harvard University Press, 2013).

41 Christiane Kunst, "William Camden's *Britannia*: History and Historiography", in M.H. Crawford and C.R. Ligota (eds), *Ancient History and the Antiquarian: Essays in Memory of Arnaldo Momigliano* (London: Warburg Institute, 1995), 117–32; D.R. Woolf, "Erudition and the Idea of History in Renaissance England", *Renaissance Quarterly* 40.1 (1987), 11–48.

42 Arnaldo Momigliano, "Ancient History and the Antiquarian", *Journal of the Warburg and Courtauld Institutes*, 13 (1950), 285–315 is the seminal article on the relation between antiquarianism and history; see also T.J. Cornell, "Ancient History and the Antiquarian Revisited: Some Thoughts on Reading Momigliano's *Classical Foundations*", in Crawford and C.R. Ligota (eds), *Ancient History and the Antiquarian*, 1–14; Peter N. Miller *Momigliano and Antiquarianism: Foundations of Modern Cultural Sciences* (Toronto: University of Toronto Press, 2015); Eriksen, "Entangled Genealogies", 93; Chantal Grell, *L'histoire entre erudition et philosophie: étude sur la connaissance historique à l'âge des lumières* (Paris: Presses universitaires de France, 1993); Joan-Pau Rubiés, "From Antiquarianism to Philosophical History: India, China, and the World History of Religion in European Thought (1600–1770)", in Peter N. Miler and François Louis (eds), *Antiquarianism and Intellectual Life in Europe and China 1500–1800* (Ann Arbor: University of Michigan Press, 2012), 313–67.

43 George Huppert, *The Idea of Perfect History: historical erudition and historical philosophy in Renaissance France* (Urbana and Chicago: University of Illinois Press, 1970); Donald R. Kelley, *Foundations of Modern Historical Scho*larship: Language, Law, and History in the French Renaissance (New York: Columbia University Press, 1970); Zachary S. Schiffman, *On the Threshold of Modernity: Relativism in the French Renaissance* (Baltimore: Johns Hopkins University Press, 1991); Claude-Gilbert Dubois, *La conception de l'histoire en France au XVIe siècle (1560–1610)* (Paris: A.G. Nizet, 1977).

44 Arnaldo Momigliano, "Gibbon's Contribution to Historical Method", *Historia: Zeitschrift für Alte Geschichte*, Bd. 2, H. 4 (1954), 450–463, reprinted in his *Studies in Historiography* (London: Weidenfeld and Nicolson, 1966); J.G.A. Pocock, *Barbarism and Religion* 6 vols (1999–2015), especially vols 1 and 2, on Gibbon and Voltaire; Pierre Force, "The 'Exasperating Predecessor: Pocock on Gibbon and Voltaire", *Journal of the History of Ideas* 77 (2016), 129–145. Pedro Faria, "David Hume, the Académie des inscriptions and the Nature of Historical Evidence in the Early Eighteenth Century", *Modern Intellectual History* 18 (2021), 299–322 suggests the hostility of the philosophic historians to Gibbon has been overstated, noting Hume's likely use of materials from the Académie des inscriptions, and that body's interest in questions of epistemology and evidence that would have appealed to Hume himself; for a similar argument in connection with Gibbon and d'Alembert, see also Anton M. Matytsin, "Enlightenment and Erudition: Writing Cultural History at the Académie des inscriptions", *Modern Intellectual History* 19 (2022), 323–48. On Hume and Macaulay see Lucy Littlefield, "Protestantism and Liberty: Catharine Macaulay's Politics of Religion as a Response to David Hume", *Intellectual History Review* 30.2 (2020), 233–52.

45 Gabriel Naudé, *Advice on Establishing a Library* [1627], ed. A. Taylor (Berkeley and Los Angeles: University of California Press, 1950), 28, 65–66; R. Whelan, "Un travail d'Hercule: Critique et histoire chez Gabriel Naudé (1600–1650), in [various

authors], *Pratiques et concepts de l'histoire en Europe XVI-XVIIIe siècles* (Paris: Presses de l'Université de Paris-Sorbonne, 1990), 59–83.

46 Miller, "Genre as Social Action", 151, 158.

47 Angus Vine, *In Defiance of Time: Antiquarian Writing in Early Modern England* (Oxford: Oxford University Press, 2010), 169–99.

48 In new editions and in collections such as Henry Savile's *Rerum Anglicarum scriptores post Bedam praecipui* (1601) or a century and a half later, Ludovico Antonio Muratori's *Rerum italicarum Scriptores ab anno æræ christianæ 500 ad annum 1500*, a publishing trend that would continue through the eighteenth century and mature in the nineteenth with series such as the Georg Pertz-edited *Monumenta Germaniae Historica* and the British Rolls series.

Bibliography

Abbattista, Guido. "The Business of Pater-Noster Row: Towards a Publishing History of the *Universal History* (1736–1765)." *Publishing History* 17 (1985): 5–50.

Alimento, Antonella & Aris della Fontana (eds). *Histories of Trade as Histories of Civilization.* Cham, Switzerland: Palgrave, 2021.

Alonso-Núñez, J.M. *The Idea of Universal History in Greece from Herodotus to the Age of Augustus.* Amsterdam: J.C. Gieben, 2002.

Aurell, Jaume. *Authoring the Past: History, Autobiography and Politics in Medieval Catalonia.* Chicago: University of Chicago Press, 2012.

Asher, R.E. *National Myths in Renaissance France.* Edinburgh: Edinburgh University Press, 1993.

Aung-Thwin, Michael. *Myth and History in the Historiography of Early Burma.* Athens, OH: Ohio University Center for International Studies, 1998.

Baragwanath, Emily & Mathieu de Bakker (eds). *Myth, Truth, and Narrative in Herodotus.* Oxford: Oxford University Press, 2012.

Barret-Kriegel, Blandine. *Les historiens et la monarchie*, 4 vols. Paris: Presses universitaires de France, 1988.

Bjørnstad, Hall, Anne Régent-Susini, & Helge Jordheim (eds). *Universal History and the Making of the Global.* London: Routledge, 2017.

Bossuet, J.-B. *Discourse on Universal History*, trans. E. Forster and ed. Orest Ranum. Chicago: University of Chicago Press, 1976.

Bodin, Jean. *Method for the Easy Comprehension of History*, trans. B. Reynolds. New York: Columbia University Press, 1945; repr. New York: Octagon, 1966.

Bolingbroke St John, Henry, & Viscount Bolingbroke. *Letters on the Study and Use of History [1738]*, new edition. London: T.Cadell, 1779.

Boturini, Lorenzo. *Idea of a New General History of North America: An Account of Colonial Mexico*, ed. S. Poole. Norman, OK: University of Oklahoma Press, 2015.

Brix, Antoine. "Aux origins des Grandes Chroniques de France: Nouveaux regards sur un succès littéraire." *Revue historique* 694 (2020): 3–39.

Bullard, Rebecca & Rachel Carnell (eds). *The Secret History in Literature 1660–1820.* Cambridge: Cambridge University Press, 2017.

Burke, Peter. *Secret History and Historical Consciousness from the Renaissance to Romanticism.* Brighton: Edward Everett Root, 2016.

Campany, Robert (ed.). *A Garden of Marvels: Tales of Wonder from Early Medieval China.* Honolulu: University of Hawaii Press, 2015.

Campopiano, Michele & Henry Bainton (eds). *Universal Chronicles in the High Middle Ages.* Woodbridge, Suffolk, UK: York Medieval Press, 2017.

Cañizares-Esguerra, Jose. *How to Write the History of the New World: Histories, Epistemologies, and Identities in the Eighteenth-Century Atlantic World.* Stanford, CA: Stanford University Press, 2001.

Christian, David. *Maps of Time: An Introduction to Big History.* Berkeley: University of California Press, 2005.

Clough, Cecil H. "Federico da Montefeltro's Concept and Use of History", in Grell, Paravicini and Voss (eds), *Les princes et l'histoire*, 297–325.

Cochrane, Eric. *Historians and Historiography in the Italian Renaissance.* Chicago: University of Chicago Press, 1981.

Cornell, T.J. "Ancient History and the Antiquarian Revisited: Some Thoughts on Reading Momigliano's *Classical Foundations*," in M.H. Crawford and C.R. Ligota (eds), *Ancient History and the Antiquarian: Essays in Memory of Arnaldo Momigliano*, 1–14.

Cortijo Ocaña, Antonio. *Teoría de la historia y teoría política en Sebastián Fox Morcillo.* Published dissertation, including an edition of Fox-Morcillo's work. Seville: Universidad de Alcalá de Henares, 1999.

Cotroneo, Girolamo. *I trattatisti dell'ars historica.* Naples: Giannini, 1971.

Cowan, Brian. "The History of Secret Histories." *Huntington Library Quarterly* 81.1 (2018): 121–151.

Davies, Kate. *Catharine Macaulay and Mercy Otis Warren: The Revolutionary Atlantic and the Politics of Gender.* Oxford: Oxford University Press, 2005.

Delahaye, Agnès et al. "The Genre of Corporate History." *Journal of Organizational Change Management* 22.1 (2009): 27–48.

Dictionnaires des 16e et 17e s, online, s.v. "genre" accessed 2023.01.24. https://num-classiques-garnier-com.proxy.queensu.ca/index.php?module=App&action=FrameMain

Dubois, Claude-Gilbert. *La conception de l'histoire en France au XVIe siècle (1560–1610).* Paris: A.G. Nizet, 1977.

Dufresnoy, N. Lenglet. *Méthode pour étudier l'histoire.* Paris: Antoine Urbain Coustelier, 1713.

Eriksen, Anne. "Entangled Genealogies: History and the Notion of Tradition." *Ethnologia Europaea* 46.2 (2016): 91–105.

Evans, W.H. *L.'historien Mézeray et la conception de l'histoire en France au XVIIe siècle.* Paris: J. Gamber, 1930.

Faria, Pedro. "David Hume, the Académie des Inscriptions and the Nature of Historical Evidence in the Early Eighteenth Century." *Modern Intellectual History* 18 (2021): 299–322.

Fear, Andrew & Peter Liddell (eds). *Historiae Mundi.* London: Duckworth, 2010.

Force, Pierre. "The 'Exasperating Predecessor: Pocock on Gibbon and Voltaire." *Journal of the History of Ideas* 77 (2016): 129–145.

Fox, Matthew. *Roman Historical Myths: the Regal Period in Augustan Literature.* Oxford: Clarendon Press, 1996.

Fox-Morcillo, Sebastián. *De historiae institutione dialogus.* Paris: Martin Iuuenem, 1557.

Frow, John. *Genre.* London: Routledge, 2005.

Grell, Chantal, Werner Paravicini & Jürgen Voss (eds). *Les princes et l'histoire du XIVe au XVIIIe siècle: actes du colloque organisé par l'Université de Versailles-Saint Quentin et l'Institut historique allemand, Paris/Versailles, 13–16 mars 1996.* Bonn: Bouvier, 1996.

Griggs, Tamara. "Universal History from Counter-Reformation to Enlightenment." *Modern Intellectual History* 4.2 (2007): 219–247.

Grafton, Anthony. *What was History? The Art of History in Early Modern Europe.* Cambridge: Cambridge University Press, 2007.

Grell, Chantal & Catherine Volpihac-Auger (eds). *Nicolas Fréret, légende et verité.* Oxford: Voltaire Foundation, 1994.

Grell, Chantal. *L'histoire entre erudition et philosophie: étude sur la connaissance historique à l'âge des lumières*. Paris: Presses universitaires de France, 1993.

Hesketh, Ian. *A History of Big History*. Cambridge: Cambridge University Press, 2023, forthcoming.

Hicks, Philip. *Neoclassical History and English Culture from Clarendon to Hume*. Basingstoke: Palgrave, 1996.

Huppert, George. *The Idea of Perfect History: Historical Erudition and Historical Philosophy in Renaissance France*. Urbana and Chicago: University of Illinois Press, 1970.

Ianziti, Gary. *Humanistic Historiography under the Sforzas: Politics and Propaganda in Fifteenth-Century Milan*. Oxford: Clarendon Press, 1988.

Ianziti, Gary. *Writing History in Renaissance Italy: Leonardo Bruni and the Uses of the Past*. Cambridge, MA: Harvard University Press, 2012.

Kagan, Richard L. *Clio & the Crown: The Politics of History in Medieval and Early Modern Spain*. Baltimore: Johns Hopkins University Press, 2009.

Kess, Alexandra. *Johann Sleidan and the Protestant Vision of History*. Aldershot: Ashgate, 2008.

Kelley, Donald R. *Foundations of Modern Historical Scholarship: Language, Law, and History in the French Renaissance*. New York: Columbia University Press, 1970.

Kunst, Christiane. "William Camden's *Britannia*: History and Historiography," in M.H. Crawford and C.R. Ligota (eds), *Ancient History and the Antiquarian: Essays in Memory of Arnaldo Momigliano*, 117–132. London: Warburg Institute, 1995.

la Popelinière, Henri Lancelot Voisin, *sieur de. L'histoire des histoires avec l'idée de l'Histoire accomplie*. Paris: Jean Houzé, 1599.

Linehan, Peter. *History and the Historians of Medieval Spain*. Oxford: Oxford University Press, 1993.

Littlefield, Lucy. "Protestantism and Liberty: Catharine Macaulay's Politics of Religion as a Response to David Hume." *Intellectual History Review* 30.2 (2020): 233–252.

Le Moyne, Pierre. *Of the Art Both of Writing & Judging of History with Reflections Upon Ancient as Well as Modern*. London: R. Sare and J. Hindmarsh, 1695.

Letter from Charles Jenner to David Garrick, 1770: OED, s.v. "genre"; accessed 2023.01.24.

Levitin, Dmitri. *The Kingdom of Darkness: Bayle, Newton, and the emancipation of the European mind from philosophy*. Cambridge: Cambridge University Press, 2022.

Liere, Katherine van, Simon Ditchfield, & Howard Louthan (eds). *Sacred History: Uses of the Christian Past in the Renaissance World*. Oxford: Oxford University Press, 2012.

Lowe, K.J.P. *Nuns' Chronicles and Convent Culture in Renaissance and Counter-Reformation Italy*. Cambridge: Cambridge University Press, 2003.

Matytsin, Anton M. "Enlightenment and Erudition: Writing Cultural History at the Académie des Inscriptions." *Modern Intellectual History* 19 (2022): 323–348.

Mandrou, Robert. *De la culture populaire aux XVIIe et XVIIIe siècle; la Bibliothèque bleue de Troyes*. Paris: Stock, 1964.

Mascardi, Agostino. *Dell'arte historica [1636]*. Florence: F. Le Monnier, 1859.

McGann, Jerome. "From Cultural Memory to Living Word: On Mather's *Magnalia.*" *New Literary History* 50.2 (2019): 171–195.

Meinhold, Peter. *Geschichte der Kirchlichen Historiographie*, 2 vols. Freiburg and Munich: Verlag Karl Alber, 1967.

Miller, Carolyn R. "Genre as Social Action." *Quarterly Journal of Speech* 70 (1984): 151–167.

Miller, Peter N. *Momigliano and Antiquarianism: Foundations of Modern Cultural Sciences*. Toronto: University of Toronto Press, 2015.

328 *Daniel Woolf*

Momigliano, Arnaldo. "Ancient History and the Antiquarian." *Journal of the Warburg and Courtauld Institutes* 13 (1950): 285–315
Momigliano, Arnaldo. "Gibbon's Contribution to Historical Method." *Historia: Zeitschrift für Alte Geschichte*, Bd. 2, H. 4 (1954): 450–463, reprinted in his *Studies in Historiography*. London: Weidenfeld and Nicolson, 1966.
Monumenta Germaniae Historica. Hanoverm Munich, etc: various imprints, 1826-.
Mortley, Raoul. *The Idea of Universal History from Hellenistic Philosophy to Early Christian Historiography*. Lewiston, NY: Edwin Mellen, 1996.
Mukhia, Harbans. *Historians and Historiography During the Reign of Akbar*. New Delhi: Vikas, 1976.
Muthu, Sankar. *Enlightenment against Empire*. Princeton: Princeton University Press, 2003.
Narayana Rao, Velcheru, David D. Shulman, & Sanjay Subrahmanyam. *Textures of Time: Writing History in South India 1600–1800*. Delhi: Permanent Black, 2001.
Naudé, Gabriel. *Advice on Establishing a Library [1627]*, ed. A. Taylor. Berkeley and Los Angeles: University of California Press, 1950.
Neddermeyer, Uwe. "Darümb sollen die historien billich fürsten bücher sein un genennet warden: Universalhistorische Werke als Ratgeber der Fürsten im Mittelalter und in der frühen Neuzeit," in Chantal Grell, Werner Paravicini, and Jürgen Voss (eds), *Les princes et l'histoire du XIVe au XVIIIe siècle*, 67–108. Bonn: Bouvier, 1998.
Ng, On-cho, & Q. Edward Wang. *Mirroring the Past: The Writing and Use of History in Imperial China*. Honolulu: University of Hawaii Press, 2005.
Monumenta Germaniae Historica, ed. G. Pertz, and G. Waitz et al. Hannover and Munich: various publishers, 1826-
Phillips, Mark Salber. *Society and Sentiment: Genres of Historical Writing in Britain, 1740–1820*. Princeton: Princeton University Press, 2000.
Preston, Joseph H. "English Ecclesiastical Historians and the Problem of Bias, 1559–1742." *Journal of the History of Ideas* 32.2 (1971): 203–220.
Pocock, J.G.A. *Barbarism and Religion*, 6 vols. Cambridge: Cambridge University Press, 1999-2015.
Pomata Gianna & Nancy G. Siraisi (eds). *Historia: Empiricism and Erudition in Early Modern Europe*. Cambridge, MA: MIT Press, 2005.
Popkin, Richard H. *The History of Scepticism from Erasmus to Spinoza*. Berkeley: University of California Press, 1979.
Priestley, Joseph. *Lectures on History and General Policy*. Birmingham: J. Johnson, 1788.
Ranum, Orest. *Artisans of Glory: Writers and Historical Thought in Seventeenth-Century France*. Chapel Hill, NC: University of North Carolina Press, 1980.
Rerum Anglicarum scriptores post Bedam praecipui, ed. Henry Savile. Frankfurt: Typis Wechelianis apud C. Marnium, 1601.
Rerum italicarum Scriptores ab anno æræ christianæ 500 ad annum 1500, ed. Ludovico Antonio Muratori, 28 vols. Milan: Milanese Palatine Society, 1723-1751.
Rapin, René. *Instructions pour l'histoire*. Paris: Sébastien Mabre-Cramoist, 1677.
Rubiés, Joan-Pau. "From Antiquarianism to Philosophical History: India, China, and the World History of Religion in European Thought (1600–1770)," in Peter N. Miler and François Louis (eds), *Antiquarianism and Intellectual Life in Europe and China 1500–1800*, 313–367. Ann Arbor: University of Michigan Press, 2012.
Sakamoto, Taro. *The Six National Histories of Japan*. Vancouver: UBC Press, 2011.
Salmon, J.H.M. "Precept, Example, and Truth: Degory Wheare and the Ars Historica", in Donald R. Kelley and David H. Sacks (eds), *The Historical Imagination in Early Modern Britain: History, Rhetoric, and Fiction, 1500–1800*. Cambridge: Cambridge University Press, 1997.

Schiffman, Zachary S. *On the Threshold of Modernity: Relativism in the French Renaissance.* Baltimore: Johns Hopkins University Press, 1991.

Seifert, Arno. *Cognitio Historica: Die Geschichte als Namengeberin der frühneuzeitlichen Empirie.* Berlin: Duncker und Humblot, 1976.

Spufford, Margaret. *Small Books and Pleasant Histories: Popular Fiction and Its Readership in Seventeenth Century England.* Cambridge: Cambridge University Press, 1985.

Skovgaard-Petersen, Karen. "Carion's Chronicle in Sixteenth Century Danish Historiography." *Symbolae Osloenses* 73.1 (2010): 158–167.

Skovgaard-Petersen, Karen. *Historiography at the Court of Christian IV (1588–1648): Studies in the Latin Histories of Denmark by Johannes Pontanus and Johannes Meursius.* Copenhagen: Museum Tusculanum Press, 2002.

Smail, Daniel Lord. "Genealogy, Ontology, and the Narrative Arc of Origins." *French Historical Studies* 34.1 (2011): 21–35.

Smail, Daniel Lord. "In the Grip of Sacred History." *American Historical Review* 110 (2005): 1337–1361.

Smith, Bonnie G. *The Gender of History: Men, Women, and Historical Practice.* Cambridge, MA: Harvard University Press, 1998.

Spiegel, Gabrielle. *The Chronicle Tradition of Saint-Denis: a Survey.* Brookline, MA: Classical Folia editions, 1978.

Spier, Fred. *Big History and the Future of Humanity.* Chichester, UK and Malden, MA: Wiley-Blackwell, 2010.

Thapar, Romila. *The Past Before Us: Historical Traditions of Early North India.* Cambridge, MA: Harvard University Press, 2013.

The New Science of Giambattista Vico, trans. T.G. Bergin and M.H. Fisch, revised edition. Ithaca, NY: Cornell University Press, 1968.

Vine, Angus. *In Defiance of Time: Antiquarian Writing in Early Modern England.* Oxford: Oxford University Press, 2010.

Wellmon, Chad. *Organizing Enlightenment: information Overload and the Invention of the Modern Research University.* Baltimore: Johns Hopkins University Press, 2015.

Whalley, Peter. *An Essay on the Manner of Writing History [1746],* ed. K. Stewart. Los Angeles: Augustan Reprint Society/Clark Memorial Library, 1960.

Whelan, R. "Un travail d'Hercule: Critique et histoire chez Gabriel Naudé (1600–1650)," in various authors (eds.), *Pratiques et concepts de l'histoire en Europe XVI-XVIIIe siècles,* 59–83. Paris: Presses de l'Université de Paris-Sorbonne, 1990.

White, Hayden. "The Politics of Historical Interpretation: Discipline and De-Sublimation." *Critical Inquiry* 9.1 (1982): 113–137.

Wickenden, Nicholas. *G.J. Vossius and the Humanist Conception of History.* Assen, Netherlands: Van Gorcum, 1993.

Woodford, Charlotte. *Nuns as Historians in Early Modern Germany.* Oxford: Oxford University Press, 2002.

Woolf, D.R. "Erudition and the Idea of History in Renaissance England." *Renaissance Quarterly* 40.1 (1987): 11–48.

Woolf, D.R. "Genre into Artifact: the Decline of the English Chronicle in the Sixteenth Century." *Sixteenth Century Journal* 19.3 (1988): 321–354.

Woolf, D.R. *Reading History in Early Modern England.* Cambridge: Cambridge University Press, 2000.

Works of Thomas Nashe, ed. R.B. McKerrow (London: Bullen, 1904), I: 194.

Index

Pages in *italics* refer to figures.